mult frequencies

plant care

pg 226

Video Field Production and Editing

Third Edition

RONALD J. COMPESI
San Francisco State University

RONALD E. SHERRIFFS
University of Oregon

ALLYN AND BACON
Boston   London   Toronto   Sydney   Tokyo   Singapore

Senior Editor: Steve Hull
Editorial Assistant: Brenda Conaway
Editorial-Production Administrator: Annette Joseph
Production Coordinator: Holly Crawford
Editorial-Production Service: Lynda Griffiths, TKM Productions
Composition Buyer: Linda Cox
Manufacturing Buyer: Louise Richardson
Cover Administrator: Linda K. Dickinson
Cover Designer: Suzanne Harbison

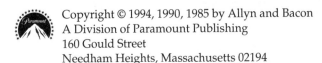

Copyright © 1994, 1990, 1985 by Allyn and Bacon
A Division of Paramount Publishing
160 Gould Street
Needham Heights, Massachusetts 02194

Previous editions of this book were titled *Small Format Television Production.*

Many of the designations used by manufacturers and sellers to distinguish their products are claimed as trademarks. Where those designations appear in this book, and Allyn and Bacon was aware of a trademark claim, the designation has been printed in caps or initial caps.

Library of Congress Cataloging-in-Publication Data

Compesi, Ronald J.
    Video field production and editing / Ronald J. Compesi, Ronald E.
  Sherriffs.
      p.   cm.
    Third ed. of: Small format television production. 2nd ed. c1990.
    Includes bibliographical references and index.
    ISBN 0–205–15505–7
      1. Video recording—Equipment and supplies.   2. Television—
  Production and direction.   3. Video recordings—Production and
  direction.   I. Sherriffs, Ronald E.   II. Compesi, Ronald J.
  Small format television production.   III. Title.
  TK6655.V5G66   1993
  778.59—dc20   93–22990
                                                              CIP

Printed in the United States of America

10 9 8 7 6 5 4 3   98 97 96 95

Credits appear on page 452, which constitutes a continuation of the copyright page.

For Cathy, Marisa, Cara, and Mary

Contents

Preface

With the publication of this new edition of *Video Field Production and Editing*, this book (formerly *Small Format Television Production*) has a new name, revised text, and completely revised figures and illustrations, featuring over 65 new photographs and all new artwork.

In the past three decades, rapid technological changes have made video equipment smaller, less expensive, and accessible to more people. These changes have revolutionized the field of video production. The introduction of lightweight, portable video field production equipment has moved television production out of the studio and into the field. The development and refinement of reliable, inexpensive editing systems has made postproduction editing more important than ever in the video production process. Also, the personal computer is finding increasing use as a video production tool.

In the time that has elapsed since the publication of the first two editions of *Small Format Television Production*, video has become an increasingly important part of American life. Portable equipment designed for broadcast use has become smaller and more sophisticated, and video camcorders and VCRs have become almost omnipresent in U.S. homes and offices. Video is widely used in education, business, medicine, and law, as well as in the traditional broadcast and cable television arena.

Video Field Production and Editing reflects the changes in technology and production processes that have taken place since the publication of the first two editions of *Small Format Television Production*. However, the central purpose of this book remains the same: to provide a text for students involved in video production, concentrating on production techniques and technology appropriate to single-camera electronic field production (EFP) and electronic news gathering (ENG). The principal features of the book include the following:

1. The single-camera/camcorder video field production process is examined, with an emphasis on portable video (8mm/Hi8, VHS/S-VHS, $\frac{3}{4}$", Betacam/Betacam SP, and M-II) equipment. This third edition is illustrated with many new photographs of the latest equipment, particularly the new generation of charge-coupled device (CCD) cameras and cam-

corders, from the major manufacturers of professional video field production and editing equipment.

2. Technical and aesthetic concerns are addressed. The book discusses production strategies and processes, as well as principles of equipment operation.

3. The elements and techniques of videotape recording and postproduction editing are fully covered. Expanded discussions of new videotape and disc-recording formats are included, in addition to new sections on desktop video production and nonlinear editing.

4. The Appendices contain a series of production exercises designed to help the potential producer develop production competence, as well as additional information on lighting and remote production planning.

5. As in the previous editions, key words are identified in boldface throughout the text. The book contains a comprehensive glossary of terms and a new bibliography of books and periodicals of interest to the video producer.

The organization of the book reflects our concern with providing a discussion of the production techniques and organization that are commonly used in video field production, as well as the technology that makes this kind of production possible. As a result, most chapters are divided into two parts: one section deals with the technical aspects of production and the other deals with production techniques or aesthetics. Although the technical discussion usually precedes the discussion of production aesthetics, the material may be read in reverse order without confusing the reader.

Throughout the book we have attempted to aim the technical discussion at the general reader who has little or no technical background in video or electronics. We hope that through your experience with the text, you will let us know whether we have hit or missed the mark.

Each chapter is a self-contained unit, and the chapters may be read out of sequence without causing problems. For example, the material in Chapter 12 may serve well as an introduction to the book, as it provides an overview of the major components of the field production/planning process. We have had success assigning that chapter early in the semester and then reassigning it as a refresher near the middle or end of the course.

One other comment deserves to be made here. The focus of the book is on video field production, but this needs to be qualified. We have primarily concentrated on what some writers have called small-scale field production, since this is the type of production in which most student and home video producers (as well as many independent and broadcast producers) are most often engaged. We are concerned with productions that involve a minimum amount of field equipment and a small crew. The video producer who has access to a camcorder or a single-camera and portable VCR, a few microphones, a small lighting kit, and a simple editing system will find that this is the level of production that we principally discuss. Although we do provide some descriptions of larger-scale productions and production equipment, this is not the primary focus of the book. We should note, however, that small-scale production does not mean amateur production. Since the line between broadcast-quality production and equipment and nonbroadcast production is a thin one indeed, we stress professional standards of production throughout the book.

ACKNOWLEDGMENTS

We owe a great debt of gratitude to the many people who have contributed to the making of this book. Bob Avery of the University of Utah has supported us from the very beginning. Without his encouragement and the foresight of Bill Barke at Allyn and Bacon, the first edition of this book might not have come to fruition. Steve Hull of Allyn and Bacon brought the same level of enthusiasm to the second and third editions and has consistently challenged us to make this a better book. His attention to detail has been greatly appreciated.

Matt Chan of KXTV, Sacramento, provided us with a wealth of information throughout the course of writing this book, and the Department of Communication at the University of Utah provided a sabbatical home base and a writing environment with few distractions during the preparation of the original manuscript. Our colleagues in the Broadcast and Electronic Communication Arts Department at San Francisco State University and the School of Journalism and Communication at the University of Oregon have provided invaluable assistance as the book has evolved through three editions. In particular, we would like to thank Hamid Khani, Bill Willingham, John Hewitt, Val Sakovich, Herb Zettl, Phil Kipper, Doug Smith, Frank Moakley, Stuart Hyde, and Art France.

We would also like to thank those individuals who read earlier drafts of the manuscript and whose comments made it a better book, including Joel Fowler (California State University, Fresno), Slawomir Grunberg (Ithaca College), Nikos Metallinos (Concordia University), Warren Pease (Pacific University), Louis Pullano (Brookdale Community College), Michael Real (San Diego State University), C. John Sincell (University of Maryland), and Larry Whitney (San Francisco State University). Lynda Griffiths of TKM Productions deserves a special note of thanks for her graceful copyediting and for shepherding the manuscript and its authors through the production process for the second and third editions.

Winston Tharp, Jerry Higgins, Peter Maravelias, and Margaret Flood (San Francisco State University), Jim Lacock (University of Oregon), and Paul Rose (University of Utah) deserve special thanks for the guidance they provided on technical matters. Thanks are also due to our many students at the University of Oregon and San Francisco State University, and in particular to Leslie Carlson. Thanks also to Pennie Sandeen, Peter Coakley, Monique Hedrick, Christie Fluken, and Susan Amacher for their help with the preparation of the revised manuscript.

We would also like to thank those people who helped us obtain many of the new photographs in the third edition: David S. Detmers and Robert Brilliant (Ampex Corporation), Stephen Godfrey (Future Video), Ellin Everson (JVC Professional Products Company), Bonnie Schwartz (Lowel-Light Manufacturing, Inc.), Thomas L. Croak (Marcus, Inc.), Maureen McConnell (Matrox Electronic Systems), Jim Wickizek and Nathalie Clark (Panasonic Broadcast and Television Systems Company), Sharon Coleman (Realtime Video), Catherine Moreau (Sony Corporation), Susan Bruner (Sun Rize Industries), Amy Gomersall (Videomedia, Inc.), Dennis Kellett, Gerard Hughes, Pedro Moreno-Carrascal, and Parul Shah. Thanks also to Rob Mertz for his assistance with computer graphics.

Special thanks are due to Cathy Sandeen for her constant encouragement and constructive criticism through three editions of this book, to Marisa and Cara for doing without their dad on the long evenings and weekends during which this revision was completed, and to Mary Sherriffs for her patience and support. This book is dedicated to them.

R. J. C.
R. E. S.

1

Introduction

The clock on the train platform reads 6:30 A.M. as I climb aboard the train and head for the city. The sun is not yet up and the usual bay fog hangs over the water as the train pulls out of the station. Today is a big day. In a few hours, I will be on the road with the crew from *Evening Magazine,* accompanying them on a remote shoot to see how things are done in the real world of television field production.

In less than 30 minutes, the train reaches the downtown station and I hop off and head for the escalator to street level. The sky has brightened considerably as I join the other morning commuters in their trek to the office. The fog has left the pavement slick, and I walk carefully as I thread my way through the downtown streets to the television station where I am scheduled to meet the field producer who has invited me along for the morning shoot. I arrive at the station at 7:30 and Mike, the producer, arrives moments later. We are not scheduled to leave until 8:30, so we duck into a restaurant across the street for a quick breakfast and some strong coffee.

Today's shoot centers on Tom K., a 24-year-old patient at a nearby medical center. Several months ago, Tom was stricken by a virus that seriously damaged his heart. Today, his heart is working at only 15 percent of its normal capacity—the damage done by the virus is severe and irreparable. He has been on the waiting list for a heart transplant for over a month.

The story being planned by *Evening Magazine* focuses on Tom and on a fund-raising effort that has been organized by some of his friends. They plan to water-ski over 70 miles in the ocean to publicize Tom's case and to solicit funds to help pay his medical bills. The story will consist of interviews with his friends, actual footage of the open-ocean water skiing, and interviews with Tom and his doctor. The latter interviews are scheduled to be recorded today. We have a 9:30 A.M. appointment with Tom at the medical center.

Mike and I finish breakfast and walk the short block and a half back to the station and go up to the *Magazine* offices. There's not much activity at this time

1

of the morning. The office occupies one corner of the floor of the building. Sections of the office have been partitioned off into small cubicle-like offices for the staff members. Two permanent rooms off to one side house the videotape editing equipment and serve as work stations for the two videotape editors. Several other offices have been assigned to the show's producer and associate producer. Large windows face out into the city and toward the bridge across the bay.

Mike makes a few last-minute phone calls as we prepare to leave the station. Rita, the camera operator, or "shooter," has arrived. We're waiting for Don, the production assistant. It's Don's job to drive the van that will carry us to the medical center, which is about an hour's drive south. At 8:30, there's still no sign of Don, and Mike begins to get a bit agitated. It's crucial that the interview be completed today, as Tom could receive the transplant at any time and the interview must be finished before the operation. Mike is getting more anxious. Finally, Don arrives.

The van is parked in the basement garage, along with other station vehicles and the employees' cars. The sides and rear are decorated with the distinctive logo that identifies *Evening Magazine.* I notice an electrical extension cord trailing out a window into a wall socket. This connection to power is being used to charge up the extra batteries carried inside the van that will power the video equipment in the field.

We all pile into the van and head toward the freeway through the early morning traffic. Three bucket seats hold the driver and two regular passengers. I get to sit on a milk carton next to the sliding door. The interior of the van is paneled and carpeted, and shows the effects of plenty of wear.

Against one wall of the van is a metal cart. On it are various pieces of television equipment: a color monitor, a portable videocassette recorder (VCR), and a forest of cables. Next to this, against the same wall, is a shelf holding half a dozen or so batteries, all locked into the charging unit. Above them is a shelf of videocassettes. On the floor at the rear of the van, on a small rectangular piece of carpet, lies the camera. The body of the camera shows signs of wear. It's scratched and dented in the places that are not covered over with decals. The *Evening Magazine* logo is evident. One side of the camera carries a decal of Chinese ideographs—a souvenir from a recent trip to the People's Republic of China.

We arrive at the medical center at 9:30 A.M. and, after some negotiation with a traffic guard, manage to park the van in a red zone near the main entrance to the hospital. Mike goes inside to confirm the interview arrangements with the publicity director of the hospital, and Rita and Don begin to take equipment out of the van.

While Mike is inside, Rita and Don talk about whether today will be a two-tape day. The discussion is important from a planning standpoint because Don has responsibility for bringing along enough blank tape to record the interviews. If he brings only two tapes and they need a third, he will have to return to the van. However more important than the planning considerations is what a two-tape or three-tape day means in terms of the amount of work the crew will be required to perform. On a two-tape day, they finish work earlier than on a three-tape day.

A few minutes later, Mike returns and indicates that everything is set—the interviews can go on as planned. For the next 10 minutes or so, he gives a quick overview of the story as he sees it. He indicates that when the story is edited, it will begin with a montage sequence built out of the water-skiing shots, and then the piece will establish the main theme—that this is a benefit for Tom. Mike talks briefly about the interview segments with Tom and his doctor and mentions some specific shots he would like to have: a shot of Tom walking down a hallway to establish him and the location, shots of Tom being examined by his doctor, and so on. At 9:45, we head into the hospital. Rita carries the camera and a tripod. Don has the portable VCR and some headphones. I'm carrying a canvas bag filled with tape, cables, batteries, extra microphones, and other miscellaneous equipment, and Mike has a large soft light and stand in hand.

We set up the equipment in a hallway and Mike introduces us to Tom. He's extremely personable and jokes about his health and his role in this program. "I've never been on TV before," he deadpans. "I feel like one of Jerry's kids."

Between 10:00 and 10:45 A.M., the crew shoots at least six different situations with Tom. The establishing shot Mike called for is staged in the hallway. Two takes are recorded, since Tom looked at the camera and laughed in the first one. The camera is moved outside, and we record several takes of Tom entering and exiting the hospital. Then it's back inside the building to record him as he is weighed on a scale in the hall, as his blood pressure is taken in an examining room, and as he talks with the nurse who has been supervising this activity. The entrance of the doctor into the examining room is staged and recorded, then his actions in the room are recorded without any rehearsal or guidance from the crew.

Throughout most of the taping, the crew members ask the nurse, the doctor, and Tom to go about their normal business and not pay any special attention to the camera. Rita, the camera operator, busily focuses on different elements of the activity. I notice on several occasions she appears to reshoot something she has just shot; for example, at one point she started a shot on a close-up of the nurse and then panned across to Tom. Apparently unhappy with the way the shot came out, she refocused on the nurse and repeated the shot.

At 10:45, Mike interviews Tom's doctor in the hall outside the examination room. The light is set up, a small microphone is pinned onto the doctor, and the interview is completed in about 10 minutes. Hospital personnel freely move through the hall as the interview takes place. Once again, Don and Rita tell the hospital personnel not to worry about interfering with the crew's work.

At 11:10, we move upstairs to the Cardiac Echo Lab, where a sonar device will be used to show what the inside of Tom's heart looks like. The output of the device is displayed on a small television monitor. It's eerie to watch Tom lying on the examination table and to see his heart beating on the nearby television screen. Rita records the image on the screen and also records the doctor as he traces over Tom's chest with the sonar device. Don uses a microphone on an extendable fishpole boom to record the sound.

We move back downstairs and out to an exterior courtyard to set up for the interview with Tom. The fog has reappeared and the day is a bit gloomy. Rita finds a bench for Tom to sit on and decides she will need to use the soft light to add some brightness to the picture. We find some exterior electrical outlets to plug in the light. A large piece of blue plastic, a conversion filter, is clipped onto the front of the lighting instrument so that its light matches the color of daylight.

Don worries about the noise being generated by air conditioners protruding from the building walls into the courtyard. He conducts an audio test and decides together with Mike that the sound is acceptable. At 11:25, Tom joins us outside and Mike conducts the interview. He has some questions written down in a reporter's notebook and asks the questions from off-camera. The interview is short—approximately 10 minutes. We thank Tom for his help and he heads back inside to wait for the day when a heart is available for transplant. We dismantle the equipment and return it to the van. Rita pops one of the videotapes into the VCR on the rack inside the van and checks the picture quality and sound on the monitor. Everything is OK. My watch reads 11:48 as we climb into the van to head back to the station. It was a two-tape day.

During the next week, two events occur that have significance to the story. First, the crew goes out in the middle of the week and shoots the ocean water-skiing footage. Unfortunately, the weather is bad and the sea is rough, and the skiers are unable to complete the planned 70-mile event. Then, one week after our interview with Tom, a compatible heart becomes available for transplantation. The operation is completed without complications. About three weeks after the interview with Tom was shot, the story is broadcast on *Evening Magazine*. It appears as a hopeful story of a young man's fight to win back the life that had hung so precariously in the balance.

The kind of production typified by *Evening Magazine* represents a relatively new approach to television production. Shooting with a single camera and a portable VCR (or a camcorder, which combines a high-quality video camera and videocassette recorder into one easily carried unit), and a relatively small crew by traditional television standards, organizations like *Evening Magazine* have revolutionized the concept of television production. Increasingly, television production is **field production**; it takes place in the outside world, rather than in a studio inside a television station (see Figures 1–1 and 1–2).

This type of production depends on reliable, portable video production equipment and on the ability of skilled production personnel to use it. The focus of this book is on such single-camera video field production—on the equipment that makes it possible and on the production techniques and strategies that can be used to create effective messages through the use of this relatively new technology.

Figure 1–1 *Evening Magazine* Crew (Field Producer, Production Assistant, Camera Operator) on Location

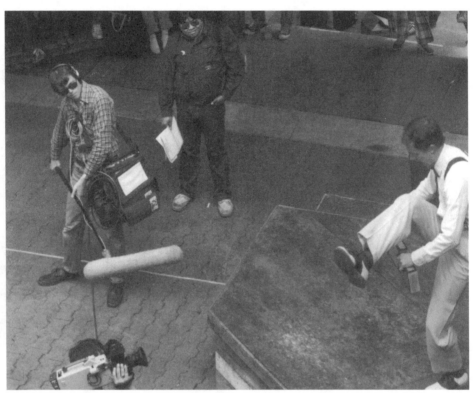

Figure 1–1 *Evening Magazine* Crew (Field Producer, Production Assistant, Camera Operator) on Location

THE CHANGING NATURE OF TELEVISION PRODUCTION

When television was introduced to the U.S. public at the 1939 World's Fair in New York, it thrilled those who saw it. The display was impressive: Technicians, cameras, lights, and the instantaneous transmission of a televised image and sound were all part of the event. Not only was the demonstration impressive but so was the equipment, particularly its size. Television cameras and television lights were very large and complicated pieces of equipment. Indeed, during the first several decades of its existence, television production was characterized by the large size of the equipment needed to produce those images.

In the early days of television (and even today for large-scale remote sports productions), a **remote production**—one staged outside a studio—was an incredibly complicated event, involving scores of technicians and an armada of

Figure 1–2   Television News Photographers Equipped with Professional Camcorders Cover the Big Event

equipment. When one went on a *remote*, essentially one took the television studio along and set it up at the remote location. The same equipment used in the studio was often rolled into a truck and used for a remote broadcast.

For many years, only two alternatives were available to a producer who wished to incorporate remote material into a production. The first alternative was a live electronic remote broadcast, with the attendant problems inherent in transporting huge amounts of television equipment to the remote location. The other possibility was to cover the event on film. And so, for many years, film had an important place in television production primarily because it was portable. Until the mid-1970s, film was used extensively in television for news and documentary production, largely because of the portability of 16mm film equipment. However, a revolution was brewing in television that would change remote production. It started quietly enough, but by the 1980s, the use of film for remote television production was largely replaced by the use of portable video equipment.

In many ways, the development of television paralleled the development of film. Just as film depended on a studio setting for recording in its early decades, so did television. Television of the 1940s, 1950s, and 1960s was essentially studio production. Live television was studio television (unless it was a sports event). The teleplays of the *Golden Age of Television* (the mid-1950s) were live television studio productions. When the first videotape recorders were introduced by Ampex in 1956, at the annual convention of the National Association of Broadcasters (NAB), they also followed the large format of studio television cameras. The videotape recorders were behemoths, weighing hundreds of pounds. Even though they came equipped with wheels, they could hardly be characterized as portable.

However, in 1965, Sony introduced the first "small-format" recording system to the market, and the video revolution began. This black and white videotape recorder used a ½"-wide tape format (compared to the 2" broadcast format) and an extremely small camera pickup tube. Although the signal quality was not technically of broadcast quality, the introduction of the equipment was a boon for people interested in video equipment and production. Television production equipment, previously accessible only to those with a large amount of capital to invest, was now available to almost anyone who wanted it. In addition, whereas television had largely been a studio enterprise prior to the introduction of small-format equipment, videomakers now could venture into the field with their electronic equipment. In 1970, ½" video formats were standardized, ½" videotape editors were introduced, and the revolution was truly underway. Table 1–1 chronicles some of the highlights in the development of video technology.

Sony's introduction of a ¾" videocassette recorder (VCR) in 1971, and the development in 1974 of a portable ¾" videotape recorder (VTR) and an automated ¾" editing system, were of great importance because the ¾" format was suitable for use both by broadcasters and other videomakers interested in nonbroadcast remote production. The portable ¾" recorder-camera-editing systems, along with the newly developed **time base correctors (TBC)** that stabilized the video signal, paved the way for the full development of broadcast electronic news gathering and the acceptance of portable small-format equipment by the broadcast community. To a large degree, developments after these breakthroughs have been refinements of existing systems: Cameras have become smaller and more sensitive; editing systems have become more precise; and portable recorders have become lighter, smaller, and more versatile.

It is important to note that video production no longer is an expensive, labor-intensive activity available only to federally licensed television broadcasters. The technological advance involving the development of more flexible and less expensive production equipment has become a communication revolution. Individuals can produce and present videotapes on topics of their own choosing, small companies can produce instructional or promotional materials to fit their specific needs, and television broadcasters can more frequently provide on-the-spot coverage of community events. Today a large variety of small-tape formats (8mm and Hi8; ½" VHS and S-VHS; ¾" U-Matic and U-Matic SP; and ½" Betacam, Betacam SP, and M-II) offer video producers a wide range of production choices.

Table 1–1   Television Technology Marches On

1939	Television introduced at New York World's Fair. Black and white only; no video-tape recording.
1941	Federal Communications Commission (FCC) accepts National Television System Committee (NTSC) standards for black and white broadcast television.
1953	FCC accepts NTSC standards for color television.
1956	Ampex introduces black and white 2" quadruplex videotape recorder (VTR) at annual National Association of Broadcasters (NAB) convention, and receives 1,000 orders for machines before the convention ends.
1956	First use of videotape on network television. On November 30, CBS uses Ampex VR 1000 to rebroadcast *Douglas Edwards and the News* to the West Coast.
1965	Sony introduces first ½" portable VTR system, including portable camera and recorder.
1966	Commercial television networks achieve full-color, prime-time schedules.
1968	Ampex introduces first color VTR.
1970	½" formats are standardized, and ½" editors are introduced.
1971	Sony introduces the ¾" videocassette recorder (VCR).
1972	Consolidated Video Systems introduces the first time base corrector.
1974	CBS begins electronic news gathering with Ikegami cameras and IVC 1" VTR.
1974	Sony introduces portable ¾" VCR and automated ¾" editing system.
1975	Betamax (½" cassette format) is introduced by Sony.
1976	VHS (½" cassette format) is introduced.
1978	Society of Motion Picture and Television Engineers' standards for type-C 1" broadcast-format VTRs are announced. Machines manufactured by Sony and Ampex.
1981	One-piece Betacam (Sony) and M-format camcorders (RCA Hawkeye and Panasonic RECAM) are introduced. Broadcast-quality camera and VCR units utilizing ½" videocassettes and component recording (incompatible with both home versions of Beta and VHS) are introduced.
1983	Beta HiFi is introduced to consumer market. VHS hi-fi follows the next year.
1983	United States Supreme Court decides that use of VCRs for off-air recording at home does not violate the Copyright Act (*Disney* v. *Sony Corporation of America*). Sales of home VCRs boom.
1984	FCC approves stereo television broadcasting. First stereo broadcasts of *The Tonight Show* and the Olympics.
1984	RCA and NEC introduce broadcast-quality CCD (charge-coupled device) cameras in which vacuum-type pickup tubes are replaced with silicon chips.
1985	Sony 8mm camcorder is introduced.
1986	Introduction of ¾" U-Matic SP and ½" Betacam SP formats.
1987	S-VHS (Super VHS) ½" tape format introduced.
1989	First successful experimental broadcast of HDTV (high-definition television) in the United States.
1990	Introduction of NewTek Video Toaster
1991	Panasonic introduces portable ½" digital tape-format camcorder.
1994 (estimate)	FCC establishes U.S. standards for HDTV.

PRODUCTION USES OF PORTABLE EQUIPMENT

The development of portable video technology has opened up the world of video production. It has pushed the world of videotape recording out of the studio, and it has also opened up the field of video production to many people who would not have had access to the large, expensive technology of earlier years. In addition, as a result of the portability and accessibility of this new technology, video has found a host of new uses. Portable video is increasingly being used for personal expression, for independent production, in educational institutions and corporations, as well as in the broadcast arena.

Personal Video

Because of its relatively low cost, portable video equipment has made video accessible to individuals in much greater numbers than ever before. In many ways, video has supplanted film as the primary medium for home and personal use. In the 1940s and 1950s, 16mm film was used as a home recording medium. That format was replaced by 8mm and super 8mm film in the 1960s and 1970s. Now, portable video has taken over. Although the ½" open reel and ¾" cassette formats never really achieved the mass popularity with consumers that had been predicted, the small cassette formats (VHS, S-VHS, 8mm, and Hi8) have made a significant impact on the home market. VCRs can be found in almost two-thirds of all U.S. homes and are one of the most popular consumer items introduced in recent years.

Personal uses of portable video equipment vary. Some people buy player-recorders for use primarily in their home entertainment systems. That is, they are used to record programs that have been broadcast or cablecast, or they are used to play back owned or rented videocassettes. A growing segment of users have purchased a portable video camcorder in addition to their home player-recorder. These low-cost camcorders have the advantage over film of producing picture and sound color recordings that are available for immediate playback. They are used extensively to record family events such as birthdays, special parties, and weddings. Sports enthusiasts use them to record and then criticize their own sports performances, such as golf swings, swimming strokes, and tennis serves. In addition, they are convenient for making visual and sound messages to send to friends or relatives who live far away (see Figure 1–3).

Independent Video Production

Independent video production refers to those organizations and individuals who either use video to make their own programs or who make their production skills and facilities available to others who want to produce and distribute messages via video. A large group of independents have used video to produce television documentaries. Almost any large or medium-sized community contains

Figure 1–3   Hi8 Camcorder—A Popular Portable Video Recording Format

individuals who are working on video documentaries that focus on various community-oriented social, economic, and political problems. These independents may have a number of goals in mind. Some may try to gain access to their local cable company or television station with their finished program, whereas others may try to distribute their material regionally or nationally. Whatever the distribution aim, the availability of relatively inexpensive equipment and facilities provides an opportunity for video production independents to express alternative viewpoints on community and national problems.

Independent artists have been using video for some time. Television is becoming popular as a medium for artistic expression, and numerous video experimenters have gained access to the medium through the use of portable equipment. Whether the artistic statement is dramatic or experimental, whether it involves the manipulation of content or formal properties of the medium (such as lighting, editing, or sound), access to the medium has been facilitated by the introduction and use of this equipment.

Many independent producers produce videotapes for clients. These may range from producing a videotape for a couple who want to record their wedding, to producing tapes for a small company that does not have its own video production facility but wants a tape that introduces a new product to a client, or trains employees in new sales techniques, new methods of product maintenance, and so on.

Educational Uses

In the past decade, numerous educational institutions have turned to television, primarily for nonbroadcast, in-house uses. For example, video is often used in schools as a supplement to instruction. Indeed, some actual instruction may be done via televised lectures live or on videotape. Speeches in public speaking classes are taped and then played back for a critique by the instructor or class. Teacher-training programs often videotape student teachers to provide a record of their classroom performance. Colleges and universities with programs in the broadcast or electronic media most frequently use portable, small-format equipment in their laboratories and cable television facilities.

Medical Television

One of the fastest growing areas of television use is in the field of medical television. Many hospitals have their own television staffs and put television to a variety of uses. It is used for the distribution of in-house information or for instruction in new medical techniques as a part of an ongoing program of continuing education (see Figure 1–4). It is also sometimes used to provide information to patients on various health problems and their treatment.

Institutions involved in providing therapeutic treatment, such as counseling or other forms of therapy, to patients with speech defects or mental or emotional problems often use video as part of therapy or to record therapy sessions.

Corporate Television

Corporate television is another significant growth area for the use of video.[1] Many large corporations use videotape to distribute electronic corporate newsletters to their employees, particularly if corporate offices are widely distributed. In-house training or staff development is another common use, as are videotapes for use at the point of sale. You have probably seen product demonstrations on cassettes being played in department stores.

Government Uses

Local, county, state, and federal government agencies also are significant users of video. Many government agencies produce videotapes to inform their constituents of new programs, policies, regulations, or accomplishments (see Figure 1–5). In some cases, these tapes may be cablecast or broadcast via local media outlets.

Figure 1–4   Typical Remote Video Production Location: The Surgery

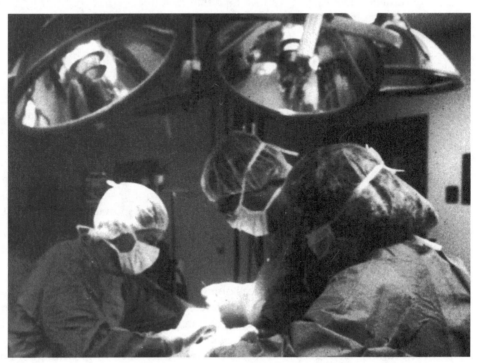

Public Access

Similarly, portable video has proved invaluable for local media access groups. Many cable systems operate public access centers in which studio or remote equipment is available to community members. A provision for community access may be included in the franchise agreement for the cable company that operates in the town or city where you live.

Broadcast Uses

The move toward the miniaturization of broadcast equipment is a strong and continuous process. Broadcast uses of portable video equipment have centered in two areas: **electronic news gathering (ENG)** and **electronic field production (EFP).** It was in the area of ENG that portable video equipment first made a significant impact in broadcasting. Prior to its introduction, broadcasters relied on film for stories that took place in the field, or on the placement of live, remote television cameras. The difficulty with film recording was the time delay involved in returning the film to the station or network, and in processing and editing the film.

Figure 1–5 Portable Video on the Moon

The introduction of lightweight, portable television cameras and recorders changed the face of television news. Most local television stations, as well as the major broadcast networks, made the transition from film to portable video for electronic news gathering in the mid-1970s. The availability of reliable ¾" portable VCRs and editing systems made large-scale commitment to ENG possible among local broadcasters.

With the development and refinement of broadcast-quality ½" tape formats (Betacam, Betacam SP, and M-II) in the 1980s and the introduction of the ½" digital tape recording format (D3) in the early 1990s, professional broadcasters had access to high-quality camcorder systems that were even more portable than the two-piece systems (separate camera and recorder) that preceded them.

Similarly, the existence of portable broadcast-quality video recorders and cameras made possible the growth of EFP. Before the introduction of this equipment, much local programming had been based in the studio or shot on film by those few stations with a commitment to remote production. The introduction of portable broadcast-quality equipment made it much easier for producers to get out of the studio. Nationally syndicated television magazine feature programs, such as *Hard Copy, A Current Affair,* and *Entertainment Tonight,* rely on remote production crews using portable cameras and VCRs. Programs such as *48 Hours,*

60 Minutes, and *20/20* are examples of network television programs that make extensive use of portable television technology. A host of "reality-based" programs such as *Rescue 911, Cops, America's Most Wanted,* and others rely as well on portable video technology for field production and editing.

These programs reflect the fact that quality production no longer depends on studio-based equipment. It may ultimately prove less expensive to contract for program production using portable equipment than to maintain costly studios in expensive, urban locations.

TELEVISION AS A MEDIUM OF COMMUNICATION

Television is both a medium of communication and a type of technology. The successful producer must understand not only the components and operation of the technology of televised communication but also the elements of the process of communication via television. As we view the process of television field production, five elements characterize this particular communication situation:

1. The unique elements of the production organization (*source*)
2. The fundamental importance of *message* design
3. The importance of the television medium as a *channel* of communication
4. The particular nature of the television *audience*
5. Audience *feedback* to the program producer

Figure 1–6 graphically displays this communication process.

Figure 1–6   Communication Process via Television and Video

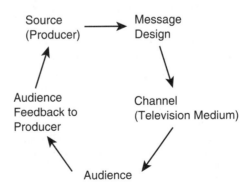

Production Organization

The television field production group is often significantly smaller than the studio production organization. Typically, the principal roles involved in producing single-camera remote productions are the **producer**, who is responsible for the overall organization of a production and for delegating responsibility to the other members of the production team; the *camera operator,* or **videographer** (sometimes called the **shooter)**, who is responsible for the visual treatment of the subject matter as well as for the physical operation of the camera; the *videotape operator* (sometimes called the **production assistant**), who is responsible for operating the videotape recorder in the field, as well as for monitoring audio, helping to set up the lights, and providing other general production support; and the **videotape editor**, who is responsible for executing the producer's vision in the process of postproduction editing. The editor has primary responsibility for physically performing the edits, and, depending on the role of the producer, the editor may have much or little responsibility for actually making editing decisions. In many cases, work roles overlap. An entire production may be produced by two or three people, with each assuming several responsibilities during the production.

The nature of single-camera field production and the small production crew it involves often creates a sense of excitement and responsibility that studio productions often lack. Each person's contribution counts. There is often intense involvement by the crew on the production, and those involved exercise greater control over the final product than their counterparts in studio production. The challenge of recording in the field, the excitement at instantly playing back images that were recorded only minutes ago, and the intense involvement demanded by the editing process all characterize video field production (see Table 1–2).

Message Design

Message design is a critical part of the telecommunication process. Ironically, one of the first elements that should be considered is the desired *effect* of the message. Who is to do what with this information? Because the goal of most commercial programming is to maximize the size of the viewing audience at a given time, many program producers and station program directors desire to design and distribute entertaining and informative programs that will appeal to the largest cross-section of the general viewing audience. Success is typically measured in terms of program ratings, which provide an estimate of the size of the audience and determine how much money advertisers can be charged to place their commercials on the air.

Producers of educational and industrial video programs frequently begin the design stage of their productions by thinking in terms of a list of specific objectives—things they hope the audience will be able to understand or do after viewing a particular program. Whether you are producing a program designed to teach language or computational skills to children, or new safety procedures

Table 1-2 Multiple-Camera Studio and Single-Camera Video Field Production Characteristics

	Studio	Remote
No. of cameras	Multiple cameras (usually 2 or 3)	Single camera
Size of crew	Large (often 8 or more) Producer Director Audio Camera operators (2 or 3) Floor director Technical director VTR operator	Small (usually 2 or 3) Producer Camera operator Production assistant
Recording method	Usually live or live on tape; a complete program or large segments	Individual segments or shots to be edited or inserted into a larger program
Amount of control over environment	Controlled studio Studio lighting Sound (acoustics) controlled Assured source of power Availability of technical support staff	Uncontrolled remote location Available light Ambient, location sound Must provide own power No technical support in field
Type of script	Usually fully or semiscripted	May be fully scripted, sometimes semiscripted

to employees in your manufacturing facility, you must have a clear understanding of the effects you expect your program to have on the viewer before you begin to produce it. Naturally, you will also need to consider your target audience as well. A program aimed at children will be approached differently than one aimed at adults, even if the subject matter is similar.

Message design is therefore concerned with the basic idea, which involves the choice of subject; a decision about how that subject will be treated as it is presented through the medium of television; and an understanding of how to control the treatment of the subject to achieve maximum impact on the audience.

The Television Medium

Perhaps more than anything else, the small screen characterizes television and video. Unlike theatrical motion pictures, where the screen may be 30 feet high and 100 feet wide, in most home, school, and institutional viewing situations television is most often watched on screens measuring 27 inches in diagonal or less. Until larger screen "home theater" and HDTV television sets become the standard, television programs will continue to be designed in close-up detail for viewing on small screens.

The audience has learned to expect close-ups and reaction shots, and the successful producer will give the audience what it expects with respect to these conventions. Close-ups provide the magnification often necessary for small-screen use. Magnification, a key to visibility, is central to most television production. Close-ups are also important because they are a means of focusing audience attention on a specific detail or relationship by eliminating all other parts of the picture.

Reaction shots are important to messages designed to persuade or generate an emotional response. The use of reaction shots evolved as media practitioners learned that the effect of a statement or action is determined by the receiver, not the sender. The quick cut to the face of a person listening to a speaker reveals how the speech is being received, whether it is being accepted or rejected. In seeing how this person reacts, the audience is, in turn, told how to react.

The Television Audience

Television is a medium of communication, and the successful producer must always keep the audience in mind as part of the process of communication. Even though television is often thought of as a form of mass communication, the successful television producer realizes that communication takes place between the message and an *individual* in the audience. Even though someone may be part of a very large audience, the individual's response to a program is always an important one. For a message or program to be effective, it must communicate individually to each person in the audience. This is no easy task, given the variations that may exist among different audience members.

The producer should also remember that the audience is composed of individuals who most often watch alone or with one or two other people. Although there tends to be little audience interaction during programs, the televised message often has to compete for attention with distractions in the home viewing environment. Therefore, the message must be designed to catch and hold the viewer's attention. In addition, since the viewing is often done alone or in a small group, the successful producer realizes that the pace of television is not based on group response timing, nor is the purpose limited to entertainment.

Theatrical production values dominate the business of network television production, and the producer of drama or comedy should note the techniques used. Producers whose purpose is to explore a phenomenon or provide specific instruction or information must understand that producing novelty or laughs instead is dysfunctional. The individual attempting to use the program for serious purposes will not appreciate the substitution.

Feedback

Feedback is that part of the communication process in which audience responses to the production are transmitted to the producers. The nature and extent of feedback is related to the type of production and the way in which it is distributed to and received by the audience. In commercial broadcast television, program ratings—a measure of the size of the audience—provide one indication of the audience response to a program. Telephone calls and letters from audience members to stations and networks are also an important part of the feedback process. For the home video producer, feedback might take the form of comments by family members on the quality of the videotape documenting a family celebration.

Feedback is extremely useful to the video producer because it provides important information about the audience's response to the program or videotape—information that the producer needs to have in order to make subsequent productions more effective.

TECHNICAL FACTORS AND AESTHETIC FACTORS

Video field production combines an understanding of the technical factors of production with the aesthetic factors of production. **Technical factors** relate to developing an operational understanding of the way in which equipment functions. To work successfully with portable video equipment, you must understand how the equipment works. This does not mean that you need to be an engineer or understand all of the electronic and physical principles that govern the operations of the equipment. What it does mean is that you must have an understanding of the way in which the system operates—the way in which different technical elements interrelate, and the way in which you can control the technical components of production. It does mean that you need to have a basic understanding of what the video signal is and how it can be controlled. All video equipment operates on similar principles; this book stresses fundamental underlying principles of operation. Since underlying operational principles vary little among brands of equipment, you should have little difficulty in adapting the general principles discussed here to the specific requirements of a particular system.

Many handbooks on television production are nothing more than manuals of equipment operation. However, it is our position that one must know not only how to manipulate the equipment but also how to manipulate the medium in which one is working: television. This brings us to the area of television aesthetics. **Aesthetic factors**, throughout this text, refer to production variables and the ways in which they can be manipulated to affect audience response to the televised message.[2]

We see the process of video field production as a combination of technical factors and aesthetic factors. Whether you are engaged in video production for personal, artistic, educational, or broadcast uses, the requirements of the technology and the medium must be considered. The fundamentals of production and the production processes discussed in this book will be helpful to you, no matter what type of video production you are engaged in.

Creative Problem Solving

If there is one phrase that expresses our idea of what is at the center of television field production, it is *creative problem solving.* Communication via television means that the producer/writer/director must understand the medium and how to use it. Finding the appropriate techniques to effectively express the idea and content of a program presents problems that must be solved creatively.

Field production also presents a unique set of logistical problems. No two days of shooting in the field are ever quite the same, since no two locations are ever the same. The ability to deal with the range of problems encountered on location is the mark of the successful field production person.

Finally, video field production presents a set of unique technical problems. People involved in field production simply must know more about the technical side of video production than their studio counterparts. All manner of technical problems arise in the field, and field producers must be able to anticipate and avoid them or correct them when they arise.

For us, the process of creative problem solving is what makes field production so exciting and enjoyable.

SUMMARY

Changes in television technology have greatly changed the way television is produced. Portable video equipment is characterized by the small size of the cameras and videotape recorders. Portable equipment has brought television production out of the studio and into the field. Video equipment has been made accessible to large numbers of people because it is relatively inexpensive and easy to operate.

Portable video equipment has found widespread use in a number of different production situations. It is often used to produce personal and artistic video and is also used in independent production. Educational and industrial users include schools, hospitals, corporations, and government agencies. Portable equipment has also found significant use among broadcasters, as it is widely used both for electronic news gathering and electronic field production.

All television production can be viewed as a method of communication, and the successful producer needs to understand the technology of television, as well as how to communicate effectively in the medium. Important characteristics of the television production communication process include the nature of the production organization, the importance of message design, the characteristics of the television audience and the television medium, and feedback to the producer.

To be successful, the video field producer must understand both the technical and aesthetic aspects of production, and possess an aptitude for creative problem solving. Technical production factors relate to an operational understanding of the way in which video equipment functions. Aesthetic production factors concern production variables and the ways in which they can be manipulated to produce more effective programs.

ENDNOTES

1. See Gayeski, Diane M., *Corporate and Instructional Video*. Englewood Cliffs, NJ: Prentice Hall, 1991. See also Dranov, P., Moore, L., and Hickey, A., *Video in the 80s: Emerging Uses for Television in Business, Education, Medicine and Government*. White Plains, NY: Knowledge Industry Publications, 1981.

2. For a full discussion of media aesthetics, see Zettl, Herbert, *Sight Sound Motion*, 2nd ed. Belmont, CA: Wadsworth, 1990, and Dondis, Donis A., *A Primer of Visual Literacy*. Cambridge, MA: MIT Press, 1973.

2

The Portable Video Camera

ELECTRONIC IMAGE REPRODUCTION

At the center of all video systems is the television camera. A marvel of modern electronics, the television camera is charged with the responsibility of producing the electronic video signal.

All television cameras have a number of standard components, including an image sensor, viewfinder, camera control unit, and lens assembly (see Figure 2–1). This chapter will focus on portable video cameras and on the function of the first three components listed above. We will look at lenses in Chapter 3.

Function and Types of Camera Image Sensors

The most important component of the video camera is its image sensor. Its function is to change light into electrical energy (see Figure 2–2). Technically speak-

Figure 2–1   Parts of a Portable Video Camera

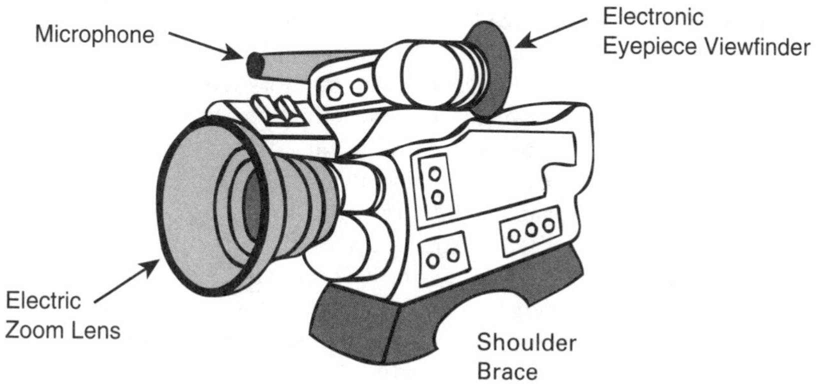

Microphone

Electronic
Eyepiece Viewfinder

Electric
Zoom Lens

Shoulder
Brace

Figure 2–2   Television Display

Video Camera

The camera changes light into electrical energy in the form of a video signal. The home television changes this video signal back into light.

ing, the camera image sensor is an **optical-video transducer,**[1] which simply means that it changes incoming light (physical input) into an electrical video signal (electrical output). By way of comparison, microphones are also transducers—they change incoming sound waves (physical input) into an electrical audio signal (electrical output).

Two types of camera image sensors are now in use: CCDs (charge-coupled devices) and vacuum tubes (usually simply referred to as pickup tubes) (see Figure 2–3).

CCD (Charge-Coupled Device) Principles

A **charge-coupled device (CCD)** image sensor is a solid-state semiconductor that converts incoming light into a video signal. In the CCD, incoming light strikes a layer of metal oxide or silicon semiconductors where it is converted into an electric charge. Each one of these conducting points is referred to as a pixel. The number of pixels in the "chip" determines the amount of detail, or resolution, the camera will be capable of producing. These pixels, or picture elements, are arranged in precise horizontal and vertical rows on the chip. High-quality CCDs often contain more than 300,000 individual pixels, or picture elements. The camera lens focuses the scene before it is on this array of pixels, each of which is responsible for reproducing one tiny part of the picture. After the incoming light is converted into an electric charge, it is transferred and stored in another layer of the chip, and then the information is read out one frame at a time in a line-by-line sequence in conformity with normal television scanning rates.

Figure 2–3   Camera Image Sensors: Pickup Tube and CCD

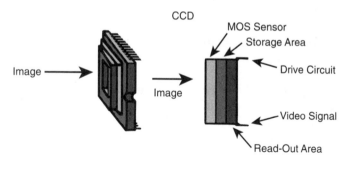

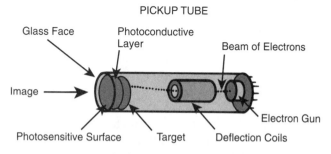

CCDs are very small. Typically, the image-sensing area of the chip is either $\frac{1}{2}''$ or $\frac{2}{3}''$, measured diagonally. CCDs are much smaller, lighter, and more reliable, and they consume less power than traditional pickup tube-type systems. Because they are much more rugged than conventional pickup tubes, CCDs have largely replaced pickup tubes in cameras and camcorders designed for the home video market. They are also used in most professional cameras and camcorders designed for remote use, where the need is for a durable camera that will stand up to more physical abuse than is typically received by a camera used in a controlled studio environment. Indeed, with continued technical improvement, CCDs may soon replace pickup tubes entirely as the imaging device in all consumer and professional video cameras.

Electronic Shutter. All CCD cameras are equipped with an electronic shutter. The electronic shutter controls the amount of time that the incoming light hits the photosensitive layer of the chip. In recording situations where the recorded image tends to flicker or become blurred because of high-speed movement of the subject in front of the camera, shutter speed can be increased to reduce these picture artifacts and improve the sharpness of the image. Although shutter speed positions of OFF, 1/60, 1/100, 1/250, 1/500, 1/1000, and 1/2000 are fairly common on professional cameras and camcorders, the number and range of shutter speed positions available will vary depending on the quality (and cost) of the camera or camcorder.

The Camera Pickup Tube

Vacuum tubes have been in use since modern television cameras were first invented, and although they have been largely replaced in new camera designs by CCDs, pickup tubes continue to be used today in a few cameras, particularly large studio-type cameras and in some cameras designed for high-definition television (HDTV). The process through which light is changed into the video signal by a pickup tube is one of the most fascinating things about television. Although it may seem complicated at first, it is really quite a simple process.

The camera pickup tube in a television camera is a small vacuum tube, usually 3″ or 4″ long and $\frac{1}{2}$″, $\frac{2}{3}$″, or 1″ in diameter. The tube has several main components. The tube itself is made of glass. Attached to the inside of the glass face of the tube is an extremely thin, transparent photosensitive coating. Next to this is a layer of photoconductive material. Immediately behind the photoconductive layer is the **target,** which has a slight positive electrical charge when the camera is turned on. Light from the scene that is being recorded is focused by the lens of the camera onto the *face* of the pickup tube. It passes through the glass and the photosensitive coating, onto the **photoconductive layer.** As light hits the photoconductive layer, it causes the charge on the target to change in proportion to the relative intensity of the light.

The video signal is produced as the target is scanned by a **beam of electrons.** This beam of electrons is emitted by the **electron gun** at the back of the pickup tube. The electron beam is focused on the target and scans it in a series of horizontal lines. Each line of the picture is composed of about 500 dots, or bits of information. Bright spots on the photoconductive layer change the charge on the target greatly, and when that particular spot is scanned by the electron beam, a greater number of electrons pass through the target than pass through in places where the image on the photoconductive layer is darker. These changes in the charge on the target plate produce the **video signal.**

Video Display

Your home television set works in much the same way as the camera image sensor, except it reverses the process. That is, instead of turning light into electrical energy as the CCD or pickup tube does, your receiver turns electrical energy into light. This is accomplished by scanning the television picture tube with an electron beam. At the back of the picture tube in your television is an electron gun, which shoots an electron beam at the inside of the face of the picture tube. The picture tube is coated with a photosensitive material that glows (becomes brighter) when it is hit by the beam of electrons. A large blast of electrons causes it to glow a lot; a small blast causes little action.

Television Scanning: Lines and Frames

The video image is composed of a number of **frames** and **lines.** Since we normally think of the television process as existing in time, we can measure the frame rate of television rather easily. In the United States, there are 30 frames of video information per second, and each one of those frames is composed of 525 lines of information.

Starting with line number 1, the beam moves across the picture tube until it gets to the end of that line. Then the beam automatically shuts off, returns to the other side of the picture tube, drops down to line number 3, and scans across that. Once again, when it reaches the end of the line, it automatically shuts off, drops down to line number 5, and repeats the process all over again. When it gets down to the bottom of the frame (line 525), it shuts off, returns to the top of the picture, and scans the even-numbered lines (2, 4, 6, 8, and so on). This process is known as *2:1 interlaced scanning*. First the odd-numbered lines are scanned and then the even ones. Each time the gun reaches the bottom of the picture, it has completed one **field,** or 262.5 lines, of information. A complete frame of information (525 lines) is composed of two individual fields: one field of odd-numbered lines and one field of even-numbered lines (see Figure 2–4).

The reason for this system of interlaced scanning is simple. The photosensitive surface on your picture tube glows for a very short time when the electron beam hits it. If the beam started scanning from the top of the frame and continued down to the bottom, by the time it got there the top of the picture would

Figure 2–4   Television Scanning Process

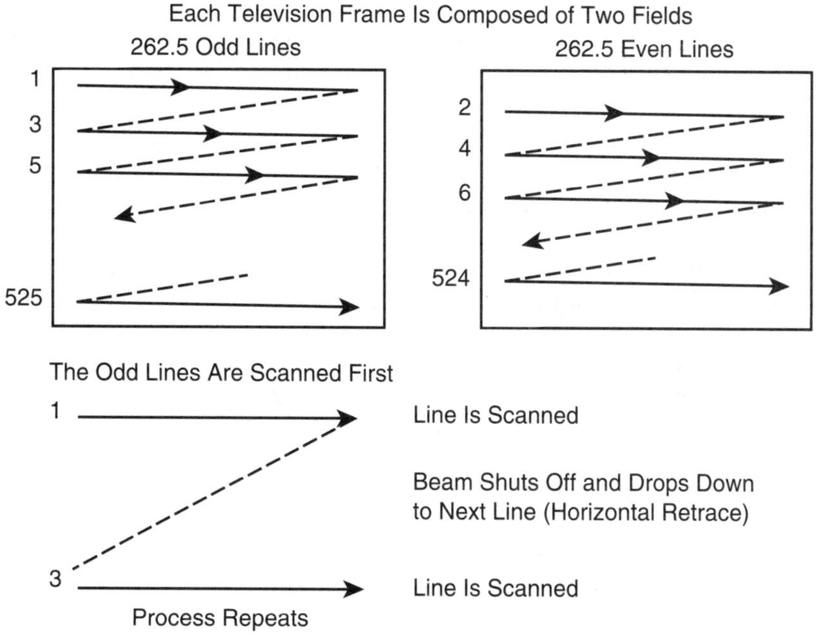

Each Television Frame Is Composed of Two Fields

262.5 Odd Lines   262.5 Even Lines

The Odd Lines Are Scanned First

1 ——————————————▶ Line Is Scanned

Beam Shuts Off and Drops Down
to Next Line (Horizontal Retrace)

3 ——————————————▶ Line Is Scanned

Process Repeats

Table 2–1   Varying Television System Standards throughout the World

Country	Frames per Second	Lines per Frame
United States, Canada, Japan, Latin America	30	525
Europe (most systems), China, Commonwealth of Independent States	25	625

already have faded to black. To keep parts of the picture from fading out or flickering, the lines are interlaced. As a result, the picture maintains its brightness throughout the program.

In a sense, the way in which frames constitute the basis of the television image is similar to the system used in film recording, except that in film the process is chemical and in television the process is electronic. If you have ever worked with 16mm film, you know that it is projected at the rate of 24 frames per second. (This is also the standard for 35mm film.) If you hold a piece of film up to the light, you can see those individual frames. Each frame is a still photo, and the illusion of motion is created when those still frames are projected rapidly onto a screen. One frame flashes on, then off, as the next frame is pulled into the projector. The projector light comes on again, the frame is flashed on, then off, as the next one comes into place, and so on. The illusion of motion—and it is an illusion because what is being projected on the screen is actually a series of still pictures—is created through the human perceptual phenomenon of **persistence of vision**. That is, you mentally connect one frame with the next, and the difference between the position of people or objects in the two frames appears to you as motion. If the film is projected too slowly, the motion will have a jerky stop-action appearance. If it is projected correctly (24 frames per second), the motion will appear to be smooth.

Similarly, each frame of video information can be looked at as a still frame. Motion becomes apparent when the picture is displayed at its normal rate of 30 frames (60 fields) per second, and this rate eliminates picture flicker.

Incidentally, the 525 lines per frame standard characteristic of U.S. television is an arbitrary standard. That is, the system could have more or less lines and still function. Indeed, many other countries use 625-line systems, which actually provide greater picture detail than 525 lines (see Table 2–1). The system used in the United States and Canada was adopted as the standard by the National Television System Committee (NTSC), which represented the major U.S. electronics manufacturers at the time television was invented. The Federal Communications Commission (FCC) adopted the NTSC recommendations for the 525-line 30-frame television standard in 1941.[2]

TELEVISION SIGNAL CONTROL

Horizontal and Vertical Sync

As we have discussed, each frame of video information is constructed by combining picture information and synchronizing information. Among the most important synchronizing control pulses are horizontal and vertical sync and blanking pulses. These pulses are generated by a sync generator that can be located as an integral component inside the camera or as a separate component outside the camera.

The **horizontal sync** and blanking pulses control the timing of each line of video information; the **vertical sync** and blanking pulses control the timing of each field and frame of information. Essentially, each line of information begins with a horizontal sync pulse and ends with a horizontal blanking pulse. Similarly, each field begins with a vertical sync pulse and ends with a vertical blanking pulse.

Thus, you can see that for each frame of video information there are 525 lines of information and 525 horizontal blanking and sync pulses. These 525 lines are arranged in two fields of information along with two vertical blanking and sync pulses. The sync pulses not only allow the system to work but this information becomes extremely important when we get to the area of videotape editing.

Internal and External Sync

When sync pulses are generated within the camera, we refer to the sync as **internal sync**. When sync pulses are generated outside the camera, we refer to the sync as **external sync**.

When a single camera is used in conjunction with a videocassette recorder (VCR), the horizontal and vertical sync pulses are usually produced internally in the camera itself. Most single-camera VCR field production units fall into this category.

In more complex multiple camera field production systems, which include a video switcher and several cameras operating simultaneously, all cameras must scan synchronously. To accomplish this, they all must have the same reference to horizontal and vertical sync. In such a situation, an external sync generator is used to regulate the timing of all the camera sources. (See Chapter 10 for a more detailed discussion.)

Sometimes the sync pulses generated by one camera can be used to "drive" the signal of another camera through a process called *gen-lock.* In this process, the second camera senses the incoming sync pulses from the first camera and then creates its own video signal synchronously with the other camera. (See Chapter 10 for a more detailed discussion.)

The Television Waveform

As this discussion has already indicated, the television signal is somewhat complex because it contains not only picture information but also synchronizing information. The picture information alone is referred to as a **noncomposite signal**. When video information and sync are both present in a signal, it is referred to as a **composite signal**.

Let's continue our discussion of the television signal by talking more specifically about the black and white picture signal. Black and white television presents a range of **brightness** only; elements in the picture are somewhere between white and black. This range of variation between white and black, or between the brightest and darkest parts of a scene, can be seen in the television waveform, which shows us what the video signal actually looks like. Figure 2–5 shows the components of one line of information of a typical video waveform.

Camera Control Unit

Control over the video signal is the function of the **camera control unit (CCU)**. Camera control units contain components that regulate the sensitivity of the tar-

Figure 2–5   Video Waveform

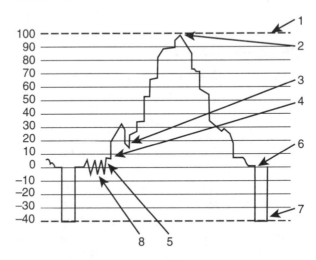

(1) Reference White—Brightest Point TV System Will Produce
(2) Peak White—Actual Brightest Point in the Scene
(3) Peak Black—Actual Darkest Point
(4) Reference Black—Darkest (Black) Possible Point TV System Will Produce
(5) Setup (Pedestal)—Determines the Point at Which Reference Black Is Set
(6) Blanking Level—Turns Off Beam of Electrons
(7) Horizontal Sync Pulse—Turns on Electron Beam
(8) Color Burst—Controls the Phasing of the Color Signal

get of the image sensor, the strength and focus of the electron beam (in cameras with pickup tubes), the size of the iris opening of the lens (described in Chapter 3), and the level of the gain and pedestal of the video signal, which we will discuss in a moment.

CCUs can be of two types: external or internal. External CCUs are completely separate from the camera. Studio television cameras utilize external CCUs. Portable television cameras almost always contain an internal CCU, which is one that is built into the camera. On some portable cameras, the functions of the CCU are fully automatic; on others, some manual adjustment of the signal is possible.

The adjustment that allows you to amplify the level of the video signal is called the **gain**. Just as you can turn up the level of sound on your car radio or home stereo, so can you turn up the level of the video signal. Increasing the gain usually has the effect of making the picture brighter. However, it may also have some negative effects. When you amplify any electronic signal, you also increase the **noise** inherent in the system. If you increase the gain of the video signal too much, the picture will become "noisy," or grainy. Picture noise is sometimes also called *snow*. This is the visual equivalent of the static or white noise that you hear when you turn up the volume on your home stereo too high. Increasing the gain on a video signal may also affect the contrast and make the picture look washed out.

The other important element of television picture signal control is the pedestal. **Pedestal** controls the black level of a picture. Every black and white picture reproduces a number of shades of black and white. These range from the brightest or whitest white, through several shades of gray, to black. The deepest black that is reproduced is controlled by the pedestal control.

The Television Waveform Monitor

To set pedestal and gain levels, television engineers use what is called a **waveform monitor**. This monitoring equipment shows the form of the video signal (the waveform). If you look at the waveform in Figure 2–5, you can see a number of the things we have discussed so far. The highest part of the wave is the **peak white**; it is equivalent to the brightest part of the scene that the camera is shooting. Peak white should not exceed 100 percent (**reference white**) on the waveform. The pedestal, or black level, is always set at 7.5 percent on the waveform monitor. An engineer will usually make the pedestal adjustment and then increase the gain until the peak white level reaches 100 percent, unless this makes the picture too noisy. The horizontal sync pulse is also visible in the waveform display.

In most portable cameras, the adjustments for pedestal and gain are controlled automatically within the camera. You do not have to adjust them at all. But in a few cases, which we will discuss in a little while, you may have the opportunity to manually adjust these controls yourself. It is therefore important to know what they do.

THE COLOR SIGNAL

Luminance and Chrominance

Up to this point, we have been talking about a black and white television signal. Today, most television programs, and therefore most video cameras, are color. Color video cameras work under the same principles as black and white cameras, but they are a little bit more complex. The two principal components of the color television signal are luminance and chrominance. **Luminance** refers to the black and white brightness information that we have already discussed. Every color television signal contains a luminance signal as well as the color information. **Chrominance** is the color information, and includes two components: hue and saturation. **Hue** refers to the color itself: red, green, blue, and so on. **Saturation** refers to the amount or intensity of the color. For example, a very light pink and a very vivid or deep red both have the same hue (red), but differ in terms of how saturated they are. Pink is a very lightly saturated red, whereas the deep red is a highly saturated red.

Additive Primary Colors of Light

Color television systems work with the **additive primary colors** of light: red, green, and blue. Do not confuse these with the subtractive primaries—the type you use when you are working with paint: red, blue, and yellow. Red, green, and blue are called primary colors of light because they can be combined to form white light, as well as any other color of the spectrum. No other three colors can do this.

Color television systems take the light that enters the lens and break it into its red, green, and blue components. There are three different ways this can be done (see Figure 2–6):

1. Incoming light can be passed through a small prism block.
2. Light can be directed through a series of dichroic mirrors that reflect certain colors and let others pass.
3. A stripe filter can be attached to the face of the image sensor to break the light into its primary colors there.

Prism Block Camera Systems

The most sophisticated color television cameras use a **prism block** to break the incoming light into its red, green, and blue components. Light is reflected off the object or person being videotaped. This light is captured by the lens of the television camera and directed into the camera itself. Inside the camera, the light goes through the prism block, where it is separated into its red, green, and blue components. Each color is then directed to its own CCD or pickup tube. So,

Figure 2–6   Three Common Color Television Camera Systems

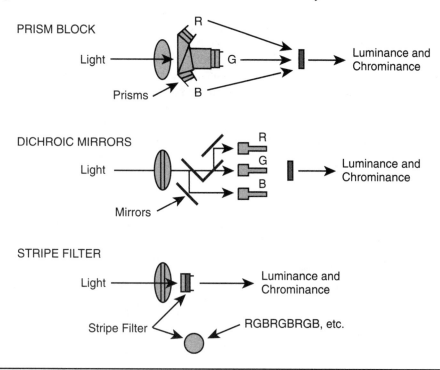

for each color, we have a separate signal. The gain and pedestal can be adjusted individually for each. It would be possible to take only the output of the red channel and send it to a television monitor, but all we would see would be red. Similarly, we could take the output of the green channel or the blue channel. Again, all we would see would be green or blue. In this state, the signal is called the **RGB signal**.

However, within the camera is a device called the **color encoder**. This device takes the output of each of the three color channels (red, green, and blue) and recombines them into one color signal, including both chrominance and luminance. This is the **encoded color signal**, and when it is displayed on a monitor or receiver, we see the scene as the camera saw it, in full color. In addition, the presence of the luminance signal ensures that the picture is seen in black and white on black and white receivers.

All of the highest-quality color cameras use three image sensors. These cameras produce the best pictures because each color is assigned to its own CCD or pickup tube, thereby ensuring the highest amount of control over the signal of each. Prism blocks are used in these high-quality cameras because the prism is the most efficient way of splitting the light into its red, green, and blue components without interfering with the signal of each.

Dichroic Mirrors

Another way of breaking the incoming light into its components in tube cameras is through the use of **dichroic mirrors**. The principle is similar to that of prism block cameras. The only difference is that the light splitting is done through mirrors rather than through the use of a prism. Dichroic mirrors are color sensitive—they reflect some colors and allow others to pass through. As with prism blocks, cameras with dichroic mirror systems utilize three image sensors—one for each of the color channels. However, cameras that use dichroic mirrors usually do not produce pictures with the sharpness of those with prism blocks. The clarity and sharpness of the picture is not as great due to loss of light and interference with the light caused by the mirrors themselves.

Stripe Filters

The third type of color camera uses only one CCD or pickup tube and a device known as a **stripe filter**. The stripe filter, which consists of extremely thin stripes of red, blue, and green filter material, is applied to the face of the CCD or pickup tube. Incoming light goes through the lens and strikes the stripe filter, which sequentially breaks it into its red, blue, and green components. The single-tube or chip camera can produce all three channels of chrominance as well as luminance. This system sacrifices picture sharpness and individual color control for decreased cost, weight, and technical complexity. For this reason, most color cameras designed for home use rely on a single CCD as the image sensor.

Color Burst and Vectorscopes

To keep the color information in proper synchronization, a special control pulse called **color burst** is used. The color burst signal ensures that the three color signals begin at the right time at the beginning of each line of video information, and the pulse can be seen on the video waveform immediately after the horizontal sync pulse. If you are not sure whether or not you have a color signal, and if you have access to a waveform monitor, you can simply look to see if color burst is present in the waveform. Figure 2–5 shows what the color burst pulse looks like.

Although color burst tells you if color is present, it does not tell you *which* colors are present. This is the function of monitoring equipment known as the **vectorscope**. Each of the three primary colors of light (red, green, and blue), and their complements (cyan, magenta, and yellow), are marked on the face of the vectorscope. By looking at the vectorscope, you can determine which colors are present in the signal and how much of each one is present (see Figure 2–7).

Since the vectorscope provides critical information about the color information in the video signal, it is an essential component of the monitoring system that is used by video engineers when color adjustments are made to cameras and VCRs. In multiple-camera shooting situations, the vectorscope is used to help

Figure 2–7   Areas of Color Display on a Vectorscope

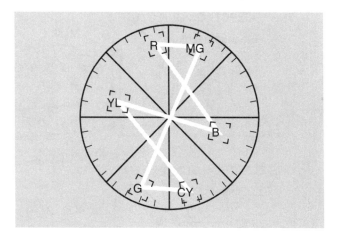

Primary Colors   Complementary Colors
R — Red   MG — Magenta
B — Blue   CY — Cyan
G — Green   YL — Yellow

match the color quality of the cameras so that the color values they reproduce are the same for each camera. In single- or multiple-camera operations, a vectorscope can assist in gauging whether or not the camera is properly white balanced; that is, adjusted to reproduce colors correctly in the lighting conditions that exist at the recording location.

Color Reproduction

The color picture that you see on a home television receiver is recreated in a way that is similar to the camera color process. The picture tube in your television set is covered with a series of phosphorescent dots. In black and white television, these dots are capable only of growing brighter or darker, depending on the strength of the electron beam that hits them. In the color set, these dots are arranged in groups of three: one red, one blue, one green (see Figure 2–8). The color television signal, as we have seen, is composed of varying amounts of these three colors, depending on the scene that is being shot. When the color video signal is fed into a monitor, it triggers the electron gun(s) to scan the face of the picture tube, and it activates the red, blue, and green dots on the screen in relation to their relative strength in the signal. What you see as you watch the screen is a full-color picture. Actually, if you get close enough to the screen of your television and stare at it, you can see there are really only three colors present: red, blue, and green. When you move away from the set, these three primary colors combine to

---

Figure 2–8   Color Television Display

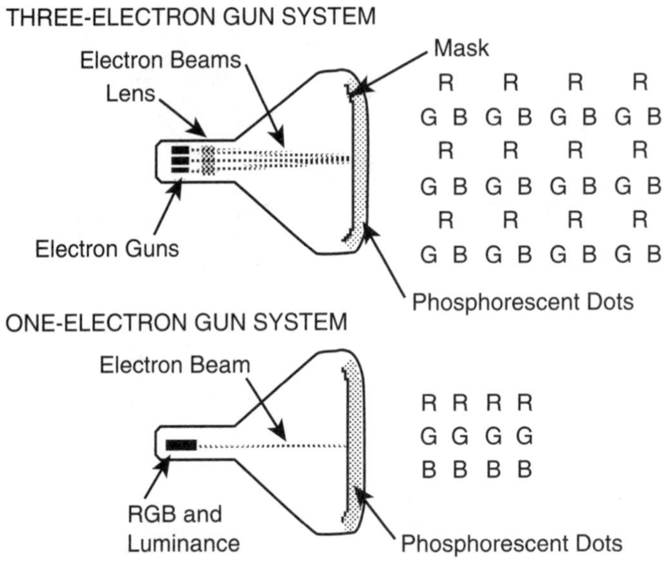

THREE-ELECTRON GUN SYSTEM

Electron Beams
Lens
Mask

R   R   R   R
G B G B G B G B
R   R   R   R
G B G B G B G B
R   R   R   R
G B G B G B G B

Electron Guns

Phosphorescent Dots

ONE-ELECTRON GUN SYSTEM

Electron Beam

R R R R
G G G G
B B B B

RGB and
Luminance

Phosphorescent Dots

---

form the other colors of the spectrum. Color mixing, therefore, is really subjective. It takes place in your head, not in the television system itself.

World Color Television Standards

Just as there are several different television frame scanning rates and line standards in operation throughout the world, so are there differences in the way the color signal is produced and recorded. The U.S. system, established by the National Television System Committee, is *NTSC* color. Critics suggest that NTSC stands for "never twice the same color," since the NTSC system allows for adjustment of color, hue, and saturation at the point of reception, with the result that color values may vary greatly from receiver to receiver. The NTSC system is used throughout North and Central America, as well as in parts of the Far East.

In other parts of the world, two other color systems are also used: *PAL* (Phase Alternation by Line), designed by the West Germans and the British and found in England, Western Europe, and throughout Africa and the Middle East; and *SECAM* (Système Électronique pour Couleur avec Mémoire), designed by the French and widely used in Eastern Europe and parts of Africa, as well as in France and Russia. SECAM is generally regarded as the best of color systems, followed by PAL and then NTSC.

As you might imagine, these different color television standards present problems when a program produced in one format is scheduled to be shown in a country that operates in another, incompatible format. Fortunately for video producers, a number of manufacturers produce VCRs with built-in conversion units that allow you to convert the VCR output to another color standard simply by flipping the appropriate switch. However, these machines are significantly more expensive than conventional VCRs.

Broadcast Quality

Technical standards exist by which engineers can determine whether or not a particular video signal is of **broadcast quality**. All broadcast signals fall under the jurisdiction of the FCC, which publishes specifications that all broadcast signals must meet. Of particular importance to the video field producer is the size of the horizontal and vertical blanking intervals. Current FCC standards require the horizontal blanking interval to be no less than 10.49 microseconds and no greater than 11.44 microseconds. (A microsecond is 1×10^{-6} seconds, or .000001 second). The vertical blanking interval limits are 10 lines (minimum) to 21.5 lines (maximum). Cameras that rely on their own internal sync generators should be periodically checked to ensure that the blanking intervals are within the specified limits, especially if the tape will be distributed to broadcast outlets.

The standards of broadcast quality for different organizations often involve variables other than the size of the blanking intervals. Program content and overall production values are as much a part of broadcast quality as technical elements. The proliferation of consumer-quality camcorders provides an interesting perspective on this issue. Although inexpensive home video camcorders are generally not considered to produce broadcast-quality recorded images, videotape of news events recorded by amateur videographers is increasingly finding its way into broadcast news programs. One broadcast news operation, the Cable News Network (CNN), actively solicited videotapes of newsworthy events recorded by amateur videographers. CNN called this its "News Hound" service. Interestingly, when the News Hound service was announced, CNN executives expressed more concern about the quality of the techniques of the camera operator than about the quality of the video signal produced by home video camcorders. In addition, concerns about technical problems such as color quality and image stability may be overlooked if the content of the videotape has extremely significant news value.

The equation with respect to the relative importance of interesting content versus technical quality extends to entertainment programs as well. One of the most popular programs on U.S. commercial television in the early 1990s has been *America's Funniest Home Videos*. Viewers submit home-made videotapes of people and animals in funny, unusual, or embarrassing situations, which are then edited for broadcast and embellished with sound effects and narration by the program's producers. As is the case with amateur news videotapes, interesting content overrides concerns about the technical quality of images recorded on consumer-level video equipment.

Although it is always a good idea to try to achieve the highest possible technical production standards, we should note that not all media outlets require that the signal be broadcast quality. Cable television systems, for example, are not regulated in the same way by the FCC as over-the-air broadcasters. Tapes produced for home viewing or for other kinds of closed-circuit distribution may deviate from the technical standard of broadcast quality, but the signal should still produce a clear, stable picture.

CAMERA PERFORMANCE CHARACTERISTICS

Not all cameras perform the same. Depending on the type and number of CCDs or pickup tubes, the internal electronics of the camera, and the type of lens attached to the camera, picture quality may vary significantly from one camera to another.

One-, Two-, or Three-Image Sensors

Most modern video cameras contain either three image sensors (CCDs or pickup tubes) or one image sensor. Cameras with three CCDs or pickup tubes are known for their excellent color reproduction and detail resolution. This type of camera is almost always used in broadcast situations. However, they are not without their disadvantages. They are larger and heavier than their single-tube or CCD counterparts and, of course, they are more expensive.

In three-tube cameras, the tubes must be kept perfectly aligned within the camera to accurately reproduce color and image detail. This process of alignment, referred to as **registration,** is usually performed daily and sometimes more often if the camera is treated roughly. CCD cameras do not have the registration problems that three-tube cameras have, because in the CCD camera system the three CCD image sensors are attached directly to the prism block in perfect registration when the camera is manufactured. Since CCDs require no maintenance and do not burn out as pickup tubes do, they are a permanent part of the image system, not a component that requires maintenance or replacement.

Camcorders and cameras with a single CCD have become the standard in consumer-quality video equipment. Single-tube or CCD cameras are known for their portability and low cost. Since they use only one image sensor, they do not have the registration problems that three-tube cameras have. However, one does sacrifice some quality when using a camera with a single-image sensor. Usually, both resolution and color quality are not as good as their three-tube or CCD counterparts.

Two CCD cameras (one for chrominance and one for luminance) offer a compromise in cost and quality but are not in wide use.

Types of Pickup Tubes

Not all tube-type cameras use the same kind of pickup tubes. From an engineering standpoint, there are two different types of tubes: image orthicon and vidicon. **Image orthicon** tubes were used in the older, large-format black and white studio cameras and some early color cameras. These tubes tended to be extremely large and are no longer manufactured. **Vidicon** pickup tubes, which have been available since the early 1950s, continue to be used in some high-quality color cameras. There are several different types of vidicons—the two most popular ones are the Plumbicon[3] and the Saticon[4] types. The principal difference between them is found in the photoconductive layer at the front of the tube. Different manufacturers use different components and give the tubes different names, but they are all variations of the basic vidicon. Pickup tubes are quickly disappearing from the popular marketplace, as most modern cameras now rely on CCDs as image sensors.

Resolution

Resolution is a term used to describe the amount of detail that a camera is able to reproduce. It is always reported in terms of lines of **horizontal resolution**. Think of a series of extremely narrow, vertical lines. If the lines are very narrow and very close together, they will be more difficult for the camera to "see" than if they are thicker and further apart. High-quality cameras have much greater horizontal resolution than low-quality cameras. For example, an inexpensive single-chip camera may only provide 250 lines of horizontal resolution, whereas a high-quality camera equipped with three CCDs may provide 600 to 700 lines. This figure is a measure of the camera's ability to reproduce fine detail in a picture. The higher the number, the greater the detail the camera can reproduce.

Video engineers use a standard resolution chart to determine how much resolution, or detail, a camera is able to produce (see Figure 2–9). High-quality cameras are generally able to reproduce much greater fine detail in a picture than low-quality cameras.

Do not confuse this measure of a camera's resolution ability with the number of scanning lines in the picture. All cameras operating in the NTSC system will produce pictures using the 525-line scanning standard; however, some cameras will produce pictures that are sharper or clearer than others. This difference in sharpness or clarity results from differences in the resolution ability of various cameras.

We should mention that the amount of resolution, or detail, apparent in the image at its final display point will only be as good as the weakest link in the recording and transmission system. Most home television receivers produce an image with approximately 300 lines of horizontal resolution; VHS VCRs record the signal with 250 to 300 lines of resolution. This may increase to 400 lines when S-VHS or Hi8 VCRs are used with compatible monitors. High-quality television studio monitors, on the other hand, may be able to resolve 600 to 800 lines.

Manufacturers have been trying for years to develop a system of high-definition television (HDTV), and several functioning systems have been introduced in the past several years. The goal of HDTV is to create a significantly improved television picture with respect to resolution.

Figure 2–9   Video Resolution Chart

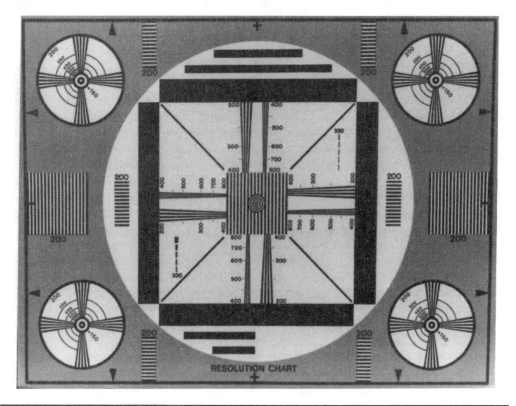

Lag

Problems with image lag and comet tails frequently occurred in tube-type cameras. **Lag**, a smearing effect that is also known as *image retention*, occurs when the camera or subject moves. It is most often associated with the use of low-cost vidicon tubes, and for that reason is also often called *vidicon lag*. Lag is often the result of insufficient lighting.

Another type of lag, called **comet tail**, is sometimes caused when there is too much contrast between light and dark areas in a picture, or when a camera pans across a light or shoots an object that is reflecting a point of light directly into the camera. This bright light source overstimulates the pickup tube and creates an effect that looks like the tail of a comet is trailing behind the subject.

Although CCD cameras are relatively free from lag and image sticking, they do exhibit a unique type of image distortion caused by very bright illumination called a *smear*, in which a bright vertical band appears above and below the bright object in the picture.

Color Reproduction

The quality of color reproduction varies depending on the type of image sensor used and the lighting conditions. Color reproduction in high-quality CCDs is exceptional and rivals or excels the performance of many tube-type cameras. However, good color quality is judged both technically and aesthetically, and the quality of a camera's picture should always be inspected closely before a decision is made to use or buy a particular kind of camera.

Sensitivity to Light and Operating Light Level

The operating light level of a camera varies with the number and type of image sensors in the camera, the type of lens, and the type of system used to break incoming light into its components for color processing. Not long ago, the operating light level for color cameras was in the range of 400 footcandles. Today, the highest-quality cameras can produce excellent pictures with 150 to 200 footcandles of light, and many cameras provide excellent color with low noise at 50 footcandles and less. (Footcandles will be discussed in more detail in Chapter 6.)

Many CCD-type cameras and camcorders can produce excellent color pictures in extremely low light. Two guidelines should always be followed with respect to the amount of light required for the optimum performance of your camera system. First, read the camera operation manual, if available, to learn the manufacturer's recommendation. Second, check with your engineering staff (if you have one!) for their recommendations.

Burn In

Burn in refers to damage done to the photoconductive surface of a *pickup tube* due to exposure to extremely bright light. The effect of a burn in on the photoconductive surface is similar to the effect of a cattle brand on the hide of a cow—a permanent mark is left. Most often, burn in occurs when the camera has been focused on a bright spot of light, such as the light from a spotlight, a reflection off chrome or water, or when the camera has been aimed directly at the sun.

A camera with a burn in the photosensitive surface will exhibit a dark mark or streak in the picture that may be a permanent feature of all subsequent video shot with the camera. For example, if you aimed the camera at a candle, the bright point of light created by the candle flame might burn a pattern into the photosensitive surface. Anything subsequently shot with that camera would also contain that pattern of the candle flame (which would look like a dark gray or black mark) superimposed over the new picture. If a tube is severely burned, the only way to fix it is to replace the pickup tube.

Although some types of vidicon tubes are more resistant than others to burn in, any camera pickup tube can be damaged if improperly used, and no pickup tube can resist burn in if it is pointed at the sun. Furthermore, power to the camera does not have to be on for burn in to occur. *The photosensitive surface can be damaged even if the camera power is off.* For this reason, the lens cap should always be used to cover the lens when the camera itself is not in use.

CCDs do not suffer from burn in. Because of their semiconductor design, there is no after-image or burn in, even when the camera is pointed directly at a bright light source.

CAMERA VIEWFINDER SYSTEMS

The camera **viewfinder** is the part of the camera the camera operator looks into to see what is being shot. *Electronic viewfinders* are found on all high-quality video cameras. The viewfinder is actually a small television screen. When you look into it, you see what the image sensor sees. Usually, viewfinders display only a black and white picture, even on most color cameras. However, an increasing number of color cameras incorporate color viewfinders. Camera viewfinders come in two configurations: studio and remote (eyepiece) (see Figure 2–10).

Studio Viewfinders and Eyepiece Viewfinders

A studio viewfinder is mounted on top of the camera. Usually it produces an image that is approximately 5" in diagonal. Studio viewfinders allow the camera operator to stand behind the camera as shots are composed and focused.

The remote **eyepiece viewfinder** is usually mounted on the side of the camera. It contains an eyepiece that allows the videographer's eye to be put firmly against the camera. This prevents natural light from hitting the small screen inside the eyepiece and washing out the picture. Viewfinders of this type are usually quite small, often approximately $1\frac{1}{2}$" in diagonal. More expensive eyepiece viewfinders can be rotated in numerous directions so that the camera can be held in positions other than on the shoulder.

Eyepiece viewfinders usually contain electronic displays that indicate whether or not the lens aperture setting is correct. They also contain indicators that monitor the status of the VCR: Is it running? Is it recording? Is it in the record-standby mode?

Finally, on most portable cameras, a scene that has just been recorded can be played back and viewed in the eyepiece viewfinder in order to check the quality of the recording. Some cameras and camcorders contain a small audio speaker that allows you to monitor the sound as well.

Figure 2–10   Portable Video Camera (A) with Eyepiece Viewfinder and (B) with Studio
Viewfinder

(A)

(B)

CAMERA CONFIGURATIONS

Modern video cameras are available in a number of different configurations. These include camcorders (one-piece unit or dockable) and convertible cameras that may be used either in a studio setting or a remote field production setting. A third group of cameras include those large-scale models designed primarily for in-studio use.

Camcorders

A combination camera and VCR, or **camcorder,** combines the camera and recorder into one easily carried unit (see Figure 2–11). This gives the camera operator much greater mobility than with a recording system composed of a separate camera and VCR, which relies on a cable connection between the two pieces of equipment. There are two different kinds of camcorders: camcorder

Figure 2–11   Professional Camcorders: (A) One-Piece Hi8 Camcorder, (B) Dockable Hi8 Camcorder, (C) One-Piece Betacam SP Camcorder, (D) Dockable S-VHS Camcorder

(A)

(B)

(C)

(D)

systems that unite a dockable camera with a variety of dockable VCR formats, and camcorder systems that are manufactured as a one-piece unit.

Most professional camcorder systems record either in the $\frac{1}{2}$" Betacam/ Betacam SP or M-II videotape formats. S-VHS, also a $\frac{1}{2}$" format, and Hi8 are finding use as well among broadcasters and video producers who seek a low-cost field recording format.

Camcorder systems designed for broadcast use high-quality cameras, usually three CCD or three-tube prism cameras equipped with either Plumbicon or Saticon tubes. These professional-quality camcorders may be one-piece systems or, more typically, dockable systems. Dockable cameras are designed to be connected to a special docking VCR to create a camcorder unit. High-quality docking VCRs are available in Betacam, Betacam SP, M-II, S-VHS, and Hi8 formats.

In all of these systems, the camera output and the VCR recording (with the help of a time base corrector) are broadcast quality. Also, sophisticated editing systems have been developed so that a full camera-recorder editing system can be purchased.

One-piece camcorders in the VHS/S-VHS and 8mm/Hi8 formats have become immensely popular and are widely used by home video producers and other producers not requiring the quality of the most expensive broadcast-quality camcorder systems. The camera portion of these consumer-level camcorders almost always utilizes a single CCD as the image sensor (see Figure 2–12).

Most one-piece consumer-level camcorders are designed to operate independently from other cameras or camcorders in a field recording situation. These portable camcorders are equipped *only* with eyepiece-type viewfinders. These eyepiece viewfinders are designed to be placed at the camera operator's eye while the camera unit is held on the operator's shoulder. The eyepiece is adjustable on some models so that the camera can be held under the arm—a method providing a different viewing angle and increased stability. The zoom lens controls (zoom and focus) are attached to the zoom lens, and the camera operator operates them with both hands.

The second characteristic of these consumer camcorders is that they cannot be operated synchronously with other cameras. That is, they are usually incapable of accepting an external sync signal and, therefore, operate independently of other cameras. The video signal is recorded directly on the camcorder's own VCR.

Convertible Studio-Field Cameras

Convertible cameras are designed to be used either in the studio with several others in a typical multiple-camera studio configuration or as a single-camera portable unit in the field. In a typical field situation, the camera is connected to the recorder by a long or short cable. In other situations, the camera output can be sent via microwave either to the recorder or back to the station for broadcast.

Figure 2–12   Portable S-VHS Camcorder (AG 450)

Two main characteristics distinguish these convertible cameras from others. First, they have the capability to be outfitted with either a studio viewfinder or a small eyepiece viewfinder. In the studio configuration (see Figure 2–13), the camera operator stands behind the camera, which is usually mounted on a tripod or camera pedestal. Since the operator stands behind the camera, the camera viewfinder must be mounted on top of the camera. Usually, the viewfinders have a fairly large (approximately 5″ in diagonal) viewfinder screen, so the camera operator can easily see the image. In addition, convertible cameras can easily be adapted so that the zoom lens controls and lens focus controls are removed from the lens itself, and are instead mounted on *panning handles* that protrude from either side of the rear of the camera. As a result, the camera operator can easily see the viewfinder image and make zoom lens and focus changes while standing behind the camera.

The second characteristic of convertible cameras is that they are capable of being operated synchronously with the other studio cameras. In order to be able to do this, the camera must be able to accept an external sync signal. Usually, the camera has a small input through which the sync generator can be connected. The sync generator provides the composite sync pulses (horizontal and vertical) to all the studio cameras. In addition, when the camera is used in a studio situation, the camera output is fed into a studio switcher rather than into its own VCR.

Figure 2–13   Portable Camera in Studio Configuration with Tripod and Dolly

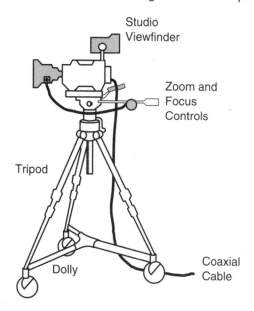

Studio
Viewfinder

Zoom and
Focus
Controls

Tripod

Coaxial
Cable

Dolly

Studio Cameras

Some television cameras are designed primarily for use in studios. They tend to be much larger than their field production counterparts, are equipped with large studio-type zoom lenses, have highly developed internal signal adjustment circuitry, and usually do not have the capability to be operated by battery power. However, cameras designed for studio use—perhaps with the exception of cameras designed for HDTV systems—are increasingly being replaced by convertible cameras, which are more versatile because they can be used in the field as well.

COMMON CAMERA CONTROLS

Power Source Selector Switch

All cameras need to have a source of power supplied to them. Power can be supplied directly to the camera from a battery attached to the camera or by using an alternating current (AC) adapter to connect to wall current. Or the power may be supplied to the camera through the portable videotape recorder. The power selector switch lets you tell the camera where its power will be coming from.

On/Off Switch

This switch turns the camera on or off. Some cameras include a third position in this switch, standby. The **standby** switch allows the camera electronics and image sensor to warm up, but it does not cause the sensor to produce an image. In this way, it increases the life of the sensor and prolongs the life of the portable battery power system. It also lets you keep your camera ready to shoot without using as much power as in the on mode.

VCR Control

All portable cameras contain a *VCR control switch*, which lets the camera operator start and stop the portable VCR when it is in the record-standby mode. This gives the camera operator control over the recording process while operating the portable camera.

VCR Compatibility Switch

The *VCR compatibility switch* found on most high-quality portable video cameras facilitates the interface of cameras and VCRs from different manufacturers. Given the proliferation of videotape recording formats, a camera may be used with any number of different format VCRs produced by different manufacturers. In order for the camera's viewfinder display to operate correctly and for various VCR functions to be controlled from the camera (start record, stop record, and so on), the VCR compatibility switch is adjusted for the particular VCR in use on a given occasion.

Automatic and Manual Gain

Many cameras give the operator the choice of operating the camera with an automatic gain control switch turned on or off. As discussed above, the gain controls amplification of the video signal. An **automatic gain control (AGC)** switch keeps the video level constant by varying the gain of the signal as the brightness of the picture changes. If the light or background suddenly gets darker, the AGC boosts the signal level. If the picture suddenly becomes brighter, it reduces the signal level. When the camera is in the *manual gain* position, the correct video level is determined by accurately adjusting the aperture of the lens.

Although AGC is sometimes useful, it can also create some big problems. For example, you are shooting an interview with someone outdoors and have adjusted your camera for the face of the person you are shooting. Then a big white truck drives by in the background. AGC automatically compensates for this additional brightness and reduces the level of the video signal. As a result, the face of the interviewee gets noticeably darker. So, in some situations, AGC poses real problems, and it is probably better to use manual rather than automatic gain.

Gain Boost

Many cameras now incorporate a special gain boost switch that is separate from the automatic-manual gain control switch. The function of the **gain boost** switch is to amplify the video signal. This is most often used in low-light situations. Color cameras have a tendency to perform poorly when they do not have adequate light. The gain boost strengthens the signal and provides somewhat better color reproduction in these low-light situations. However, the benefit is not without a cost. As with any radical adjustment of the gain, the picture quality is usually somewhat degraded due to the increase in visual noise in the signal.

Filter Wheel

The **filter wheel** allows the camera operator to compensate for changes in the color temperature of the light. As you know, the actual color of white light varies. Some lighting instruments produce light that appears to be reddish or bluish, depending on the type of bulb used. The color of daylight varies from morning through evening. This is particularly apparent very early in the day and very late in the day. Color television cameras are extremely sensitive to these changes in the color temperature of light. (Color temperature is discussed in more detail in Chapter 6.) Cheaper cameras typically contain a two-position electronic filter with settings for indoor or outdoor light. Professional cameras contain a filter wheel built into the camera between the lens and the prism block with positions for a variety of lighting conditions, as well as one or more neutral density filters that can be used to reduce the amount of light passing through the lens without affecting color temperature or the lens iris setting.

White Balance

In conjunction with the filter wheel, and because of changes in the color temperature of light, all high-quality cameras have a white balance switch. **White balance** enables the camera operator to adjust the relative intensity of the red, green, and blue channels to allow the camera to produce an accurate white signal in the particular light in which the camera is shooting. White balance adjustments can be automatic or manual. *Automatic white balance* adjustment allows the camera operator to quickly white balance the camera: You simply focus the camera on a white card or object in the light that you plan to record in and press the automatic white balance switch. The camera automatically corrects the color signal so that the camera produces a white picture. Many cameras equipped with automatic white balance also incorporate a memory system that retains the white balance information when the camera power is off.

Manual white balance controls require the camera operator to make the appropriate color corrections. Again, the camera is pointed at a white card in the light that will be used and the camera operator manually adjusts the camera to achieve the proper white balance. Usually, such cameras have the gain and pedestal controls for the color channels externally mounted on the side of the camera. By twisting the controls and watching a white balance meter in the camera viewfinder, the proper white balance can be achieved.

Although automatic white balance controls are often preferred for their speed and accuracy, there is an advantage to using a camera with manual controls. Such manually controlled cameras give the camera operator the opportunity to **paint** the picture. If the camera output can be viewed in a color monitor, the camera operator can make subtle changes in the color of a scene to achieve a particular mood or effect. Such painting is routinely done by professional video engineers as part of their control of studio television cameras.

Some of the more expensive and versatile professional cameras contain an automatic white balance control, as well as a set of RGB paint controls. This offers the camera operator the best of both worlds. White balance can be set effortlessly with the automatic white balance control, and then minor adjustments in the color of the picture can be made with the paint controls.

Color Bars

Most professional and industrial-quality cameras now available have a color bar switch. This switch causes the camera to generate a standard NTSC color bar output. These **color bars** are a standard pattern of yellow, cyan, green, magenta, red, and blue bars, and are used as a standard color reference by television engineers. It is a good idea to record some color bars generated by your camera at the head of each field tape. This can be used as a color reference when it is time to play back your tape.

Automatic Camera Setup

Many of the professional-quality cameras now on the market have a full set of controls that allow the camera operator to quickly set the correct electronic parameters for proper signal recording within the camera. Auto centering, also called automatic **registration,** correctly aligns the three pickup tubes in tube-type cameras in order to guarantee accurate image and color reproduction. Automatic white balance (auto white) is a standard feature on these cameras, as is automatic **black balance** (auto black), which automatically sets the black level of the picture. In addition, many cameras now have a microcomputer memory system to retain this information, even when the camera is turned off. This eliminates the need to reset the camera each time it is turned on.

CAMERA MOUNTING EQUIPMENT

Perhaps the most common image that people have today of television cameras is the image of the electronic news gathering (ENG) crew on a remote shoot, with the camera held on the shoulder of the camera operator, and a news reporter chasing down a potential interviewee. This brings us to the area of camera mounting equipment. Exactly what options are there for physically supporting a camera?

Shoulder Mount or Brace

One of the most common ways to support a portable camera or camcorder is to carry it. Early portable camera designs were awkward and had to be held in front of the camera operator (usually because the viewfinder was mounted on the rear of the camera), but current models with a side-mounted viewfinder allow the camera to be carried on the shoulder of the camera operator. These cameras utilize a **shoulder mount** or brace to cushion the operator's shoulder from the weight of the camera. They consist of a contoured piece of metal with foam padding attached to the bottom of the camera.

Some cameras contain braces that can be changed to accommodate right-handed and left-handed operators. In addition, well-designed cameras take camera balance into account—the camera should rest evenly on the operator's shoulder. The weight of the lens at the front of the camera should be counterbalanced by the battery pack at the rear of the camera. The camera should not have a tendency to fall forward or back, but should rest squarely on the operator's shoulder.

The shoulder mount gives the camera operator the greatest amount of flexibility in the movement of the camera. The operator can walk easily with the camera, and all types of lateral or vertical camera movement are possible. However, even the strongest camera operator can tire of holding a shoulder-mounted camera, and even the best camera operator will have trouble holding a steady close-up shot for any great amount of time. For this reason, a tripod is used.

Tripod

Tripod mounts—or **sticks**, as they are often called because of the wooden legs on some models—are widely used in remote productions. If camera movement is not important (for example, in an interview with the subject remaining in one position), a tripod-mounted camera provides the greatest amount of control (see Figure 2–13).

The tripod provides a steady base for the camera. The shoulder brace is removed from the bottom of the camera, and the camera is then attached to the head of the tripod. Many tripods contain telescoping legs, so that the height of the camera can be adjusted.

Tripod heads come in two types: friction heads and fluid heads. **Friction heads**, which are the less expensive of the two types, give fair control over camera panning (from left to right) and tilting (up and down). Smooth camera operation is achieved by using a tripod head that is designed to accommodate the specific weight of the camera you are using, and through practice on the part of the camera operator. Professional camera operators always use tripods with **fluid heads**.

These are more expensive than friction heads but are designed so that it is virtually impossible to make a jerky horizontal or vertical camera movement. For very smooth, solid camera operation, the tripod-mounted fluid head is the usual choice.

Two attachments for the legs of the tripod are often used. A *spreader* is used to spread the tripod legs out to their widest stance and hold them firmly in that position. A *tripod dolly* is a wheeled base that can be attached to the tripod legs if movement of the tripod is desired.

Monopods

While the shoulder brace method allows for maximum mobility of the camera, and the tripod gives maximum stability, the monopod provides a compromise between the two. A **monopod** is a telescoping rod that is attached to the base of the camera and is inserted into a special belt pouch. The monopod takes the weight of the camera off the shoulder of the camera operator but also allows for movement.

Monopods were originally designed for use with cameras with rear viewfinders, but they may be used on cameras with side-mounted viewfinders as well. The main disadvantage to the monopod is that some vertical camera movements are rather awkward to achieve. To tilt up, the camera operator must literally bend over backwards. To tilt down, the operator must bend forward. Although these movements may have a yoga-like appeal, in practice they can be difficult and sometimes even dangerous.

Steadicam

The perfect compromise between mobility and stability appears to have been achieved by the mounting device known as the **Steadicam**.[5] This camera-mounting system, designed specifically for use with portable film (35mm) and video cameras, won an Academy Award for its design in 1978. A number of different models of Steadicam are available, depending on the weight of your camera/camcorder. Models include an EFP model for use with professional video cameras and camcorders, as well as Steadicam JR, designed to be used with consumer camcorders (8mm/Hi8 and VHS/S-VHS C formats) weighing less than four pounds.

NEW DEVELOPMENTS

Digital Video

Much of the current system of television signal processing is based on an analog system. Digital technology has seen great developments in the past few years, and the development of an all-digital camera is expected in the near future. In the not-too-distant future, all video cameras and recorders will operate in the digital domain.

Most television cameras produce an **analog signal**. That is, the output of the video signal is proportional to the brightness of the light entering the lens. The output signal, then, is *analogous* to the input signal. In **digital signal** video, the analog signal is converted into numbers—bright areas receive high numbers, dark areas low numbers.

There are several advantages to converting the analog signal to a digital one, or to recording it digitally in the first place. First, the digitized signal can be processed by a computer and manipulated in various ways simply not possible with an analog signal. Most of the striking visual effects now seen on television are digital effects. Second, since the digital signal is a group of numbers, rather than a varying electrical current, it can be stored, replayed, and copied with greater accuracy and less noise than an analog signal.

High-Definition Television

Much recent research and development activity has been dedicated to the development of **high-definition television (HDTV)**. HDTV systems differ from existing conventional television systems in several significant ways. The first difference is in the shape of the screen. The conventional television frame maintains an aspect ratio of 3:4 (height:width). The HDTV system provides a wider angle of view, with a screen ratio of 9:16 (see Figure 2–14). Second, the number of horizontal scanning lines has increased to provide greater image detail and resolution, thus giving rise to the term *high-definition* television. Third, the quality of the audio signal has greatly improved over existing systems.

A working HDTV system has been developed by NHK (Japanese Broadcasting), which began regular HDTV transmissions in Japan in 1989. These events caused significant concern among U.S. equipment manufacturers and television broadcasters, because the Japanese system utilizes 1,125 scan lines and is incompatible with conventional receivers in use in the United States and elsewhere. As a result, a number of U.S. equipment manufacturers have developed HDTV systems that are compatible with existing transmission and receiving

Figure 2–14   Conventional and HDTV Screen Shapes

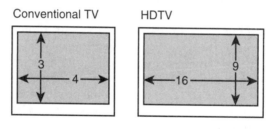

equipment. A decision from the U.S. Federal Communications Commission on the technical specifications for HDTV in the United States and a time table for conversion of network and local broadcasting to a fully digital HDTV standard is expected shortly, if it has not already been implemented since this book went to press.

SUMMARY

The principal components of the portable television camera include the image sensor, viewfinder, camera control unit, and lens assembly. Two types of image sensors are now in use: CCDs (charge-coupled devices) and pickup tubes. The image sensor produces the electronic video signal by changing light into electrical energy. The U.S. television standard is based on a system of 525 lines per frame and 30 frames per second, which is controlled by a series of horizontal and vertical electronic synchronizing pulses within the camera.

An analog representation of the video signal called the television waveform can be seen with the use of a waveform monitor. Control over the video signal is provided by the camera control unit (CCU). Most portable cameras contain an internal CCU, whereas studio cameras utilize external CCUs.

Most portable cameras are color cameras. They produce a television signal with two important components: luminance (the black and white or brightness part of the signal) and chrominance (the color information). To produce the color signal, incoming light must be broken into red, blue, and green, the additive primary colors of light. High-quality, professional three-CCD or tube cameras most often use prism blocks or dichroic mirrors to break the incoming light into its primary components, whereas single-CCD or tube cameras most often use a stripe filter attached to the face of the image sensor. The color burst pulse keeps the color information in proper synchronization and the vectorscope monitors the color signal.

The type and number of image sensors influence the performance of the camera. Most modern cameras contain either three image sensors or one image sensor. All cameras manufactured for use in the United States operate on the NTSC color system, which differs from the color systems found in some other countries.

Portable cameras are designed in several typical configurations: one-piece or dockable camcorders, or convertible cameras.

Camcorders, recording systems that combine a camera and videocassette recorder into one unit, are used extensively in professional television field production as well as for home video recording.

Convertible cameras can be used either as a single camera with a VCR in the field or in conjunction with several cameras in a television studio. Large-scale studio cameras still find use in some production applications.

The principal performance characteristics of cameras include resolution, lag, color reproduction, sensitivity to light, and burn in.

The camera viewfinder produces an image so the camera operator can see what is being shot. All high-quality cameras use electronic viewfinders. Studio viewfinders are large and mounted on top of the camera, but all portable cameras designed for use in the field are equipped with small eyepiece viewfinders, usually attached to the side of the camera.

The principal controls found on most portable cameras include the power source selector switch, on/off switch, VCR control switch, automatic or manual gain control, gain boost for extra sensitivity in low light, filter wheel, white balance, and color bars. Automatic camera setup is a feature found on many broadcast-quality cameras.

The most common method of supporting a portable camera is by carrying it on a shoulder mount or brace. Greater stability can be achieved by using a tripod, monopod, or Steadicam.

Camera systems are changing rapidly, and in the near future we are likely to see conversion to a digital rather than analog system of signal processing, and the continued replacement of analog pickup tubes with solid-state pickup devices such as charge-coupled devices.

HDTV (high-definition television) promises to provide television pictures with higher resolution and a wider aspect ratio than the existing conventional television system.

ENDNOTES

1. Ennes, Harold E. *Television Broadcasting: Equipment, Systems and Operating Fundamentals,* 2nd ed. Indianapolis: Howard W. Sams & Co., 1979, p. 23.

2. Head, Sydney W., and Sterling, Christopher H. *Broadcasting in America,* 4th ed. Boston: Houghton Mifflin, 1982, p. 184.

3. Plumbicon is a registered trademark of N. V. Philips, Inc.

4. Saticon is a registered trademark of Hitachi Denshi, Inc.

5. Steadicam is a registered trademark of Cinema Products Corporation.

3

Lenses and Visualization

PART ONE:
LENSES

In Chapter 2, we concentrated on the role the camera plays in producing an electronic television image. In this chapter, we will look at the function of the lens and the way manipulation of the camera and lens functions as a part of the process of visualization in television. We are concerned here with the technical elements of lens operation and manipulation, as well as the aesthetic impact that results from that manipulation. Television is not only an electronic phenomenon that produces a video signal, it is also an artistic or aesthetic phenomenon that produces images that audiences respond to. Any discussion of lenses, therefore, should contain a discussion of these complementary components.

LENSES: FUNCTIONS AND TYPES

The lens is the camera's eye. What it sees and how it sees it form the basis of the visual element of television. The camera **lens** functions to gather light that is reflected off the scene being recorded and to direct an image onto the pickup device within the camera.

Focal Length

Camera lenses are often described by their **focal length**, which is defined as the distance from the optical center of the lens to the point where the image is in focus (the face of the pickup tube or CCD). When we talk about lenses, we usually describe them in terms of how long or short they are. *Long* and *short* refer both to the focal length of the lenses and to their relative physical length, since long focal length lenses are actually longer than short focal length lenses.

Figure 3–1   Lens Focal Length and Angle of View

Short Focal Length; Wide Angle of View   Medium Focal Length; Medium Angle of View

Long Focal Length; Narrow Angle of View

The focal length of the lens determines the angle of view of a scene that the lens will reproduce. Short focal length lenses have a wide angle of view (they show you a wide expanse of a scene) and therefore are referred to as **wide-angle** lenses. Long focal length lenses have a narrow angle of view; they magnify a scene by making distant objects appear large and close, and they are often referred to as *narrow-angle* lenses, or more commonly, **telephoto** lenses (see Figure 3–1). The focal length of the lens also affects depth of field. We will talk about this a little later in this chapter.

Types of Lenses

Two basic types of lenses are found on video cameras: zoom lenses and fixed focal length lenses. Almost all portable color video cameras come equipped with zoom lenses. A **zoom lens** is a lens that has a variable focal length. That is, by making an adjustment on the lens, you can vary the focal length, thereby changing the magnifying power of the lens. By adjusting the zoom control, you can *zoom in* (make an object appear larger and closer) or *zoom out* (make the object seem to decrease in size or move farther away) (see Figures 3–2 and 3–3).

The focal length of a lens is generally measured in millimeters (mm). At the wide-angle setting, the zoom lenses on most portable video cameras have a focal length of 10 to 15mm. The focal length of the lens when it is zoomed in—that is, when it is in its narrow angle or telephoto setting—depends on the **zoom ratio**, or zoom range, of the lens. For example, a zoom lens with a wide-angle focal length of 12mm and a zoom ratio of 6:1 has an effective focal length of 72mm (6 × 12mm) when it is zoomed in all the way. However, a lens with the same wide-angle focal length of 12mm and a zoom range of 10:1 has an effective focal length of 120mm when it is zoomed in all the way (10 × 12mm). This provides greater magnification than the 6:1 lens; small objects appear larger and objects that are far away appear closer when they are shot with the 10:1 lens zoomed in all the way into its 120mm narrow-angle position.

A zoom lens with a zoom ratio of 10:1 or more is particularly useful for outdoor shooting. Distant objects can be magnified simply by zooming in to them. On the other hand, a lens with a 6:1 ratio may be more than adequate for indoor shooting. Because the optical system in the 6:1 lens is less complex, it requires less light than the 10:1 lens. And since the camera is always held relatively close to the subject indoors, it probably provides adequate magnification.

Most high-quality field production cameras are equipped with zoom lenses with a minimum zoom ratio of 10:1 or 12:1. Consumer-quality cameras and camcorders are typically equipped with lenses with a zoom ratio of 6:1 or 8:1. Some

Figure 3–2   Zoom Lens Components

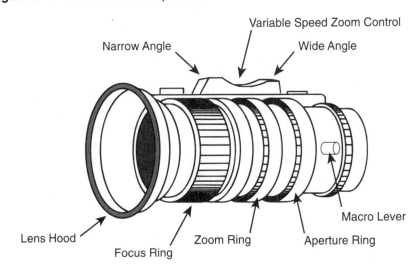

Figure 3–3   Optical Elements in a Zoom Lens

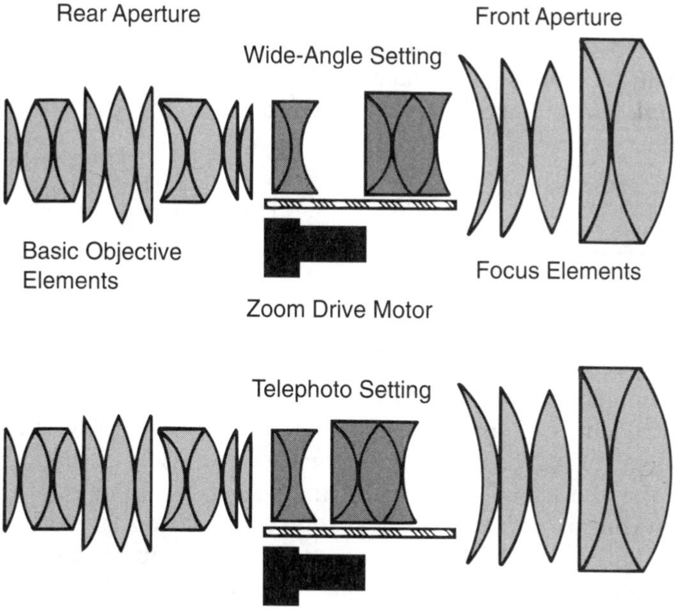

Rear Aperture   Front Aperture

Wide-Angle Setting

Basic Objective
Elements   Focus Elements

Zoom Drive Motor

Telephoto Setting

inexpensive consumer cameras may contain zoom lenses with extremely small zoom ratios (2:1 or 3:1) and should be avoided. Since the magnification power is so small, there is no significant advantage to using such a lens.

The other basic type of lens is the *fixed focal length* lens. This kind of lens, which is found on most still-photography cameras, does not have a zoom control. If you want to make an object appear larger or smaller by changing from a close-up to a wide-angle shot, you must either change the lens or physically move the camera closer to or farther away from the object being photographed.

A number of different kinds of fixed focal length lenses are available for use in special situations. Extreme wide-angle lenses, or **fish-eye lenses**, produce a 180-degree angle of view of a scene as well as extremely dramatic distortion of objects (or faces) placed close to the lens. Special **periscope lenses**, or **snorkel lenses**, allow the camera operator to move the camera lens around small objects and are used extensively to photograph products for television commercials.

Lens Mounts

Two different types of systems are used to attach a lens to a video camera. Most portable cameras contain a **bayonet mount**. In this system, the lens is inserted into the lens mount opening in the camera head and turned until it locks into place. Because different cameras use image sensors of different sizes (typically

$\frac{1}{2}''$ or $\frac{2}{3}''$ CCDs), bayonet mounts and lenses are designed in both the $\frac{1}{2}''$ and $\frac{2}{3}''$ formats.

C-mount lenses, more commonly found on film cameras, feature a threaded design in which the end of the lens is screwed into the lens mount opening. On most consumer-level camcorders, the lens is integrated with the camera housing and is not designed to be easily removed or interchanged with another lens.

ZOOM LENS COMPONENTS

How a Zoom Lens Works

A zoom lens, as we have said, is a variable focal length lens. The focal length of the lens can be changed by adjusting the zoom control, which moves the internal elements of the lens. The advantage to a zoom lens is that it combines the benefits of a short focal length lens and a long focal length lens. By adjusting the zoom control, you effectively change the lens from a wide to a narrow angle of view. This is accomplished in a smooth, continuous action and produces the sensation of zooming in or out, continuously magnifying or decreasing the size of the image. The ability to change the angle of view without moving the camera or changing lenses makes the zoom lens extremely versatile, and for that reason it is widely used in television production.

If you look at the zoom lens on a portable video camera, you can see its three major components: the focus ring, the zoom ring, and the aperture control. Each of these components plays a major role in controlling the quality of the image delivered to the camera's image sensor (see Figure 3–2).

Focus Ring

The **focus ring** is at the far end of the lens. By turning the focus ring clockwise or counterclockwise, you can focus the image that the lens is capturing. An image is *in focus* when the important parts of the image are seen in sharp detail, and *out of focus* when it is seen as fuzzy and unclear. The correct focus depends on what it is you are trying to communicate. This is what dictates which part of the picture is most important and must be kept in focus. If you are shooting an interview, you usually want the person who is talking to be seen in focus. If you are shooting a sporting event, you usually want the large area of action to be in focus. You can tell whether something is in focus or not simply by looking at the image in the viewfinder of the camera to see if the focus is sharp, and by adjusting the focus ring if it is not.

The focus ring on all professional and industrial-grade cameras is operated manually. Most consumer-grade cameras, however, are equipped with **automatic focus (auto focus)** mechanisms. These auto focus systems work by emitting a beam of infrared (invisible) light or ultrasound (inaudible sound). The beam bounces off the object being videotaped and travels back to the camera, which calculates the distance from the camera to the object. A **servomechanism** then automatically adjusts the focus ring for correct focus.

Although use of auto focus cameras often carries the stigma associated with nonprofessional camera work, they can be helpful, particularly for inexperienced camera operators. Auto focus guarantees sharp focus in shooting situations that may be difficult for novice camera operators. For example, the continuously emitted focusing beam keeps the subject in focus, even if it or the camera moves, or if the lens is zoomed in or out. In extremely low-light conditions, when it is difficult to see the image on the camera viewfinder, auto focus often provides more reliable focus than manual focus.

These benefits notwithstanding, some serious disadvantages are associated with the use of auto focus cameras. Most auto focus devices tend to focus on large objects located centrally in the frame. This is fine if you are shooting Grandpa as he tells ribald stories at the dinner table. However, if your subject is small or not centrally located in the frame, the camera will probably focus on some other part of the picture. If there are two similar-sized objects at different distances from the camera, and both are positioned in the center of the frame, the auto focus device will not know which one to focus on. If the auto focus device is ultrasonic and the object you want to focus on is behind a glass window, the ultrasonic beam will be reflected back from the glass and will focus on the window rather than on the object behind it.

For these and other reasons, if you are considering buying an auto focus camera, you should look for one with an auto focus mechanism that can be turned off and on. A camera that allows you to focus automatically and manually is preferable to one that only works in the auto focus mode. Manual focus gives the camera operator more control over the camera, and in situations where it is important to focus only part of the picture, manual focus is essential.

Zoom Ring

The middle part of the lens contains the **zoom ring**, which can usually be controlled either manually or automatically. When the control is manual, you turn the zoom ring by hand to zoom in or out. Manual control gives you very good control over the zoom speed. You can go as fast or as slow as you want.

Automatic zoom lens controls are motor driven. A small motor drives the lens elements when you activate it. Some automatic zoom lens controls have one or two preset speeds that allow you to set the speed selector switch for a fast or slow zoom. Depending on the preset speed setting, you automatically zoom in or out at a fast or slow speed when you push the button that activates the zoom lens. More sophisticated automatic zoom lenses have continuous variable speed motors hooked up to the lens. With these devices, a control switch is mounted on the zoom lens itself. The control has a *zoom in* position at one end and a *zoom out* position at the other end. The lens zooms in or out when you depress the appropriate side of the control. In addition, the zoom speed is controlled by the amount of pressure put on the control—the zoom speed increases with increased pressure and decreases with decreased pressure. This guarantees extremely smooth zooming over the whole zoom range of the lens.

Aperture Ring

The **aperture ring** is mounted at the end of the lens next to the camera. The aperture ring controls the size of the **iris** opening of the lens. The iris of the lens works like the iris of your eye. In low-light situations, the iris needs to be opened up to allow more light to hit the image sensor. In bright situations, the iris needs to be closed, or shut down, to reduce the amount of light hitting the sensor.

Technically speaking, the aperture ring controls the size of the f-stop of the lens. **F-stops** are a standard calibration of the size of the aperture opening. F-stop numbers are printed on the lens itself, and usually vary from about 1.4 to 22 (see Figure 3–4). Smaller f-stop numbers correspond to large aperture openings. Therefore, a lens that is set at f-1.4 (a small f-stop number) is one in which the aperture is open very wide. A lens that is set at f-22 (a large f-stop number) is one in which the aperture is extremely small. This inverse relationship is one that you should memorize. Though this may seem confusing at first, the relationship between f-stop numbers and aperture size should become clear as soon as you take your camera in hand and work with it for a few minutes.

Figure 3–4   F-Stop Numbers and Aperture Size

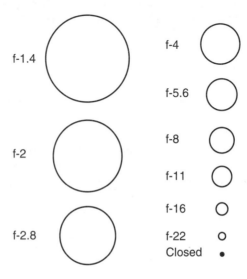

The f-stop settings on most high-quality lenses are a series of **click stops**. As you change from one f-stop to another, the lens clicks into place at the new setting. This helps you to determine how many stops you have opened or closed the lens. Typical f-stop settings on a lens are: f-1.4, f-2, f-2.8, f-4, f-5.6, f-8, f-11, f-16, f-22, and closed. It is not necessary to set the aperture precisely at one of the click stops. You may set it at any position on or between f-stops because the aperture size varies continuously as the aperture ring is turned.

In addition, most lenses also have an iris setting in which the aperture can be completely closed. Normally, the iris is left in the closed position when the camera is not in use. The closed iris setting can also be used for aperture **fades**, in which an image is faded up from black by opening the aperture or faded out to black by gradually closing it.

Many consumer-quality camcorders eliminate manually operated apertures and f-stop settings in favor of an automatic iris system. In some cases, the automatic system can be overridden by using the "back light" control, which opens up the aperture one or two additional stops to correct lighting problems when the background light is brighter than the subject you are trying to photograph. An additional manual override for the automatic iris may also be present, but on inexpensive camcorders the range of possible adjustments to the iris is often limited. Both the back light and manual iris controls are usually found on the side of the camcorder housing rather than on the lens assembly.

Other Lens Components

Before we begin our discussion of the control of the aesthetics of the image, several other lens components ought to be mentioned. The **lens hood**, attached to the end of the lens, works like the visor on a hat to prevent unwanted light from hitting the lens and causing lens flare. A **lens flare** is an optical aberration that is caused when light bounces off the elements within a lens. Most often, it is caused by pointing the camera directly at the sun or a light source with the effect of causing a glaring point of light to appear in the picture. The **lens cap** is a covering that can be attached to the end of the lens. The lens cap has two functions: It protects the glass in the lens from damage when the camera is not in operation and it prevents any light from hitting the image sensor. The lens cap should *always* be used when the camera is not in operation. It should be used when transporting the camera and when the camera is turned off between shots. It is the single most important safety feature on a portable camera. A **macro lever** is a device that converts the lens to a **macro lens**, which allows you to take extreme close-up shots of very small objects. In the normal zoom lens mode, most lenses are not capable of focusing on objects less than two or three feet from the end of the lens. When the macro lens switch is activated, you can focus the camera on objects that are only inches away from the lens, and magnify their size so that they fill the television frame. A macro lens is extremely useful if you plan to shoot a large number of small objects.

Lens Filters and Extenders

A variety of lens filters and range extenders are available for use with existing lens systems. Many camera operators attach a clear filter to the front of the lens to protect the outside lens element from physical damage such as scratching or chipping. Other special effects filters are used to change the quality or amount of light passing through the lens, allowing the camera operator to manipulate the incoming light in a number of ways. Among the most commonly used special effects filters are *fog filters* and *star filters*. *Range extenders* or reducers are small elements that can be attached directly to the front of the lens in order to extend or reduce the focal length of the lens.

Lens Care

In addition to placing the lens cap on the lens for protection when the camera is not in use, care should be taken not to damage the face of the lens. In some shooting conditions, the lens may get wet or dirty; by looking through the viewfinder and by closely examining the lens, if it becomes apparent that dust or dirt is present, the lens should be cleaned. Special lens-cleaning solutions are available from photographic or video supply houses. The solution can be sprayed onto the lens and then removed with special nonabrasive lens paper. Common tissue paper should not be used to clean the lens. It usually leaves some lint residue behind and, depending on the quality of the paper, may be abrasive as well.

ZOOM LENS OPERATION

Zoom Lens Focus

Presetting the focus on a zoom lens is a fairly simple matter. Turn on the power to the camera (so that an image is visible in the viewfinder) and, with the camera in the automatic aperture mode, zoom in as close as possible to the object you plan to shoot. Turn the focus ring until the image appears to be in focus. Then zoom out and frame up your shot. Do *not* adjust the focus ring again. You can now zoom in and out on the subject, and it will remain in focus as long as its position remains constant in relation to the camera. If you move the camera or if the subject moves, you must reset the zoom focus.

Correct Exposure

Since the aperture setting affects not only the quality of the image but also the level of the video signal, it is extremely important to set the aperture accurately by finding the correct exposure for a scene. Opening the aperture too wide and letting too much light hit the image sensor washes out the details in the picture and causes extreme color distortion. In addition, overexposure often produces very bright, glowing spots, known as **hot spots**, in the picture. Image detail and correct color are lost in hot spots.

Hot spots are unacceptable for several reasons. First, the loss of image detail (unless this is a desired special effect) is extremely distracting to the viewer and unflattering to the subject. Second, in terms of the video signal, these hot spots represent places in which the video signal is driven far above the maximum point for the peak white. Therefore the video signal, as well as the image, is somewhat distorted. Finally, on tube-type cameras, continued overexposure may damage the pickup tube itself, causing the image to burn in.

If the exposure is too low, it will produce a picture with a lot of electronic noise, muddy or gray colors, and an inadequate video signal.

How can you know which aperture setting is correct? There are a number of approaches you can take. Perhaps the most commonly used method is eyeballing. With this method, you literally look at the viewfinder image to see what the scene looks like. With the lighting you will use in place, open the aperture until the viewfinder produces the best picture, one with good contrast between the bright and dark areas, and without any hot spots. If you have a color monitor, it is extremely helpful to look at the color picture to see whether or not the colors are reproduced accurately. Slight corrections in the aperture setting often make dramatic changes in color reproduction.

Most cameras are equipped with a **light meter** built into the camera viewfinder (see Figure 3–5). The light meter tells you whether the scene is too bright, too dark, or just about right. However, remember that the light meter works as an averaging meter. The light meter senses the brightest and darkest

Figure 3–5   Camcorder Viewfinder Display

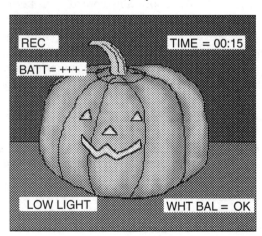

parts of the image and sets the exposure at a middle point. The average brightness on the scene may or may not give the correct exposure for the most important part of the scene—that is, the center of interest you are shooting. Usually, the light meter tells you if you are in the ballpark as far as exposure goes, and then you can make minor adjustments for the correct aperture setting.

Some camera viewfinders contain a **zebra stripe** exposure indicator. In this system, a series of black and white lines appear over the brightest portion of the picture when the maximum video level has been reached. In some camera viewfinders, the zebra stripes are set to appear when correct exposure for skin tone is achieved.

The most accurate way to set the aperture is to use a waveform monitor in conjunction with a good camera monitor. This allows you to monitor the parameters of the video signal. Some camera viewfinders produce a waveform display superimposed over the viewfinder image. However, remember that the way the image looks is every bit as important as how good the waveform looks. You do not want to adjust every scene so that the peak white is at 100 percent if you have some scenes that are indeed darker than others. A scene shot in outdoor daylight looks different (aesthetically and technically) from a scene shot in a candlelit room. The waveform is extremely useful, however, in determining whether or not you are exceeding the 100 percent video level. Exceeding this level distorts the picture, and the waveform can help you avoid this distortion and keep the signal within its normal limits.

APERTURE CONTROL AND DEPTH OF FIELD

Aperture Control

The camera iris, like the zoom lens control, can be operated manually or automatically. With manual aperture (or manual iris) control, the camera operator looks into the viewfinder and manually adjusts the aperture until a good picture appears in the viewfinder. In a camera equipped with an **automatic aperture** (or automatic iris), a small light meter in the camera controls the size of the aperture opening. The picture area is sampled for brightness and an average brightness is calculated. The iris opening is then adjusted automatically for this scene. If the lighting changes, the camera automatically responds and makes the appropriate iris correction.

Automatic aperture can be a helpful feature to have, but the videographer should always keep two things in mind: contrast range and center of interest. **Contrast range**, expressed as a ratio of brightness to darkness, refers to the television system's ability to reproduce a range of different values of brightness. A contrast ratio of between 30:1 and 40:1 is normal for most portable color television cameras. That is, the brightest part of the scene must not be any more than 30 times brighter than the darkest part of the scene. If the ratio is greater than

40:1, the camera is not able to handle it, and the very bright parts of the scene will wash out or turn into glowing hot spots. Compare the television contrast ratio with the contrast ratio possible with the human eye (100:1).[1] The eye is significantly better able to handle extreme contrast than a television camera.

We mention contrast ratio here (as well as when we discuss lighting) because it is very important when one is trying to find the correct aperture setting. When the camera is set on automatic aperture, it samples the picture for brightness and, as stated, averages these brightness values to set the correct iris setting. The automatic iris, however, cannot determine the brightness only for the part of the frame most important to you. Let's assume that you are videotaping a dancer in front of an open window. If you are indoors, it is very likely that the background (window) will be considerably brighter than the dancer (see Figure 3–6). With the iris on automatic, the camera will sample the scene and adjust the aperture for a point between the brightness of the dancer and the brightness of the background. In all likelihood, this will result in the dancer being darker than she should be. If you were to adjust the aperture manually, you could set the correct exposure for the dancer. However, it is then likely that the background would be too bright and would wash out.

This situation is a good example of how different a scene can appear depending on the aperture setting. The automatic aperture setting device does not know which part of the picture is the most important. It simply takes an average reading. Sometimes a particular spot or point in the frame is important in terms of what you are trying to communicate; it is the **center of interest** in the frame. To correctly expose for it, you may have to set the aperture manually.

As we mentioned, when the aperture is set on automatic, the camera compensates for any change in the lighting or brightness of the image. Let's use the same example of the on-site interview given in Chapter 2. With the camera on automatic aperture, you are shooting an interview outdoors when a large white truck drives by in the background. The automatic aperture responds to the

Figure 3–6 Silhouetting Caused by Window in Background

increased brightness caused by the presence of the truck and closes down the iris accordingly. When the truck disappears from the frame, the aperture adjusts again and reopens to the previous setting. The effect of the aperture closing and opening is that the face of the person being interviewed gets darker when the truck enters the frame and then brighter again when the truck leaves the frame. At best, this is very distracting to the viewer.

Some cameras have a feature called **automatic aperture lock**. This locks in the setting first calculated by the automatic aperture and prevents the camera from responding to any subsequent changes in brightness. Going back to our same example, with the camera in the automatic aperture mode, you prepare your shot of the person to be interviewed. You focus the shot and then engage the aperture lock. This holds the facial exposure that has been automatically set. When the white truck drives by in the background, the camera does not respond to it, and the exposure on the subject's face remains constant.

A word of caution is necessary at this point. If the lighting changes radically while the camera is in the aperture lock mode, picture quality will suffer greatly. The camera operator must constantly monitor the image and make aperture corrections when necessary.

Depth of Field

Depth of field refers to the portion of the scene that is in focus in front of the camera (see Figure 3–7). Depth of field can be very long or very short, depending on the aperture setting, the distance between the subject and camera, and the zoom lens setting. Table 3–1 shows these relationships. It is somewhat beyond the scope of this book to explain *why* these relationships work out like this, but a number of good books on lenses are available for a more technical explanation of this phenomenon.[2]

Table 3–1   Depth of Field Relationships

+ amount of available light + f-stop number (– aperture size) – focal length of the lens + distance from camera to subject	Depth of field *increases*[a]
– amount of available light – f-stop number (+ aperture size) + focal length of the lens – distance from camera to subject	Depth of field *decreases*[b]

[a]Read as: With increase in amount of available light, f-stop number also increases (aperture size decreases) and depth of field increases. With decrease in focal length of lens, depth of field increases. With increase in distance from camera to subject, depth of field increases.

[b]Read as: With decrease in amount of available light, f-stop number also decreases (aperture size increases) and depth of field decreases. With increase in focal length of the lens, depth of field decreases. With decrease in distance from camera to subject, depth of field decreases.

Figure 3–7   Depth of Field: Area in Focus in Front of Camera

This picture has a very short depth of field. The nails in the center of the picture are in focus, but the foreground and background are out of focus.

Perhaps the easiest way to explain these depth of field relationships is through the use of examples. We will consider two different lighting situations: one outdoors, in which the depth of field is long, and one indoors, where the depth of field is shallow.

Example 1: Daylight Outdoors. Let's briefly discuss the way the elements of aperture, focal length of the lens, and distance from camera to subject affect the depth of field. Let's assume that you plan to videotape a football game. You take the camcorder to the field and are given a camera position on the 50-yard line at the top of the grandstand. This puts you and your camera at a considerable distance from the action. It is a bright, beautiful autumn day.

Now, let's analyze each of the variables that affect the depth of field. First, let's consider the amount of light falling on the scene. Since it is early afternoon on a beautiful, cloudless day and you are shooting in full sunlight, we can assume you have more than enough light to shoot your video. Since you have a lot of light, you set your camera iris at f-8 or f-16, both fairly normal settings for a bright day. These aperture settings (high f-stop numbers) give you a fairly small aperture opening. This makes sense because on a very bright day you want to limit the amount of light hitting the camera image sensor so that you do not overexpose the scene (see Table 3–1). Our first rule of the relationships among amount of available light, f-stop number, and depth of field tells us that as the amount of available light increases, the f-stop number increases, aperture size decreases, and, as a result, depth of field increases. These relationships are apparent in the example, and you will discover that your depth of field under these conditions is quite long.

Next, let's consider the focal length of the lens. From your vantage point, you are able to zoom in or out on the scene below. To provide a cover shot of the action, you can zoom out the lens to its widest possible shot. This effectively sets the zoom lens on its shortest focal length and enables you to cover a great deal of the field. In this position, the second relationship becomes apparent: As focal length of the lens decreases (lens is zoomed out to a wide shot), depth of field increases. In the light described, all of the action below is in focus with the wide-angle lens setting. As a matter of fact, everything from about three feet in front of the lens to infinity in the distance is in focus. You are shooting in a situation that gives you approximately the greatest possible depth of field.

Depth of field is enhanced because the camera is positioned a considerable distance from the action. Again, as distance from the subject to the camera increases, so does depth of field. All of these factors contribute to great depth of field as you shoot this football game.

Now let's consider changing one variable: the focal length of the lens. At times during the game you want to zoom in on the action, thereby effectively increasing the focal length of the lens. The zoom in makes the lens act like a long focal length telephoto lens. It magnifies the scene, and instead of showing you all the action in a long shot, it shows only a part of it in close-up detail. As you zoom in, you notice that the depth of field decreases significantly. On the long shot, you were able to keep all the action across the field in focus. Now as you shoot while zoomed in, you find that some of the field and players in the fore-ground (closer to the camera) are out of focus, as are some of the players in the background. You have to work the focus ring to keep the center of interest—the player with the ball—in focus, particularly if he runs toward either side of the field (toward or away from the camera) rather than in a straight line toward the end zone.

Example 2: Low-Light Indoors. Let's contrast the brightly lit outdoor scene with another scene in which all the elements contribute to give you very short depth of field. Let's assume that you are now recording an evening scene indoors, using only the light available in the room. The room in which you are to record is dimly lit. To produce an acceptable picture with your camera, you are forced to open the aperture as wide as it will go, in this case to f-1.4. In addition, since you are working in a small room, your camera is significantly closer to the action than it was at the football game when you were positioned high in the grandstand.

All these elements produce a situation in which the depth of field is extremely short. There is very little available light, and to compensate for this and give the camera enough light to make an acceptable picture, you have opened up the aperture (large aperture = small f-stop number). In addition, the distance from the camera to the subject is short. As you look through the viewfinder, you find that if you focus on one person, the background and foreground go out of focus. It is very difficult to keep all the people standing at different distances in front of the camera in focus. This becomes even more apparent when you zoom in (increase the focal length of the lens) on the scene. The only way to improve the situation—to increase the depth of field—is to increase the amount of available light, which allows you to shut down the lens slightly (decrease the aperture size). However, this is not possible because you have been asked not to use any additional lights. So, you keep very busy trying to maintain focus as people move about the room.

PART TWO:
VISUALIZATION AND COMPOSITION

AESTHETICS OF VISUAL COMPOSITION

Have you ever noticed that not all television programs look alike? Different programs and different movies often have a particular look or style that results from the way that particular program or film was visualized by the camera operator. The most significant elements of visualization include the impact of lighting and editing (to be discussed in later chapters) and the way in which the camera and its lens are used to create the visual images to which we respond. The rest of this chapter will concentrate on this last element.

How does the camera operator decide whether or not a shot is good? We have standards that determine if something is *technically* good (Is the color accurate? Is the video signal adequate? Is the contrast range accurate?), but we seldom talk about the *aesthetics* of visual composition. At a seminar given several years ago, a leading Hollywood camera operator said that he trained his eye for composition by going to art museums and looking at the paintings. (We should note here that he was a fan of portraits, not modern art.) His point, however, was an interesting one: How do you know how to shoot a scene? What should it look like? Some people seem to know intuitively, and we often say that a good photographer has a "good eye." But how does someone get a good eye? Is it something that you are born with? Or is it something that is learned? It is probably a combination of both.

This discussion will examine some of the factors you should take into consideration when composing images for television, including screen size and aspect ratio, focus, field of view, framing and balance, and camera movement. This is not a comprehensive list, but it will help you get started in thinking about the ways to structure the composition of the individual images in your production.

SCREEN SIZE AND ASPECT RATIO

Two primary considerations for anyone working with television images are the size and aspect ratio of the television screen. There are two inescapable constants: most television screens are small and they all have the same aspect ratio. By **aspect ratio**, we mean relationship of the height to the width of the screen. For television, this is a fixed ratio of 3:4 (three units high by four units wide) (see Figure 3–8).

Let's talk about size first. The screen size of most television sets in use in the United States today is approximately 27 inches or less in diagonal. Although large-screen systems have become more popular in recent years, they constitute a small percent of the actual number of television display systems. For now, when you think of a television screen, think small.

What does this mean in terms of the composition of images? For one thing, it means that close-ups are important. Since the screen is so small, a long shot cannot provide a lot of detail. Therefore, if detail is important to your produc-

Figure 3–8   Aspect Ratio

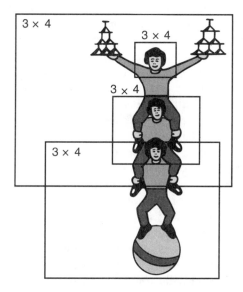

tion, it usually must be shown in close-up. If you are producing a tape about a new medical procedure or a new type of electronic component, to effectively present your subject matter to the audience you are going to have to shoot it in close-up detail. A long shot of the operating room or manufacturing facility may help establish the location, but a transition to a close-up of the event is essential to communicate your subject matter effectively to your audience.

The lens plays some important functions with respect to image size; the zoom lens or a fixed focal length macro lens can be used to magnify objects. This magnification is important because it makes elements of the scene more visible by magnifying them. It also eliminates or reduces other visual distractions, since a close-up often eliminates the other elements in the frame from the field of view.

The fixed 3:4 aspect ratio of the television screen is important in defining the visual potential of the medium, since the screen is always wider than it is tall. The screen has a basic stable, horizontal orientation that approximates the normal field of vision produced by our eyes. However, this horizontal screen orientation makes it somewhat difficult to accurately shoot extremely vertical subjects such as buildings, tall people, and so on. In using the camera to frame something that is taller than it is wide, we usually have to cut off part of the object or person to make it fit into the aspect ratio of the screen (see Figure 3–8).

Focus

The use of the lens **focus** is important in directing the audience's attention to what is important in a shot. If everything in a shot is relatively the same size and everything is in focus, all parts of the shot appear to be of equal importance to the viewer. Focus can be used to isolate the more important parts of a shot from those less important or to direct the audience's attention to one part of the shot.

Focus and Depth

We see the world in three dimensions when we look at it through our eyes. However, the world as it is presented on television has only two dimensions: height and width. The third dimension, depth, is really an illusion, since the television screen surface is actually flat. Since our normal experience of the world is in three dimensions, television images seem more realistic when they also appear to be three dimensional. To create the sense of depth on the television screen, it is important to construct images that are divided into distinct foreground, middleground, and background areas. Focus is one technique that can be used to separate these three planes. The technique through which the camera focuses on one of these planes and lets the others go out of focus is known as **selective focus** (see Figure 3–7). Selective focus is most commonly used with a short depth of field created through the use of a telephoto lens (or a zoom lens zoomed into the telephoto position).

Field of View

A basic terminology is used to describe the types of shots found in television production. The following shot descriptions refer to the field of view apparent in the shot (how much of the scene the shot shows) and to the number of people visible in the shot. It is important to have a terminology for shots, since these shot descriptions are used by television writers to describe shots in written scripts and by the director or videographer to communicate to the other crew members how they want a shot or scene to look (see Figure 3–9).

Extreme Long Shot. The **extreme long shot (XLS)** gives the audience an over-all view of the large scene. It provides a panorama of the elements of the scene or shot. Although we may not be able to see all of the significant individual details in the shot, the XLS is nevertheless important for establishing the relationship between the parts and the whole or creating impact through the use of wide open spaces.

Long Shot. The **long shot (LS)** is not as wide as the extreme long shot. When people are involved in a LS, it shows us the positional relationship between the actors and their setting. Extreme long shots and long shots are often referred to as **establishing shots**, because they establish locale and the relationships between the individual parts of the shot.

Medium Shot. The **medium shot (MS)** is tighter (closer) than the long shot but not as tight as a close-up. The medium shot is used to show the relationship between people in a shot or scene but generally does not present as much information about the setting as a long shot. When people are shown in a medium shot, they are usually cut off somewhere between the knees and the waist.

Figure 3–9   Fields of View Terminology

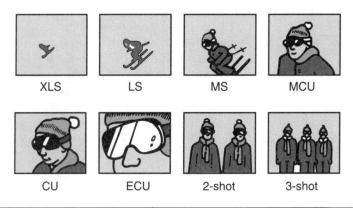

Medium Close-Up. The **medium close-up (MCU)** is one of the most frequently used shots in television. It consists of a head and shoulders shot that ends at the chest of the subject. The medium close-up gives full face detail on the subject but without the extreme impact of the close-up.

Close-Up. The **close-up (CU)** is an extremely powerful shot that gives an extremely tight shot of the subject's head. A close-up of an object practically fills the screen. The close-up is one of the most effective shots available for providing a close view of the details of a face or object.

Extreme Close-Up or Tight Close-Up. The **extreme close-up (ECU)** or **tight close-up (TCU)** is the tightest shot possible for your subject. On a person, the extreme close-up frames the subject's eyes and nose or mouth. If both the eyes and mouth will not fit in the frame, it is usually better to frame the shot to include the eyes and nose rather than the nose and mouth.

1-Shot, 2-Shot, and 3-Shot. This terminology refers to the number of people seen in a shot. Thus, a medium 2-shot is a medium shot that includes two people; a long 3-shot is a long shot that includes three people; and so on.

Composition through Framing

Framing refers to the placement of a person or object within the television frame. When a person is the subject of a shot, two compositional elements related to framing are headroom and noseroom. **Headroom** refers to the distance between the top of the person's head and the top edge of the television frame (see Figure 3–10). In gauging the correct amount of headroom, the camera operator usually tries not to leave too much or too little space at the top of the frame. With too little headroom, the person appears to stick to the top of the frame. This simply looks wrong to the viewer. Similarly, if the subject is placed too low in the frame, the person appears to be sinking out of the frame. There is no formula for determining how much headroom is correct, although more headroom is appropriate on longer shots, and less headroom works better on close-ups.

Figure 3–10 Headroom

None   Too Much   Comfortable

You should pay particular attention to headroom whenever you zoom in or out on a subject. Typically, as you zoom out and the subject becomes smaller, headroom will increase. Therefore, you will need to tilt the camera down to compensate for this. On the other hand, as you zoom in and the subject becomes larger, the amount of headroom will decrease. In this situation you may need to tilt up to correct the framing.

The concept of noseroom is similar to the concept of headroom. **Noseroom** refers to the distance between the edge of the nose of the person in the shot and the edge of the television screen. In reality, **eyeroom** might be a better term than noseroom, since it is the person's eyes, not the nose, that creates a powerful force within the frame. Correct framing is based on the direction of the eyes (where they are focused), the dynamics of the story being told, and the graphic composition of the picture.

For example, if the subject looks to one side of the frame, the rules of normal composition dictate that the camera pans slightly to allow sufficient eyeroom (or noseroom) so that the person does not appear glued to the frame's side (see Figure 3–11). If, however, within the context of the story we know that the subject is being pursued and is about to be overtaken, framing the person without sufficient eyeroom reinforces the idea that this person is trapped. This technique is commonly used in horror films and television programs of that genre; when the picture cuts to a close-up as the subject struggles to escape, the end is near. Similarly, if the camera pans to create space *behind* the subject, rather than in front, the audience knows something is going to happen in the space behind the subject.

Finally, the camera operator should pay attention to the outlines of people or objects in a shot. Since most shots commonly have a background with detail in it, the outline of foreground objects should *overlap*, rather than *coincide*, with the outline of background objects. For example, consider a shot of someone sitting in a chair with a painting on the wall in the background. It is best to frame the shot so that the outline of the head either does not touch the bottom of the painting or instead blocks part of the painting from view. If the outline of the top

Figure 3–11 Eyeroom

Attention Focused behind
Subject

Attention Focused in Front
of Subject

Figure 3–12   Foreground/Background Coincident Lines

BAD: Coincident Lines Are Distracting   BETTER: But Does Not Express Depth

BEST: Overlap Expresses Depth

of the head touches the outline of the bottom of the painting, the resulting image will be distracting, if not comical (see Figure 3–12). Trees and poles in the background that appear to grow out of someone's head should also be avoided for similar reasons.

Framing and Balance

The way in which a shot is framed and composed affects the viewer's perception of the balance of the shot. **Balance** refers to the relative weight created by objects or people in the frame. These weights may be distributed evenly (*symmetrical balance*) or unevenly (*asymmetrical balance*) (see Figure 3–13). Symmetrical framing, in which the graphic weight of objects in the frame is symmetrically balanced, is very stable and tells the viewer that the situation is at rest or under control. Asymetrical framing, in which the graphic masses are asymmetrically balanced,

Figure 3–13   Symmetrical and Asymmetrical Balance

Symmetrical   Asymmetrical

creates a sense of imbalance and instability. It produces tension and suggests that something is about to happen.

CAMERA MOVEMENT

Camera Head and Zoom Lens Movement

There are two basic types of camera movement: (1) movements of the camera head or zoom lens, with the camera itself in a fixed position; and (2) movements of the entire camera and its support system.

The two most common camera head movements are panning and tilting. A **pan** is a horizontal movement of the camera head only. The word *pan* is short for panorama, and the purpose of the pan is to reveal a scene with a sweeping horizontal motion of the camera head. A **tilt** is a vertical movement (up and down) of the camera head. Again, it is usually accomplished with the camera in a fixed position. The **zoom** is accomplished by simply moving the zoom lens assembly, causing the lens to zoom in or zoom out. The effect of the zoom is to bring the scene closer to the viewer or to move it farther away from the viewer.

Zoom lenses were developed to allow the camera operator to change the field of view without changing lenses. Thus, technically speaking, the zoom lens was a device that made production more efficient because the camera operator could get new shots set up quickly. However, the zoom movement itself found considerable popularity in television productions and is particularly useful when shooting with a single camera.

A word of caution is in order here: Do not overuse the zoom. The zoom can be extremely effective when it is used properly, but the zoom must have a reason for its existence. The scene must call for it—it must be motivated or introduced to present new information in a shot. It is extremely bad practice to simply zoom in and out to add movement to a scene. Not only will constant zooming nauseate your audience but it will also create difficulty when editing the videotape, since it is usually easier to cut between two still shots than between two moving shots.

Zoom speed is also an important variable. A fast zoom draws attention to the zoom and the image, whereas a slow zoom may hardly be noticed, as it subtly directs the viewer's attention to the content of the shot.

Movement of the Camera and Its Support Unit

Movement of the camera and its support unit (often a tripod with a three-wheel dolly attached to the legs) produces the movement of dolly, truck, and arc. A **dolly in** or **out** is actual movement of the camera and its support toward or away from the scene. A **truck left** or **right** is horizontal movement of the camera and its support in front of the scene. An **arc** is a semicircular movement of the camera and its support around the scene. These terms can also be used if the camera is hand held, although the movements will not be as smooth because the up and down walking motion of the camera operator will be visible in the shot.

Smooth, effective camera motion can also be achieved by using some rather untraditional methods of moving the camera. Grocery carts, wheelchairs, and bicycles can provide steady support for moving camera shots, as can shooting out of the window or sunroof of an automobile.

Hand-Held Versus Tripod-Mounted Camera Movement

There are differences between movements accomplished with a hand-held or shoulder-mounted camera, and those done with a camera mounted on a tripod dolly or other stable, movable mounting device. The differences are both physical and psychological. A camera mounted on a tripod is extremely stable. Since it is so stable, the camera becomes an invisible, objective observer of the scene. The purpose of the camera in television studio presentations such as news programs and interviews is to record what happens, not participate in the event. For this reason, tripod or pedestal-mounted cameras are almost always used for these kinds of programs.

If the lens is zoomed out all the way, it is easier to control the perceived effect of camera movement than if it is zoomed in. Nevertheless, when the camera is hand held, it becomes significantly less stable. As a result, the viewer becomes aware of the movement of the camera, and consequently also becomes aware of the presence of the camera. The camera participates significantly more in the event because its presence is apparent. It is no longer an invisible observer without an effect on the scene. The effect of the camera is now visible and the viewer can see how it responds to the scene. Thus, the decision to mount a camera on a tripod or to hand hold it should be made with a great amount of forethought.

SHOOTING TO EDIT

In almost all single-camera field productions, the camera operator shoots material that will be edited together in postproduction. The camera operator has a responsibility to give the editor material that can be coherently assembled. The following guidelines should be considered when shooting material that is going to be edited in postproduction.

Shoot Establishing Shots

The function of the establishing shot is to set the scene; it tells the viewer where the action is happening. Establishing shots, most often in the form of extreme long shots or long shots, show the relationship of the parts to each other and to the scene as a whole. An establishing shot is essential if the viewer, who otherwise has no knowledge of the scene or setting, is to make sense of the scene.

Cover the Action

When you look at a situation or scene, try to identify the principal action or events. Break scenes or events down into their principal components and then try to cover them. For example, if you are commissioned to videotape a friend's wedding, you could break that event into components like these:

1. Prewedding activities—bride dressing, arrival of groom at church, bride's drive to church, and so on
2. Ceremony—arrival of bride, walk down the aisle into church, ceremony including exchange of rings and traditional kiss, and so on
3. After ceremony—walk down the aisle and out of church, throwing rice or birdseed at bride and groom, drive to reception, reception line, cutting the cake, and so on

By breaking down the event into component parts, you can determine what you need to cover to faithfully capture the essence of the event. Breaking down an event into components also tells you if you need one camera or more. If you have only one camera, you can decide which parts of the event are most important and plan to cover these.

Repeat the Action if Possible

If you have only one camera to shoot an event, and the participants are willing and able to repeat the action, you can shoot the same event from different angles. In traditional Hollywood film-style shooting, the director provides a master shot of the entire scene shot on a wide-angle lens. Then the scene is repeated from several additional angles to provide close-up detail of the major characters or actions in the scene. In a television studio program utilizing multiple cameras, one camera usually holds a wide shot and the others are set on close-up of the details of the action. The director then cuts from one camera to another as the scene unfolds.

Since you probably have only one camera for shooting in the field, it is helpful to shoot multiple takes. This is often easy to arrange. For example, if you are recording a musical group, you can do one take of a song on a wide shot, then shoot a close-up of the lead singer, and then perhaps do a third take, shooting close-ups of the instrumentalists during their solo segments (see Figure 3–14). For editing, this provides a cover shot (the long shot of the whole group) plus repeated action of the significant details from which to assemble your segment.

Whether or not your subject can repeat the action depends to a certain extent on the nature of the action. Product demonstrations and dramatic scenes lend themselves quite readily to multiple takes of repeated action. You will mostly likely have more success in arranging multiple takes with the music recording session just described than with your local hockey team's score of a game-winning goal. Instant replays, unfortunately, are not a characteristic of real life.

If you are shooting a program from a script that involves dialogue or action, then the technique of **overlapping** should be used. Begin each new shot by repeating the action or dialogue that ended the previous shot. This technique of shooting overlapping action and dialogue greatly simplifies the editor's task.

Shoot Essential Details

In addition to the overall action or principal elements of a scene, what are the essential details? Shoot close-up shots of essential details of the event to be used

Figure 3–14 Multiple Takes of a Musical Performance

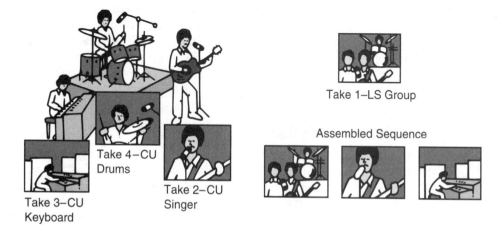

Take 1–LS Group

Take 4–CU Drums

Take 3–CU Keyboard

Take 2–CU Singer

Assembled Sequence

as **cut ins**, and shoot other related details, not a part of the scene itself, to be used as **cut aways**. For example, if you are shooting an interview with a painter who is discussing current projects, you might also shoot some footage of the artist at work. Shots at work might include wide shots of the painter in the studio as well as close-ups of the brush moving against the canvas. A cut from a shot of the painter talking on camera during the interview to a shot of the painter at work is a cut away. A cut from the wide shot of the artist in the studio to a close-up of the brush moving is a cut in.

Another common type of cut away shot in an interview scene is the **reaction shot**. Shoot some footage of the interviewer responding to the painter. A cut away from the painter to the reaction shot will show the audience how the interviewer is responding to what is being said.

If the artist demonstrates the techniques used, you should shoot some close-ups of this activity. You can then cut in from a wide or medium shot of the artist in the studio to a close-up shot of the artist's hands at work.

Shoot Material for Transitions

You should have a good idea of the way in which you are going to achieve your transitions from one segment or scene to another when you go into the field to shoot. Let's assume that you are constructing a program out of interviews of people involved in the debate over the safety of nuclear energy. You shoot a series of interviews in two towns that are several hundred miles apart. The people in town A are almost unanimously opposed to nuclear energy because there have been several accidents at the reactor in their community, and they fear for their own safety and the safety of their children. The people in town B get most of their electrical energy from the plant but live far enough away to not have to worry about radiation leaks. They are almost unanimously in favor of nuclear energy and the continued operation of the plant in question.

When you assemble your program, how will you make the transition from the anti-nuclear interviews to the pro-nuclear interviews? This is the function of transitional material. Perhaps you will use an on-camera narrator to bridge the gap. Or you might use a cover or establishing shot of the locale, or a shot taken from the window of a car driving down the main street of the town. Whatever device you use, you should have an idea of what it is going to be before you go out to shoot so that you can be sure to get the appropriate footage on tape.

Shoot Segments Long Enough for Editing

The mechanics of video systems require that any segment of tape to be used during editing must have *at least* 5 seconds of preroll material. This means that you must focus your camera and begin recording for a minimum of 5 seconds before you will have usable video. This is necessary for at least two reasons. First, it usually takes about 5 seconds for the tape to get up to speed and for the image to stabilize. Second, most editing control units need this preroll time to cue up and execute edits. All shots should therefore be 10 seconds or longer to ensure that you have at least a few seconds of usable video.

Shoot Shots That Utilize Matched Camera Movements

If, for example, you are shooting a series of still photographs to be incorporated into a profile of a local photographer, start with a long shot of the first photograph and hold it for 10 or 15 seconds. Then zoom in slowly to the important detail in the picture and hold that; then zoom out slowly at the same rate you used to zoom in to your original wide shot, and hold that again. Repeat the procedure with all the photographs you record. Your editor can then choose from a series of long shots, slow zooms, and close-ups of all the relevant photographs.

Similarly, if you are shooting landscapes, you may want to use the same technique of holding the long shot and then zooming in. Or you may want to record a series of pans across significant details of the landscape, all shot at the same panning speed. These shots can then be cut together into a most effective sequence of shots with matched camera action.

Specific Suggestions for Shooting Interviews

One of the most common single-camera situations is the on-site or remote interview. Some specific camera blocking (position) setups are discussed in the next few pages, but here we would like to focus on some basic strategic decisions that should be made before you begin shooting. First, decide if the interviewer is going to be seen on camera. Also decide whether or not the questions are going to be heard on camera or if you plan to edit them out and allow your audience only to hear the subject's answers. If the questions are to be heard on the tape, will the interviewer be seen?

Let's assume that you want to see the interviewer ask the questions and that you plan to edit the questions and answers together into a continuous sequence. Shoot the interview with the camera generally focused on the subject. Vary the lens angle (zoom in and out) at appropriate points in the interview. For example, you might want to pull out a little when a question is asked and then zoom in as the question is answered. Or, if the subject makes a startling or personal revelation, you might want to slowly zoom in for emphasis.

Since you have kept the camera focused on the subject during the interview, you will need to shoot some additional material for cut aways. After the interview is over, shoot several **over-the-shoulder shots** (also called *reverse shots* or *reversals*) of the interviewer and interviewee. You do not even need to record sound. Just shoot both people from several different angles (see Figure 3–15). After the interview is over, you can shoot the interviewer asking the questions. This technique of **question re-ask** is frequently used in television news and documentary production. Make sure the questions are re-asked in the same location and with the same background as the original interview. Also make sure that the re-asked questions are the same as the original questions! If the questions are in

Figure 3–15   Over-the-Shoulder Shot Interview

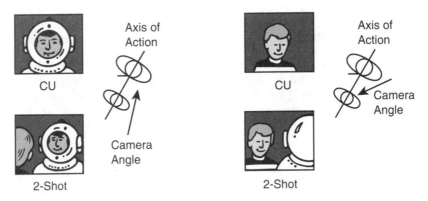

a script, the interviewer can simply re-ask them into the camera after the real interview has been completed. If the questions are ad-libbed, a production assistant should make a record of the questions while the interview is in progress. If there is any doubt about what actually was asked, you can always refer to the video itself, since the subject's microphone will have picked up the questions even if the interviewer did not wear a microphone. News producers have an ethical and legal responsibility to make sure that the questions that are re-asked, and the answers that are given in the edited version of the program, correspond to what was actually asked and answered in the original interview.

SUBJECT-CAMERA RELATIONSHIPS

Above, At, and Below Eye-Level Position

Because camera position has a profound impact on the audience's perception of the subject, determining the position of the camera in relation to the subject is extremely important. So-called objective videography places the camera at the eye level of the subject. **At eye-level camera position** makes the viewer and the subject equal in terms of their relative height. The viewer looks directly at the subject rather than up or down. At eye-level camera position is probably the most commonly used camera position in television. Almost all studio presentations shoot at eye level, and most typical kinds of remote footage—such as news, documentaries, and on-site interviews—place the camera in this neutral, objective position.

When the camera is positioned above or below the eye level of the subject, the dynamics of the audience's perception of the subject change radically. When the camera is placed in the **above eye-level camera position**, it shoots down at the subject. Since the audience views the shot from the perspective of the camera, the audience assumes a position of superiority over the subject. If you want to make someone seem smaller, less significant or important, shoot from above the eye level of the subject.

Conversely, when the camera is placed in the **below eye-level camera position**, it shoots up at the subject. Again the audience views the shot from the perspective of the camera, which now places the viewer below the subject. The viewer looks up at the subject who now towers over the camera. Below eye-level camera position increases the power, significance, and perceived size of the subject. The effect is almost the exact opposite of shooting from above eye level.

Objective and Subjective Camera

The camera can either observe an event or participate in it. When the function of the camera is simply to observe an event, we classify it as an **objective camera**. The perspective of the objective camera viewpoint is from outside the scene. The camera acts as an unseen observer, and the participants within the scene seem unaware of its presence. Two examples of the use of the objective camera are a documentary in which the camera records an event and a dramatic program such as a soap opera in which the characters play to each other and are oblivious to the camera. Most television programs are shot from this perspective.

Subjective camera refers to the use of the camera as a participant in the scene. This may take a number of forms. The camera may act as the eyes of a person in a scene or the characters may talk directly into the camera. A classic episode of the television series "M*A*S*H" used the subjective camera technique quite effectively. The entire episode was shot from the point of view of a wounded soldier who was brought to the medical unit for treatment. The audience saw everything through the eyes of the wounded soldier, from the time he arrived via helicopter at the beginning of the episode, to the time he left the hospital at the episode's conclusion. Throughout the episode, the camera acted as the soldier's eyes and made the audience experience the scene through its (the camera's) and his (the soldier's) point of view.

When used appropriately, the subjective camera is an extremely powerful production technique. The portable television camera has the mobility demanded by the subjective camera technique and is therefore easily used in this context. However, care must be exercised so that the technique is not overused, as overuse may well diminish its effectiveness.

Many programs use a combination of both objective and subjective camera viewpoints. An easily understood example of a type of programming that frequently combines these techniques is the on-site television news report. Typically, at the beginning of the report, the reporter introduces the story by speaking directly to the camera and the audience. This is a classic example of the use of subjective camera. Then, a voice-over accompanies shots of the event that is being reported. Here, the camera assumes the position of the objective observer. The techniques complement each other to present a news report that is both personal and informative.

Principal Action Axis

When shooting any type of dramatic scene, interview, or event that will be edited in postproduction, the videographer must determine the position of the **principal action axis**. The camera must be kept on one side of the principal action axis while recording the scene to maintain continuity in the direction of action and position of the scene. This principal action axis is sometimes referred to as the *principal vector line*,[3] and keeping the camera to one side of the axis is sometimes called the *180-degree rule*. These three terms are interchangeable.

To identify the principal action axis, look at the direction of the action in a scene and draw a line tracing it. For example, in a football or basketball game, the principal action moves the ball and the players from one end of the field or court to the other. This motion from one end and back again creates the principal action axis (see Figure 3–16). To position your camera correctly and maintain continuity of direction from shot to shot, the camera must shoot all coverage of the action from one side of the action axis. The camera may be positioned on either side of the action axis, and as long as all action is shot from the same side of the line, directional continuity will be maintained. If, however, the camera moves to the other side of the line, the action will appear to be reversed (see Figure 3–17).

On-Site Interview Setup

One of the most common remote shooting situations is the on-site interview. Since television equipment has become so portable, it is a rather simple operation to travel to the home or office of the person you want to interview and shoot the interview in the subject's normal environment, rather than in the artificial television studio environment. Almost all on-site interviews are shot with a single camera, and as a result, the videographer must shoot all the angles needed to

Figure 3–16 Principal Action Axis—Football Game

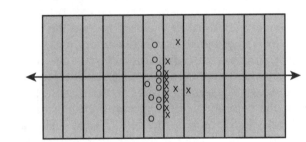

Figure 3–17   Possible Camera Positions: Side A or Side B

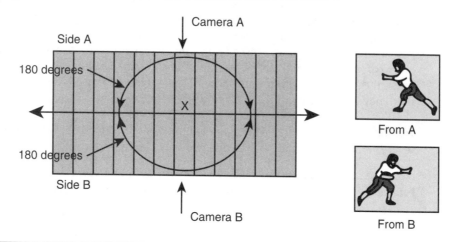

edit the interview into a coherent sequence. The interview must have both content and visual continuity. The remainder of our discussion here will focus on visual continuity.

The following factors should be considered when setting up an on-site interview.

1. Position of the subject
2. Position of the interviewer
3. Position of the camera
4. Principal action axis

Position of the Subject. When you travel to the home or office of the subject of your interview, you are able to show the subject in his or her normal working or living environment. The subject should be placed comfortably, facing the camera, where you can take advantage of the surroundings to provide rich background detail to the interview. In many cases, particularly when the interview takes place in an office, your subject will be sitting behind a desk. In the home, the subject will normally be sitting in a chair or on a couch. With your subject in position for the interview, examine the background to be sure that it does not distract from the subject. Lamps and pictures on the wall often provide unwanted distractions. If they interfere with the composition of your shot, move them into a more favorable position.

Be careful not to position the subject in front of a window. If there is a window in the background and you cannot move the subject so that the window is out of the shot, close the window blinds or draperies when shooting during the day to avoid silhouetting the subject.

Position of the Interviewer. There are two possible positions in which to place the interviewer—next to the subject or somewhat in front of the subject with the interviewer's back to the camera. The best place for the interviewer is in front of the subject, back to the camera (see Figure 3–18). Placement of the interviewer next to the subject may make the subject feel more comfortable, since this approximates a normal sitting position for conversations, but it will consistently present the camera with a poor view of the subject because he or she will have a tendency to turn toward the interviewer and away from camera.

Position of the Camera. The camera should be positioned slightly behind the interviewer and off to one side. In this position, the camera can easily shoot a three-

Figure 3–18   Blocking the On-Site Interview and Resulting Shots

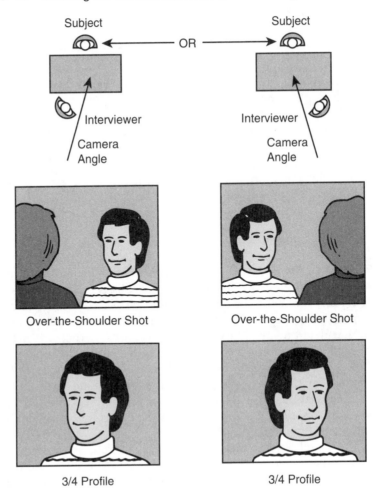

Subject   Subject

← OR →

Interviewer   Interviewer

Camera   Camera
Angle   Angle

Over-the-Shoulder Shot   Over-the-Shoulder Shot

3/4 Profile   3/4 Profile

quarter profile of the subject, as well as an over-the-shoulder shot of the interviewer and subject. From this position, the subject will always be able to maintain easy eye contact with the interviewer and will present the camera with an almost full-face shot. Figure 3–18 diagrams this setup and the shots possible from it.

When you are setting up the position of the interviewer and the subject, try to keep the distance between them relatively short, and keep the camera a few feet behind the interviewer. The camera should be able to zoom in to a tight close-up on the subject, and at the same time the interviewer should be in focus when you zoom out to the over-the-shoulder shot.

Principal Action Axis. A principal action axis is formed in an interview setting, just as it is in an action-oriented scene. The principal action axis extends from the subject to the interviewer (see Figure 3–19). To maintain continuity when you shoot question re-asks or reaction shots, the camera must remain in the 180-degree semi-circle formed by the principal action axis. If you keep this in mind, you will be able to move the camera during or after the interview to shoot additional material of your subjects from different angles and still present your editor with material that retains continuity when edited.

Figure 3–20 presents another blocking diagram of an interview; however, this one is not arranged as well as the previous example. In news or on-the-street interviews, where the interviewer is forced to hold the microphone that is recording the sound, or when the interviewer must face the camera directly to introduce the subject, it is common for the interviewer to stand next to the subject. The difficulty with this blocking arrangement is that it is natural for the subject to talk to the interviewer rather than to the camera when answering the questions. As a result, the camera is left with a poor shot of the subject—the infa-

Figure 3–19   Principal Action Axis—On-Site Interview

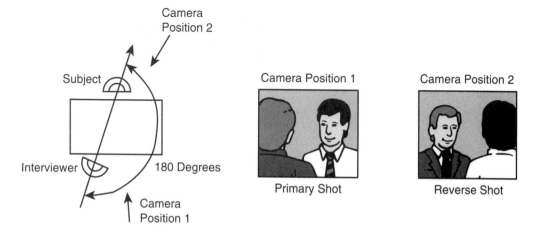

Camera
Position 2

Subject

Interviewer   180 Degrees

Camera
Position 1

Camera Position 1

Primary Shot

Camera Position 2

Reverse Shot

Figure 3–20   Poor Composition (The Great American Ear Shot)

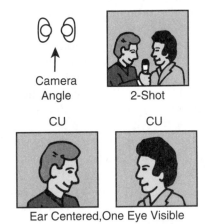

Figure 3–21   Foreground/Middleground/Background Objects

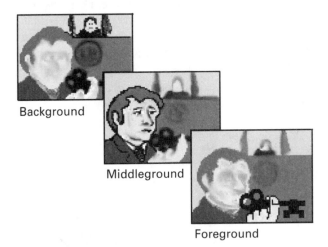

mous **ear shot**—in which any zoom into a close-up reveals the subject's face in profile rather than from the front. Since the eyes of the subject convey significantly more information to the audience than an ear, try to avoid this situation whenever possible.

Shooting for Depth

As mentioned earlier, we try to increase the sensation of depth in television images to make them seem more realistic, since we know that objects in the real world are three dimensional rather than flat. Following several simple shooting rules can increase the sense of depth in television images. First, always try to compose images that have a distinct foreground, middleground, and background. Place objects between the camera and your subject, as well as behind your subject, to draw attention to depth. Second, when staging a scene, or even when simply setting up the position of interviewer and subject, try to stage for depth by placing the subjects at different distances away from the camera. And third, whenever possible, bring action toward or away from the camera rather than moving it horizontally in front of the camera (see Figure 3–21). Although it is not possible (or advisable) to adhere to these rules all of the time, you can improve the look of your video presentations by using them in situations that call for them.

SUMMARY

The camera lens functions to gather light that is reflected off a scene being recorded and to direct an image onto the image sensor (pickup tube or CCD) inside the camera. Lenses are described by their focal length, which determines the angle of view of a scene that the lens will reproduce.

The two basic types of lenses are fixed focal length lenses and zoom lenses. Almost all portable video cameras come equipped with a zoom lens, which is a variable focal length lens that allows the camera operator to zoom in and out on a scene simply by moving the lens elements.

The three major components of a zoom lens are the focus ring, zoom ring, and aperture control. The focus ring is used to bring the image into focus. The zoom ring controls the movement of the lens elements and zooms the lens in or out. The aperture ring controls the size of the iris opening of the lens. Focus, zoom, and aperture controls may be automatic or manual, depending on the type of camera. Other lens components include the lens hood, lens cap, and macro lever.

Correct zoom lens operation includes presetting the lens focus and adjusting the aperture for correct exposure. Control of the aperture is critical, as it affects not only exposure but also depth of field. Correct exposure is determined by adjusting the exposure for the center of interest in the frame. Depth of field varies depending on the amount of available light, the focal length of the lens at a particular zoom position, the size of the aperture opening, and the distance between the subject and camera.

Some of the principal factors to consider when composing visual images with a television camera include screen size and aspect ratio, focus, depth, field of view, framing, and balance.

Images may be recorded with the camera in a stationary position or with the camera moving. Camera movement may be achieved in a number of ways. Panning, tilting, and zooming are accomplished by moving the camera head or zoom lens elements, with the camera itself in a fixed position. When the camera and its support unit move, the camera may dolly, truck, or arc. Many field cameras are often hand held, and they may also be mounted on a tripod to lend stability.

Many single-camera field productions are shot in pieces and the final program is assembled in postproduction editing. Guidelines to follow when shooting for editing include shoot establishing shots, cover the action, repeat the action, shoot essential details, shoot material for transitions, shoot segments long enough for editing, and shoot shots that utilize matched camera movements.

When shooting interviews, pay strict attention to camera and subject blocking. Reversals of the interviewer are always shot to aid in editing. Question re-asks, in which the interviewer's questions are recorded after the interview is completed, also aid in editing and give the appearance that the interview was recorded by more than one camera.

The relationship between the subject and the camera may influence the audience's perception of the subject. The camera may be placed above, at, or below eye-level position. The camera may be an objective observer of an event or it may participate in the scene (subjective camera).

If you are shooting a scene that will be edited in postproduction, the correct position of the camera is determined by identifying the principal action axis of the shot or scene. This is important when shooting interviews as well as when shooting action sequences. In all shooting, attention to maximizing the perception of depth in a scene adds an important dimension of realism to the image.

ENDNOTES

1. Millerson, Gerald. *The Technique of Lighting for Television and Motion Pictures.* London: Focal, 1974, pp. 24, 52.

2. For example, see The Editors of Time-Life Books. *The Camera.* New York: Time-Life Books, 1976, pp. 97–130; and Lipton, Lenny. *Independent Filmmaking*, revised ed. San Francisco: Straight Arrow, 1973, pp. 140–185.

3. Zettl, Herbert. *Sight Sound Motion*, 2nd ed. Belmont, CA: Wadsworth, 1990, pp. 308–313.

4

Videotape Recording

In the early days of television, all programs originated from one of two sources: They were live broadcasts or they were broadcasts of programs that had originally been produced on film. Initially, there was no electronic means of storing the television image, and those programs that were aired live often disappeared forever— they were seen once at the time of the broadcast and then they were gone for good. The only way to save a live broadcast was to record the picture and sound by pointing a film camera at a television monitor during the live broadcast. Today, these film recordings of television programs, called **kinescopes**, provide the only record of many early television broadcasts.

Although kinescope recordings were useful in providing a historical record of what had been broadcast, they were less useful as a production device because their picture and sound quality was greatly inferior to that of the television system. What was needed was a means of electronically recording and editing the television signal. Such a system would preserve the electronic character of the television image and not distort it the way kinescope recording did. However, it was not until 1956 that the Ampex Corporation introduced the first practical videotape recorder. It provided the first all-electronic storage and production medium for television programs.

DEVELOPMENT OF VIDEOTAPE RECORDING

The Magnetic Recording Process

The development of a practical means of electronically recording the video signal was a goal of many small and large companies in the 1940s and 1950s. The principles applied in audiotape recorders acted as a model for these potential inventors. Successful audiotape recording systems had been developed in which the audio signal was fed to an audio head and then transferred to a piece of magnetic tape. The **head** was a small electromagnet, and the strength of the magnetic field produced by the head varied in proportion to the variations in the current—the audio signal—fed into it. The signal could be stored on magnetic tape because the variations in the magnetic field produced by the head were recorded by the particles embedded in the tape.

The way in which the head works to encode the signal onto a piece of magnetic tape can be explained fairly easily using a simple scientific experiment on magnetism. You probably remember conducting this experiment as a child. You place a pile of iron filings or small pieces of metal shavings on a piece of paper and then pass a magnet under the paper. This results in the metal filings arranging themselves in a pattern that corresponds to the movement of the magnet under the paper. If the magnet is moved in a straight line, it creates a straight line of iron filings; if it is moved in a circle, it creates a circular pattern of iron filings. The process of recording on audiotape or videotape works on the same principle of magnetism of metal particles.

An audio or video recording head is really a small electromagnet. Both sides of the head are wrapped with a coil of wire, and a current passing through the wire causes an electromagnetic charge to be emitted at the **gap**—the space between the two sides of the head (see Figure 4–1). Magnetic recording tape is plastic tape coated with metal particles that store the charge emitted by the head as it passes over the tape.

Engineers found that the quality of a recording could be improved by varying two factors: the gap in the head and the speed of the tape. The gap in the head is a microscopic space between the two sides of the electromagnet. The smaller this gap, the higher frequency signal it is capable of recording. Similarly, as the speed of the tape increases, so does its frequency response. For example, tape moving at

Figure 4–1   Video Recording Head

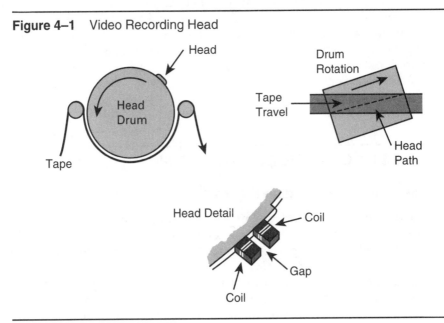

15 **inches per second** can record a greater range of frequencies than tape moving at $7\frac{1}{2}''$ per second. This occurs because when the tape moves past the heads at a faster speed, more magnetic particles on the tape are available to store the signal, since more of them come in contact with the heads at the higher speed. A tape moving at 15" per second can store more information than tape moving at $7\frac{1}{2}''$ per second. As a result, the 15" per second recording sounds and looks better than the recording made at a slower speed. This is one reason why the quality of recordings produced on professional audiotape recorders operating at 15" per second is significantly better than what you are able to achieve on your home audiocassette deck, which operates at $1\frac{7}{8}''$ per second.

Early Attempts at Videotape Recording

Recording the video signal presented a major problem to video engineers because it is so much more complex than the audio signal. The video signal contains not only the picture (remember, that's 525 lines of information) and sound information but all the signal synchronizing information as well. In addition, the range of frequencies necessary to create the video image is considerably wider than the range of frequencies found in audio. In audio recording, the frequency range of the recorded signal falls between 15 hertz (or cycles per second) and 20,000 hertz, for a range of about 20,000 cycles per second. But the range of frequencies in the television signal varies from about 30 hertz to 4.5 million hertz—a range of over 4.5 million cycles per second.

Nevertheless, video engineers reasoned that they could successfully record the video image if they could figure out a way to manipulate the same variables (head gap and tape speed) that had been successfully manipulated to achieve audio recording. In one of the early recording attempts, Bing Crosby Productions actually modified an audiotape recorder so that it would accept a video signal. Rather than use only 1 head, they arranged 11 recording heads across a tape. Even with these 11 heads, the Bing Crosby team was not able to achieve an acceptable recording until it increased the tape speed. The system they finally developed used 11 stationary video heads and a tape that moved at 100" per second.[1] RCA also attempted to develop a recording system at this time; like the Bing Crosby team, their efforts centered on moving the tape extremely fast across a stationary head assembly. In the RCA system, only 1 video head was used, but to make a satisfactory recording, the tape had to move at 360" per second.

The BBC (British Broadcasting Corporation) was also involved in early VTR development experiments, and in 1955 began broadcasting with a system called VERA (for vision electronic recording apparatus).[2] However, it suffered from the same problem as the U.S. systems. With a recording speed of 200" per second, a 30-minute program required approximately 30,000 feet of videotape on a reel 5 feet in diameter. Thus, while these systems were capable of recording and playing back the television signal on videotape, they simply were not practical because they required huge amounts of tape.

Solution to the Problem: Moving Heads

At about the same time that these experiments were being conducted, Ampex Corporation, a small electronics company in Redwood City, California, hit on the idea that tape-to-head speed could be maximized not only by moving the tape past the heads but also by moving the heads themselves. They developed a recorder that utilized four rotating heads mounted in a drum that spun as the tape moved across it. With the tape speed set at 15" per second, and the heads rotating at 14,400 revolutions per minute, an effective tape-to-head speed greater than 1,500" per second was achieved. Using this system, it was possible to record 60 minutes of material on a reel of tape 2,400 feet in length and about 1 foot in diameter. To understand the magnitude of this development, consider this: If the heads were stationary and the tape speed was increased to achieve the tape-to-head speed of 1,500" per second, it would take almost 500,000 feet of tape to record those same 60 minutes of material.[3]

The system invented by Ampex became the broadcast industry standard. The tape was 2" wide, and the process of using four heads to record the signal was called **quadruplex** recording. Until the development of 1" VTRs in the late 1970s, the term 2" *quad* was synonymous with the broadcast standard of recording.

Another term for tape-to-head speed is *writing speed*. Writing speed is determined by the speed at which the heads rotate, the speed at which the tape is pulled through the VCR, and the size of the head drum. In general, the higher the writing speed, the higher the quality of recording. Consequently, the quality of recordings produced by 2", 1", and the professional-quality $\frac{1}{2}$" component VCRs (Betacam and M-II) is significantly better than the quality of the recordings made on small-format systems such as $\frac{3}{4}$" VCRs, $\frac{1}{2}$" VHS/S-VHS VCRs, and 8mm/Hi8 VCRs.

HELICAL SCAN RECORDING

Transverse and Helical Scan

Although 2" machines worked well in broadcasting, a host of other potential video users found the 2" machines impractical because of their size and cost. Recording engineers focused on ways to make smaller and cheaper machines. Once again, they came up against a basic problem: How does one make the components of the system smaller and still record the complex video signal? The solution was to be found in the way the signal was physically put down onto the videotape.

The 2" recorders utilized a process known as **transverse scan**; that is, the video signal was recorded in vertical lines of information on the tape (see Figure 4–2). Each one of the four heads laid down 16 to 17 lines of picture information per pass of the tape, and it took eight revolutions of the head drum to lay down one full frame of information. The video engineers discovered that they could decrease the width of the tape significantly by laying down the video information at an

Figure 4–2 Transverse Scan and Helical Scan

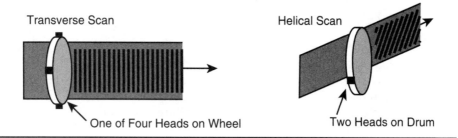

Transverse Scan

One of Four Heads on Wheel

Helical Scan

Two Heads on Drum

angle on the tape. In addition, they also found a way to reduce the complexity of the head assembly from four heads to two by allowing each head to lay down one entire field of information (262.5 lines) per pass of the tape.

The process of recording the video information at an angle is known as **helical scan** recording. This name is used because the videotape is wrapped around the head drum inside the machine in the form of a helix. Sometimes this type of recording is called **slant track** recording, as this describes the angle of the video information on the tape (see Figure 4–3).

Two-Head VCRs

The video heads are mounted on a bar that spins inside the head drum. The heads protrude from a slot cut in the drum. This is where they make contact with the videotape.

Most helical scan systems use two rotating heads in a head bar that rotates at 1,800 revolutions per minute (or 30 revolutions per second). Since the head bar contains two heads, and the bar rotates at 30 revolutions per second, you can see that the heads come into contact with the tape 60 times per second (two heads per revolution multiplied by 30 revolutions per second). These 60 contacts per second

Figure 4–3 Helical Scan Tracks

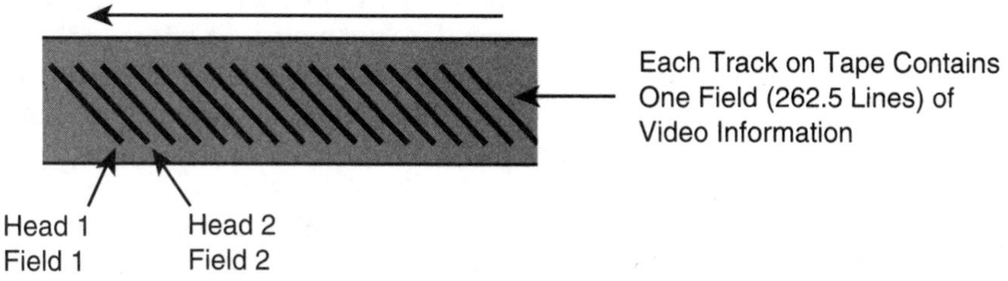

Each Track on Tape Contains One Field (262.5 Lines) of Video Information

Head 1
Field 1

Head 2
Field 2

correspond to the 60 fields of information displayed in one second of video information.

Tape Speed

The development of $\frac{1}{2}$" VHS, Beta, and 8mm format machines reflected another breakthrough in engineering. (The Beta formats referred to here are the consumer-quality Betamax/SuperBeta formats and not the professional-quality Betacam format that also uses $\frac{1}{2}$" tape. Although the $\frac{1}{2}$" Betamax format has all but disappeared from use in the United States, it is still used in other countries throughout the world.)

Long-play recordings can be made on VHS, 8mm, and Beta systems by decreasing the speed at which the videotape moves through the machine. The tape speed in some machines is relatively fast (2" tape speed, 15" per second; 1" tape speed, 9.6" per second; $\frac{3}{4}$" tape speed, 3.75" per second; $\frac{1}{2}$" Betacam tape speed, 4.67" per second; $\frac{1}{2}$" M-II tape speed, 2.67" per second). However, in Beta and VHS format machines, the tape moves very slowly in the standard play mode (Beta tape speed, 1.57" per second; VHS tape speed, 1.30" per second). In the extended long-play mode, this speed decreases to 0.523" per second for Beta tapes and 0.437" per second for VHS tapes. In the 8mm recording format, tape speed in the standard play mode is approximately 0.56" per second.

Four Heads Are Better than Two

Many VHS machines now on the market contain four heads. A look at the head drum assembly of these machines reveals that the heads protrude from the head drum at 90-degree intervals. However, this is not a quadruplex system like the early 2" machines.

Many VHS machines have several play and record modes in which the speed of the tape is varied: Standard play (**SP**) is the two-hour mode; long play (**LP**) is the four-hour mode; and standard long-play/extended play (**SLP/EP**) is the six-hour mode. Increases in playing or recording time are achieved by slowing the speed at which the tape runs through the machine. Changing the tape speed also changes the **track pitch**, or width of the track available for each track or field of video information. The track pitch (width) in SP is three times greater than in SLP/EP. Because of these differences in track width, the heads designed to record and play back the signal at one speed will not work properly at other speeds. This is because the width of the head gap does not match the width of the track of video information. Four-head machines, therefore, contain one pair of heads maximized for record and playback in the SP mode, and another pair maximized for the SLP/EP mode. Only one pair of heads is used at a time, and which pair is used depends on the mode in which the machine is operating.

In early models of VHS machines with multispeed capability, the heads were maximized for the SP mode. As a result, the quality of the recording and playback image in the SLP/EP mode was significantly lower than in the SP mode. Four-head machines have greatly improved the quality of the image in the longer-play modes, but SP still gives the highest-quality recording because tape speed, and consequently writing speed, are higher than in the other modes, thereby providing the greatest frequency response in the recording.

CONTROL TRACK

As we have discussed above and in Chapter 2, the stability of the television image produced by the camera is related to a series of sync pulses controlling the timing of the horizontal and vertical scanning of the images. As long as we are dealing with a live system, these horizontal and vertical timing controls are sufficient to ensure that the image seen by the camera is reproduced correctly by the home receiver. The horizontal and vertical sync pulses that drive the camera are encoded into the television signal and transmitted to the home receiver, where they also drive the scanning beam in the television receiver. But what happens when a signal is recorded onto videotape? How can we guarantee that the speed of the videotape will be precisely controlled so that it plays back at precisely 30 frames per second? And how can we guarantee that the playback heads precisely trace over the tracks of recorded information on the videotape and faithfully play back the recorded signal?

The problem of precisely controlling the speed of the playback medium is one that plagues anyone who works with the recorded image or sound. Film, of course, solves the problem through the use of sprocket holes. These sprocket holes guide the speed of the film and regulate the action of the camera or projector shutter. But in audio and video recording, there are no sprocket holes in the tape. How, then, can the system be regulated?

Controlling Tape Speed—The Capstan

In an audiotape system, the tape moves but the heads do not, so the problem is relatively simple. All one has to do is control the speed of the movement of the tape. If the record and playback speeds are the same, the system will work. Since no sprocket holes are used on the tape itself, how does it move through the machine? The solution is simple—the tape is driven by the **capstan**, a rotating shaft driven by the recorder's motor. The tape is sandwiched between the capstan and a rubber pinch roller, and the friction of the two against the audiotape literally pulls the tape through the machine. The speed of the capstan is regulated so that the speed of the audiotape is correct for the system: $1\frac{7}{8}''$ per second for audiocassettes and $3\frac{3}{4}''$, $7\frac{1}{2}''$, or $15''$ per second for reel-to-reel machines.

In video, however, the problem is more complex. Not only must the movement of the tape be controlled but the movement of the video heads must be precisely synchronized so that they accurately hit the tape on the tracks of video information. Any change in tape speed must also be reflected in a change of the movement of the heads, or the recording will not play back correctly.

Function of Control Track Pulses

Some way had to be found to synchronize the movement of the head assembly with the movement of the capstan. This is the function of the control track. The **control track**, a series of electronic impulses recorded directly onto the videotape, regulates the playback timing of the system.

In most helical scan systems, there are 30 control track pulses per second. One control track pulse is recorded for each frame of video information. In the record mode, these control track pulses are timed off the vertical sync pulses of the video signal as it enters the VCR. Since there are 60 vertical sync pulses per second, every other one causes a control track pulse to be recorded. These control track pulses are recorded onto the videotape in their own track, separate from the audio and video signals (see Figure 4–4).

At this point, a review of some video basics is probably in order. As you will recall from our discussion in Chapter 2, one frame of video information (525 lines) is composed of two fields, each containing 262.5 lines of information. The two fields are interlaced during the playback of the signal to ensure that the image does not flicker.

When a video signal is recorded onto videotape with a two-head helical scan system, each head lays down one field of information (see Figure 4–5). The recording of the video information is coordinated with the recording of the control track pulses. First, a control track pulse generated by the incoming vertical sync pulse is recorded, and then field 1 of the video information is laid down by the first video head. Next, the second head comes into contact with the tape and lays down field 2 of the video information. Then, the next control track pulse is recorded and the process repeats itself.

Do not confuse control track with horizontal or vertical sync. Horizontal and vertical sync regulate the timing of the beam as it scans the image and are part of the video signal. They are recorded in the slanted tracks of information along with the picture information. Control track pulses, on the other hand, are found only on videotape, where they function to regulate the playback of the signal by control-

---

Figure 4–4   **Control Track Pulses**

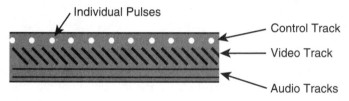

Figure 4–5   Video Frames, Fields, Tracks, and Control Track Pulses

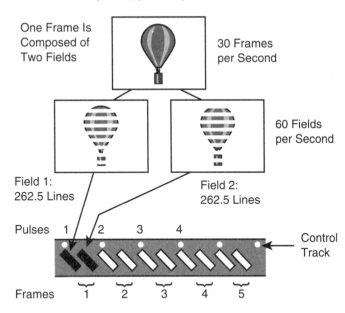

ling the movement of the capstan and the heads. There are no control track pulses in a live television signal.

Capstan and Head Drum Servos

The playback speed and scanning of the video information are controlled by the capstan and head drum servos. The capstan is driven by a motor connected to a servo (an abbreviation for servomechanism). The **capstan servo** senses the control track pulses on the tape and adjusts the speed of the motor that turns the capstan to maintain the correct tape speed.

The **head drum servo** then adjusts the position of the video heads so that they rotate in phase with the tracks of video information on the tape. Not only must the heads be positioned directly over the tracks of information on the tape but they must spin in such a way that they begin and end their movement across the tracks in precise synchronization with the actual beginning and end of each track.

CONTROL OF PLAYBACK SIGNAL

For a tape to play back correctly, at least three conditions must be met: The tape speed must be correct, the video heads must trace over the recorded tracks to pick up the signal, and the tape tension around the head drum must be correct. As we discussed, the playback speed of the tape is controlled by the capstan and pinch roller and is regulated by the capstan servo. Two other controls, **tracking** and **skew**, also help to maximize the quality of signal playback.

Tracking Control

Normally, any tape will play back correctly on the machine on which it was recorded. However, when you record a tape on one machine and then play it back on another, you sometimes run into problems caused by small differences in the machine speeds. This results in slight differences in the way the heads hit the tape. To ensure that the video heads are correctly in line with the tracks of information on the tape, many machines contain a **tracking control**. The tracking control adjusts the relationship between the heads and tracks of video information on the tape to optimize the level of the playback signal (see Figure 4–6).

You can tell if a VCR is tracking properly simply by looking at the picture on a monitor. If the tracking is correct, the picture will be clear and stable. If the tracking is not correct, the picture will contain a large band of noise running through it. This band of noise indicates that the heads are not in proper alignment with the video information tracks.

Figure 4–6   Tracking

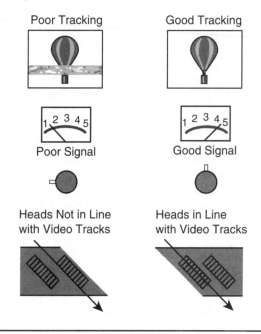

Many machines incorporate a **tracking meter**. By twisting the tracking control until the meter reaches its maximum point, you can adjust the machine for the best playback of the signal. An exception to this is found in the 8mm/Hi8 format, which substitutes automatic track finding (ATF) for the traditional control track pulses. The ATF signal is recorded in the tracks of video information on the videotape. During playback, the VCR automatically senses the ATF signal and adjusts the VCR for the best playback of the video information recorded on the tape.

Skew Control

Correct tape tension is also critical to the correct playback of video information. All machines have built-in components that automatically adjust the tension to its correct setting. However, sometimes tape tension problems result in a distortion of the playback image.

Tape tension problems cause the top of the picture to bend either left or right. This picture bending is referred to as **flagging**, and it can be corrected by adjusting the **skew control** on the VCR.

VIDEOTAPE RECORDING FORMATS

As the preceding discussion has indicated, there are now a number of different videotape recording formats in use. Tape format is determined by the width of the videotape; its configuration (reel to reel or cassette); the arrangement of the tracks of audio, video, and control track information on the tape; and the speed at which the tape moves through the recorder. Three different tape widths—$\frac{1}{2}''$, $\frac{3}{4}''$, and 8mm—are widely used in a variety of professional, industrial, and consumer VCRs (see Figure 4–7). All of these tapes are housed in videocassettes, which greatly simplify the tape loading process in comparison to reel-to-reel machines. An additional variable to consider is whether the video signal is recorded onto the tape as composite video or component video.

The following is a brief description of a number of different videotape recording formats now in use.

8mm and Hi8

The 8mm video systems feature the smallest videocassettes currently available. Since the tape is only approximately $\frac{1}{4}''$ wide, camcorders and VCRs can be made quite small. As a result, 8mm has become quite popular as a home video recording format. Equipment for 8mm video systems is widely available from a number of manufacturers, as standards for this format were jointly developed and agreed upon by a number of equipment producers. These systems achieve high-quality

Figure 4–7   Videocassette Recorders: (A) Hi8 VCR (Sony EVO-9800), (B) ½" VHS/SVHS
VCR (JVC BR-S622U), (C) ½" VHS/SVHS Videocassette Player (Panasonic AG-7650), (D)
¾" UMatic VCR (Sony VO-9800 SP), (E) Betacam SP Videocassette Player (Sony PVW-
2600), (F) M-II Studio VCR (Panasonic AU-65H)

(A)

(B)

(C)

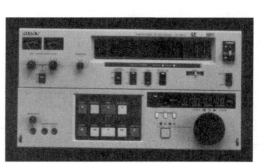

(D)

(E)

(F)

recording by using metal particle tape. High-fidelity audio is recorded by the rotating video heads.

Hi8 format equipment, introduced by Sony in 1989, incorporates the capability to record time code (see Chapter 8) along with resolution and color that exceeds the standard 8mm format. The availability of up to two high-fidelity (AFM) and two digital (PCM) audio tracks allows for very high-quality recording. Despite the fact that Hi8 is sometimes classified as a consumer-level recording format, it is finding increasing use among documentary and news producers, even at the network level, because of its low cost, extreme portability, and the very high quality of first-generation recordings.

An extremely compact Hi8 desktop editing system is now available. In addition, a Hi8 player/recorder can be used as the source machine in a $3/4$" editing system with a Sony edit controller and editing VCR, allowing Hi8 field tapes to be edited into a $3/4$" master.

$1/2$" VHS and S-VHS

VHS (video home system) emerged as the dominant format for home video recording in the early 1980s. Most VCRs in the United States that are used in the home to play back rented movies available on videocassette are in the VHS format.

S-VHS (Super-VHS) was introduced by Victor Company of Japan (JVC) in 1987 and is marketed by several manufacturers. Although not a true component recording system like Betacam and M-II, S-VHS VCRs process the luminance and chrominance signals independently within the system and improve the resolution (approximately 400 lines versus 240) and color recording over conventional VHS systems. Indeed, the potential resolution capability of S-VHS is greater than that of either conventional $3/4$" U-Matic or U-Matic SP formats. High-quality VHS/ S-VHS VCRs offer two channels of longitudinal audio as well as two channels of high-fidelity audio. A limitation of this format is the lack of a dedicated address track for time code separate from the two available longitudinal audio channels.

Because relatively low-cost, high-quality editing systems are available in both the VHS and S-VHS formats, these formats are widely used in a number of production situations. Although VHS is often classified as a consumer video format, S-VHS appeals to industrial and broadcast users as well. With the continued development of high-quality dockable camcorders, the S-VHS format will find wider use in these applications.

Betamax/SuperBeta/ED Beta

The $1/2$" Betamax videocassette format was developed for the home video market; however, it never achieved much popularity in the United States in the face of competition from VHS. SuperBeta and ED Beta improved the resolution and color recording capabilities of the original format and still find limited but declining use in the consumer and "prosumer" (between consumer and professional) video markets.

³/₄" U-Matic

The ³/₄" U-Matic tape was the format that initially made possible broadcast-quality television field production. This format is still used in some broadcast applications as well as in educational and industrial/corporate video applications. It is a reliable format that can be used for field production, editing, and tape distribution. An improved version of this format developed by Sony, ³/₄" U-Matic SP (Superior Performance), records the signal with more resolution than the conventional ³/₄" format and is fully compatible with it. All ³/₄" systems contain two longitudinal audio tracks. Professional "broadcast" VCRs contain an additional address track for time code as well.

Due to the width of the tape and the size of the cassettes used in the ³/₄" format, it has not been possible to develop a practical camcorder. Given the development of lightweight camcorders in a number of other formats, many of which record a higher-quality signal with smaller tape, use of the ³/₄" format for field recording is decreasing. Where once it was the standard for electronic news gathering, it has now been supplanted by Betacam/Betacam SP, M-II, and even in some instances by S-VHS and Hi8.

Nevertheless, some estimates of the number of ³/₄" format VCRs sold over the past two decades are in the range of two to three million machines. Many of these machines are still in operation; thus, ³/₄" will continue to be a viable production format in the foreseeable future, particularly in those production facilities that have invested heavily in this format and among users who cannot afford the cost nor need the quality of the more expensive Betacam and M-II formats.

Betacam SP and M-II
(¹/₂" Component Video Recording)

Betacam SP (Superior Performance) and M-II are professional, broadcast-quality ¹/₂" recording formats. Because of the small size of the videocassettes and the VCRs that are used for recording, they have found very wide use in camcorders used for television field production. In both of these formats, the video signal is recorded onto ¹/₂" videocassettes using the component recording process.

Four audio tracks are available in the Betacam SP and M-II formats: two longitudinal tracks and two high-fidelity tracks. In addition to providing broadcast-quality field tapes, Betacam SP and M-II perform extremely well as editing formats where multiple generation recording is necessary.

Betacam SP represents the second generation of development of this format, succeeding the original Betacam format (both developed by Sony). Similarly, M-II is the second generation of the original M format developed by Matsushita. Whereas Betacam and Betacam SP remain compatible with each other, M and M-II are incompatible. And since the position of the tracks of information on the videotape as well as the tape speed differs between the Betacam/Betacam SP and M/M-II formats, the Betacam formats are incompatible with the M formats. M-II format machines require the use of a special metal particle videotape; Betacam SP can record with either conventional metal oxide or special metal particle tape, but the highest-quality recordings are achieved with the special tape.

1" (Type C) and HDVS

Although our principal interest is in describing the smaller recording formats that are most suitable for field production, there are also a number of larger formats that are in use today.

Although not generally considered to be a so-called small format, 1" reel-to-reel tape is widely used in video production today, particularly in television studio operations and in videotape editing. Although a portable 1" VTR is available, this format is not widely used in field recording situations due to the size and expense of the machines. Despite increasing use of Betacam and M-II in the field, 1" tape remains one of the standards in high-quality editing systems. Many tapes that are shot in the field on Betacam or M-II are edited onto 1" tape.

With the advent of high-definition television, appropriate recording systems are being developed as well. The high-definition video system (HDVS) developed by Sony records the HDTV format developed by Japan Broadcasting System (NHK) (1125 horizontal scanning lines in a wide aspect ratio). This system (or another standard similar to it) is expected to find wide use as a production format that will rival the quality of 35mm film.

Digital Formats (D-1, D-2, and D-3)

Thus far, all of the videotape recording formats that have been discussed are analog formats. In addition to these formats, several high-quality (and high-cost) digital videotape recording formats are currently available. Utilizing special 19mm videocassettes (approximately $\frac{3}{4}$"), D-1 format machines record a component digital signal, whereas D-2 machines record a composite digital signal. Digital VCRs are found where the highest-quality editing is needed, as they produce the least amount of quality loss in the editing process. A portable digital VCR is also available, but it is quite large in comparison to conventional analog VCRs.

The decision to adopt either the component D-1 format or the composite D-2 format is often influenced by the type of equipment that is already in place in a production facility. For example, if the existing equipment is composite and the facility wishes to upgrade to digital editing, composite D-2 equipment with analog inputs can be installed with no modification to the existing facilities. In order to receive the full benefit from the component D-1 format, all other recording and signal processing equipment (VCRs, video switchers, time base correctors, distribution amplifiers, and so on) should also be capable of processing a component signal.

As its name indicates, the $\frac{1}{2}$" D-3 digital tape format uses a small $\frac{1}{2}$" cassette that records four channels of digital audio and a composite digital video signal. Time code and control tracks are recorded as well. The small size of the tape has allowed development of a relatively lightweight camcorder in addition to the larger studio-type recording/editing VCRs.

Composite and Component Recording

Major differences in the ways in which the video signal is processed and recorded can be seen when we examine several of the popular videotape recording formats now in use. The conventional way to record the signal is to record a *composite*, NTSC-encoded video signal. Each track of video information on the tape (the equivalent of one field of video information) contains the luminance (Y) and chrominance (C) parts of the signal mixed together with all the synchronizing information: color burst and horizontal and vertical sync. This type of recording is used in the conventional $\frac{1}{2}$" VHS, $\frac{1}{2}$" Betamax, and $\frac{3}{4}$" U-Matic and U-Matic SP videotape recording formats.

Another type of recording process is called *component* recording. In component recording systems, the luminance (brightness) and chrominance (color) components of the signal are recorded on different tracks on the tape. To do this, one group of video heads lays down the luminance information, and then the chrominance information is laid down in an adjacent track. To record one frame of video information, four tracks on the tape are used: Two tracks contain the two fields of luminance information and two tracks contain the two fields of chrominance information.

By recording the luminance and chrominance signals separately, instead of mixing them together and recording them simultaneously on the same track, component VCRs do not lose the high-frequency signal components that are lost in the conventional recording process. As a result, the picture quality of component recording is superior to conventional $\frac{3}{4}$" and VHS recordings, and rival the recordings made with professional-quality 1" VCRs.

Another term used to describe the way in which the video signal may be processed within a VCR is **Y/C signal processing**. In the 8mm, Hi8, and S-VHS formats, luminance (Y) and chrominance (C) channels of information are processed separately within the VCR in order to achieve better color purity and image detail than is possible in conventional VHS and $\frac{3}{4}$" recording systems. The luminance and chrominance signals may actually be output from the VCR as two separate signals and displayed on special video monitors equipped with an "S-Video" input connector. However, insofar as the videotape recording process is concerned, Y/C signals in 8mm, Hi8, and S-VHS VCRs are recorded as composite signals with luminance and chrominance recorded together in the same track of video information on the tape, and not on separate tracks as is the case with true component systems.

Choosing a Tape Format

As the preceding discussion has indicated, there has been a large growth of tape formats, particularly in the past few years. This can be very confusing to the video producer who is trying to make an informed decision about which format to use. Although the student producer may not have a choice to make because laboratory equipment has been purchased and assigned for student use, other producers can benefit by considering what their production needs are and how much they can afford to spend to buy or lease equipment. Generally speaking, tape use falls into three large applications: acquisition (field or studio production), postproduction editing), and distribution. Different tape formats present different advantages and disadvantages.

Because of the extremely low cost of tape and VCRs and the remarkably good quality of first-generation recordings, the consumer-level VHS and 8mm formats are widely used in camcorders and VCRs dedicated to home video use. VHS is the standard in the United States for movies that are rented for home use. Because VHS VCRs are almost omnipresent, VHS is an excellent format for distributing tapes for viewing in the home or workplace.

S-VHS and Hi8, by virtue of their Y/C signal processing and high-quality tape, are excellent low-cost acquisition formats. Tapes and camcorders are extremely small and portable. Relatively high-quality editing is available, and the final product is usually acceptable up to the third or fourth generation, after which signal loss begins to become noticeable.

U-Matic and U-Matic SP formats do not offer camcorders, but high-quality portable VCRs and very rugged editing VCRs are available. Only one manufacturer (Sony) continues to produce these machines, as this format is gradually being supplanted by higher-quality systems in a variety of other formats.

Betacam, Betacam SP, and M-II are extremely high-quality acquisition formats (camcorders and portable VCRs are both available). Betacam/Betacam SP is the more popular of the formats, but as a result, M-II equipment is available at a lower cost and produces a comparable product. Editing and dubbing in both formats is quite good up to 8 to 10 generations from the original recording.

The highest-quality original recordings can be made in the digital formats, and $\frac{1}{2}''$ digital offers a very portable camcorder. The digital tape formats excel in the area of editing and dubbing, where little or no signal loss will be apparent, even when the final tape is many generations removed from the original. Where complex, multilayered special effects are required, the digital formats will provide superior performance over the analog formats.

LOCATION OF SIGNALS ON VIDEOTAPE

All videotapes contain the following tracks of information: video, control track, and one or more audio tracks. In addition, some videotape formats also include a special cue or address track. The placement of these tracks of information varies from one tape format to another. Figure 4–8 illustrates the location of each of these tracks of information for the most popular small-tape formats ($\frac{3}{4}''$ U-Matic, VHS/S-VHS, and 8mm/Hi8mm) and for the $\frac{1}{2}''$ Betacam and M-II component formats as well.

Figure 4–8   Location of Tracks on Videotape

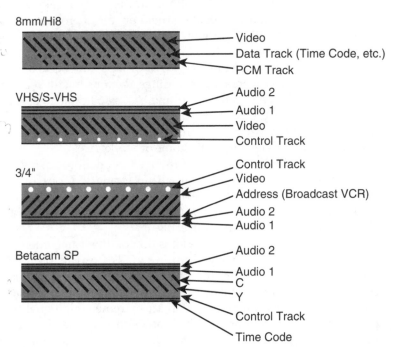

Video

Video information is always centrally located on the tape, and the tracks of video information occupy most of the tape surface. Differences in formats are found in the angle at which the tracks lie on the tape and whether or not guard bands are used to separate tracks of video information.

In the 1″ and ³⁄₄″ formats, each track of video information is separated by an area of tape with no information recorded on it. This blank-space between video tracks is called the **guard band**. Since video heads tend to read the information next to tracks of video information, as well as the information in the track itself, the possibility of picking up interference from a directly adjacent video track is removed through the use of this guard band area. It is a safety zone like the median strip between traffic lanes on a freeway.

No guard band is utilized in the VHS and 8mm formats. By eliminating the blank space between video tracks, more information can be crammed onto the tape. Therefore, these VCRs are able to use narrower tape that runs at a slower speed.

How, then, is the problem of interference between adjacent video tracks removed? The solution lies in what is known as the slanted **azimuth recording** system, which is used in VHS and 8mm format machines. The azimuth refers to the position of the head gap in relation to the tracks of video information on the tape. In the $^3/_4$" and 1" systems, the gap of the video head is positioned so that it is perpendicular to the tracks of video information. Video information laid down in the track by each of the video heads cuts directly across the track. Figure 4-9 shows what this looks like.

In the slanted azimuth recording system, the gap of the video head is not perpendicular to the video track. In fact, it is angled slightly off the perpendicular line.

Recording with the slanted azimuth process eliminates the need for guard bands between tracks of information because the video information within each track is recorded at different angles. When playing back, each video head reads only the information it recorded. Head 1 reads track 1 because the information in that track is at the same angle relative to the angle of the head gap. Head 1 is unable to read the information from track 2 because the angle of that information does not correspond to the angle of its head gap. Only head 2 can read that information. Therefore, there is no chance that information laid down by one head will interfere with either the playback or recording of information laid down with the other. As a result, the separating function of the guard bands is no longer necessary and more of the surface area of the tape can be used to record video information.

Control Track

Control track information in the $^3/_4$" and $^1/_2$" formats is recorded at or near the edge of the videotape by a stationary control track head. Although it is easier to record the control track at the edge than in the interior of the tape, edge recording

---

Figure 4–9   Conventional and Slanted Azimuth Helical Scan Recording

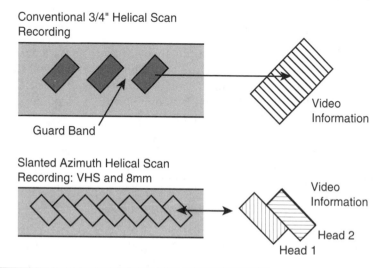

Conventional 3/4" Helical Scan
Recording

Guard Band

Video
Information

Slanted Azimuth Helical Scan
Recording: VHS and 8mm

Video
Information

Head 2

Head 1

presents a problem because the tape edge sometimes wrinkles in the machine. If the tape sustains any damage to the edge and the damage extends into the area where the control track has been recorded, the tape may be unstable when played. Great care should be taken to prevent the tape edge from damage. In the 8mm and Hi8 formats, a control signal (automatic track finding) recorded in the tracks of video information by the rotary video heads replaces the traditional control track pulses.

Audio Tracks

Depending on the tape format, audio information can be recorded with a stationary recording head in one or more longitudinal tracks (VHS/S-VHS, $\frac{3}{4}''$, Betacam, M-II) or high-fidelity audio can be recorded along with video information in the video tracks via either the rotary video heads or a special rotary head dedicated to audio (S-VHS, 8mm/Hi8, Betacam, M-II). There is little consistency in the way the longitudinal audio channels are numbered or in which channel sound picked up by a camera microphone is recorded.

In different tape formats, the audio track against the edge of the tape is sometimes called audio channel 1 and at other times audio channel 2. The problem with recording at the edge of the tape, whether it is control track or audio information, lies in the fact that the tape edge is susceptible to damage. Just as wrinkling of the tape edge that has control track information recorded on it may affect tape stability, so damage to the edge with audio information may affect the quality of the audio playback. In cases of severe tape edge damage, distortion may be introduced into the tape or the audio information may be altogether erased.

It is important to identify the safest audio track on the format you are using. Use that track to record your principal audio, regardless of whether it is called channel 1 or channel 2.

Cue or Address Track

Some $\frac{3}{4}''$ VCRs contain an additional cue or address track that is used to record SMPTE (Society of Motion Picture and Television Engineers) time code information. Time code information provides an accurate identification code for each frame of video information and is widely used in videotape editing. This is discussed in greater detail in Chapter 8.

COMPATIBILITY

Compatibility refers to the capability of a given VCR to play back a particular videotape. If a videotape can be played back on a VCR, the two are compatible; if it cannot be played back, the two are incompatible. Compatibility is determined by the format of the videotape recording and the playback machine. Tapes recorded on any 8mm VCR should be compatible with all other 8mm VCRs. Similarly, any VHS tape should play back on any other VHS machine. However, remember that a tape must be played back at the same speed at which it was recorded. A tape recorded in the six-hour SLP/EP mode will not play back on a machine equipped with only two-hour (SP) and four-hour (LP) record/playback speed modes.

Tapes may be incompatible with certain VCRs for two reasons. First, the physical configuration of the tape may not be acceptable to the VCR. Second, the tape format may be incompatible with the VCR. The question of compatible physical configuration is easy to understand.

For obvious reasons, an 8mm cassette will play back only on another 8mm VCR but not on a $\frac{1}{2}$" VHS VCR. However, Betacam and M-II cassettes, which are both in the $\frac{1}{2}$" cassette configuration, are incompatible because of differences in the format. The location of the video tracks and the speed at which the tapes move through the VCRs are different in both formats. Therefore, $\frac{1}{2}$" Betacam cassettes play back only on Betacam VCRs, and M-II tapes play back only on M-II VCRs.

The terms *upward compatibility* and *downward compatibility* are used to describe compatibility issues that arise between conventional tape formats and their improved performance successors. For example, conventional $\frac{1}{2}$" VHS has been modified to create a higher resolution Super-VHS tape format. Conventional VHS recordings can be played back in S-VHS machines, thus they are upwardly compatible. However, S-VHS tapes cannot be played back in conventional VHS machines, thus we can say that S-VHS is not downwardly compatible with conventional VHS. Conventional $\frac{3}{4}$" format recordings and $\frac{3}{4}$" SP recordings are both upwardly and downwardly compatible, as are Betacam and Betacam SP recordings.

Dubbing

What, then, do you do if you have a tape in one format but have a machine in another, incompatible format? The answer is to make a dub. A **dub** is simply a copy of a tape. Since all VCRs have a series of standard video and audio inputs and outputs, it is possible to take a tape in one format and make a copy of it in another format. For example, you can dub a $\frac{3}{4}$" cassette onto a tape in a $\frac{1}{2}$" VCR, you can dub an 8mm tape to VHS, and so on. To make a dub, you need the original tape and a machine capable of playing it back. In addition, you need another machine in the format you want to dub to and a blank tape. Put the original tape into the machine that will play it back, and connect the video and audio outputs of that machine to the video and audio inputs of the other machine. The machine with the original tape in it is called the **source VCR**, and the machine on which the information will be rerecorded is the **record VCR**. Figure 4–10 diagrams the connections between machines for dubbing from an 8mm to a $\frac{1}{2}$" VCR.

Through the process of dubbing, copies of any tape can be made in any other format. However, there is always some quality loss in the copy. Small-format systems are particularly susceptible to quality loss when copies are made of tapes.

Figure 4–10   Dubbing from 8mm to $\frac{1}{2}$" VCR

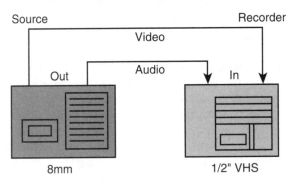

This quality loss appears first as noise in the video picture. The copy may appear a little grainy and fuzzy. If a copy is made of the copy, the signal will continue to degrade, losing definition and color values. The further away from the original your copy is, the poorer the quality of the tape.

The original tape is referred to as a first-**generation** tape. The first copy made from the original is a second-generation tape; a copy made of the second-generation tape is a third-generation tape; and so on. Small-format systems are capable of producing good-quality copies only up to the second, and sometimes the third, generation. After that, the quality of the signal becomes noticeably poorer, and by the fourth or fifth generation, even the color of the original may be unrecognizable. Green faces and red grass hint at how many generations away from the original the copy may be.

One of the principal motivations for developing improved resolution recording formats such as $\frac{3}{4}$" SP, S-VHS, and Hi8 has been to improve the ability of those formats to produce higher-quality images in terms of detail and color reproduction, even when they are several generations removed from the master tape. Indeed, one of the reasons that the digital tape formats are used so extensively in videotape editing is their ability to produce high-quality copies of the original tape, even when the copy is many generations removed from the original.

TYPES OF VIDEOCASSETTE RECORDERS

Some VCRs are portable; others are not. The difference is primarily one of size. There are three types of full-sized VCRs: video players, player-recorders, and editing VCRs. (Portable VCRs are discussed in the next chapter.)

Video Players

Video players are VCRs incapable of recording—they can be used only to play back a videotape. The principal reason for buying a playback-only VCR lies in its cost. They are considerably cheaper than player-recorders since they do not contain the extra circuitry that makes recording possible.

Video players are used wherever it is not important to have recording capability. For example, if a VCR is going to be used only to play back a videotape demonstrating a particular product in a department store, a player, rather than a recorder, would be appropriate. Similarly, video players are sometimes used as source machines in videotape editing systems.

Player-Recorders

Probably the most common type of VCRs are the **player-recorders**. Any VCR with the capability to record and play back a videotape is a player-recorder. These machines are extremely versatile. They can record signals from video cameras and switchers. If they are equipped with a television tuner—the device that picks up broadcast or cablecast television signals—they can also record programs off the air or cable.

The player-recorder is essentially the larger counterpart of the portable VCR; in many cases, it duplicates the design of the portable machine. The major differences between the two lie in the fact that the full-sized player-recorder utilizes somewhat heavier motors and components and is therefore more durable. In addition, the full-sized VCR accepts both full-sized and mini-cassettes, whereas the portable VCR (in $3/4''$ and VHS type-C formats) accepts only mini-cassettes. In addition, the full-sized VCR has full range of video and audio inputs, outputs, and meters, whereas the portable VCR sometimes does not.

Editing Videocassette Recorders

The third type of machine is the **editing VCR**. It is equipped with special electronic circuitry that enables it to edit the video signal. We will discuss how this works in considerable detail in Chapter 8.

VIDEOTAPE

The storage medium employed in most video recording systems is videotape, as we have mentioned. **Videotape** is simply a very thin strip of plastic (polyester or mylar) that is coated with metal oxide particles. Videotape works in the same way as audiotape. The picture and sound received by the camera and microphone are generated in the form of electrical impulses. These electrical impulses are directed to the videotape, where they are stored magnetically. A series of video and audio **heads**, which in effect are very small electromagnets, magnetize the metal particles (usually iron oxide or chromium dioxide) on the tape in a pattern that corresponds to the electrical input signals. Once these particles have been magnetized by the heads in the correct pattern, the signal is safely stored on the tape. Playback of the stored signal simply reverses the process. As the tape is played back, the video and audio heads read the information recorded on the tape. If the VCR is connected to a monitor, you see the image and hear the sound.

Most tape manufacturers produce several different grades of videotape. The higher-quality (and higher cost) tapes usually contain higher-quality magnetic particles and more of them than the lower-quality tapes. This generally produces a better recording.

Improvements in tape quality have been a significant factor in the development of recording formats with enhanced detail and color qualities (S-VHS, Betacam SP, U-Matic SP, 8mm, and so on). High-quality recordings are obtained in these formats by using special metal tapes. These tapes feature higher-quality recording particles than conventional tapes. The particles tend to be smaller and more uniform in size than those on conventional tapes. The orientation of the particles on the tape (that is, the direction in which the particles face on the tape) is more regular and more highly controlled. All of these factors create a recording surface that is much more densely coated with recording material and capable of recording a broader range of frequencies (and consequently better picture detail and color) than conventional videotape.

Size

The size of a videotape refers to its width. Videotape comes in a number of different widths. The most common portable field production systems use tape that is either 8mm, $\frac{1}{2}$″, or $\frac{3}{4}$″ wide (see Figure 4–11). The trend is toward smaller tape size for a number of reasons: It is more economical to use because it costs less money to produce; the machines used to record and play back the video signal can be made smaller because narrower width tapes do not require the massive head drum assemblies that the older large format tapes required; and the tape is smaller and requires less space to store it.

In many cases, due to improvements in the way in which the signal is recorded, smaller-format tapes provide better-quality recordings than their larger-format predecessors. The 1″ machines can do everything that the old 2″ machines could do—in fact, they can do it better and cheaper. The same can be said for $\frac{1}{2}$″ S-VHS in comparison with the $\frac{3}{4}$″ format. The $\frac{1}{2}$″ Betacam and M-II component formats offer performance characteristics that are vastly superior to $\frac{3}{4}$″ tape (at a significantly greater cost). Nevertheless, while picture quality and stability in the 8mm/Hi8, $\frac{1}{2}$″ (VHS/Beta), and $\frac{3}{4}$″ tape formats is generally not as good as their broadcast counterparts, the fact that they are smaller and cheaper makes them appealing to a large number of video users.

So, the proliferation of formats should not be read only as the difference between less expensive and more expensive systems, or high-quality and poor-

Figure 4–11   (A) Tape Size Varies by Format ($^3/_4$", $^1/_2$", and 8mm), (B) 8mm/Hi8 Cassette Format

(A)

(B)

quality systems. In many ways, the development of these smaller-type formats reflect significant advances in electronic technology. The move toward miniaturization in all other areas of electronic technology has also had a dramatic impact on the design of video gear.

Configuration

The other important aspect of videotape is its configuration. Configuration refers to the physical design of the tape. Is it an **open-reel** tape? Or is it a **cassette**? The 1" systems use open-reel tapes, and the machines are reel-to-reel recorders, just like old audiotape recorders. All the other contemporary formats use cassette tapes. The principal advantage to the use of a cassette tape is that the machine automatically threads the tape into the machine. On the other hand, reel-to-reel systems require that the tape be manually threaded into the machine.

If you are working with a portable video system, you are working with videotape in the cassette configuration. That is why you will find two different terms used to refer to video recorders. Some people call them *videotape* recorders, or *VTRs*, which simply indicates that videotape is used to record the video signal. Others will make a point of referring to their *videocassette* recorder, or *VCR*. Although VCR is more precise than VTR, the two terms are used interchangeably.

Mini-Cassettes

Some ½" systems, most notably VHS/S-VHS type-C (compact) camcorders, require the use of a special mini-cassette (see Figure 4–12). These mini-cassettes contain normal ½" tape, but the tape housing is smaller than that normally used for full-size camcorders and studio VCRs. The type-C mini-cassettes usually con-

Figure 4–12   Comparison of Standard VHS and VHS-C Mini-Cassettes

tain 20 minutes of tape, whereas $\frac{1}{2}$" VHS/S-VHS tapes in the standard full-size housing usually contains 30, 60, or 120 minutes of tape.

Type-C mini-cassettes can be inserted into full-size machines with the use of a special mechanical adapter. A few full-size machines are also available that do not require the use of the adapter: VHS-C tapes can be inserted directly into them.

If you have a conventional $\frac{1}{2}$" VHS or S-VHS system, all tapes are in the same-size housing. Full-size portable VCRs and full-size camcorders use the same tapes as the nonportable table models. The only difference among tapes is in the amount of tape contained within the cassette. Remember, however, that while type-C mini-cassettes can be used in full-size machines with the use of an adapter, full-size tapes cannot be used in type-C machines.

All portable $\frac{3}{4}$" VCRs record on mini-cassettes. Unlike VHS-C tapes, no special adapter is needed to insert a $\frac{3}{4}$" mini-cassette into a full-size VCR. Like the VHS-C mini-cassettes, the $\frac{3}{4}$" mini-cassettes usually contain 20 minutes of tape, whereas $\frac{3}{4}$" tapes in full-size housings usually contain 30, 45, or 60 minutes of tape.

The 8mm and Hi8 cassettes offer standard tape length of 30, 60, 90, and 120 minutes. Regardless of tape length, all 8mm and Hi8 tapes use the same-size housing—there are no mini-cassettes in this format.

Tape Thickness

One other factor to consider with regard to videotape is the thickness of the tape. Tape thickness is one of the elements that manufacturers vary to be able to fit more tape onto a reel or into a cassette. The other factor that is varied is simply the amount (length) of the tape on the reel or in the cassette. For example, in the $\frac{1}{2}$" VHS/S-VHS formats, the tape in a 120-minute cassette is simply twice as long as the tape in a 60-minute cassette. Longer-playing, full-size cassettes with up to 180 minutes of tape are available. However, in these long-playing cassettes, the tape is actually thinner than the tape used in the 60- and 120-minute cassettes. The thinner tape takes up less space on the reels inside the cassette, and so more of it can fit into the cassette.

You should be very careful when working with videotape that is thinner than normal. Thinner tape is not as strong and more likely to stretch or break than normal tape, particularly if it is subjected to heavy stress. These thin tapes will not stand up to the pressure put on them by an editing system, or still framing, and should therefore not be used if you plan to edit your field tapes. Use only tapes with extended still-framing capability that have been designed for use in editing VCRs and that are capable of withstanding the pressure of fast and reverse motion tape shuttling and still framing.

Record Safety Devices

Since information is stored on videotape as magnetic impulses, the videotapes can be used over and over. It is quite simple to erase an entire tape by exposing it to a

bulk eraser, a powerful electromagnet that randomizes the arrangement of the particles on the tape, thus eliminating the recorded signal.

In addition, all VCRs contain several **erase heads**. When a machine is put into the record mode, the erase heads engage and erase the previously recorded signal before the record heads pass over the tape to lay down the new signal. Because it is so easy to erase tapes, and since accidental erasure of material is something that everyone who works with video wants to avoid, all cassette tapes contain a **record safety** (see Figure 4–13). When the record safety device is removed from the tape housing, it is impossible to accidentally record over the material on a tape. On VHS/S-VHS and 8mm/Hi8 tapes, the record safety is a small tab or switch on the side of the housing. On $^3/_4$″ cassette tapes, the record safety is a small red button on the underside of the tape housing. In each of these tape configurations, you can record when the record safety device is in place but not if it has been removed or set.

A bulk eraser will erase a tape whether or not the record safety has been removed. Tapes can be bulk erased, or bulked, simply by passing the tape over the surface of the bulk eraser. There is no way to prevent the bulk eraser from doing its job. The best protection against accidental bulk erasure of tapes is through correct, clear labeling of tapes. If you know what is on the tape and clearly mark it "DO NOT ERASE," you stand a greater chance of preventing accidental erasure than if the tape does not carry such a warning. Finally, since any electromagnet can act as a bulk eraser, it pays to store tapes away from telephones, fan motors, and so on.

Figure 4–13   Videocassette Record Safety Devices

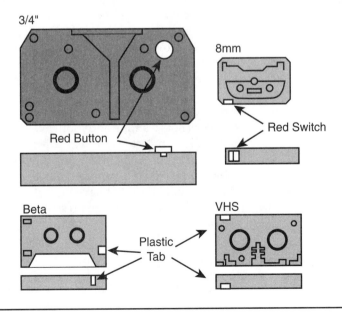

Care of Videotape

Videotape should be handled and stored with care. The oxide surface of the tape can easily be damaged, so you should handle it with care. Videotape should never be touched with bare hands. Fingers leave an oily deposit that can damage the tape. If you must touch the tape, wear cotton gloves.

Videotape should be stored under conditions similar to those comfortable for people. Temperature should not vary excessively, as extreme heat and cold will damage the tape. Similarly, extreme humidity can cause great problems by making the tape sticky. This may cause it to bind together within the cassette, or cause excessive friction against the head drum of the VCR, making tape playback and recording impossible.

Protection from dust and smoke is also important. Both of these elements can seriously damage the recording surface of the tape, as well as the video heads within the VCR.

Videotapes should be stored on end, rather than on their side. Do not lay them down flat and stack them up one on top of another; instead, stand them up side by side. Also make sure that tapes are wound to the beginning or end of the spools for storage.

Dropouts

Videotape begins to wear out as it gets old. One sign of wear is the dropping out of information in the picture. **Dropouts** occur when parts of the oxide coating that hold the magnetic information fall off the tape, leaving a hole in the picture. These can easily be seen on a monitor, where they appear as small black specks in the picture. Tape with a lot of dropouts should be discarded. Excessive dropouts not only affect the picture quality but may also affect picture stability and sound quality.

Many high-quality VCRs contain dropout compensators. A **dropout compensator** detects the loss of information caused by tape dropouts and corrects the problem by replacing the lost information with the line of information that immediately preceded it.

Excessive oxide dropouts can cause the video heads to clog. If there is **head clog**, the heads do not record or play back, and need to be cleaned with a head-cleaning solvent. The VCR heads may become clogged if the videotape is old and the oxides are falling off, or if the VCR is left in the pause mode for an excessive period. If this happens, the heads are in continual contact with one spot on the tape. This tends to damage the tape by wearing off the oxide particles at that point, leaving a blank spot that will no longer hold signal information.

Cleaning the Heads

As the video heads come in constant contact with videotape during record and playback, they tend to get clogged with oxide particles that drop off from the tape.

Consequently, the heads must be cleaned regularly to guarantee high-quality signal recording and playback.

You can tell when the video heads are getting dirty simply by looking at the picture produced by the VCR on a monitor. Clean heads produce a clear, sharp picture. When the heads are dirty, the picture looks fuzzy or noisy. In extreme cases, the heads become completely clogged, and the machine may fail to play back or record anything. All you see on the screen is *snow*, or electronic noise.

Heads should therefore be cleaned regularly, depending on use. If you use your VCR infrequently, you may need to clean the heads only every month or two. If you use the machine heavily, or if you are using old tape stock, you will certainly need to clean them more often—perhaps weekly, if not daily.

Many video service centers provide a head-cleaning service, but it is a rather simple process to clean the heads yourself. Obtain a foam-tipped swab and some video head cleaner from a video supply store. Dip the swab into the liquid and then insert it into the VCR through the opening where the videocassette is usually inserted. (Make sure the power is off.) *Gently* move the swab in a *horizontal* pattern, back and forth against one of the heads. Rotate the head drum and repeat the process for each of the remaining heads. The head cleaner will dissolve the oxide particles and remove them from the head.

When cleaning the heads, observe the following precautions. *Never* clean the heads by moving the swab vertically (up and down) against the head. The head is very fragile and vertical pressure will most likely damage it. *Never* use a cotton-tipped swab to clean the heads. The cotton threads tend to come off and stick to the heads and this may interfere with subsequent recording and playback.

In addition to head-cleaning liquid, head-cleaning cassettes are available commercially. These look like regular videotapes and are inserted into the VCR in the play mode to clean the heads and the various guides that hold the tape in place.

Two kinds of head-cleaning cassettes are available. One kind is a wet system that requires the addition of a small amount of head cleaner to the cassette each time it is used. The cleaning solution wets a nonabrasive material that gently cleans the heads, head drum, and tape guides. The second type of head-cleaning cassette is a dry system that uses a mild abrasive to grind the dirt off the heads. We do not recommend the use of the abrasive head-cleaning cassettes. Although they have been improved in recent years and are not as abrasive as they used to be, they are still somewhat abrasive and continued use can reduce the life of the heads.

In a sense, an abrasive head-cleaning cassette works in much the same way as sandpaper. If you needed to clean a fine wooden table or floor, you would probably use a mild detergent. It is unlikely that you would decide to sand the surface with sandpaper to clean it. As with the fine table, in most cases you can clean the heads of your VCR much more gently and with little or no damage to their surface by using the correct nonabrasive cleaning solution.

VIDEO DISC RECORDERS

Although videotape has been the principal medium for recording the electronic video signal for almost 40 years, new technologies are evolving that will ultimately replace videotape as the recording medium of choice. A number of these technologies are in use now.

Still video recorders record still images—the electronic equivalent of a still photograph or slide—rather than moving images. Unlike VCRs, which use videotape as the recording medium, still video recorders use a small magnetic floppy disk to record the video signal, similar to the disks used in many personal computers. One current system is capable of recording 25 single-frame (two fields each) still pictures, or 50 single-field still pictures on one still video floppy disk (see Figure 4–14).

Video information can be fed into the still video recorder from a variety of sources, including a color video camera, a VCR, a video disc player, or a personal computer. By recording only one frame of a moving image, the effect of a still frame is achieved. The output of the recorder can be displayed on a monitor or through a projection system, or it can be printed out on paper with a video printer. Still video images can be recorded onto videotape and edited into a taped program, or the signal can be sent to a video switcher (via a time base corrector) to be integrated into a production with other synchronized video sources.

Figure 4–14   Still Video Recorder (Sony MVR-5500A)

Figure 4–15   Videodisc Recording System (Sony LVS-5000)

Another disc-based recording medium is the computer **hard disc**. Like the floppy discs used in still video recorders, computer hard discs store the video signal as magnetic information. In addition, because computers work with digital rather than analog signals, the video and audio signals are converted from analog to digital before they are recorded. The use of computers in video production is discussed in more detail in Chapter 10.

Video disc systems that can record and play back video signals are also finding increasing use in production situations (see Figure 4–15). Like the compact discs (CDs) that are widely used to distribute recorded music, these systems use a laser to read information from the disc. However, unlike audio CDs, which are a playback medium only, the video disc systems can record information as well. Because no recording heads touch the disc, they are much more reliable than taped-based systems, and they also have the added advantage of allowing almost instantaneous random access to information anywhere on the disc. Current systems are capable of recording about 30 minutes of full motion video on a single disc.

SUMMARY

Videotape recording is an electronic process. After much experimentation, a practical recording system utilizing video heads that scanned the videotape at high speed was introduced in 1956.

Old-style videotape recorders used a system of transverse scanning of the tape, whereas all contemporary systems use the more economical helical scan system of recording, also known as slant track recording. 8mm/Hi8 and VHS/S-VHS VCRs use a system of slanted azimuth recording, which eliminates the guard bands between tracks of information and reduces tape speed to allow for long-playing recordings.

Control track pulses are recorded onto videotape whenever a video recording is made. These pulses work in conjunction with the capstan and head drum servo to guarantee stable playback of the video signal.

For a tape to play back correctly, the tape must run at the correct speed and the tracking and skew controls must be set properly.

Two different signal recording techniques are used in modern videotape recording. In composite recording, luminance, chrominance, and synchronizing information are recorded together in the tracks of video information. In component recording, luminance and chrominance are recorded on separate tracks on the videotape.

Videotape format is determined by the width of the videotape; its configuration; the arrangement of the tracks of video, audio, and control track information recorded on the tape; and the speed at which it moves through the VCR. The most common field production formats are 8mm and Hi8, $\frac{1}{2}$" VHS and S-VHS, and $\frac{3}{4}$" U-Matic. Broadcast-quality camcorders use either the Betacam/Betacam SP format or M-II.

The video signal is recorded onto videotape. The size of a videotape refers to its width, and most small-format systems use tape that is 8mm, $\frac{1}{2}$", or $\frac{3}{4}$" wide. Tape configuration refers to whether the tape is on an open reel or in a cassette. Most contemporary video systems use cassettes. Some VHS/S-VHS camcorders and all portable $\frac{3}{4}$" VCRs record on small mini-cassettes. In some tape formats, the tape thickness is varied to fit more tape onto a reel. Most videocassettes contain a small record safety device to prevent accidental erasure.

Compatibility refers to the capability of a given VCR to play back a particular videotape. It is determined by the size and physical configuration of the tape as well as the recording format. Tapes from one format may be dubbed to another format, but dubbing usually results in some signal quality loss.

VCRs may be portable or full size. There are three types of full-size VCRs: video players, player-recorders, and editing recorders. In addition to videotape recorders, a number of magnetic and laser disc-based video recording systems are now in use.

ENDNOTES

1. Robinson, Richard. *The Video Primer*, revised ed. New York: Quick Fox, 1978, p. 248.

2. Kybett, Harry. *Video Tape Recorders*, 2nd ed. Indianapolis: Howard W. Sams & Co., 1978, p. 10.

3. Robinson, p. 249.

5

Portable Videocassette Recording Systems

The purpose of this chapter is to give you a brief introduction to the function and operation of the portable **videocassette recorder (VCR)**.

THE BASIC SYSTEM

A basic portable video recording system contains two components: a video camera and a portable videocassette recorder. With these two components, you can shoot and record electronic images. The camera, as we have already discussed, produces the basic video signal, which is an electronic representation of an event that has taken place in front of the camera. But what happens to the signal after it has been produced by the camera? In portable video systems, the signal is sent to a portable videocassette recorder (VCR), a lightweight piece of equipment designed to record picture and sound in the field. Videotape is the recording medium.

Most portable VCRs can record and play back video signals; however, some machines are record-only machines. Record-only VCRs are smaller and lighter than their record and playback counterparts. They are used primarily in electronic news gathering, where it is more important to have an extremely light machine than it is to have a machine that will play back the recorded signal in the field.

Two kinds of portable video recording systems are in wide use. In one type of system, the portable video camera and the portable VCR are separate components that are connected with a camera cable. In camcorder systems, the camera and VCR are combined into one easily carried unit (see Figure 5–1). The camera and VCR may be manufactured as a single unit in which camera and VCR are

Figure 5–1 Recording in the Field with a Professional Camcorder

Figure 5–2 Portable Video Recording Systems

One-Piece Camcorder

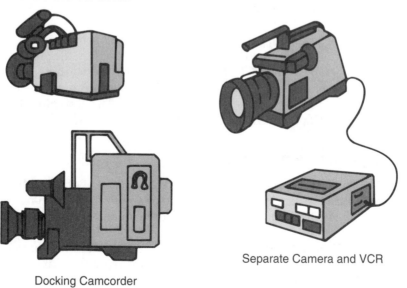

Docking Camcorder

Separate Camera and VCR

inseparable (as is most often the case with home video camcorder recording systems) or the camera and VCR may be manufactured as separate dockable units in which the camera outputs and VCR inputs can be directly connected together to create the camcorder unit (see Figures 5–2 and 5–3).

In addition to these principal components, the system may have any number of auxiliary components. These auxiliary components may include power components (including both batteries and alternating current [AC] adapters), monitoring devices (equipment that lets you see the picture and hear the sound), lighting instruments, and additional audio equipment. Lighting and audio are the subjects of separate chapters, and we will not treat them in any great detail here. Rather, we will focus on the portable VCR and the auxiliary field production components of power and monitors.

EXTERNAL VIDEOCASSETTE RECORDER CONTROLS AND INPUTS

The four important parts of any portable VCR, whether the VCR is configured as a separate component or as a part of a one-piece or dockable camcorder system (see Figure 5–4), are the following:

1. Tape transport controls
2. Audio and video inputs and outputs
3. Power inputs
4. VCR meters and warning lights

The tape transport controls govern the movement of the videotape in the machine, and video and audio inputs and outputs are the places where the signal enters and exits the VCR. The various meters and warning lights give the VCR operator information about the status of various parts of the system, such as audio and video record level, battery level, and so on. The power inputs are where direct current (DC) power enters the deck.

Tape Transport Controls

The tape transport controls regulate the movement of the videotape within the VCR and are arranged like the tape transport controls on most audiocassette recorders. The following controls are found on most portable VCRs.

Eject. This button is used to eject the tape from the machine or to insert a tape into the machine. Most VCRs have a safety device to prevent you from ejecting the tape while the machine is running, but it is nevertheless a good idea never to eject the tape unless the machine has been stopped.

Figure 5–3 Portable VCRs and Camcorders: (A) $^1/_2$" S-VHS Camcorder (Panasonic AG 460U), (B) $^1/_2$" S-VHS Dockable VCR (JVC BR-S411U), (C) $^1/_2$" S-VHS Dockable Camcorder (JVC KY17 and BR-S420CU Dockable VCR), (D) $^1/_2$" S-VHS Portable VCR (JVC BR-405U), (E) $^3/_4$" U-Matic Portable VCR (Sony VO-8800 SP), (F) Hi8 Dockable Camcorder (Sony EVW 325)

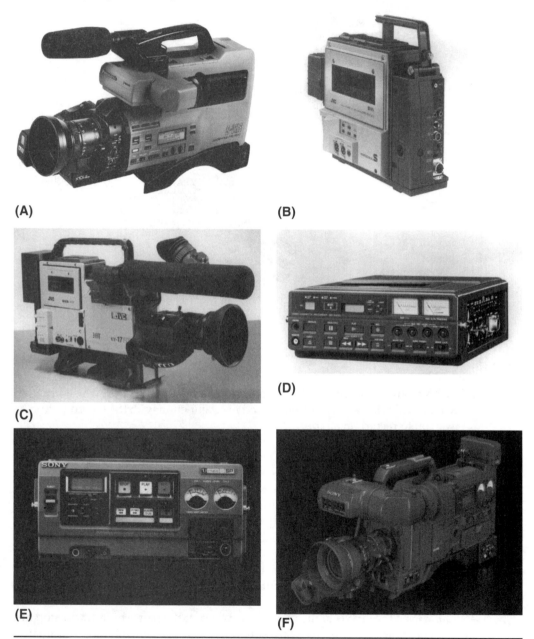

Figure 5–4   Parts of a Portable VCR/Camcorder

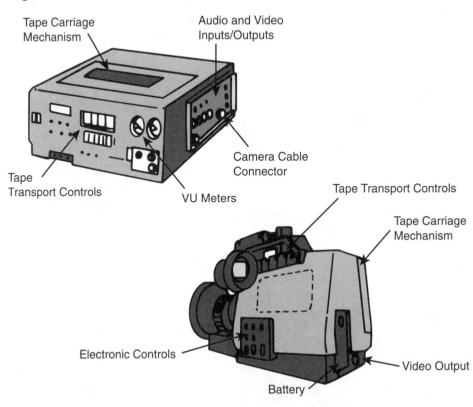

Tape Carriage Mechanism

Audio and Video Inputs/Outputs

Tape Transport Controls

Camera Cable Connector

VU Meters

Tape Transport Controls

Tape Carriage Mechanism

Electronic Controls

Video Output

Battery

Play. This causes the tape to move forward at a normal speed; it is used to play back a tape. When the play button is used in conjunction with the record button, it allows you to record on a tape.

Stop. To stop the movement of the tape in any mode, press STOP.

Fast Forward. This causes the tape to move forward at a fast rate of speed. You do not see the picture or hear the sound when the VCR is engaged in fast forward because the tape is not in contact with the heads. Use the fast forward button when you want to find a spot that is a considerable distance into the tape.

Rewind. This functions the same as the fast forward except it moves the tape in the opposite direction. The rewind button also disengages the tape from the heads.

Pause. When the tape is in the play mode, pressing the pause button will stop the movement of the tape and give you a still frame. The tape remains engaged against the heads so that you can still see the picture. Do not leave the tape in the pause mode for more than a few minutes, as this may damage the tape by subjecting it to excessive wear. Many machines will automatically stop and release the tape from the heads if the machine is left in the pause mode for more than a few minutes.

Record. The record button is used to record new audio and video onto videotape. To go into the record mode, first press the record button, which engages the recording circuits. Then push the play button while continuing to hold in the record button. When the tape is engaged by the machine, you can release both buttons, and the tape will now be locked into the record mode.

Audio Dub. This is used to record new audio information onto a prerecorded tape without erasing the video information already recorded on it. It is engaged in the same way as the record button: Press the audio dub button in conjunction with the play button.

Forward Search and Reverse Search. Many machines incorporate forward and reverse search controls. These allow you to forward or reverse the image at a high speed. Unlike the fast forward and rewind controls, the tape is not released from the head drum. As a rule of thumb, this mode should be used only to move the tape relatively short distances in either direction. If more than a few minutes of forward or reverse movement is necessary, use the fast forward or rewind button.

Audio and Video Inputs and Outputs

Since VCRs record both picture and sound, there are a number of audio and video inputs and outputs on these machines (see Figure 5–5).

Camera Input. The camera input is the place where the cable from the portable camera is connected to the VCR. If the camera is equipped with a built-in microphone, this cable will deliver both audio and video to the portable VCR. No camera cable is needed when working with a camcorder, as the camera and VCR are an integrated unit.

Video Inputs and Outputs. Sometimes a video source other than a camera provides the video signal to the portable VCR. For example, the signal from another VCR may be transferred to your portable VCR or camcorder and recorded on it. In this case, the auxiliary video input (also called the **video in**) would be used. The video output (**video out**) can be used to connect the output signal of the portable VCR or camcorder to a monitor or to send the signal to another VCR. In addition to conventional video inputs and outputs, S-VHS VCRs have **S-Video** inputs and outputs where the luminance and chrominance signals are kept separate.

Figure 5–5   Audio and Video Inputs and Outputs

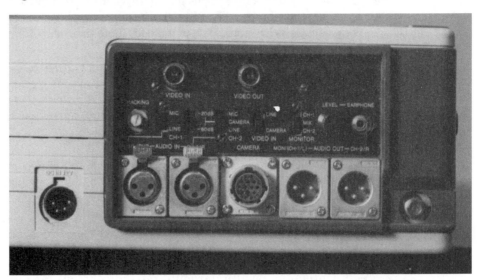

Audio Inputs and Outputs.   If audio is generated by a source other than the camera microphone, a number of additional inputs are available to route the signal into the VCR. Microphone-level inputs are used for unamplified sources, and line-level inputs are used for sources that have been amplified.

An external microphone can be connected to the **microphone in** connection; line-level audio signals from another VCR, audio tape recorder, and so on, can be connected to the **audio in** (line) jack. Audio outputs can be used in conjunction with the video output or independent of it. The audio output signal, **audio out** (line), can be connected to a monitor so that the sound can be heard. Or it can be connected to another VCR or audio recorder to record the audio output signal. Professional-quality camcorders contain the normal series of audio and video inputs and outputs on the body of the camcorder. On consumer-quality camcorders, connectors for additional line-level audio and video inputs and outputs are frequently found on the AC power adapter.

Radio Frequency Output

Some systems contain a **radio frequency (RF)** output. The RF signal mixes the picture and sound together and makes it possible to see and hear your recording on a regular television set. To do so, you must tune the television to the channel to which the RF converter has been preset (usually channel 3 or 4). On consumer-quality camcorders, the RF output is usually found on the AC power adapter.

Power Inputs

All portable VCRs are powered by a 12-volt **direct current (DC)** power source rather than standard household 110-volt **alternating current (AC)**. If AC current is used, a special AC adapter that converts household current to 12-volts DC is needed. Since the batteries used with portable VCRs all deliver 12-volts DC, no special adapters are needed for their use. You will find two typical power inputs on a portable VCR. On older VCRs and some camcorders, internal batteries connect to a single-pin input inside the VCR itself. On more modern equipment, the electrical contact points on the internal battery are exposed, and the proper connection is made simply by inserting the battery into the VCR or camcorder. External batteries and AC adapters usually connect to a special four-pin connector on the outside of the case.

Meters, Warning Lights, and Tape Counters

All high-quality machines contain a series of meters for monitoring different machine functions. In many camcorder systems, even the most inexpensive consumer-level systems, displays for many of these metering functions (with the exception of audio levels) are shown in the camera's viewfinder while recording.

Battery Meter. The battery meter is used to monitor the level of power in the battery. Typically, this meter has a red zone to indicate that battery power is low, and a black or green zone to indicate acceptable battery power. In addition, since many camera viewfinders also contain a battery indicator, you may have a double warning system for low battery power.

Volume Unit Meters. All professional equipment contains a **volume unit (VU) meter** to monitor the level of the audio and/or video input. A VU meter contains a scale that is a standard calibration of signal strength used in all broadcast and non-broadcast media facilities. A small needle indicates how high or low the signal is.

There is only one rule of thumb to be observed when reading a VU meter: Keep the signal level high but keep the needle out of the red zone. For example, if the audio level consistently peaks in the red, the sound will be distorted and scratchy. If the video level peaks in the red, colors will be distorted. If you can manually control the input signal level, check to make sure that it falls within the acceptable range on the VU meter. (See Chapter 7 for a more detailed discussion.)

Warning Lights. Many machines come equipped with a variety of warning lights that tell you if something is wrong. The **dew lamp** warns you that moisture or condensation has formed on the head drum. Since the videotape must glide smoothly over the head drum, and moisture can make the tape sticky, the dew indicator is extremely important. If it comes on, it means the head drum is damp and the VCR will not make a satisfactory recording. Sometimes this happens if the machine has been stored in a damp place or if it has been moved from outside to indoors. If the dew warning lamp comes on, push the eject button, remove the tape, and allow air to circulate inside the machine. The problem will usually correct itself in a few minutes.

Some machines contain a **servo lock warning light**. This light tells you when the machine has reached its proper recording speed and the picture has stabilized. A few machines contain a tape end warning light that lets you know when you are a minute or two from the end of the tape.

Tape Counters. Three types of tape counters are found on portable VCRs. The most common is the simple *numerical counter* that begins running when the tape is moving and stops when the tape is stopped. The counter numbers generally have no relationship to minutes or seconds of tape and are useful only in providing a rough estimate of the location of shots on a tape. There are usually differences in the calibration of counters from one machine to another. Thus, it is often difficult to find a specific place on the tape when you play it back on another VCR, even when you know the counter number associated with the visual event on the tape.

Another type of counter is the *real-time frame* counter. This type of counter displays a read-out in hours, minutes, and seconds, and works by counting off the control track pulses on the videotape. Real-time frame counters are accurate so long as you remember to reset the counter to zero at the beginning of the tape. Also, you must be careful not to hit the reset button while you are playing a tape, since this will return the read-out to zero. The counter will then begin counting in time from that new zero point.

The most accurate type of counter is the **time code** counter. With this system, each frame of video information is assigned its own unique time code number in hours, minutes, seconds, and frames. Since this information is actually encoded onto the videotape, you can always find the precise frame of information you are looking for. Also, since the information is actually encoded on the tape, hitting the reset button does not affect the read-out. The meter will always display the actual time code number for the particular frame of information that is being played back. Time code counters are available only on professional-quality machines.

Other Controls

Several other extremely important external controls can be found on most portable VCRs.

Video Input Selector. The video input selector switch tells the VCR where the input video signal is coming from. The switch typically has two positions: camera and line. To record from a portable camera, the switch must be in the camera position. When using the VCR to record a video signal from another VCR, the line position is used.

Camera Input Selector. On S-VHS VCRs, when the camera output is an encoded NTSC video signal, this switch is set to the ENC position. It is set to Y/C when the signal coming from the camera is sent as separate luminance and chrominance channels. (*Note:* Not all cameras are capable of sending a Y/C signal.)

S-VHS Record Mode Selector. S-VHS VCRs are capable of recording in either the conventional VHS mode or in the S-VHS mode. In order for an S-VHS recording to be made, the S-VHS selector switch must be properly set and an S-VHS tape, rather than a conventional VHS tape, must be used in the VCR. With the S-VHS selector switch in the "on" position and with an S-VHS videotape in the VCR, an S-VHS recording will be made. If the selector switch is in the "off" position, the recording will be made as conventional VHS, regardless of the type of tape used. Some selector switchers contain an "auto" position. When this is selected, the recording will be S-VHS when an S-VHS tape is used, and conventional VHS when a conventional VHS tape is used.

Audio Input Selector. This control tells the VCR where the audio signal is coming from—microphone, camera, or line.

Audio Mode Selector. The audio mode selector can usually be set to "normal" or "high fidelity" on S-VHS VCRs and to "AFM" or stereo "PCM" on 8mm/Hi8 VCRs. This selector controls the audio output of the VCR and the VU meter display on VCRs that are capable of recording and playing back normal and high-fidelity (or digital) audio signals.

Audio Monitor Control. On VCRs with two audio channels, the audio monitor control determines which audio channel is heard in the earphones or headphones when they are connected to their jacks. In the channel 1 position, only audio channel 1 is heard; in the channel 2 position, only channel 2 is heard. In the mix position, both channels are heard simultaneously. The audio monitor control does not affect the way the audio signals are recorded; it only affects what you hear when you are monitoring the audio during recording or playback.

Tracking Control. The **tracking control** is used in the playback mode to maximize the quality of the playback image by compensating for slight differences in the way different VCRs record and play back a signal. Without adjusting the tracking control, something recorded on one machine may not play back correctly on another machine due to the slight mechanical differences between the VCRs.

The tracking control should always be set in the fixed position when recording. This position is usually marked on the control and there is a small notch in the fixed position where the control clicks into place.

Speed Control. On $\frac{1}{2}$" VHS recorders, the record speed control varies the speed at which the videotape runs through the machine. A slow record speed allows you to record for a longer period of time on a given videotape but results in a poorer quality recording than one made at a faster speed. For that reason, field recordings should always be made in the fastest mode available on the VCR.

Playback Mode Control. The playback mode control operates only in the playback mode and can usually be set in one of three positions: B&W, auto, or dub. The control should be set on B&W (black and white) to play back a black and white recording. The normal setting for playing back a color recording is auto (automatic). The dub setting is used when the portable VCR is the source or playback machine for dubbing a color program to a tape on another VCR.

Color Lock. This is also a playback control. **Color lock** controls the phase of the playback color to compensate for differences between machines. In the record mode, the color lock control should be set in the fixed position.

Remote Controls. Some VCRs contain a remote control input that allows the operator to control the tape transport system with a remote control unit. The remote controls often duplicate the standard tape transport controls. Some remote control units include controls for slow- or fast-motion tape playback.

SPECIAL FEATURES OF VIDEOCASSETTE RECORDERS

Most portable VCRs contain special features that deserve at least brief mention.
  Automatic backspace editing gives clean cuts from shot to shot when you are recording and using the camera trigger at the beginning and end of each shot. When you pull the trigger at the end of a shot or sequence, the VCR stops and then automatically backs the tape up a few frames. When you pull the trigger to begin recording the next shot, the tape rolls and then begins the new recording in sync with the previously recorded material. The effect is that of a clean cut, or edit, from one shot to the next, without any blank tape or image break up and between the two shots.
  Video insert (called *video dub* or *video add* on some machines) allows you to insert new video into a previously recorded segment without erasing the previously recorded audio. This feature gives a clean entrance to and exit from newly inserted video. Somewhat along the same lines, *sound-on-sound* allows the VCR operator to add new sound to a previously recorded soundtrack without erasing the old sound. The level of the old sound is suppressed somewhat, the new sound is recorded at a slightly higher level, and the effect of a multiple source sound mix is achieved.

MAKING CONNECTIONS: BASIC SYSTEM SETUP

Now that we have some basic vocabulary established, let's move on to the setup of the system and the operation of the machines. To record on a portable VCR or camcorder, you need to hook up the machine to power, insert a blank videotape, and put a video and/or audio signal in the machine. Let's start with power.

Power for the Videocassette Recorder or Camcorder

All portable VCRs and camcorders can be powered by a battery or by standard AC power through the use of a special AC adapter. Your choice of power source depends on the recording situation and the available equipment. If you are using a consumer-quality camcorder to record your grandmother's eightieth birthday party indoors at home, you can choose between an internal camcorder battery or external AC power because of its availability. However, if you're recording an interview with a geologist who is surveying an earthquake fault at a remote mountain site, you will probably have to rely on batteries. Most camcorders use internal batteries that are inserted into the camcorder or clip-on battery packs that attach to the back of the camcorder with a special adapter. Both provide about one to two hours of power. Portable VCRs may use internal or external batteries.

Internal batteries are designed to fit into the machine itself. They usually power the equipment for a very limited time—seldom more than 60 minutes (see Figure 5–6). External batteries, in the form of clip-on battery packs or battery belts,

Figure 5–6   Internal and External Batteries

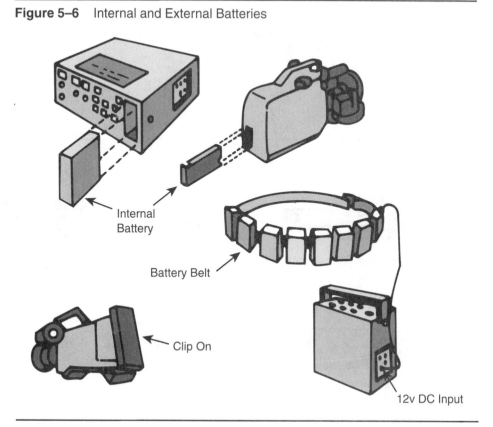

Internal
Battery

Battery Belt

Clip On

12v DC Input

usually provide power for a significantly longer time. Depending on the type of external battery system used, you may be able to power the deck and camera for three to four hours or more.

The external battery (DC) input on many portable VCRs is either a four-pin Deutsche Industrie-Norm **(DIN) connector** or a four-pin **XLR connector** (also called a Cannon connector). The XLR connector is slightly more rugged than the DIN connector, and for that reason XLR connectors are typically found on professional-quality machines. DIN connectors are used most often on consumer and industrial machines. Figure 5–7 illustrates these power connectors.

As mentioned earlier, AC adapters convert 110-volt household alternating current into the 12-volt direct current that video recorders and cameras run on (see Figure 5–8). One end of the AC adapter plugs directly into a wall outlet and is equipped with a standard two- or three-pronged AC connector. The other side of the AC adapter is equipped with a connector that attaches to the VCR or camcorder. The AC adapter also has an on/off switch. Two cautions should be observed when connecting the AC adapter to a portable VCR or camcorder:

1. Make sure that the AC adapter is turned off when you plug it into the wall and the VCR. Do not turn it on until you have made all connections correctly.
2. When you connect the AC adapter to the portable VCR, make sure you make the connection correctly.

If the pins of the AC adapter are not inserted into the correct holes on the VCR, you might blow a fuse in the deck and will be unable to operate the

Figure 5–7   DC Power Connectors

Single-Pin (2.5mm or 3mm)

Four-Pin DIN

Four-Pin XLR

Four-Pin Twist Lock

Figure 5–8　AC Adapter

machine until the fuse is replaced. The pins are arranged so that you can only insert the connector correctly in one way. In addition, the DIN connector typically is equipped with a guide and groove, and the XLR on more expensive machines is equipped with a twist-lock mechanism that makes improper connection difficult.

At this point, a suggestion with respect to making connections is in order: *Don't force anything.* Many of the receptacles (and some of the plugs) found in portable equipment are made out of plastic. If forced into an incorrect connection, they will break. Always examine the pin configuration before you attempt to connect it to a piece of equipment.

Camera/VCR Interface

In two-piece portable video systems (separate camera and VCR), the most important connection to make to the deck after power has been connected is the camera connection. The camera cable carries the video signal from the camera to the VCR, as well as the audio signal if the camera is equipped with a built-in microphone. In addition, the cable carries the electrical power needed to run the camera from the VCR to the camera. The camera cable also carries remote control operation signals back to the VCR.

In dockable camcorder systems, the camera/VCR connection is automatically made once the portable VCR has been attached to the dockable camera. And, of course, in one-piece camcorder systems, no special connections between camera and VCR need to be made.

Most portable VCRs are designed to allow the VCR to be controlled at the camera. The degree of control available depends on the type of equipment. On most portable systems, the camera operator can stop or start the VCR when it is in the record mode by pushing a trigger or button on the camera. VHS/S-VHS and 8mm/Hi8 camcorders contain a full range of remote controls. From a small control panel on the camcorder, the camera operator is able to put the VCR into the play or record modes, accomplish insert edits, and view the tape in the reverse search, forward search, or slow search modes.

The Camera Cable

The camera cable in two-piece portable systems is not one solid wire but rather a cable with a number of individual lines running inside it (see Figure 5–9). Several kinds of camera cables are in use, and depending on the manufacturer and the type of camera, the cable may have 14, 26, or 32 different lines inside it (three of the most popular types in current use). Figure 5–10 illustrates the pins and their corresponding signals in a typical 14-pin connector.

As you might expect, connectors vary on VCRs as well. The 14-pin type is widely used on professional S-VHS and U-Matic VCRs, but other configurations are also used. Therefore, before you can connect the camera to the portable VCR, you must make sure that you have the appropriate camera cable to connect the specific camera and VCR with which you are working. For example, one popular camera with a 14-pin connector requires the use of different camera cables depending on whether the camera is connected to an S-VHS VCR, a VHS VCR, or a U-Matic VCR.

Inserting the Videotape

All videocassettes have a top and a bottom. The top of the cassette is a smooth piece of plastic; the bottom contains the recessed portion of the tape spools. In addition, each tape has a front and a back. The back of the cassette is a solid piece of plastic and the front has a small metal or plastic door.

In order to insert the tape into the machine, push the eject button on the VCR or camcorder. This will cause the tape carriage (the part of the machine that holds

---

Figure 5–9   Camera Cable Connectors

Fouteen-Pin Plug and Chassis Mount

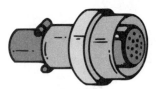

Figure 5–10   Fourteen-Pin Cable Configuration

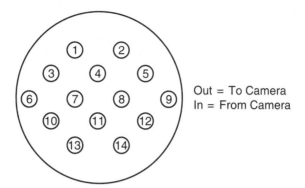

Out = To Camera
In = From Camera

Pin	Function
1	Power – Ground
2	Power – 12V DC Out
3	Audio – MIC In (X)
4	Audio – MIC In (Y)
5	Audio – Ground (Shielded)
6	Video – Video In (X)
7	Video In – Ground (Shielded)
8	Video Out – Ground (Shielded)
9	Video – Video Out (Y)
10	Battery Indicator Signal Out
11	Not Used
12	Record and Warning Signal Out
13	VCR Start/Stop Signal In
14	Power Signal In
	Audio Monitor Out

the tape) to pop open. (*Note:* In most portable systems, the eject button will not work unless the camcorder or separate VCR has been connected to battery or AC power.) Carefully insert the tape into the carriage with the door away from you and the open spools to the bottom. Many VCRs also have a guide in the carriage assembly that corresponds to a groove in the videocassette. Match the guide and the groove, make sure that the cassette door goes into the machine first, and then insert the tape as far as it will go. Then push down on the carriage assembly to lock the tape into position.

If you are using a new videotape for recording, it is a good idea to fast forward the tape to the end and then rewind it before recording. This process, known as *repacking the tape*, loosens up the tape within the cassette and allows the tape to move through the VCR at a uniform speed when you begin to record. Since videotape sometimes has a tendency to bind or stick to itself when it is stored, this is a good practice to adopt before recording with any tape.

The Mysteries of Tape Movement

What happens to the videotape when you insert it into the tape carriage and push it down into the machine? Several things happen inside the VCR or camcorder. First, as the tape carriage is depressed, the small door on the front of the videocassette opens automatically. The door acts as a shield to protect the tape when it is outside the machine. But, for the tape to operate within the machine, the tape must be withdrawn from the cassette and brought into contact with the video heads. So, a small device triggers the door to release, and the door pops open. (If you want to see how this works, you can manually trigger the door to release. Take a blank videocassette and hold it with the door facing you and the open part of the spools facing the floor. Slightly off to the side of the door you will see a small, rectangular opening, and immediately inside the opening you will see a small piece of metal or plastic. Carefully take a pencil or other small object, insert it into the opening, and press down on the release. The door should pop open and reveal the video-tape to you. Be careful not to touch the tape with your fingers, as this may damage the oxide coating. Also make sure that you close the door completely before you attempt to insert the cassette into the VCR.)

What happens after the tape is inserted into the VCR and the door is opened depends on the mode or function selected for the VCR. In the stop mode, the tape stays within the cassette and does not move. In the fast forward and rewind modes, the tape is driven forward or in reverse at a high speed. Again, the tape remains entirely within the cassette housing. In the play mode, however, something very different happens.

In order for a VCR to play back a tape or record onto a tape, the videotape must be brought into contact with the video heads. As we have already mentioned, the video heads lay down the signal in the record mode and read the signal on the tape in the play mode. The video heads are located within the **head drum**—a stainless steel cylinder inside the VCR. In order for the tape to make contact with the heads, a mechanical arm reaches inside the cassette, physically pulls the tape out of the cassette, and wraps it around the head drum. This is a complicated mechanical operation and demands that the mechanical arm and tape guides be precisely adjusted and aligned (see Figure 5–11).

In reality, this mechanical method of extracting the tape from the cassette housing is one of the greatest trouble areas with portable equipment, particularly older ³/₄" VCRs. When the mechanism malfunctions, the tape gets "eaten" by the machine. Anyone who has ever worked with portable equipment for any amount of time has seen a tape chewed by a VCR. Your day will come. However, you may be able to delay the time if you understand the mechanics of the system.

If you have access to a VCR repair or engineering facility, or if you have a table model VCR from which the top can be easily removed, it can be quite instructive to have the top taken off and to watch what happens to the tape in various modes of operation. *Do not attempt to do this without engineering supervision! If you take apart your machine, you may void the warranty.*

Figure 5–11 Tape-Loading Schematics: (A) $1/2$" VHS/S-VHS and 8mm/Hi8, (B) $3/4$" U-Matic

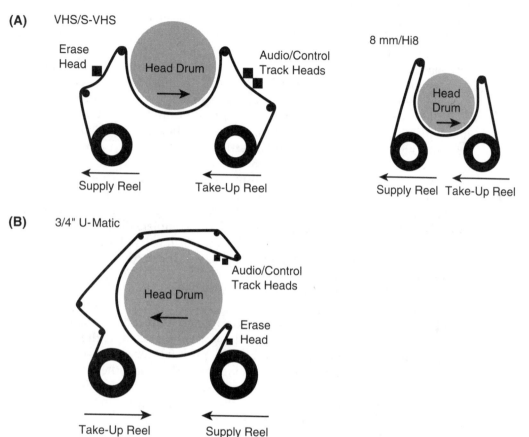

(A) VHS/S-VHS

Erase Head

Head Drum

Audio/Control Track Heads

Supply Reel

Take-Up Reel

8 mm/Hi8

Head Drum

Supply Reel   Take-Up Reel

(B) 3/4" U-Matic

Head Drum

Audio/Control Track Heads

Erase Head

Take-Up Reel

Supply Reel

Let's assume that the top of the machine has been safely removed. Insert the cassette. Notice how the door is automatically opened and the videotape is exposed.

Push the play button. Watch the mechanical arm pull the tape out of the cassette and wrap it around the head drum. The VCR is now in the play mode, and if it is connected to a monitor you will see the image on the screen.

Push the pause button. This stops the movement of the tape in the play mode. The tape is held against the head drum, but the video heads keep spinning and reading the information from one place on the tape. For this reason, you can see a still frame of the image on the monitor.

Now push the stop button. The tape comes off the head drum and returns to the cassette.

You will notice that whenever you push the play or stop button, it takes the machine several seconds to respond fully to your command. When you engage the play button, you can hear the mechanical mechanism within the VCR moving, but you will not see the image for a few seconds. This is the time that it takes to withdraw the tape from the cassette housing and wrap it around the head drum. Similarly, when you push the stop button (in the play or pause mode), it takes the machine a few seconds to come to a complete stop. The image on the monitor disappears as soon as you press the stop button, but the VCR continues to make noise for a few more seconds. This is the time that it takes to return the tape to the cassette housing.

Now, with the tape in the stop mode, press the fast forward button. You will notice that the tape is not withdrawn from the cassette. The tape spools are simply driven at high speed in the forward direction. By pressing stop, you can stop the fast forward action. The rewind button works in the same manner. The tape is not withdrawn from the cassette; rather, it simply moves inside the housing.

Now, put the machine into the ready-to-record mode. First, hold in the record button. Notice that the video heads start spinning. You can actually hear the motor that drives the heads begin to work. Now, complete the function by pressing the play button. At this point, the mechanical arm will pull the tape out, wrap it around the head drum, and if the camera trigger is correctly set, the tape will go into the pause mode. If you are working with a table model VCR, the machine will go into the record mode and the tape will move past the heads.

In older VCRs with mechanical tape transport controls, a very good rule of thumb was to always push the stop button after each function was complete. For example, if you wanted to fast forward and then play a tape, the best way to approach the machine was to insert the tape, push fast forward, then push stop, and then push play. Entering the stop mode ensured that all other functions were canceled. This allowed the machine to go safely from one mode to another. Pushing fast forward and then play, without first pressing stop, would either break the machine or cause the machine to destroy the tape.

Modern VCRs incorporate soft-touch controls. When touched, these controls relay a signal to a small microprocessor within the VCR that analyzes the command and figures out how to execute it.

For example, if you push fast forward and then play, the machine executes the fast forward command upon receiving it. To execute the play command, however, the machine first goes into the stop mode. The microprocessor automatically sends a signal to the machine to stop. When this command is executed, it then sends a signal to the machine to play. This results in fast, error-free operation of machine functions.

TWO SIMPLE VIDEO RECORDING SYSTEM SETUPS

Let's assume that you simply want to record some video and audio information onto videotape with your portable recording system. To make matters even simpler, we will assume that you plan to use the microphone that is either built in or attached to your camera or camcorder. How to proceed varies slightly, depending on whether you will be using a camcorder or a system with separate camera and VCR connected via a camera cable.

Camcorder System Setup

In general, the following steps apply to the setup of most simple one-piece camcorder systems.

Step 1. With the power switch off, make sure the camcorder is secure (either mounted on a tripod or resting safely on a hard surface).

Step 2. Connect the camcorder to power by inserting the internal battery into the camcorder.

Step 3. Turn on the power to the camcorder. The power light should illuminate.

Step 4. Open the tape carriage door by pushing the eject button. Insert the videocassette carefully and correctly. Lower the tape carriage. Rewind the tape to the beginning.

Step 5. Set the filter and white balance controls to their proper positions for the lighting conditions in which you will be recording. Set the gain boost to normal.

Step 6. Uncap the camcorder lens. An image should be visible in the viewfinder.

Step 7. Look through the viewfinder. Frame up and manually focus the image (or set to autofocus). Set the iris to automatic (or manually adjust the aperture for correct exposure).

Step 8. Push the record trigger button to begin recording. Make a brief test recording.

Step 9. Push the record trigger button to stop the recording. Press the rewind button to return the tape to the beginning. Push the play button to check your recording by watching it in the viewfinder. Use an earphone to monitor the recorded audio.

Separate Camera and VCR System Setup

The following steps apply to the setup of most separate camera and VCR systems.

Step 1. Make sure that all power switches on the camera and VCR are turned off and that the camera is secure (either mounted on a tripod or resting safely on a hard surface).

Step 2. Connect the VCR to power. Choose *one* of the following alternatives:

1. Insert the internal battery pack into the VCR and connect it to the power input in the deck.
2. Strap on your external battery belt and connect it to the four-pin DC input on the outside of the VCR.
3. Making certain that the AC adapter is off, connect it first to the four-pin DC input on the side of the VCR. Then plug it into the wall socket and turn on the power switch on the AC adapter.

Step 3. Turn on the power to the VCR. The VCR power light should come on.

Step 4. Raise the tape carriage in the VCR by pushing the eject button. Insert the videocassette carefully and correctly. Lower the tape carriage.

Step 5. Check to make sure that the machine works. Push the play button. If you hear the VCR starting, wait a few seconds and then push the stop button. Then rewind the tape to the beginning. It will stop automatically. Reset the counter to zero.

Step 6. Connect the camera cable to the camera and to the input on the VCR. You will need to push it into the receptacle and then tighten down the threaded sleeve. Tighten the connection, but not so tight that it cannot be unscrewed.

Step 7. Turn on the camera power. Check your instruction manual to see whether the camera should be turned on with the camera lens capped or uncapped. If the instructions call for the camera to be uncapped, make sure that it is defocused and pointed at a dull object or surface to protect against burn in.

Step 8. Put the VCR into the ready-to-record mode. This is accomplished as follows: Push in the record button on the VCR, and while you are holding it in, also push the play button. When you hear the machine engage the tape, release both buttons. The tape should now be engaged around the heads and it should pause; that is, the tape should not be moving. If the tape is moving, push the trigger on the camera to pause the tape. If everything has been connected properly and all your equipment is compatible, you are almost ready to record. There should be an image in the camera viewfinder and the audio and video from the camera should be going into the VCR. Before recording, remember to white balance the camera for your particular lighting situation.

Step 9. The system is now ready to record. When the camera trigger is pushed, the VCR will begin to record continuously until the trigger is pushed again. The trigger is like an on/off switch. It does not need to be held in for the duration of the shot. Simply depress it and release it to begin recording, then depress it and release it to stop recording.

Step 10. When you are finished recording, cap the camera lens and push the stop button on the VCR. To review what you have recorded, press rewind and then push play. The image should appear in the camera viewfinder. Audio can be monitored by connecting an earphone or monitor jack on the VCR.

If the image in the camera viewfinder appears as a still frame—that is, you see the image but it is not moving—pull the camera trigger once and release it. When a tape is played back into the camera viewfinder, the camera retains its remote control over the VCR, and the image can be paused or advanced by using the camera trigger.

Camera-VCR Compatibility

We would like to make one additional comment about camera-VCR compatibility. As previously noted, if you are connecting a camera to a portable VCR with a cable, you must be sure that you have the appropriate cable specified by the camera manufacturer for use with the particular format and model VCR that you are using. In addition, you must correctly set the *VTR interface switch* on the video camera to the appropriate position as specified by the manufacturer.

Most camera viewfinders contain either a light or a visual display to indicate if the VCR is ready to record or if it is actually recording. Since this information is carried through the camera cable, and since different manufacturers use different pin configurations within the cables, sometimes you will find that even when you are using the correct cable and the camera interface switch is correctly set, the information displayed in the viewfinder does not correspond to what is actually happening. For example, the light in the viewfinder may indicate that the VCR is in the record mode with the tape moving when it is actually in the ready-to-record mode (tape not moving). Or the opposite may occur—the light may indicate the VCR is ready when in fact it is already recording.

Many equipment manufacturers, aware that consumers often match one type of camera to another manufacturer's VCR, have built in a compatibility device to correct these signal polarity mismatches. This small **compatibility** switch can usually be found on the bottom of the camera or on the side input panel of the VCR. It is marked with a plus (+) sign on one side and a minus (–) sign on the other side. If your camera viewfinder is displaying incorrect information, locate the compatibility switch and switch it to the other position. This should solve the problem.

AUDIO AND VIDEO CONNECTORS

Quite often in field production you need to go beyond the simple setup of camcorder or VCR. Most VCRs contain a series of auxiliary audio and video inputs and outputs. These additional inputs and outputs are used when you want to record a video or audio source other than the camera or camera microphone into the VCR, when you want to monitor the output of the VCR, or when you simply want to play back a tape into a monitor to check its quality.

A big problem with auxiliary inputs and outputs on portable VCRs is that the connectors used have not been standardized. As a result, you need to become familiar with the range of video and audio connectors in use, and in particular, you need to know which specific connectors are used on your equipment. Figure 5–12 illustrates the most common audio and video connectors found on portable video equipment.

Audio Connectors

The most common use of additional inputs is for recording audio. Since the quality of the audio recording can be enhanced by using an external microphone rather than the camera microphone, and since more than one microphone is often used in a recording situation, some way of getting the signal into the VCR is needed. Therefore, it is extremely important that you know what the audio input and output connectors are on your equipment.

The variety in audio connectors in use in portable equipment is guaranteed to drive you crazy. Professional equipment uses a three-pin **XLR** (Cannon) connector for all audio inputs and outputs. Consumer-quality ½″ and 8mm equipment utilizes the **RCA/phono connector**, a small pin surrounded by a metal

Figure 5–12   Audio and Video Connectors

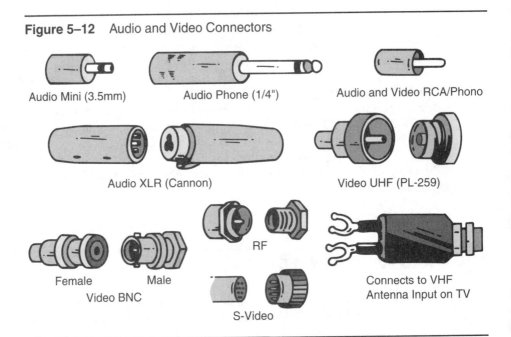

Audio Mini (3.5mm)   Audio Phone (1/4")   Audio and Video RCA/Phono

Audio XLR (Cannon)   Video UHF (PL-259)

RF

Female   Male   Connects to VHF
Video BNC   Antenna Input on TV

S-Video

sheath, for line-level audio inputs and outputs. (Line-level signals will be discussed further in Chapter 7.) Microphone inputs are typically **mini-plugs**, small single-pin connectors. Mini-plugs are also used for the earphone jack, which is used to monitor the sound as it is being recorded. Once very popular, but now becoming less widely used, are **phone plugs**. These large pin-type plugs are often used as headphone connectors on home stereo systems and also as headphone connectors on $3/4''$ studio VCRs but are seldom found on any other portable equipment.

Video Connectors

Most VCRs have a series of video inputs and outputs that are independent of the video input from the camera. For example, if you want to dub a videotape from one machine to another, the video output from one machine can be connected to the video input on another machine. On high-quality VCRs, video inputs and outputs will either be in the form of UHF connectors or BNC connectors (see Figure 5–12). **UHF** (ultra high frequency) **connectors** are barrel-type connectors with a center pin. The male side of the connection has a threaded sleeve that screws onto the threaded barrel of the female side. **Bayonet (BNC) connectors** are bayonet twist-lock connectors and are the type of connector used on almost all professional equipment.

The third type of connector used for video is the RCA/phono connector. This type is most often found on consumer-quality 8mm and VHS machines; it is the same type of connector sometimes used for audio.

And finally, VCRs with S-Video inputs and outputs use a special four-pin connector that is used to make direct S-Video connections (separate luminance and chrominance signals) between VCRs, cameras, and monitors that are equipped with similar connectors.

Other Connectors

Two other types of connectors deserve mention. The radio frequency (RF) output of all portable VCRs is carried by a coaxial cable with an **F-connector**. The RF output carries audio and video superimposed onto a carrier current, which allows you to play back a videotape and watch it on a conventional television. If you have cable television, you are already familiar with the F-connector—the cable ends in a small sleeve and a small, thin copper wire protrudes from the center of the cable. If your television has a female F-connector on the back, you can connect the cable (or VCR RF output) directly to the television. If it does not have this input, a small **VHF** (very high frequency) **twin lead adapter** is used to connect the VCR output to the antenna inputs on the back of the television.

Finally, some full-size VCRs come equipped with a rectangular eight-pin connector that allows connection of the audio and video output directly to a television monitor.

MONITORING THE RECORDING

Video field producers are always concerned about the scene being shot actually being recorded on the videotape.

What options are available to the field producer for monitoring the quality of the signal and recording? First, the visual quality of the image (in black and white) can be monitored in the camera viewfinder. This shows the camera operator what the picture that the camera is sending to the VCR looks like. Second, the audio quality can also be monitored like the video. Headphones, or an earphone, can be connected to the VCR. Or the side panel of the camera/camcorder may be equipped with a built-in **earspeaker**—a small speaker that allows the camera operator to hear the sound input directly without the use of headphones or an earphone. Again, this monitors the quality of the audio input and tells the camera operator what the audio input signal sounds like.

Meters

Audio and video can also be monitored through the use of the volume unit (VU) meter on portable recorders. This meter indicates the level of the signal going into the deck.

Some portable VCRs contain a video-level meter, but this is becoming less common, as all video-level controls are automatic on most VCRs. The exception to this is on professional-quality machines that typically include a video-level meter.

All high-quality VCRs contain VU meters for audio. The level of the audio input signal can be controlled automatically through the use of the audio automatic gain control (AGC). On some VCRs and camcorders, the AGC can be overridden and switched to manual gain control. Usually, there is a small **potentiometer**, or pot, built into the VCR to allow the operator to increase or decrease the audio level. Since control of the audio is critical to good field production, manual control of the audio signal level is extremely valuable. It is unfortunate that most 8mm and VHS consumer camcorders do not contain either audio VU meters or manual audio gain controls, because this deprives the serious producer of an element of fundamental control over the signal.

Confidence Heads

Carefully monitoring the audio and video levels through the VCR meters, and the quality of the picture and sound through the viewfinder and headphones, only tells you what is coming from the camera and microphone. Until recently, there was no way of actually monitoring the quality of the recording without playing back the tape after the recording session. However, several professional models of portable VCRs and camcorders now incorporate what the manufacturers call video **confidence heads**. These are a second set of video heads positioned immediately behind the principal set of recording heads. As the record heads lay down the signal, they are immediately followed by the confidence heads, which can play back the signal while the machine is still in the record mode. Simply stated, this allows you to monitor the visual quality of the recording as it is being recorded.

Field Monitors

Since most machines do not have confidence heads, how can you actually monitor the quality of the recording? There is only one foolproof method of checking the quality of a recording, and that is to play back the videotape immediately after it has been recorded.

Most field producers will make a short test recording with the equipment at the beginning of the day, and then immediately play it back to see that the equipment is working properly. The recording can be played back into the camera viewfinder, and audio can be monitored through the use of headphones. All you need do is rewind the tape to the beginning of the recorded test section and then play back the tape. The camera viewfinder will automatically display the image, and the sound can be picked up by hooking up the headphones to the appropriate jack on the VCR.

However, since most camera viewfinders on portable cameras are black and white, this method of monitoring does not allow you to check the quality of the color of your recording. To check the quality of the color that was recorded, as well as your recording's sound and image, you need to bring a portable color monitor into the field (see Figure 5–13). A portable color monitor is a small color television

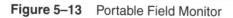

Figure 5–13 Portable Field Monitor

monitor. For field use, these monitors should be small (a 5" diagonal screen is usually sufficient), lightweight, rugged, and capable of being operated either via AC or DC (battery) power. A monitor capable of operating only on AC wall current is not very useful out in the field, far from a source of AC power. As the previous discussion indicates, there are several different types of devices that can be used to view television programs or to display the output of a VCR. These devices include receivers, television monitors, and combination monitor/receivers.

A television **receiver** is the type of television most common to all of us. Its function is to pick up a signal that is either **broadcast** (over the air) or **cablecast** (over a wire) and to display that signal as picture and sound. Television signals that are broadcast or cablecast are RF modulated. That is, the actual video signal and audio signal are superimposed on a carrier that oscillates at a particular frequency. These different carrier frequencies correspond to different channels on home television receivers. For example, within your local community, you probably have access to several local television stations. Each station is assigned to a different channel, which in effect corresponds to the wavelength carrier that station uses to transmit its signal.

Television **monitors**, on the other hand, work by displaying video and audio signals that are not superimposed on a carrier. The output of all VCRs, when labeled *video line out* and *audio line out*, are straight video and audio outputs without the RF carrier currents. To monitor video and audio line outputs, you need a monitor—not a receiver—that is capable of displaying them.

Let's assume that you want to monitor what you are recording in the field through the use of a combination *monitor/receiver*. This type of equipment has the capability to act either as a receiver or a monitor. To operate it as a monitor, switch it to the monitor mode and connect it to power. Then connect the audio and video outputs on the VCR or camcorder to the audio and video inputs on the monitor. To make the connections correctly, you will need to pay attention to the types of connectors used on both the VCR outputs and the monitor inputs (see Figure 5–14). Once these connections have been made, you can simply insert a tape into the VCR or camcorder and play it back. Picture and sound should appear on the monitor.

In addition to monitoring picture and sound after they have been recorded, you can also use the monitor to display picture and sound while you are recording. The signal going into the VCR from the camera will automatically be routed through the VCR to the monitor if you have made all the connections properly. In many portable systems, the VCR does not even have to be recording for you to monitor the camera output.

As long as the power to the camera and VCR or camcorder is turned on (even if the VCR is in the stop mode), the output signal of the camera will be looped through the VCR to the monitor. This is particularly useful if you want to warm up the camera or practice camera moves without actually engaging the tape around the head drum. It saves wear and tear on the video heads and the videotape.

One word of caution is needed here: Remember to keep the audio speaker on the monitor turned down if you have a live microphone nearby. If the audio speaker is turned up too high, the audio components will begin to produce **feedback**. This is

Figure 5–14   Schematic for Field Monitor Connection

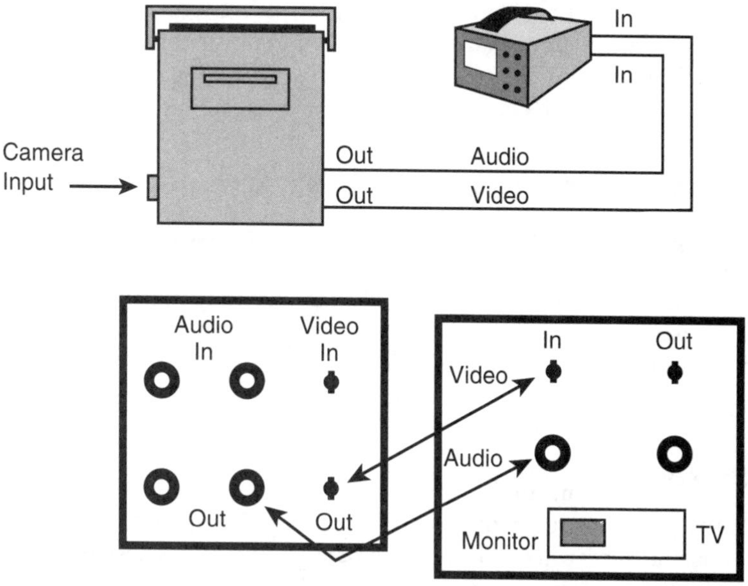

a loud, squealing audio noise that occurs when the microphone picks up its own sound from the speaker, which is then reamplified by the audio circuits in the VCR.

Some VCRs have a built-in RF unit and RF output. If your VCR has an RF output, then the VCR output can be viewed on a regular television receiver. The RF output unit will contain a small switch that indicates which channel the output can be viewed on, usually channel 3 or 4. Switch the output to the channel that is *not* used by a local station in your area. If you have a local channel 3, switch the VCR output to channel 4 so that the local station's signal does not interfere with the VCR output. If your area has a local channel 4, then switch the VCR RF output to channel 3 for the same reason.

On consumer-quality camcorders, line-level and RF video outputs can usually be found on the AC adapter rather than on the camcorder itself. These outputs can be used only when the AC adapter is being used to power the camcorder, either during the time the recording is being made or when the camcorder is being used to play back the tape.

CARRYING THE EQUIPMENT

If you are fortunate enough to be working with a camcorder system rather than a system with a separate camera and VCR, you will quickly see the advantage that camcorders have over two-piece systems in terms of their portability. Nevertheless, much field production continues to be done with two-piece systems, using either $\frac{1}{2}$" or $\frac{3}{4}$" portable VCRs. If you are working with a two-piece system, it should be apparent that even a relatively simple remote shoot involves the use of a significant amount of equipment. How does one carry all this gear around? A number of solutions are readily available.

Carrying Case with Shoulder Strap

Most portable VCRs are equipped with a carrying case and a shoulder strap. If yours is not, cases in a variety of sizes are commercially available. These carrying cases and straps are useful not only because they make it easier to carry the VCR but also because they offer the VCR some protection from shock and dust. Remember not to swing the VCR by its strap. Such motion can create a gyro effect, which may produce an unstable recording.

Backpack

If one person is required to carry both the camera and the VCR, then it might be advisable to mount the VCR into a **backpack** frame. These frames, which are made out of lightweight aluminum tubing, allow the VCR camera to be carried on the operator's back. Although it is sometimes difficult to operate the tape transport controls with the VCR in this position, this is a small price to pay for the extra mobility that the backpack provides the camera operator.

Carts

For an extremely complicated remote shoot, or in a situation where the portable camera and VCR will be augmented with the use of a field monitor, extra batteries, and additional audio or lighting equipment, *wheeled carts* (sometimes called *crash carts*) are frequently used. The carts are usually designed to hold the VCR, AC adapter monitor, and other auxiliary equipment, and they provide convenient access to the operating controls of each piece of equipment. The camera may be attached to the VCR with a long camera cable, allowing the camera operator a reasonable degree of mobility from the home base of the equipment cart. Some carts may even have a tripod head mounted directly onto them if stability, rather than mobility, is a primary concern.

Problems

Recordings made in the field will be more reliable and stable if the portable camcorder or VCR remains stationary while the recording is in progress. Obviously, this is not always possible. However, if you are carrying the camcorder or VCR or moving it around in a wheeled cart, try to minimize the amount of motion that is subjected to the recorder. If the VCR or camcorder is violently swung or bounced, this will almost certainly affect the speed at which the tape is moving through the VCR and introduce some instability into the recording.

SUMMARY

The basic portable video recording system contains two components: a video camera and a portable videocassette recorder. The portable video camera and VCR may be separate pieces of equipment connected by a cable, or they may be combined into one unit as a camcorder.

The video signal is stored electronically on videotape by the videotape recorder. Since videotape in portable systems is most often found in the form of cassettes, these recorders are called videocassette recorders, or VCRs. Videocassette recorders used in the field are portable and usually record and play back the video signal. Some VCRs include special features such as automatic backspace editing and video dubbing.

All VCRs contain a number of external controls and inputs, including the tape transport controls, audio and video inputs and outputs, power inputs, meters, warning lights, and tape counters. Other controls may include the video input selector, camera input selector, S-VHS record mode selector, audio input selector, audio mode selector, tracking control, speed control, audio monitor control, playback mode control, color lock, and occasionally a remote control.

To record on a portable VCR, equipment must be connected and set up properly. Principal steps include connecting the VCR or camcorder to battery or AC power, inserting a videotape into the VCR, and connecting the VCR to the camera with the appropriate camera/VCR cable when working with a two-piece field recording system.

A complicated mechanical device extracts the videotape from the cassette and wraps it around the head drum for recording and playback.

To set up a camera and VCR for recording, first the VCR and then the camera should be connected to power and turned on, following the proper step-by-step sequence. Remember to white balance the camera before recording and to make a test recording to check that your system is operating correctly. Some cameras and VCRs contain interfaces or compatibility switches that must be set correctly to use a camera manufactured by one company with a VCR manufactured by a different company.

All VCRs contain a series of audio and video inputs and outputs. There is little standardization of connectors, so familiarity with a range of them is necessary. Principal audio connectors include the XLR (Cannon), RCA/phono, mini-plug, and phone plug connectors. Video connectors include the BNC, UHF, RCA/phono, and S-Video connectors. Other common connectors include the F-connector for RF output and a rectangular eight-pin video/audio connector that is found on some full-sized VCRs.

Picture and sound can be monitored while recording by looking at the image in the viewfinder and by connecting an earphone or headphone to the VCR. Audio and video can also be monitored through the use of the VU meters on the portable recorder and by the use of a portable monitor in the field. Some decks are equipped with confidence heads for immediate confirmation of the integrity of the recording.

Several options exist for carrying the equipment in the field. Carrying cases with shoulder straps, backpacks, and portable carts are often used.

6

Lighting

PART ONE:
PHYSICAL FACTORS OF LIGHTING

Whether one is producing a video picture in a studio, forest, surgical facility, or fishing boat, the physics of light remain the same. This is not to say that those versed in studio production have little to learn about lighting remote locations. In truth, they have much to unlearn before they become proficient at lighting in the field. Specifically, field producers need to expand their concepts of visualization beyond those used in the studio—in the field, action need not be forced into the standard camera height, setting, or light plot. Video production is becoming less dependent on the studio in the interests of greater authenticity and viewer interest. Although the same rules of illumination and illusion via controlled lighting apply, the conditions of circumstance, equipment, and time change radically in field production.

Generally speaking, remote production can be divided into two categories: the generation of materials for use in news programs (electronic news gathering—ENG) and the creation of complete programs or program segments (electronic field production—EFP). Each requires the integration of video materials with those gathered or produced elsewhere. Audiences are all too familiar with the poorly produced news insert that features a purple reporter describing the activities of the green people seen in the background. In the face of such overwhelming visual distraction, no one remembers the significance of the topic. Lighting for remote production, then, begins with avoiding such distractions and meeting audience expectations efficiently and inexpensively.

While the *craft* of lighting focuses on generating colors and visible detail acceptable to viewers in the laboratory, boardroom, classroom, or at home, the *art* of lighting involves controlling the aesthetic factors central to persuasive productions. Lighting for scanning bank checks, steam gauges, or parking lots must only provide sufficient illumination for sharp focus at the prescribed distance from the lens. However, to attract and maintain the attention of your viewers, you must help them see what they have not seen before. You do this by establishing expositional details of time and place, by expressing relationships among people or between people and objects, and by conveying senses of textures and atmospheres. This chapter will discuss how you achieve this in your video productions through the use of lighting.

BASE ILLUMINATION

Baselight

As you remember from our discussion in Chapter 2, the television CCD or pickup tube creates the television picture by changing light that is reflected off the scene into electrical energy—the video signal. For this process to take place, the camera requires that a certain minimum amount of light be present on the scene that is being recorded. The minimum amount of light that must be present for the camera to operate properly is called the **base illumination** level, or **baselight**. Baselight, then, refers to the amount, or intensity, of the light that is required to make the camera function properly.

Unfortunately, television cameras are not as efficient as the human eye when it comes to seeing the event in front of them. The human eye is much more sensitive than a video camera and requires less light to make a picture than does a camera. Similarly, some scenes that look fine to the eye may contain too much light/dark contrast for the camera to process without distortion.

Since the eye responds differently to light than the camera, a mechanical way to measure the light present is needed to determine if it is sufficient for the camera to make everything visible. The **light meter** does this (see Figure 6–1). The light meter

Figure 6–1   Incident Light Meter

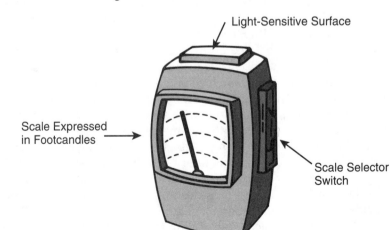

provides a rough indication of the amount of light striking the photosensitive surface of the CCD or pickup tubes, and expresses the amount in **footcandles (fc)**.

Increasingly, camera light-level requirements are expressed in **lux** instead of footcandles. Lux are calculated in the same manner as are footcandles except one meter replaces one foot in the formula. Since one footcandle equals about 11 lux and since most of the world uses the metric system of measurement, manufacturers express the low-light capacity of their cameras in whole number lux rather than in fractions of a footcandle—for example, 10 lux instead of .9 footcandle. (See Appendix 2 for a more thorough discussion of light measurement.)

Incident and Reflected Light

Light meters can be used to measure the amount of light falling on a scene, called **incident light**, or the amount of light reflected off a scene, called **reflected light** (see Figure 6–2).

Incident light is measured by placing the light meter in the subject's position and pointing it at each lighting instrument. This results in a relatively high reading, which, although crude, is reliable. As long as subjects or materials of the same general reflectance are used, incident light can be used as the measure of the basic illumination on a scene. Some incident light meters have a light-sensitive area that is hemispherical rather than flat. The sphere approximates the shape of the human face and can be used to measure all the light falling on a subject from various directions.

A more precise method of measuring the intensity of the light present involves placing the light meter in the camera position and measuring the light reflected from the subject to the camera. This is called reflected light.

Although both types of light meters are widely used in video production, incident light meters are probably the most common, largely because baselight

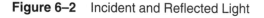

Figure 6–2   Incident and Reflected Light

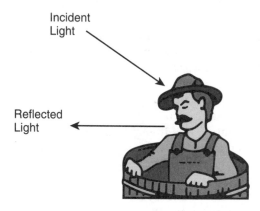

Incident Light

Reflected Light

requirements for cameras are most often reported in terms of the amount of incident light that they require.

Camera Development and Baselight Requirements

We can identify four cycles in the development of television (video) cameras with respect to the amount of illumination required by the cameras to function properly. Cycle 1 began with the development of the first broadcast-quality black and white studio cameras, cycle 2 with the development of studio color cameras, cycle 3 with the development of portable video cameras, and cycle 4 with the development of the CCD.

Cycle 1: Early Black and White Cameras. The black and white studio cameras of the 1950s required enormous amounts of light to function. Without such light, a recognizable picture was not produced. With the development of the image-orthicon pickup tube, a black and white studio camera evolved that could function with much less light. These cameras were restricted largely to studios because of their size and weight.

Cycle 2: Color Cameras. With the development of the studio color camera in the mid-1960s, cycle 1 was repeated. The first color cameras were extremely large and heavy and required extreme illumination levels, often in the range of 400 footcandles, to function in a marginally acceptable way. The lights used for video productions were so hot that desktop microphone stands would be hot to the touch before the conclusion of a 30-minute interview program. All this discomfort was aggravated by the fact that the color produced was far from the photographic standard set by the motion picture industry. As long as color television was a novelty, however, it was good enough.

There is a lesson here. Audiences are soon spoiled by technical accomplishments and come to expect whatever has become possible. Anything less becomes a distraction. Once a technical standard is established in the "big bucks" entertainment field, for example, even the special interest audiences associated with nonbroadcast video expect it. More than one in-house sales presentation or training tape has failed to achieve management's objectives because viewers found it poorly produced by the standards of the day.

Cycle 3: Tube-Type Portable Video Cameras. Early versions of tube-type portable video cameras suffered from many of the problems of their studio predecessors—high lighting requirements, particularly among less expensive cameras, and a marked tendency in low-light situations for the image to exhibit a lagging or smearing effect when the subject or camera moved.

Eventually, advancing pickup tube technology produced portable color cameras that operated efficiently in low light. The development of Saticon and Newvicon pickup tubes all but eliminated the lag problem of the earlier Vidicons.

Baselight requirements of this generation of portable color cameras were in the 150 to 200 footcandle range (approximately 2,000 lux) when the solid-state CCD-type cameras became available.

Cycle 4: CCD Cameras and Camcorders. Solid-state CCD pickup devices have found wide and increasing use in broadcast-quality and consumer-quality video cameras and camcorders since the mid-1980s. The highest-quality cameras and camcorders designed for broadcast use utilize a three-chip design, with light requirements in the 150 to 200 footcandle range. At the other end of the spectrum are the least expensive, single-chip cameras and camcorders that have been designed for home or consumer use. These units have been designed to operate under "normal" lighting conditions and are capable of producing truly remarkable pictures outdoors, as well as indoors under normal incandescent and fluorescent lighting conditions.

CONTRAST RANGE

In spite of the technical improvements made during the last 30 years, video systems are not able to match the **contrast range** capabilities of film, let alone those of the human eye. In this regard, the video camera cannot record reality as seen both in film and in our everyday experiences. As a rule of thumb, think of video as operating within a 30:1 ratio of light to dark. This can be understood as the difference between very light, highly reflective surfaces like a white wall and total darkness, or the lack of reflective light—black. The video camera's inability to process a full range of contrasts accurately is most often seen on tape as faces turning into silhouettes as

Figure 6–3   As Background Becomes Brighter, Foreground Subject Becomes Silhouetted

Figure 6–4   Effect of Bright Foreground Object on Background

If foreground object becomes too bright, even medium shadows appear black.

the sky or wall behind them brightens, or becoming heavily shadowed and grainy as an extremely bright object appears in the foreground (see Figures 6–3 and 6–4).

The technical term used to describe the camera's ability to reproduce the tonal gradations, or contrast range, of a scene is called **gamma**. Since gamma is constant in most inexpensive field cameras (no adjustment of this factor is possible), it is necessary to control the brightness of subjects within a scene to generate an acceptable picture. This control is next to impossible in some circumstances: Moving from the interior of a dark chapel to a bright outdoors courtyard in a single shot, for example, exceeds the capacity of most cameras. The camera automatically compresses part of the contrast range and loses something. If the scene is too bright, everything from middle gray to black is processed as black. This could include the natural middle brightness shadows on the face that combine to create a three-dimensional, or modeling, effect.

This is an area of great concern to video camera manufacturers, and important advances are announced with increasing frequency. The ability to accurately reproduce a scene with a high contrast range distinguishes high-quality industrial grade and professional cameras from their less expensive counterparts. Although most portable color cameras can produce a bright, clear, and attractive picture, sometimes more expensive cameras can do it in a greater range of circumstances and with less time-consuming attention to manipulation of the environment.

COLOR

Although baselight and contrast range deal with the amount of light and its effect on a scene in terms of its overall black and white brightness, most television cameras today are color cameras. To operate effectively, the successful producer must understand the complexity that color adds to light and video production.

Additive and Subtractive Color

Two complementary theories of color must be understood before proceeding further. One, termed *additive*, concerns the mixing of colored light; the other, called *subtractive*, concerns the mixing of pigments.

Additive Color. Physicists have demonstrated that visible light is really electromagnetic radiation that can be manipulated (see Figure 6–5). A beam of light can be bent with a magnet, and different colors are formed through adjustment of the electromagnetic frequencies. Each color is formed by a different frequency. When all of the frequencies in the visible spectrum are added together, white light is formed. Along the way, some surprises occur. For example, mixing red and green light (adding the frequencies) produces yellow light.

The **additive primary colors** of light—red, green, and blue—are the minimum colors necessary to mix all other colors. Inspection of a color television picture reveals that the illusion of a picture is created through the presentation of many thousands of colored dots in sets of three. Each set contains a red, green, and blue dot. Varying the intensity of each dot in the set generates a general impression of the desired color.

Subtractive Color. The other theory of color important to the video producer is that of **subtractive color**. It concerns the mixing of pigments, paints, inks, dyes, and so on. The subtractive primary colors are magenta, cyan, and yellow. In your grade-school water-color set, you probably knew these subtractive primaries as red, blue, and yellow (red and blue approximate magenta and cyan closely).

In theory, mixing all the colors in your paint set together would have resulted in black. Why? Because each color really absorbs all of the frequencies of light

---

Figure 6–5   Frequencies of Visible Light

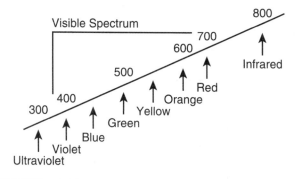

except that which it reflects and therefore appears to be. An orange appears to be orange because it absorbs (and changes into heat) all frequencies except orange. Black absorbs the most frequencies (and generates more heat) than does white (which reflects most frequencies and remains cooler). You have tested the truth of this theory if you have ever walked barefoot on pavement in the summer—the white lines on an asphalt road are always significantly cooler than the black asphalt next to them.

When does an orange not appear orange in color? When it is illuminated by a light containing no orange frequencies to be reflected; green light will do the trick. Under a green light, the orange fruit appears black and no amount of adjusting the intensity of the green light will change the orange from black.

This is extreme, but the principle applies to the illumination of the human face just as clearly. In field production, that illumination can come from the sun and fluorescent lights simultaneously; one side of the subject's face will be in yellow light, the other in blue. Skin pigmentation will not be reproduced accurately in video. The nature of the light distorts the reality of the subject. Sometimes this acts in a positive way; most of the time it creates a problem.

Video producers must remember that the subject (a clothed person, in most cases) is a collection of many pigments and that available illumination also is a collection of direct light and light reflected from nearby surfaces, each of which can change the quality of light in the scene.

Remember, the *quality* of light (its constituent frequencies) and the *intensity* of light (its overall brightness) are different, and different means of control are necessary. Remember also that light meters measure light intensity, not the quality of light.

Color Temperature

In addition to the relative brightness of objects in a scene and the consequent attention that must be given to the contrast range capabilities of the camera, the remote producer must also control or accommodate the quality of light in a scene. Unlike studio production, where this element is under complete control, field production is characterized by a lack of unity in the quality of light, especially when multiple locations are integrated into a single program.

These changing circumstances result in pictures that do not match in important respects, the most obvious being the colors of skin, clothes, grass, bricks, sky, and anything already known to the audience. The reason for this is that the light available in different locations does not consist of the same mix of electromagnetic frequencies. Therefore, a different mix is reflected from the subject to the camera. Remember not to confuse this with brightness or contrast range; it concerns the inherent quality of the light itself, not how much of it there is.

Automatic white balance circuitry in camcorders is designed to adjust the signal as conditions change; thus, video color values are maintained even when different color temperatures dominate the beginning and ending of a single shot. Automatic aperture controls respond to changes in the intensity of light.

The appearance of color is determined by the pigments present in the object being photographed and the quality of the light illuminating them. What appears to be white light to the human eye does not always appear white to the television camera. For example, consider the qualities of light emitted by a fluorescent light and a standard household light. The household light has a tendency to be redder or warmer than the fluorescent light, which has a cool, blue-green quality. These variations in the quality of what appears to be white light are called differences in **color temperature**, and they are measured in a system of degrees kelvin (°K). Video cameras are particularly sensitive to changes or differences in the color temperature of light. Some further explanation of this phenomenon is necessary.

Laboratory experimentation has shown that the extent to which a filament is heated (by passing an electric current through it) is related directly to the color it turns and the color of the light it radiates. At low temperatures, the filament glows red and casts a reddish light. Increasing the current increases the heat, and the filament glows yellow. Enough heat causes the filament to become white hot and to cast a white or seemingly colorless light—a light that contains all frequencies and therefore does not change the appearance of the pigments it illuminates.

To further complicate matters, not only do different types of lighting instruments differ in color temperature (fluorescent versus incandescent versus tungsten-halogen lights, for example) but they all differ from natural sunlight. In addition, not even sunlight has a constant color temperature—it changes depending on the time of day and whether it is a cloudy or a clear day!

Television studios solved the problem of color temperature in a simple way. All lighting instruments are matched at 3,200 degrees kelvin so that colors remain constant regardless of camera position or time of day. Since offices, factories, stores, or exteriors are illuminated by a complex range and mix of light sources, this stands as a major difference between studio and remote production. The remote video producer must learn to recognize the sources and qualities of illumination available on location and make the necessary adjustments in order to produce pictures with accurate color.

Since hand-held color temperature meters, or **kelvinometers**, are not widely used in remote video production, attention continues to be focused on the source of the illumination in question. Rough guides disseminated by equipment manufacturers translate the numerical degrees kelvin of various light sources into descriptive adjectives that nonphysicists are likely to recognize. Table 6–1 presents a list of common light sources and the color temperature of the light they emit.

White Balance

Adjustment of the television camera for the color temperature of the dominant light source is accomplished either through built-in automatic circuitry or by using the appropriate filter for the lens, and then by white balancing the camera. Built-in **filter wheels** allow the camera operator to accommodate the existing lighting conditions. Inexpensive cameras may have a simple indoor-outdoor, two-position filter. More expensive cameras typically have filters to accommodate a variety of

Table 6–1   Color Temperature of Various Light Sources

Color Temperature[a]	Light Source	General Description
1,800°K	Open flame	Warm (red evident)
2,000°K	Household lamp—warm shade	
2,800°K	Unshaded frosted white household lamp	
3,200°K	Television studio standard (tungsten-halogen) lamp	
3,500°K	Home-type photo floodlight	
4,800°K	Fluorescent lamp	
5,400°K	Direct sunlight (noon)	
6,500°K	Overcast daylight	
8,000°K	Blue sky	Cool (blue evident)

[a]Color temperature given in degrees kelvin.

lighting situations: television standard tungsten-halogen lights (3,200 degrees kelvin), fluorescent lights (4,800 degrees kelvin), or an overcast day (6,500 degrees kelvin). In addition, one or more **neutral density filters** may be built into the filter wheel. These do not change the color temperature of the light but simply reduce the quantity of light hitting the image sensor. They are most frequently used when existing light is simply too bright for the camera to handle.

To adjust the camera for the color temperature of the existing light, a white card is held in front of the camera in the actual light that will be used in the scene or shot. If the camera has automatic white balance circuitry, it is engaged. If not, the correct filter must be selected for the existing conditions. Then, the camera operator zooms in to fill the frame with the white card and sets the **white balance**. On most cameras this is an automatic adjustment: The switch used to set the white balance is depressed until the appropriate viewfinder display indicates that the camera has adjusted itself to the light. The electronic adjustments automatically made inside the camera guarantee that the white card will have the proper ratio of red, blue, and green in the video signal. Since the camera now knows what white looks like, it will also accurately reproduce any other colors in the scene. This process of white balance adjustment is made with each change of lighting, scene, or location.

Gels

In some situations, you can adjust the quality of light found in the field by using filters of one sort or another. The most common type of filters are called **gels**, from the word *gelatin*, which is the substance from which they used to be made. Today's products are made of plastics or polyester. They can be used on a window or a lighting instrument to change the color temperature of the light.

Blue gels, or **dichroic filters** (filters that allow only certain frequencies of light to pass), can be applied to lamps emitting light in the range of 2,000 to 4,800 degrees kelvin to convert them to the color temperature of average daylight. This is necessary if you need to augment natural daylight on a scene with additional illumination from tungsten-halogen lamps.

Similarly, amber gels can be placed on windows to convert the color temperature of the light coming through them on a sunny day to the color temperature of interior lights. The color temperature of outside light will be too high, and consequently much bluer than the interior lights, and the amber gels will correct this.

Neutral density gels (similar in function to neutral density lens filters) are available if windows causing brightness problems must appear in the shot. These gels appear to be transparent, but they reduce the amount of light passing through the window into the room without affecting the color temperature.

There are several things to keep in mind if you use gels on a light source: The greater the correction attempted, the less light actually reaching the subject; the less light produced by an instrument, the more instruments needed; the more instruments used, the more power cables, adapters, stands, and electrical circuits needed; the more equipment used, the larger the crew to be hired and the longer the hours they will work; ad infinitum. Clearly, accurate assessment of the problem is needed in the first place, as well as selection of the proper equipment for the job. Those who, through study and experience, can make these judgments correctly are an invaluable production resource.

LIGHTING EQUIPMENT

Obviously the capabilities of the equipment are important in determining the lighting problem. Light can be manipulated to make up for camera shortcomings where base illumination, contrast range, and color temperature are concerned. Of course, each manipulation requires time and the results may not be known until the finished videotape is later examined on a waveform monitor and vectorscope in the editing facility. These technical devices display data relative to the strength and purity of the signal recorded. Given the small size of the typical remote production crew and the premium placed on speed—for example, one ENG crew may cover four stories in a single morning—such technical inspections are not the order of the day.

Portable waveform monitor units containing a color TV and waveform monitor are appearing on the market. Their use promises to reduce further the quality gap between field and studio production.

Basic Lighting Instruments

The remote video producer must recognize the nature of the light on location as well as the capacity of the portable instruments available. The basic lighting instruments used in remote productions include **spotlights**, which produce a narrow beam of hard, focused light, and **floodlights** (also called *broadlights*), which produce a wider beam of softer unfocused light.

Depending on the complexity of the production, the lighting instruments used in the production will vary widely. An ENG cameraperson may well use only one small camera-mounted spotlight to illuminate a single individual who is the subject of an interview. A small-scale EFP crew working on a magazine-style program might use a combination of spotlights and floodlights to illuminate the subject and background areas. On a very large-scale production, a full array of open-face spotlights, reflectors, and diffusers, as well as an electrical power generator, might be employed.

With improvements in light-gathering capacity and contrast range of cameras, changes have been made in basic lighting needs. Increasingly, cloth reflectors are replacing spotlights as the major illuminator. Light reflected from aluminized cloth can be used to provide a bright yet diffused light that models the subject or reduces the contrast created by deep shadow areas.

Portable Lighting Instruments

Lamps. Two types of lamps (or bulbs) are commonly found in television lighting instruments. **Incandescent lamps** are similar in construction to common household bulbs. They have a tungsten filament within an evacuated glass bulb and are relatively inexpensive.

Tungsten-halogen lamps, sometimes called *quartz-halogen* or *quartz lights*, are the industry standard and are found in most professional lighting equipment. The filament in these lamps is tungsten, and the quartz glass bulb is filled with halogen. The halogen prevents the tungsten filament from evaporating and coating the inside of the bulb with particles of tungsten that would affect the color temperature of the light. Unlike conventional incandescent lamps, whose color temperature decreases with age as the glass bulb becomes coated with particles of the filament, the tungsten-halogen lamp maintains a constant color temperature throughout its life (see Figure 6–6).

Figure 6–6   Tungsten-Halogen Lamp

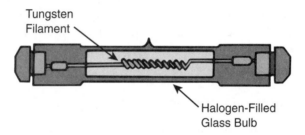

Tungsten
Filament

Halogen-Filled
Glass Bulb

The most popular lighting instruments for remote use are lightweight, bright, and easy to set up. They are open face (have no lens), contain a 500- or 750-watt tungsten-halogen lamp rated at 3,200 degrees kelvin, and operate on common 110-volt, 60-cycle power.

While the older incandescent parabolic aluminized reflector (PAR) lamps are occasionally still used, the tungsten-halogen lamp is now the industry standard because it maintains a constant and higher color temperature throughout its life. It is also smaller and can fit into an open-face instrument (see Figure 6–7). On the negative side, the tungsten-halogen lamp must never be touched by bare fingers—if oil from the skin is deposited on the glass, it may cause the bulb to explode when it gets hot.

Fixed and Variable Beam Spotlights. Two types of spotlights are commonly used in remote production: variable beam spotlights and fixed beam spotlights. On *variable beam spotlights*, the width of the beam of light produced by the instrument can be adjusted by moving a control on the back of the light. This moves the lamp toward or away from the reflective surface inside the instrument, causing the width of the beam to increase or decrease (see Figure 6–8). A narrow beam produces a hard spotlight effect, whereas a wider beam produces a softer floodlight effect. Variable beam spotlights are extremely versatile and for that reason are extensively used in field production.

Fixed beam spotlights do not allow adjustment of the beam width. The position of the lamp within the instrument is permanently set; therefore, the width of the beam of light produced is constant.

Most spotlights are equipped with **barn doors**. These metal flaps can be attached to the light to control the way the light is thrown onto the scene. The barn doors can be opened to allow the light to hit the scene unobstructed, or they can be partially closed to restrict the light from hitting certain parts of the set (see Figure 6–7).

Light Quality—Hard and Soft Light. Variable and fixed beam spotlights are designed to cast a hard light, one that creates sharp-edged shadows. The light created is highly directional. This kind of light is useful in that its directional quality and sharp shadows are good for modeling—delineating the three-dimensional nature of people and objects.

In addition to spotlights, floodlights (or broadlights) have been developed that produce a softer light, one that casts a diffused, unfocused light with less apparent edge to the shadows. Fitted with a tungsten-halogen lamp, the reflector is shaped so that the light comes from each part of it rather than through a central point. These are used to fill in shadows that are too dark, which create too great a light-dark contrast range to be accommodated by the camera (see Figure 6–7).

Soft Lights. A variety of folding-reflector floodlights are available today that are extremely useful to the field producer. The cloth reflector is aluminized or coated with other highly reflective substances and stretched over an umbrella-like frame.

Figure 6–7   Portable Lighting Instruments: (A) Variable Beam Spotlight with Barn Doors (Lowell Omni-light), (B) Floodlight with Flag Mounted on a Door (Lowell Tota-light), (C) Floodlight with Gel Mounted on a Floor Stand (Lowell Tota-light), (D) Softlight with Barn Doors (Lowell Softlight 2)

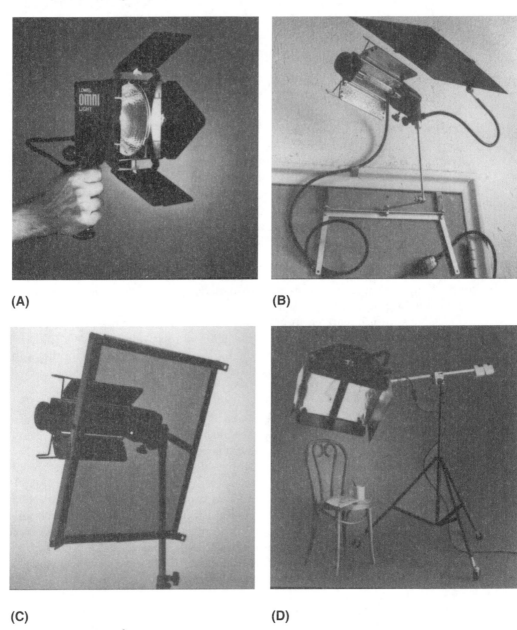

(A)

(B)

(C)

(D)

Figure 6–8   Changing Light Intensity with an Adjustable Beam Instrument

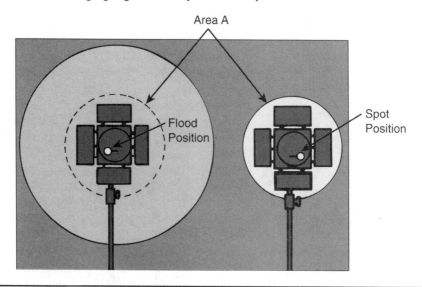

Area A

Flood
Position

Spot
Position

Known as **soft lights**, they provide a bright light that is even more shadow free than open-face floodlights. When erected, they occupy more workspace than open-face floodlights, but in some situations they produce superior illumination (see Figure 6–7).

Lighting Umbrellas. Lighting umbrellas are widely used in conjunction with open-faced spotlights and floodlights to soften and diffuse the quality of light produced by those instruments. The small umbrella is opened and attached to the lighting instrument. As is the case with a soft light, the lamp faces into the umbrella, which then reflects the light out to the subject. The quality of the light that results from this technique is much softer and less harsh than the quality of light produced by the same instrument aimed directly at the subject (see Figure 6–9).

Halogen-Metal-Iodide Lights. A problem is created when natural light in an exterior scene proves to be insufficient and needs to be boosted. The AC-powered tungsten-halogen spotlights and floodlights provide the wrong color temperature (3,200 degrees kelvin), and the mix with natural daylight (6,000 degrees kelvin) may prove troublesome. Dichroic filters are available to convert the 3,200 to 6,000 degrees kelvin—close enough to the color temperature of daylight for video purposes—but then additional instruments may be necessary.

The industry responded to this problem with a filterable light to serve remote production purposes, the halogen-metal-iodide (HMI) light. It is twice as efficient in terms of footcandles per watt as tungsten as a basic source of illumination, and four times as efficient when tungsten is filtered from 3,200 degrees kelvin

Figure 6–9 Spotlight and Umbrella Combination

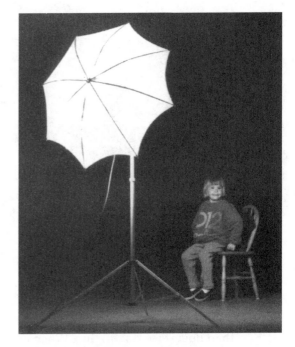

to the equivalent of daylight. However, HMI lights are not widely used in ENG operations because they are a pulsed light that must be synchronized with the camera to avoid flicker in the picture. Therefore, extra safety precautions must be taken in their use. In addition, the required auxiliary support system needed for HMI light operation is very heavy.

Light Supports

When external lights such as those previously described are used in remote productions, some means of supporting the lights must be provided. Typically, one of the three following methods is chosen.

Floor Stands. Most portable lights can be attached to telescoping **floor stands**. These stands are usually made of lightweight aluminum and they provide a reasonable amount of stability for the lighting instrument. Since they telescope upwards, the height of the lighting instrument can be adjusted to control the angle of light as it falls on the subject. One word of caution: The higher the stands are extended, the more unstable they tend to become. Be careful not to bump into the stand or tug on the power cord, as even a slight force may cause the light and stand to fall.

Camera Mounted. Camera-mounted lights attach directly to the camera and are used when a crew member is not available to hold the lighting instrument, where the action being videotaped prevents the use of a floor stand (because of movement, for example), or when the camera operator simply wants to ensure constant, direct illumination of the subject. Camera-mounted lights are often used in ENG operations. They are also extremely useful to the home video producer who consistently shoots indoors and does not want to be bothered with setting up the more cumbersome floor stand-supported lights.

Hand Held. Hand-held lights are often used in remote productions. The lighting instrument must be equipped with a small handle that is insulated from the heat of the bulb. A crew member holds the instrument. The principal advantage to using a hand-held light over a camera-mounted light is that the angle from which the light strikes the subject can be varied. The camera-mounted light always illuminates the subject from the direction of the camera, but the hand-held light can be moved up or down, or from one side to the other to provide better modeling of the subject.

POWER REQUIREMENTS

Electrical power for lights, cameras, and videotape recorders is not available at every remote location. Although offices, hospitals, and factories have sufficient power available for video production, the outlets may not be in the most convenient locations, and three or four power cables and adapters may be needed. Permission to lay such cable in hallways may be required and may be granted only if rubber mats are taped in place over the cables as a pedestrian safety measure. Other locations, such as exteriors and some interiors in old buildings or warehouses, may not have any electrical power available. In these cases, the video producer must augment natural light with mechanical means, such as reflectors, or rely on battery-powered instruments.

Each solution has its limitations. There may be insufficient light to reflect, especially in late afternoon or at night, and batteries are reliable only for minutes, not hours. Lighting instruments lose intensity and the color temperature drops as batteries weaken. The time constraints of ENG make battery-powered lighting instruments useful on an individual production basis, but they may become a source of concern if a number of stories are to be covered in a single morning. ENG crews carry replacement batteries because of their short service life, and as soon as the crews return to the station, they immediately begin recharging the batteries. Many ENG vans are equipped with a rack of batteries and a battery-charging system so that a ready source of battery power is always on hand.

Formula for Alternating Current Power

The video producer must also consider the capacity of the alternating current (AC) electrical circuits available. Depending on the wattage of the lamps being used, two or three instruments may be powered by one household circuit. If at all possible, cameras and videotape recorders should be powered on separate circuits so that the act of turning on the VCR will not overload a circuit already operating at capacity.

You can calculate how much power is available to you by using a simple formula:

$$watts = amps \times volts$$

To use this formula, first determine the number of amps that the electrical circuit is rated for. In most homes and offices, this is a standard 15-amp circuit. (The amp rating is listed on the fuse box or circuit breaker.) The line voltage of most household electrical power in the United States is 110 volts. Therefore, you can determine the wattage of the circuit by plugging the numbers into the equation. Since watts = amps × volts, using the figures above your circuit would deliver 1,650 watts (watts = 15 amps × 110 volts).

Next, examine your lighting instruments. If you have 650-watt lamps, you will be able to run only two of them safely on any one circuit (2 × 650 watts = 1,300 watts). Three lamps will blow the fuse or trip the circuit breaker because they will exceed the capacity of the line (3 × 650 watts = 1,950 watts).

Most rooms have a number of electrical outlets but seldom more than two circuits or electrical lines. A room with four outlets is typically arranged so that there are two outlets on two different circuits (see Figure 6–10). An easy way to determine whether different outlets are on the same or different circuits involves the use of a simple light. Plug a light into an outlet and then turn off the circuit breakers one at a time at the main power source. When the light goes out, you will know which circuit it is on and which circuit breaker controls it. Repeat the procedure for all the outlets in the room. If there are multiple electrical lines (circuits) in the room, you will be able to identity each, the outlets on each circuit, and the circuit breakers that control them.

In calculating the amount of power you need, don't forget to compute the power drawn by the camera and VCR. Figures for the power consumption of this equipment can usually be found among the list of technical specifications in the operating instructions manual.

CONTROLLING THE INTENSITY OF LIGHT

Light intensity can be adjusted through the use of dimmers, by varying the beam width on those instruments with focus controls, by changing the lamp-to-subject distance, and through the use of diffusers.

Figure 6–10   Electrical Circuits and Outlets

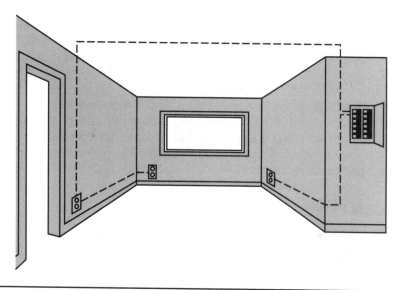

Dimmers

Dimmers work by varying the wattage supplied to the lighting instrument. In this way, the intensity of the light can easily be changed. If a light is too bright, the wattage can be reduced until the light is at the proper intensity. Dimmers are extensively used in television studio production; however, they are seldom used in field production because of their weight and size.

Few field producers are in a position to carry dimmers for their lighting equipment. In a sense, this is just as well because they affect the color temperature of the lamps being dimmed. As a lamp is dimmed, the color temperature decreases and the light it produces becomes progressively redder. The effect is more noticeable on incandescent lamps than on tungsten-halogen lamps, but it is nonetheless present for both. Dimming can cause significant problems with color balance, and for this reason some producers avoid using them altogether.

Varying the Beam Width

The variable beam found on many portable spotlights is extremely valuable for field production. Without changing the position of the instrument, the intensity of the light can be increased or decreased by adjusting the beam width. No dimmers are involved, and the light generated by a constant flow of electrical power can be spread widely or focused on a narrow area. The intensity of the light at any point within the beam depends on how concentrated the beam is.

Lamp-to-Subject Distance

Another easy way of altering the intensity of a specific light source involves simply moving the light. A change in the distance from the lamp to the subject affects the intensity of the light falling on the subject. Doubling the distance reduces the intensity of the light reaching the subject to one-fourth of its original strength (see Figure 6–11). This is the **inverse square rule**, and it is an important tool in remote video production (see Appendix 2).

Adjusting the lamp-to-subject distance is often the most effective way of changing the intensity of a light that does not have the variable beam feature. However, adjusting the lamp-to-subject distance often has a negative side effect: The angle of the light relative to the subject also changes, and with it, aesthetic properties are changed. This will be discussed in greater detail later.

Light Diffusers and Reflectors

Light **diffusers**, also called **scrims**, are often used in remote productions to change the amount and quality of the light. Professional lighting instruments are fitted with slots or frames to hold these diffusers, although a clothes pin can safely be used to hold a diffuser in front of a lamp that lacks slots.

Common aluminum window screening can be placed in front of a lamp to reduce its effective intensity and soften the edges of the shadows slightly without changing the color temperature of the light appreciably. Several layers of screen can be used if the problem is extreme. The commercial diffusers on the market provide a more subtle range of control.

A variety of **reflectors** are also available. The principles upon which they operate are simple, and they can be constructed at home with excellent results.

Figure 6–11   Inverse Square Rule

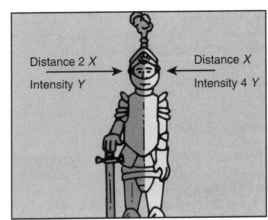

Commercial products are sturdier than home-made reflectors, but to make your own, you need only find a piece of cardboard or Styrofoam at least three feet by four feet. Cardboard curls and Styrofoam breaks, so commercial products do have their advantages. Glue aluminum foil to one side, avoid wrinkles, and make it as flat and shiny as possible. This will reflect a hard light. On the other side, glue a pebble-grained or finely wrinkled foil; this will diffuse the light it reflects and soften the edges of the shadows. In either case, the color temperature of the light being reflected is not affected.

White Styrofoam by itself is an effective reflector. The light reflected is soft and lightens the shadow on the subject's face. However, it is easily damaged by clamps and soils from everyday use.

A white bedsheet can be used to reflect or diffuse light, and a lightweight folding frame can be constructed to hold it. A small opening in the center of the sheet provides access for the camera for special shots.

Colored reflectors, usually gold, are available or can be constructed for special purposes. The light they reflect is warm and matches the color temperatures associated with open flame, incandescent lights, and sunsets.

Flags and Silks. The well-equipped field producer also may have a variety of flags and silks. **Flags** are opaque cards of assorted sizes with handles that facilitate mounting on floor stands and other equipment to create a shadow by interrupting a beam of light (see Figure 6–7). They are often used to keep the light from one instrument from illuminating the wrong part of the set or to keep direct sunlight off a subject.

Silks are giant diffusers used to control light intensity and color temperature in outdoor productions. They are used like an awning or tent—above the picture but situated to filter all the light from the sky. Since they are difficult to rig and keep in adjustment, they are associated only with the most expensive productions. At best, they facilitate production in bright sunlight by creating an even effect of a hazy day; at worst, they can become the subject of a comedy feature.

OTHER EQUIPMENT

Every description of the remote video producer's equipment includes two essential items: duct tape and aluminum foil. The uses for the tape are many and constant; subjects who cannot remain in position or in the light can even have their shoes taped to the floor! Aluminum foil can be used to extend barn doors on lighting instruments, to act as a hard or semisoft reflector, or to flag an errant light source. Producers who venture into the field without tape and foil should be prepared for a long stay.

A substance once common in television production, but now out of favor, is **dulling spray**. Designed to reduce the intensity of reflections from chrome and glass, it was an accepted treatment when remote telecasts were a novelty and thus were tolerated at any expense. Today's typical interview subject, however, is likely to balk at the prospect of having the office sprayed in exchange for a 20-second appearance on the evening news when alternatives are available. The discerning video producer changes subject-camera blocking and lighting angles to reduce the reflections that find their way to the lens, thereby leaving no unpleasant dulling spray residue at the scene of the production.

Finally, **three-to-two-prong AC adapters** are of paramount importance when lighting in the field (see Figure 6–12). All professional lighting equipment comes equipped with the familiar three-pronged plug. However, many older homes and offices are still outfitted with two-pronged outlets. Safe operation of electronic equipment requires that all equipment be grounded properly. This is the function of the round third prong on three-prong plugs. Failure to properly ground electronic equipment may result in damage to the equipment and severe electrical shock to anyone who comes into contact with the equipment. *Under no circumstances should the ground pin be removed from a power cable to enable a three-pronged plug to be connected to a two-pronged outlet.*

The astute field producer always carries a number of these three-to-two-pronged adapters to ensure a fast and safe AC hookup. After connecting the adapter to the three-pronged plug on the power cable to your equipment, be sure to connect the small wire or clip on the adapter to the small center screw on the faceplate of the electrical outlet. If the outlet has been installed properly, connection of this ground wire or clip will effectively ground your equipment.

LIGHTING SAFETY

A few practical warnings are in order with respect to lighting safety. Caution is imperative when lighting on location. For this reason, it is usually best to delegate responsi-

Figure 6–12   Three-to-Two-Prong AC Adapter

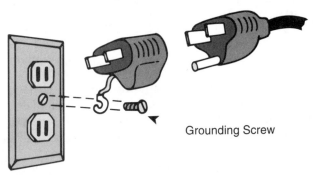

Grounding Screw

Caution: Always connect the ground wire to the screw in the center of the outlet faceplate.

bility for lighting supervision to one member of the crew who will see to it that safety requirements are met. Consider the following points when lighting on locations:

1. *Do not overload electrical circuits.* Always calculate the amount of power your lighting instruments draw, and compare that with the amount of power the electrical circuits deliver. At best, an overloaded circuit can result in a blown fuse or circuit breaker; at worst, the outcome is a fire.

2. *Make sure all electrical cables are properly grounded.* Always connect three-pronged plugs to grounded outlets. If you must use a three-to-two-pronged adapter, always connect the ground wire or clip on the adapter to the center screw on the faceplate of the electrical outlet.

3. *Keep fingers off tungsten-halogen lamps.* Finger oil on the quartz bulb may cause the lamp to explode. Always use a soft cloth or the piece of foam rubber supplied with the lamp to shield it from your skin if you have to touch the lamp (for example, when replacing a burnt-out lamp).

4. *Make sure lights are securely mounted.* If you are using floor stands, make sure that the telescoping rods are securely fastened. If possible, tape the floor stand down. Tape the electrical cord to the floor at the base of the floor stand; if someone accidentally pulls on the cord, the shock will be absorbed by the tape and the light might remain standing.

5. *Keep the face of the lighting instrument a safe distance away from any flammable surface.* Lights get extremely hot. Be careful when operating them near draperies or any other flammable material. Keep lights a good distance away from people, and after your shoot, make sure you do not touch the instrument until it has cooled down.

6. *Carry insulated electrician's gloves.* If you have to move a hot light in an emergency, insulated gloves will protect you from the instrument's heat.

Always observe the standard rules of electrical safety. Avoid water, tape exposed wires, tape all cable securely to floor or walls, and try to keep children and animals well away from electrical equipment.

PART TWO: AESTHETIC FACTORS

MODELING

Once the remote video producer recognizes the principles of illumination, the camera requirements, and the capacities of the lighting equipment, attention can be focused on the aesthetic factors. These make the picture effective in the context of the news being reported, the report being submitted, or the story being told. Chief among these aesthetic factors is creating an illusion of space and of three-dimensional subjects and objects on the two-dimensional piece of glass that is the television screen. The process of creating this illusion through lighting is called **modeling**.

Scenic painters and grade-school artists approach the problem of illustrating space in the same way: They simply invent objects and relationships that illustrate the idea. The remote video producer, however, must use real elements of the existing location to capture the illusion and bring it to the viewer's attention. Many techniques are available: the use of diminishing size, overlapping planes, changing focus, darkening colors, and diminishing brightness. In addition, the video artist can enhance the separation of objects by contrasting their apparent textures.

Remember, the viewer is not a static unfeeling being; the viewer wants to experience the dynamic qualities of the special location you are using. The successful producer, through manipulation of the elements in the picture, provides an unusual experience for the viewer. This is as true in the presentation of the workings of a hot air balloon factory as it is in the presentation of a can of soup.

Illumination

Much of the special feeling we can generate for familiar objects is related to the manner in which they are presented. For example, the pine cone is a common, undistinguished brown object found throughout the forest. Some may even believe it litters paths and, along with dead leaves and decomposing matter, contributes to the generally unkempt appearance of things. Remove this pine cone from the forest, place it in a gallery on a polished black marble pedestal in front of a soft ivory wall, illuminate it with a single shaft of light from above, and you will have produced art. By its presentation, the viewer can savor its eternal qualities and the genius of its design. So it can be with the presentation of people and objects via the video medium. Light can dominate our attention, describe form, and express mood.

Attention to the base illumination requirements of television has led to the observation (often true) that the picture appears flat and lifeless. Base illumination is half of the lighting problem, modeling is the other. **Base illumination** is light that is everywhere but that comes from no particular direction. Away from direct sunlight, nature creates this effect; with a collection of floodlights and receptors, we can achieve the same effect. Instruments are placed so that the same intensity of light reaches every object in the scene and shadows caused by one instrument are neutralized by light from another. The even brightness provides no clues to the relative placement, dimension, shapes, or surface textures of the objects.

By varying the illumination, attention can be invited to one object among many. Generally, the eye is attracted to the brightest object in the scene unless that impulse is countered through manipulation of focus or inclusion of an unusual silhouette (see Figure 6–13). Therefore, the human face is most often the brightest object in a scene.

Figure 6–13   Control of Attention: Brightness and Silhouette

Face   Silhouette

Directional Light

Careful control of relative brightness can enhance the visibility of objects, but it is not the whole solution to the problem. If placed properly, the addition of a **directional light** can give an object substance or solidity by emphasizing the facets that form the third dimension. The directional light does not automatically create the illusion. It must be placed so that the pattern of highlights and shadows it creates can be interpreted by viewers as representing the normal patterns they experience in real life.

The pattern of shadows created by the directional light depends on the hardness of the light (the extent to which it represents illumination radiating from a single point) and the relative positions of the subject, the light, and the camera. The illusion of depth is a function of the contours of the object, the camera positions, and this dominant light. Because of its importance, it is termed the **key light**. Remember, there is no standard position for this light: Its effectiveness is relative to the position of the camera and the desired effect (see Figure 6–14).

Camera Position

In contrast with theatrical motion picture production, video production is complicated by the use of several cameras or camera angles in a given scene or interview. To light the scene effectively from one camera angle is to weaken the effect from another angle. If time is not a factor and coverage is of continuing action—live action that can be restaged—television can use **film-style lighting**.

Figure 6–14 Three-Dimensional Image: Position of Key Light

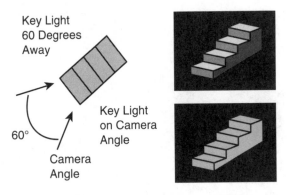

Key Light
60 Degrees
Away

60°

Key Light
on Camera
Angle

Camera
Angle

That means each scene is lit for each camera angle. In film-style lighting, the lighting setup is changed each time the camera position is changed, and lighting is done shot by shot. Film-style lighting gives the video producer a great deal of control over the lighting within a production. However, such attention to lighting detail has a price: time. Film-style lighting is a slow and meticulous process.

To get the most out of a given situation or location, the remote video producer determines where the camera is going to be placed before attempting to light the scene. If multiple angles are to be used, all camera positions must be determined before the lighting is set.

What factors determine camera position? First, the producer considers the reason for the choice of location. If that reason encompasses more than the location of a certain person, and includes interest in a specific activity or facility, the camera must be placed where that action or facility can be seen and understood by viewers. The atmosphere of the actual location should be communicated to the viewer. The remote video producer's task is to provide more than what is already common knowledge to the viewers, and more than what is possible in the studio.

Once the optimum angle or angles are chosen, an inventory of possible distractions should be made. Are there brightly illuminated windows in the background that could cause contrast range problems in the picture? Are there highly reflective glass or metallic surfaces that could ruin the picture? Next, are sufficient circuits available to power the instruments necessary to the videotaping? Is there enough room for the necessary lighting instruments? Will the instruments be too close to the subjects to maintain control of brightness? When these questions are answered satisfactorily, the production can proceed. The ENG producer has as little as five minutes to make these decisions; the EFP producer will visit the site prior to the production date to survey the location so these questions can be answered.

THREE-POINT LIGHTING

In theory, lighting to create the illusion of the third dimension involves three tasks: establishing the form (the key light), separating the object from its background (the back light), and reducing the intensity of the shadows created by the key light (the fill light or lights). This technique is known as *three-point lighting* (see Figure 6–15).

It is important to understand that these "three points" identify the functions of light that you will need to manipulate to produce the desired effect. Field production differs from studio production in that some light or combinations of sources of illumination already exist and are identifiable as part of that remote location. Field video production augments this existing illumination; illumination must be created in its entirety in studio production.

The augmentation of existing, or "location," light may address concerns with base illumination, modeling of subjects, apparent forms or textures of objects in the scene, the range of light-dark contrast in the scene, or a need to separate a subject from the background. Control of these functions of light can require the use of extra lighting instruments, reflectors, and diffusers. Such control may also involve staging action in a different direction relative to location light sources, such as waiting for clouds to move or the sun to progress a few degrees. Does all this seem complicated? It can be unless you scout the location well ahead of the scheduled shoot.

Key Light

The **key light** is the brightest, and therefore often the most important, light on a scene. The key light has the primary responsibility for establishing the form of the object being videotaped. It does this by providing bright illumination for the subject and by producing the shadows on the object. In many situations, it is the distribution of shadows on an object, rather than general illumination itself, that provides the most significant information about the object's form.

Figure 6–15   Three-Point Lighting

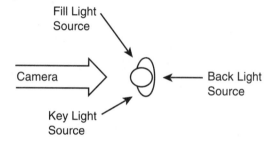

As a consequence of viewing television for some 40 years or so, the public has come to expect certain types of presentations. News or formal announcements are commonly delivered by a person facing the camera in a studio setting—in nowhere, so to speak. A medium shot or medium closeup is used. There is nothing of note concerning time or place. One announcement looks like any other, regardless of station or time of day. The key light conveys no expositional information and the subject is meant to appear absolutely normal, as if it was about 2:30 in the afternoon on a hazy day. To accomplish this, the key light is placed on a line from 30 to 45 degrees above the camera-subject axis, and from 30 to 45 degrees to the right or left of that axis (see Figure 6–16). A pattern of highlights and shadows created by the key light on the face of the subject that makes the subject appear normal is found somewhere within these angles (see Figure 6–17).

For many field production situations, this type of lighting may be all that is needed. If there is sufficient existing light for proper camera operation, and if the production features only one camera angle and one reporter in a city hall lobby, a single key light might provide enough modeling, brightness contrast, and sparkle to do the job.

If the scene is to be shot outside on the steps, the reporter should be placed so that the sun acts as the key light. If the steps are out of the direct sunshine, the key light might be in the form of a reflection from a nearby white wall or a portable reflector (aluminum or white) held outside the field of view of the camera. Remember to adjust the camera filter for daylight. If a lighting instrument is used in this situation, a gel may be necessary to maintain a constant color temperature by converting the color temperature of the instrument to the color temperature of daylight.

Figure 6–16 Typical Angle of Key Light

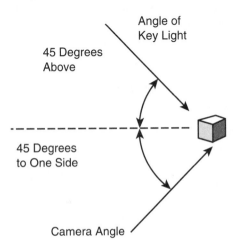

Figure 6–17 Effect of Key Light

Fill Light

Many scenes are more complex than this and involve the use of several lighting instruments. In a location that is too dark for video production, using only a key light might aggravate the situation by creating extreme contrasts between highlights and shadows. You may be tempted to use two bright lights, one on each side of the camera axis. This will illuminate the subject, but if the lights are of equal intensity, the effect of modeling will be neutralized completely.

The solution to the problem lies in the use of a fill light. **Fill lights** increase the overall light level on a scene, and fill in somewhat, but not completely, the shadows created on the subject by the key light (see Figure 6–18). Fill lights should be adjusted to produce from one-half to three-fourths of the intensity of the key light. Set the intensity of the fill light no lower than the base illumination level required for the camera. It may be higher if it is used in a portion of the scene that should be brighter than the rest for purposes of attracting attention.

Color television production is notorious for its use—and in many cases, overuse—of fill light. This situation evolved because of the problems many color cameras have in accurately reproducing colors in shadow areas. Rather than reproducing a shadow area simply as a darker shade of the same color in a lit area, quite often a color shift takes place in the shadow area. The shadow area on a face, for example, might reproduce as green or some other unsuitable color rather than simply as a darker shadowed area of skin.

To prevent such unsightly distractions, enormous amounts of fill light are often added to eliminate the shadow areas. Examples of this type of overfilling can

Figure 6–18   Effect of Fill Light

be seen in many television situation comedies. The characters and their environment are uniformly bright, shadowless, and flat.

Fortunately, the rapid improvement in light-gathering capacity of field cameras (represented by the CCD technology) reduced the need for so many picture-flattening fill lights. The subtle blending of skin tones from highlight to shadow is captured effectively by most cameras using only one soft light to augment natural illumination of the scene.

Whether the key light is provided by the sun or a lighting instrument, examine the quality of color reproduction in the shadow area to determine if fill light needs to be added by an additional light or through the use of a reflector.

Back Light

The **back light** has two functions: It acts to separate the subject from the background by outlining the subject's head and shoulders with a thin line of bright light and it supports the modeling effect (see Figure 6–19). The back light is extremely valuable in giving form to hair or clothing that would otherwise blend into the background. Because so little of it is reflected to the lens, the back light is maintained at an intensity level at least equal to that of the key light, and often brighter. It is placed behind and well above the subject. If it is placed too high, it will illuminate the subject's hair and nose out of proportion to the rest of the picture. If it is too low, its light on the subject will be lost to the camera. If it is even lower, it will radiate light directly into the lens and produce distracting lens flare, or it may even damage a pickup tube.

Figure 6–19   Effect of Back Light

The position of the back light presents a real challenge to the location lighting director. Since most portable lights are mounted on floor stands, a back light set up directly behind the subject may appear in the shot. If this proves to be too distracting, the light, subject, or camera will have to be repositioned to eliminate the offending stand from view. Two other solutions to the problem are also commonly used. The back light can be suspended above and behind the subject rather than mounted on a stand. This should put it out of the camera's field of view. (Make sure the light is fastened securely.) Another solution is to use **bounce light** as back light. Aim a lighting instrument at the ceiling or the wall behind the subject so that the light bounces off that surface onto the back of the subject. If the rear wall is used as the reflecting surface, make certain that it does not appear in the shot, as it will undoubtedly be too bright and will create a distraction.

Because of the problems of positioning the back light, it is not frequently used in field production. Technically, the separation of the subject from the background and modeling of the subject can be seen as being different problems. A well-placed back light can solve both problems simultaneously.

Three-Point Lighting: Ideal Versus Real

The ideal concept of three-point lighting is easily illustrated, but in reality the lighting setup may differ considerably from the ideal. Ultimately, the final decision about whether or not the lighting has been set correctly is a subjective one that should be made on the basis of how the scene looks on camera (or on a monitor), and not by whether or not the position and intensity of the various lights correspond to the ideal formula for three-point lighting (see Figure 6–20). The lighting relationships previously discussed, then, provide a point at which to begin lighting a scene rather than the point at which one must always end.

Motivated and Unmotivated Lights

Key lights, back lights, or both can be unmotivated (as in a neutral news set) or motivated. *Motivated lights* are related to a light source identified with the location of the remote videotaping, such as a window to the sunlit world, a streetlight, or the light from a blast furnace, welder, or nuclear reactor. The audience is conscious of its presence (assuming the producer lets them see the remote location in a long or establishing shot), and accepts the domination of the scene by that source via the key light or back light.

Table or desk lights solve the problem of identifying a motivating light. If the lamp has a translucent shade, or if the light from it strikes an object close by, it will violate the contrast range limits of the shot and create a major visual distraction. If the light is necessary to the scene, it is customary to place a 15-watt bulb in it for effect (and to reduce color temperature complications) and to apply directional lights from outside of the scene. Be careful to avoid casting a full shadow on the wall of the lamp that is supposed to appear to be illuminating the scene. In reality, table lamps seldom cast full shadows of themselves on nearby walls!

Figure 6–20   Effect of Key, Fill, and Back Lights

Lighting for Texture

In addition to controlling the brightness of the background relative to the subject, care must be taken to bring out any textures or architectural features that contrast with the subject. This makes the whole scene more interesting and adds to the visibility of the subject. Fill light alone usually does not make the actual textures apparent to the viewer.

Just as a directional light is needed to model a human face, a directional light is also needed to create a pattern of highlights and shadows that form a recognizable texture. The closer this directional light comes to paralleling the plane of the background, the more visible the shadows become (see Figure 6–21). Draperies, tile, brick, paneling, cork, and plaster all have recognizable textures that contrast effectively with the human face. This background element is important for identifying the spatial quality of the location, and should be featured.

The directional light used to reveal natural texture is most effective if it seems to come from an existing motivating element—commonly a lamp or window. A wall next to a window is often chosen to serve as a background for two reasons. First, the window is a troublesome background, because it is too bright and transmits a different color temperature. Also, the window functions as a mirror and reflects the production crew and the lights back at the camera. Second, the window on a side wall often provides the directional light necessary to present the background texture. Color temperature shifts on the wall caused by the light from the window will not be a problem as long as the audience does not know what color the wall was supposed to be, and as long as the subject is illuminated separately.

Background Shadows

When selecting the camera position, which influences the location of lighting instruments, the producer must be careful to provide as much space as possible between the subject and the background. The greater the space, the less likely the shadow of the subject will appear on the wall. In the minds and experience of the audience, such a shadow is unusual and calls attention to the facts of the produc-

Figure 6–21   Lighting for Texture

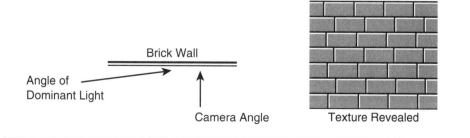

tion rather than to its purpose. Note also that the smaller the office or other remote location, the more difficult it is to control all the elements that may affect the picture quality. When each pictorial improvement brings distractions with it, it may be best to concentrate on the subject's face and to keep everything else gently out of focus. Lower than normal light levels facilitate this. In such a situation, the f-stop on the lens will have to be opened and, as a consequence, the depth of field will become more shallow.

Using Background Light to Indicate Time and Mood

Background light is probably the most important lighting variable that can be manipulated to influence the viewer's perception of the time of day or mood of a scene. **Background light** is different from back light; background light falls on the background of a scene, not on the subject.

Our everyday experience tells us that there is a big difference between day and night in terms of light. It's bright during the day and dark at night. If television cameras processed light as efficiently as the human eye, then creating the illusion of night would be relatively simple—we could simply turn off all the lights. Unfortunately, when this is done, the camera no longer produces a usable picture. A common mistake made by many beginning producers is to equate light with daytime and to equate no light with nighttime.

The key to creating the illusion of night lies in control of the background light. A scene set at night should have a fairly dark background, even if it takes place indoors. A scene taking place during the day should have a bright background. In both scenes, night and day, the foreground illumination should provide enough light to satisfy the minimum baselight requirements of the camera, although the night scene might be lit with a few more foreground shadows than the day scene.

Similarly, background light can be an effective determinant of mood. Bright backgrounds, typical of daytime, tend to be bright also in mood. Dark backgrounds, on the other hand, introduce significantly more contrast into a shot or scene and are somewhat more ominous and mysterious. Again, in both scenes the foreground lighting may remain constant from one situation to the next. It is the background light that determines if the scene is a bright, happy comedy or a deep, dark mystery or drama.

LIGHTING PROBLEMS

Multiple Subjects

Thus far, we have focused on the problem of lighting a single subject in a remote location. Illuminating a conversation between two subjects poses several problems. First, at least two camera angles may be used. Second, there may not be enough lights, circuits, or time to light each subject separately.

The producer will probably not place the camera perpendicular to the subject-to-subject axis because this results in all close-ups being profiles of each subject (the great American ear shot). Also, from this camera position, wider shots place the subjects at opposite ends of the screen, like bookends. This camera position unfortunately lacks the dynamic quality valued by producers (see Figure 6–22). The practice of placing the lighting instrument or instruments next to the camera makes the resulting picture even more bland. The faces will appear flat and featureless. Do not practice this technique.

A second method the remote video producer might follow is the common studio practice of facing the subjects at a 90-degree angle from each other. This allows close-ups of each face and provides a pleasing 2-shot. It also requires the use of three or four lights in addition to the fill, and is not particularly flexible insofar as placing the subjects in a special location is concerned. With this subject and camera blocking, two key lights are used—one for each subject—and each subject's face is illuminated toward the other. Neither person is hiding in the shadows during the conversation (see Figure 6–23).

Given the difficulty of controlling the radiation of unwanted light in the constricted space characteristic of many remote production sites, the use of spotlights with this *cross-keying* method does not produce the most attractive modeling. The illumination levels become too high to exercise the subtle shadings that produce a rich picture. Multiple softlights or reflectors, however, can produce an effective picture.

A third method has evolved that uses as few as two lights beyond the fill and background requirements, produces attractive modeling, and lends itself to the comparatively dynamic z-axis camera and subject blocking treatment. The **z-axis** is an imaginary line extending from the camera into the scene. The arrangement of people or objects in the scene at different points on the z-axis increases the sense of depth in a scene. In this method, the subjects face each other, and the key and back lights are combined, as each instrument serves two purposes. One light serves as a

---

Figure 6–22   Weak Composition and Flat Lighting

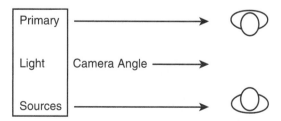

When the light source is parallel to the camera angle, minimal shadows are created, which "flattens" the contours of faces.

Figure 6–23   Lighting for Standard Composition

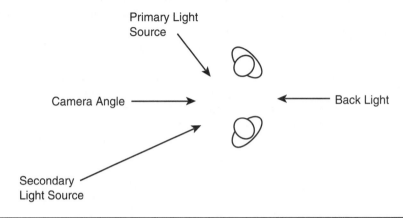

key for subject A and as a back light for subject B. The other light keys subject B and backs subject A. The camera can be placed for an over-the-shoulder shot in either direction as long as one light is on each side of the camera-subject axis (see Figure 6–24). This method generates a theatrical touch that fits the purpose of videotaping on location. The directional highlights seen on the subjects suggest motivated light of some sort and, in so doing, make the location seem more interesting. The subjects do not seem to be illuminated by the same hazy sky that illuminates so many other locations.

A soft light or large reflector can be substituted for one of the instruments with good results. The sun or other location light source can be used in place of one light and a soft light or large reflector can substitute for the other.

Figure 6–24   Lighting for Dynamic Composition

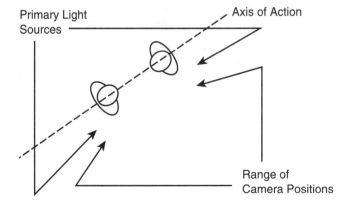

The action in the scene is arranged along the camera axis with this method. The foreground subjects appear larger and overlap each other, and the scene beyond them is reduced even further in size. The subjects can be seated on opposite sides of a desk or on the same side of a lathe. It is easy to include elements of the remote location with this blocking and lighting method.

Planning

Competence and speed in lighting for remote production develop through systematic practice in determining the dimensions of the problem, the application of basic principles, the capacities of the equipment and materials available, and the conscientious observation of the nature and quality of light produced in each setup. Classrooms offices, cafeterias, and service stations each provide opportunities to plan for remote video production. A purpose is established for each of these potential remote locations, and the producer identifies the opportunities and problems associated with each. Camera and subject **blocking diagrams** and tentative **lighting plots** should be prepared along with detailed equipment and materials lists (see Figure 6–25). This planning should precede the actual use of the equipment and will help you to use it more efficiently.

Once the equipment is in hand, the accuracy of the plan is tested. Detailed records of changes needed provide a base for discovering new techniques. Through a rigorous approach such as this, the producer learns that some effects can be achieved without the optimum equipment. Through comparison of the amended plan with the actual picture, as it appears in the video monitor, the producer learns to identify and solve production problems—and to turn production problems into eye-catching production opportunities.

Figure 6–25   Sample Light Plot and Blocking Diagram

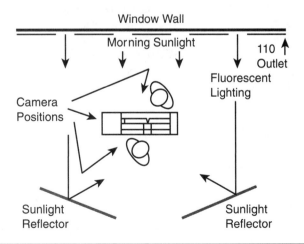

Table 6–2   Common Lighting Problems

Problem	Probable Cause	Solution
Dull colors; everything looks grayish, grainy, or noisy.	Not enough light; aperture not open wide enough.	Add light; open aperture.
Colors too bright; pictures have hot spots that are white and glowing.	Too much light; aperture open too wide.	Reduce light; use a scrim; flood out the light; close aperture.
Weird skin tones; people look blue, green, or other unusual colors.	Filter wheel incorrectly set; improper white balance.	Check filter wheel; reset white balance.
People and faces appear in silhouette and are darker than the background.	Too much light on the background. Is subject in front of window, sky, or a white wall?	Change the background; cover it up so it appears to be darker, or move.
Inaccurate colors in shadow areas.	Too much shadow.	Use fill light to reduce the density of the shadows.
A strange green line outlines brightly lit objects.	Too much contrast between lit and unlit areas.	Try to even out the lighting and reduce overall contrast.
Flare appears in viewfinder.	Backlight (or other light) is shooting directly into the camera lens, creating lens flare.	Use a lens hood; change the position of the offending light, or move the camera.
All the power goes out when you turn on lights.	Circuit is overloaded; circuit breaker has tripped.	Unplug something from the circuit and try again.
Glare from lights is being reflected directly into the camera by glass on pictures on the wall.	Angle of lights and reflective surface.	Change either the angle of the picture or the light, so that light is reflected away from camera.
Distracting shadows being cast on rear wall by actors or set pieces.	Angle of light; action too close to the wall.	Move actors and set pieces away from the wall; raise lights so shadows are thrown onto the floor, not walls.

Common Lighting Problems

Location lighting, perhaps more than any other part of television field production, gives the field producer the opportunity to become a creative problem solver. Those who enjoy the challenge flourish, and those who do not quickly turn to other pursuits.

The number of problems encountered while shooting on location are as varied as the locations themselves. However, a number of common lighting problems are often encountered by beginning producers. Table 6–2 lists 10 of these common problems, along with their probable causes and possible solutions.

SUMMARY

Good lighting is absolutely essential in television field production. Consumer-quality cameras are much less forgiving of variations in lighting than more expensive professional cameras. In addition to visualization and composition, lighting plays an important role in influencing the audience's perception of a shot or scene.

From a technical standpoint, a minimum baselight level of light is necessary to produce an acceptable image. A light meter is used to measure baselight in terms of the number of footcandles of incident light falling on the subject. As cameras have become more sophisticated, required baselight levels have fallen, and the most recent generation of portable cameras can operate efficiently in relatively low light. Nevertheless, attention must be paid to the contrast range of any scene, as most cameras will operate effectively only within a 30:1 ratio of light to dark.

Almost all portable cameras are color cameras. Color television works on the principles of additive primary colors rather than on the principles of subtractive color. Of major importance is the color temperature of white light. Since different light sources operate at different color temperatures, cameras need to be adjusted to each lighting situation by adjusting the white balance of the camera. The color temperature of different light sources can be changed by using gels.

The basic lighting instruments used by many television field producers include spotlights—which produce a narrow beam of hard, focused light—and floodlights and soft lights—which produce a wider beam of unfocused light. Portable lighting instruments most frequently use tungsten-halogen lamps, sometimes called quartz lights, that burn at a constant color temperature of 3,200 degrees kelvin, the color television standard. Spotlights may produce a fixed beam of light or a more versatile variable beam. Light quality tends to be hard for spotlights and softer for floodlights. The softest light of all is produced by instruments called soft lights, which are widely used in field production.

Lights may be supported by floor stands, mounted on the camera itself, or hand held. Portable lights use a considerable amount of power. Power consumption can be calculated by using the formula: watts = amps × volts.

Light intensity can be adjusted with dimmers, by varying the beam width of a spotlight, by changing the lamp-to-subject distance, and by the use of screens or diffusers. Barn doors, flags, silks, and reflectors can also be used to control the quality and direction of light falling on a scene.

Other useful equipment for lighting includes duct tape, aluminum foil, dulling spray, and three-to-two-prong AC adapters. When shooting in the field, avoid accidents and injury by always paying attention to the rules of lighting safety.

Lighting is an art as well as a craft. A principal component of lighting aesthetics is modeling, the illusion of three dimensionality created through lighting. Modeling is affected by illumination, directional light, and the position of the camera in relation to the subject and light source. In film-style lighting, the lighting setup is changed each time the camera position is changed.

Three-point lighting is a classic lighting technique that can be reduced to three well-placed sources of illumination that provide control of form, contrast range, and separation of picture elements. Three-point lighting is an ideal that presents a point from which to begin lighting a scene rather than a point at which one must always end. Other factors to consider when lighting include motivated and unmotivated lights, lighting for texture, background shadows, and the use of background light to indicate time and mood. Thorough planning can eliminate many common lighting problems.

7

Sound

PART ONE:
TECHNICAL FACTORS

There is a tendency to concentrate almost exclusively on the picture portion of the message when talking about television and video production. Indeed, the words *television* and *video* are both derived from the Latin word *videre* (to see). Yet, television is an audiovisual medium—one in which both picture and sound are important.

Unfortunately, television sound has for many years been the weakest part of television. The poor quality of television sound is the result of the way in which television has been produced and the way in which the sound is reproduced at the point of reception—the home television receiver.

Multiple-camera television studio production, particularly dramatic production, requires that microphones be invisible to the viewer. As a result, they are away from the performers (the source of sound). This reduces the quality of voice pickup and results in the pickup of ambient studio noise—air conditioners, camera noise, and the movement of equipment and people in the studio.

At the point of reception, the limited fidelity of television sound is often masked by the poor quality of the speakers found in most television sets. Although we have become accustomed to high-quality sound reproduction in our home stereo systems and FM radios, the quality of television sound is still extremely poor by comparison. Not only does television sound lack the fidelity of these other systems but it is often monaural rather than stereo.

Despite these problems, a number of improvements have been made in television sound and more are coming. The use of stereophonic sound in television broadcasts has been steadily increasing since its introduction in the United States in 1984. Many television receivers are now capable of reproducing stereo sound on their own high-quality speakers. Some televisions feature audio outputs that allow the sound signals to be routed through a home stereo system. The development of HDTV carries with it not only the promise of improved picture resolution but the delivery of CD (compact disc) quality digital sound.

Ironically, many of these improvements in broadcast television sound have been available for years to field producers working with portable video recording systems. Many VCRs are now available with a high-fidelity sound option that dramatically improves the quality of the sound they can record and play back. In addition, most VCRs now contain two audio channels, making them capable of recording and reproducing stereophonic sound.

The technique of single-camera video field production frequently allows much more precise positioning of microphones than multiple-camera studio production. Furthermore, use of natural location sound adds a realistic dimension to field productions that studio productions consistently lack.

SOUND IN VIDEO FIELD PRODUCTION

In general, video field producers are concerned with sound in three different situations: location recording, adding sound to prerecorded videotape, and sound manipulation during postproduction editing. In all three applications of sound production, the video producer must have a clear understanding of the nature of sound, the capabilities and limitations of the equipment used to record it, and the impact of the manipulation of sound on the audience's perceptions.

Necessity for Clear Sound

Since the sound portion of a program carries a significant amount of information, at a very simple level of operation there is a necessity for all programs to have good, clear clean sound. We can define **sound** as any aural component of a program that is intentionally present. **Noise**, on the other hand, interferes with sound—it obscures it and makes it more difficult to understand. In many cases, noise is an unintentional element that has been introduced into the program.

In many ways, recording sound for television is similar to lighting for television. Just as it is fairly easy to make an image visible to the camera, so it is easy to record sound. However, there is quite a difference between simply recording *any* sound and recording *effective* sound. Indeed, the art of recording and manipulating sound for television may be compared to playing the guitar. It is one of the easiest things to do poorly and one of the hardest things to do well.

SOUND: TECHNICAL BASES

Sound can be thought of simply as a pattern in the vibration or movement of molecules of air. When a sound is made, air is moved in waves (thus the term *sound waves*). Although the propagation of sound waves is a complicated phenomenon, we will discuss only two characteristics of sound waves: amplitude (intensity) and frequency (pitch). For our purposes, these two characteristics of sound are the most important.

Sound Intensity

Differences in the loudness, or **intensity**, of the sound can be seen as differences in the **amplitude**, or height, of the sound wave (see Figure 7–1). Loudness is measured in **decibels (db)**. Decibels are the standard unit, or ratio, of measure used in all audio equipment to gauge the relative intensity of sound.

The decibel scale is a logarithmic scale. This means that a sound that is 3 db greater than another is twice the intensity of the first sound. In reality, a 3 db change in intensity is very difficult to perceive, and a sound may have to increase in intensity as much as 6 db before we perceive it to be twice as loud as the previous sound.

The human ear responds to a great range of sound intensities, from 0 db (the threshold of hearing), to 120 db (the threshold of pain). Sounds louder than 120db can be heard but they may cause pain and/or deafness.

Sound Frequency or Pitch

The other important characteristic of sound is its pitch. **Pitch** refers to the way in which some sounds are higher or lower than others. For example, women's voices are usually higher in pitch than men's voices. (Remember, this is not a difference in loudness, although such a difference might also exist. Rather, it is a difference in the quality of the sound.)

Differences in pitch are visible in sound waves as differences in the frequency of the waves. **Frequency** refers to how often the wave repeats itself in a given period of time (see Figure 7–2). Each complete pattern of the wave—from

Figure 7–1   Differences in Amplitude of Two Sound Waves

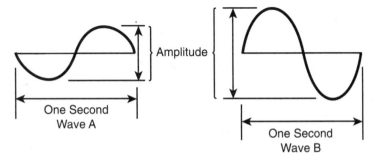

Wave A and Wave B have the same frequency—one cycle per second. The amplitude and intensity of B is greater than A.

Figure 7–2   Differences in Frequency of Two Sound Waves

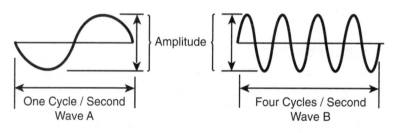

one peak to the next—is called a cycle. When we talk about the frequency of different sounds, we use a standard unit of measure: **cycles per second (cps)**. These are sometimes called **hertz (Hz)** in honor of the German scientist Heinrich Hertz, whose influential work on electromagnetic wave theory in the late 1800s led to the invention of radio.

Humans can hear a range of frequencies that extends from a low of about 20 cycles per second up to a high of about 16,000 cycles per second. A 20 cps sound is extremely deep and bassy; a 16,000 cps sound is extremely high.

Not only are the concepts of sound intensity and frequency important in the theoretical sense but they are also important because they have practical applications in almost all areas of sound production. **Volume unit (VU) meters**, for example, are calibrated in decibels and are used in audio production to determine the relative strength of the audio signal. Different microphones vary from one another with respect to their frequency response. Some microphones are more sensitive to certain frequencies of sound than others. The frequency response of a microphone, then, becomes an important variable to consider when attempting to decide which microphone to use in a particular recording situation.

Audio-Level Meters

A VU meter contains a scale that is a standard calibration of signal strength used in all broadcast and nonbroadcast media facilities. The scale is calibrated in decibels, and ranges from a low of –20 db to a maximum of +3 db. Ordinarily, the –20 db to 0 db range of the scale is represented in black, and the 0 db to +3 db range is presented in red. Sometimes the scale also contains a percent scale, with –20 db representing 0 percent and 0 db representing 100 percent. A small needle indicates how high or low the signal is.

Two types of VU meters are used: analog VU meters, such as the one shown in Figure 7–3, and LED (light emitting diode) VU meters in which the moving needle is replaced with a series of small lights (diodes) that correspond to the various points on the VU scale.

Another type of meter sometimes found on audio equipment is the **peak program meter (PPM)**. Peak program meters are somewhat more accurate than

Figure 7–3   Analog VU Meters

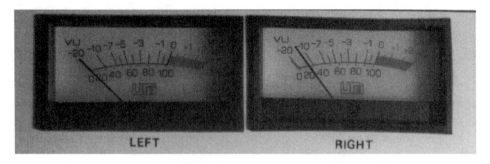

LEFT   RIGHT

VU meters in terms of responding to rapid changes in the peak level of an audio signal, but they tend to be used more widely on studio equipment rather than on equipment designed for portable use in the field.

MICROPHONE CHARACTERISTICS

Location sound is picked up and channeled into the video recording system with a microphone. A **microphone** is a transducer, just as a CCD is a transducer. However, the function of the CCD is to change light into electrical energy, whereas the function of the microphone is to change sound into electrical energy.

Sound is often difficult to control in the field because the real environment is unpredictable. Jet planes fly overhead, train whistles blow in the distance, wind and clothing rub against microphones, and so on. The world is not silent, and the microphone does not discriminate between wanted sound and unwanted noise as it picks up sound on your location shoot. Therefore, one of the most important elements that can be controlled to ensure a good recording of field sound is the microphone. The choice of a particular microphone and its placement depends on the particulars of the recording situation. Several characteristics of microphones should be considered before deciding which microphone to use.

Microphone Pickup Patterns

The **pickup pattern** of a microphone refers to the directions in which it is sensitive to incoming sound (see Figure 7–4). Microphone pickup patterns are important to understand and use in production because microphones, unlike the human ear, are not selective about what they hear. They respond to all incoming sound; they cannot distinguish between important sound and unimportant sound. If you are standing in the middle of a large group of people who are all talking, and you are

Figure 7–4   Microphone Pickup Patterns

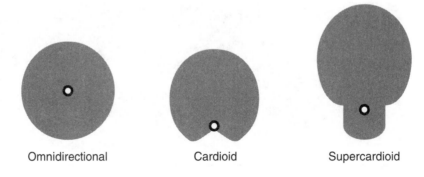

| Omnidirectional | Cardioid | Supercardioid |

particularly interested in hearing the conversation of only a few people, you could listen selectively to them and mentally block out all the other conversations. We practice this type of selective perception all the time. Place a microphone in the middle of a crowd, however, and no such selective perception is possible, unless the pattern of sound picked up by the microphone is controlled. If the microphone is sensitive to sound coming in from certain directions, and insensitive to sound coming in from other directions, then a kind of selective pickup can be achieved.

Microphones that are sensitive in all directions are called **omnidirectional** microphones. Some microphones are sensitive in the front and back but not on the sides. These are **bidirectional** microphones. Other microphones have a heart-shaped pickup pattern. They are extremely sensitive out front but somewhat less sensitive to the sides and rear. These are **cardioid** pickup patterns. **Supercardioid** microphones exaggerate the sensitivity in front. They are very directional and generally are most sensitive to sounds in a very narrow angle in front of the microphone. Because these microphones are often extremely long and narrow, they are referred to as **shotgun microphones**.

Omnidirectional, cardioid, and supercardioid microphones are the kinds most often used in video field production. Omnidirectional microphones are useful if sound needs to be picked up from a wide area or if one microphone is needed to pick up sound from several people. Cardioid and supercardioid microphones are useful if more selectivity in the pattern of sound pickup is desired. For example, if you want to isolate sound pickup to a narrow area—one person in a group, for instance—a microphone with a narrow pickup pattern would be used.

Microphone Types

In addition to differences in pickup patterns, microphones also differ with respect to the way they are constructed. Microphones work by sensing changes in the sound waves created by the sound source. Within each microphone is a diaphragm that is sensitive to these changes in sound intensity and quality. The diaphragm converts the sound waves into an electrical audio signal. Not all micro-phones use the same type of mechanism to change sound into electrical energy. These differences in the microphone mechanisms provide one of the principal ways to distinguish microphone types.

The two most popular microphone types found in video field production are dynamic microphones and condenser microphones (see Figure 7–5). The **dynamic microphone** contains a diaphragm that is attached to a coil of wire wrapped around a magnet. When the diaphragm moves, so does the coil, and this causes a change in the magnetic field within the microphone. This is the audio signal.

Dynamic microphones are extremely rugged and may be the most widely used microphones in television production. They are relatively inexpensive (for professional-quality microphones) and usually have good frequency response. However, they tend to be somewhat less sensitive to high-frequency sounds than condenser microphones.

Condenser microphones require either AC or battery power to operate. They use an electric capacitor, or condenser, to generate the signal. This consists of a moving faceplate at the front of the microphone and a backplate in a fixed posi-tion behind it. Both plates are electrically charged, and sound hitting the faceplate causes a change in voltage.

Figure 7–5   Microphone Construction

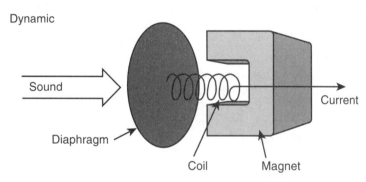

Dynamic

Sound

Diaphragm

Coil

Magnet

Current

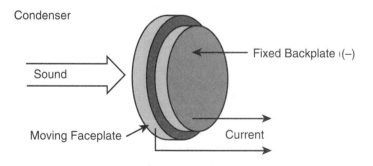

Condenser

Sound

Moving Faceplate

Fixed Backplate (–)

Current

Electret condensers are a popular type of condenser microphone. They differ in construction from conventional condenser microphones. Electrets are manufactured with a permanent electric charge in the capacitor, and therefore only require the use of a very small battery as a power source to boost the output signal of the microphone to a usable level. As a result, electret condensers tend to be significantly smaller than other condenser microphones. They are frequently used as built-in microphones on portable cameras and in other situations requiring a small, inconspicuous microphone. Some electret condensers operate from phantom power. Power is supplied to the microphone via the microphone cable from an audio mixer or other power supply unit. This eliminates the need to check and replace microphone batteries since no microphone batteries are used in these systems.

Professional-quality condensers and electret condensers are widely used in broadcast television production. Many dramatic productions use very high-quality shotgun condenser microphones for sound pickup. Electret condensers are often used as clip-on microphones. Because of their small size, they are very unobtrusive.

Condenser microphones have several advantages. They are highly sensitive, particularly to high-frequency sounds. In addition, they can be made extremely small. On the negative side, they are often very expensive, fragile, and need a power source. If the particular condenser microphone you are using needs an AC power supply rather than battery power, it most certainly will cause problems in remote productions.

Another type of professional microphone is the **ribbon microphone** (sometimes called *velocity microphone*). However, due to the physical construction of these microphones—they contain a thin ribbon of metal foil between the two sides of a magnet—they are extremely large and bulky. Designed originally for radio—where they are still extensively used because of their excellent voice pickup—they are very seldom used in television field production because of their size and extreme fragility.

Finally, the least expensive and poorest-quality microphones use crystal or carbon elements to generate the audio signal. Designed primarily for voice pickup (carbon microphones are commonly used in telephones), neither of these microphones provide the high-quality sound that professional production demands.

Frequency Response

The way in which the microphone is constructed is important to the field producer because it determines how the microphone will perform. The **frequency response** of the microphone refers to its ability to accurately reproduce a wide range of frequencies. No microphone is capable of capturing the full spectrum of frequencies from 16 Hz to 16,000 Hz. However, professional-quality microphones are generally able to pick up a wider range of frequencies than inexpensive microphones. This wider frequency response extends both down to lower frequencies and up to higher frequencies. An inexpensive microphone may well pick up middle-range frequencies but exclude the highs and the lows. In addition, many microphones are designed with specific uses in mind. A microphone designed for voice pickup will not have the high-frequency response that characterizes microphones designed for music pickup.

Specifications for microphone frequency response are provided by the manufacturer along with the microphone. Correct microphone usage and selection depends on matching the proper microphone—in terms of its frequency response—to your particular recording situation.

It is important to note that the frequency response of a microphone also depends on correct placement of the microphone. Reflected sound—sound that bounces off one or more room surfaces—sounds different to the microphone than sound picked up directly from the sound source. The distance of the microphone from the sound source also affects frequency response: The farther away it is placed, the poorer the sound pickup quality. In addition, the direction from which the incoming sound is coming must match the microphone's pickup pattern to maximize frequency response. For example, a microphone with a very directional supercardioid pickup pattern responds better to high-frequency sounds hitting the sensitive front of the pickup pattern than similar sounds coming from the side or rear of the microphone.

Microphone Impedance

Finally, the field producer must consider the impedance level of the microphone. **Impedance (Z)** is a measure of the amount of resistance to electrical energy in a circuit. Impedance is measured in **ohms** (Ω), and two impedance categories are commonly found in audio equipment. **Low impedance**, also called **low Z**, refers to equipment rated at an impedance of 600 ohms or below. **High impedance**, or **high Z**, is rated above 600 ohms.

All professional-quality microphones are low impedance and are usually rated at 150 ohms. Similarly, most VCR audio inputs on small format VCRs are low impedance inputs. However, some microphones (usually inexpensive crystal microphones) are high impedance, and some VCRs and other audio components have high impedance inputs or outputs. The rule of thumb is simply to match the impedance levels of the audio sources that you are connecting. Low impedance sources connect to low impedance inputs, and high impedance sources connect to high impedance inputs.

The principal advantage to using low impedance microphones and other sources is that the audio signal can be sent over several hundred feet of cable with very little loss in signal quality. High impedance lines, on the other hand, tend to noticeably affect signal quality if cable lengths exceed 25 feet or so.

USE OF CAMERA-MOUNTED MICROPHONES

The **camera microphone** is a standard feature of many portable video cameras and camcorders. In inexpensive consumer cameras, the microphone is commonly built into the camera. In industrial and professional-quality cameras, the microphone generally is attached to the camera but can be removed. In all these systems, the camera microphone can be used to record the audio simultaneously with the recording of the picture. Indeed, this is one of the great advantages of videotape over film—not only are picture and sound recorded simultaneously but they can be played back as soon as the recording has been completed. In addition, no special cables are needed to route the audio signal into the VCR. In portable systems with separate camera and VCR, the signal from the camera microphone is usually carried to the VCR through one of the wires inside the camera cable.

Built-In Microphones

Built-in camera microphones are most often electret condensers by construction. They are often located on the front of the camera body above the lens. On consumer-quality camcorders, they are sometimes located at the front of the camcorder's pistol grip.

Attachable Microphones

Professional-quality cameras frequently contain a mount into which a microphone may be inserted. If no mount exists, gaffer's tape may be used to attach a microphone to the camera. Typically the rear of the camera is equipped with an XLR (Cannon) input, thus making it possible to connect any professional-quality microphone to the system's audio input through the camera (see Figure 7–6).

Obviously, cameras that can accommodate a professional-quality attachable microphone allow for better sound recording than those equipped with a fixed position, built-in microphone. Good sound pickup depends on the use of the correct type of microphone. Since microphones vary with respect to sensitivity and pickup pattern, a microphone suitable for use in one situation may be the wrong one to use in another situation. The use of attachable microphones gives the videographer flexibility that does not exist in cameras with built-in microphones.

Advantages and Disadvantages of Camera Microphones

The most significant advantage to the use of camera-mounted microphones is in the convenience they provide. They are particularly useful if only one person is operating the field production system (camcorder or separate camera and VCR). No special provisions need be made for recording audio. You simply point the camera and shoot, and the camera microphone picks up the sound from the direction in which it is pointed, subject to its sensitivity, frequency response, and pickup pattern.

A camera-mounted microphone is very convenient to use but presents some significant disadvantages. The most important disadvantage lies in the distance of the microphone from the principal sound source. Unless the camera is precisely at the sound source, the microphone will be a considerable distance away from the

Figure 7–6 (A) Audio Inputs on a Professional Camcorder, (B) Camcorder with Shotgun Microphone Attached

(A)

Four XLR connectors are used to connect audio inputs and outputs to this professional quality M-II camcorder.

(B)

sound. Since the quality of a recording usually demands that the microphone be close to the principal sound source, this is a significant problem.

The second principal disadvantage to using a camera-mounted microphone lies in the fact that sound sources close to the microphone tend to be the prominent ones in the recording. Unfortunately, the sound sources closest to the camera are seldom what one wants to record: The sounds of the electrical motors that drive the zoom lens and lens focus mechanisms, breathing or talking by the camera operator, and other ambient noise close to the camera microphone will all achieve prominence in the recording. Unfortunately, close sounds tend to be louder than sounds farther away. Since the microphone has no way of knowing what is intentional sound and what is noise, all sound is recorded as it is received. Although the problem of intrusive proximate noise can be reduced somewhat by using a shotgun microphone on the camera instead of an omnidirectional one, it cannot be eliminated. Camera-mounted microphones usually provide recordings with inferior sound quality and levels than those produced with properly placed and selected external microphones.

Camera-mounted microphones can be used advantageously if all one wants to pick up is general, rather than selective, sound from a location. A camera-mounted microphone will effectively pick up the sounds of a cheering crowd as the camera pans the grandstands, or the noise of traffic on the freeway as cars and trucks whiz by the camera. If, however, you want to isolate sound pickup to a particular person in the crowd or if you want to selectively pick up the voice of the on-camera reporter who is standing on the freeway overpass, then microphone choice and placement must be more selectively controlled.

USE OF EXTERNAL MICROPHONES

External microphones are any microphones that are not built into or mounted onto the field camera. Once the field producer decides which type of microphone is best suited to the field recording situation at hand, a decision needs to be made about where to position the microphone and how to place it in that position. Microphones can be hand held, pinned onto the performer's clothes, hidden on the set, supported on booms off camera, hung from the ceiling, or attached directly to the object making the sound. Field producers use all these techniques and others.

Hand-Held Microphones

Hand-held microphones are commonly used in ENG-type productions, particularly when an on-camera newscaster conducts an interview and only one microphone is available. Hand-held microphones are usually dynamic microphones with a barrel that is relatively insensitive to sound. This does not mean that it is totally immune to picking up barrel noise—no microphone is. (If you tap your fingers along the barrel, it most certainly will pick up this sound.) However, in comparison with other microphone types, the hand-held microphone is relatively insensitive along the barrel and therefore is widely used (see Figure 7–7).

When using a hand-held microphone, it is important to remember that the person who holds the microphone controls the quality of the sound pickup. The on-camera interviewer must remember to speak into the microphone when asking a question and to move it when the respondent answers. Failure to position the microphone correctly reduces the quality of the sound pickup.

The cardinal rule to follow when using a hand-held microphone is to never relinquish control of the microphone to the person you are interviewing. Some interviewees instinctively grab the microphone when it is their turn to talk. Control of the interview, and the microphone, should be maintained by the on-camera interviewer.

Lavaliere Microphones

Lavaliere microphones are very small microphones that are pinned onto the clothing of the person who is speaking. The literal definition of *lavaliere* is a pendant worn on a chain around the neck, and some lavaliere microphones are actually hung around the subject's neck with a string. However, most current models have a small clip that pins the microphone onto the subject's clothing (see Figure 7–8).

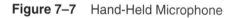

Figure 7–7 Hand-Held Microphone

Figure 7–8   Lavaliere Microphone

Most lavalieres are either electret condensers or dynamic microphones. The electret condensers are the smaller of the two varieties and are widely used in field (and studio) production. The dynamic microphones are slightly larger but considerably more durable.

When using a lavaliere, try to position the microphone close to the subject's mouth. Quite often, they are pinned onto a jacket lapel or shirt collar. However, be careful when positioning the microphone to avoid placing it where the subject's clothing or jewelry may rub against it and create distracting noises.

When using a condenser lavaliere, be careful not to place it too close to the subject's mouth. Condensers are extremely sensitive and if the sound source is too loud (which often happens if it is too close to the microphone), it may distort the audio signal. This is known as **input overload distortion**.

If you are using a battery-powered electret condenser, remember also to check the battery before you begin recording. Make sure that it is correctly placed inside the microphone's battery compartment. If the positive and negative poles of the battery are not correctly seated in the compartment, the microphone will not work. Always carry a spare battery or two in case one of the microphone batteries gives up the ghost during your production.

Surface-Mount Microphones

Although several manufacturers have developed boundary effect microphones of one design or another during the past two decades, the success of one is such that the trade name now identifies the microphone type. That name is Crown International's **PZM (pressure zone microphone)**.

These microphones are designed to be placed on the hard surface of a wall, desktop, or floor where, in theory, the sound waves are not disturbed by reflections from other nearby surfaces. Multiple reflections of sound waves can act to change the volume and frequency of those waves. Reduction of this source of audio distortion results in comparatively clean processing of the human voice.

The pickup pattern of this microphone type is hemispherical. When mounted on the floor, it is often placed at a distance from a speaker equal to his or her height. For musical or theater groups, the microphone can be used effectively at a distance equal to the width of the group.

PZM-type microphones are used in confined spaces with excellent results. If such a space does not have a hard surface onto which to mount the microphone, it can be mounted on a flat piece of rigid plastic that is placed in the scene outside of camera range. Scenes in automobiles, aircraft cabins, canopied beds, or the like can be recorded in this manner.

The PZM microphone also delivers better sound in city exteriors than can be obtained with the traditional omni-on-a-pole method. If the program type or camera usage is such that the PZM will not be in the scene or not matter if it is, it is the best choice. If camera work or dramatic illusion cannot be compromised in order to use a PZM, wireless microphones or fishpoles provide the best alternatives.

Shotgun Microphones

Shotgun microphones are widely used in remote production (see Figure 7–9). Since they have a very directional pickup pattern, they are often held off camera and aimed at the principal sound source. Thus, they do not intrude into the picture but they provide sound pickup on a precise spot. They can be used to isolate sound pickup to one or two people in a crowd or to a particular location where activity is taking place.

Most shotgun microphones are extremely sensitive to barrel noise. For this reason, some have **pistol grips** attached to the microphone, which are used when it is hand held. When shotguns are attached to microphone booms, **shock mounts** are often used to insulate the microphone from the noise of the boom, and a **wind screen** is almost always needed when shooting outdoors.

Contact Microphones

Contact microphones are microphones that attach directly to an object. For example, say you want to clearly pick up the sound of roller skates or snow skis during an action sequence that is out of the range of a shotgun microphone. You can

Figure 7–9   Shotgun Microphone with Windscreen

attach a microphone (perhaps a small condenser lavaliere) directly to the skate or ski. This will give very good pickup of the sound, even when the action takes place at a considerable distance from the camera.

Hanging Microphones

Hanging microphones are sometimes used indoors in remote production. These microphones are hung directly over the area where the action will take place or hung slightly in front of the action area and then aimed at it. In either case, by hanging the microphone you can usually get it out of the field of view of the camera. However, sound pickup usually suffers because the microphones tend to pick up a lot of the ambient background noise on the location.

Microphone Stands and Mounting Devices

Various types of stands and mounting devices are used to support microphones (see Figure 7–10). Stands have the advantage of holding a microphone securely in a fixed position. They also insulate the microphone from noise on the surface where it is positioned. **Desk stands**, for example, are small stands used to hold microphones on a desk or table in front of the person or persons who will speak.

One microphone on a desk stand can be positioned to pick up the sound from two or more people. **Floor stands** are taller stands that telescope upwards. They consist of a base, which supports the stand, and a telescoping rod, which allows the microphone height to be adjusted for correct sound pickup. Microphones on floor stands are frequently used to pick up sound from musical instruments and from people standing up to speak.

Fishpoles are extremely popular in field production. A fishpole is a metal rod that extends to allow placement of the microphone close to the sound source. It has many of the advantages of a hand-held microphone but it is insulated from barrel noise and allows the person holding it to remain off camera and move with the person who is talking.

A **boom**, a three-legged contraption that sometimes comes equipped with wheels and a telescoping boom rod, allows the microphone to be aimed, extended, and retracted. Booms are primarily used in dramatic production, where the movement of the actors is tightly controlled and limited to a relatively small action area.

Most field production situations use a variety of microphones and microphone supports. At a recent televised university gymnastics meet, we noticed the following kinds of microphones in use by the remote television production crew: Sportscasters used hand-held omnidirectional microphones to conduct interviews with gymnasts; shotgun microphones were taped onto each portable field camera to provide background sound pickup for each camera shot; contact microphones were taped to the floor at intervals along the runway the contestants used when they sprinted toward the vault; a shotgun microphone on a floor stand was aimed at the vault to pick up the sound of contestants hitting it; and shotgun micro-

Figure 7–10 Microphone Stands

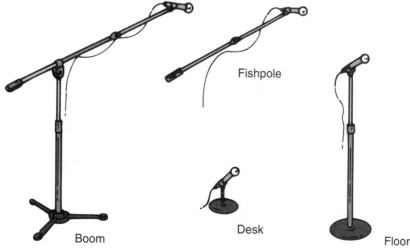

Fishpole

Boom

Desk

Floor

phones on floor stands were aimed at the parallel bars and balance beam to pro-vide precise sound pickup in each of these action areas (see Figure 7–11).

WIRED AND WIRELESS MICROPHONES

By this point, you are probably wondering how the signal gets from the micro-phone to the VCR. Two types of systems are used: wired and wireless micro-phones. By far, the most common method of transmitting the signal is through an audio cable. Microphones that are connected by cable are called **wired micro-phones**.

Wired Microphones

Wired microphones are widely used in field recording because of their ease of operation and reliability. After connecting a cable to the microphone and the appropriate audio input on the VCR, you can begin recording.

Although this type of recording arrangement works well in most situations, the presence of the microphone cable sometimes causes problems. If the subject moves around a lot or is at a great distance from the VCR, or if the presence of microphone cables will spoil the appearance of the event, you should use another method of transmitting the signal from the microphone to the VCR.

Figure 7–11   Using a Variety of Microphones

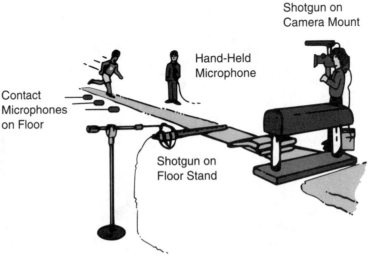

Wireless Microphones

Wireless microphones—also called radio microphones—eliminate many of the problems associated with the use of microphone cables; therefore, they are extremely popular in field production. A wireless microphone sends its signal to a receiver via RF (radio frequency) transmission rather than through a cable. That is, it actually broadcasts the audio signal to the receiving station and thereby eliminates the need to use long cables to connect these two points. Wireless microphones contain three components: the microphone itself, a small transmitter attached to the microphone that transmits the signal, and a small receiver that receives the transmitted signal. The output of the receiver is then connected by cable to the appropriate audio input on the VCR (see Figure 7–12).

Many types of microphones—hand held, lavaliere, and shotgun—can be obtained in a wireless configuration. Most wireless systems designed for field use are battery powered, with both the transmitter and receiver operating off battery power. However, in some systems the transmitter may be battery powered while the receiver is powered by AC.

Figure 7–12   Wireless Microphone System (Panasonic WX-PR 410/RP700) (Left) Transmitter and Microphone, (Right) Receiver

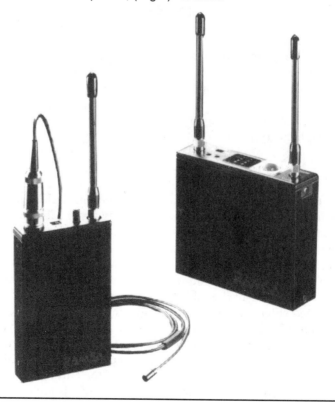

Wireless microphones have several great advantages. They do not restrict the movement of the sound source, the microphone remains in the same relationship to the sound source even if the sound source moves, and there are no obtrusive cables to be seen. A wireless lavaliere microphone attached to a referee in a football game is always less than 12 inches from the referee's mouth, no matter where the referee is on the field. This ensures better sound pickup than a shotgun microphone on the sidelines aimed at the same official. No matter how the official moves or turns, the wireless lavaliere is always there to pick up the sound. In addition, since no cable is used, there is no chance of interfering with the movement of the players during the game.

Wireless microphones do present some problems, however. Since they demand power, either adequate AC or battery power must be available. More than one production has been ruined by failing batteries late in the day.

Although the transmitting part of the wireless unit is small, it nonetheless must be carried by and concealed on the sound source. Depending on how the subject is dressed, this may present problems. If you plan to use a wireless microphone for sound pickup as you videotape a wedding, you may find that the transmitter and microphone can be easily concealed on the groom, whose jacket offers a good hiding place. But the bride's dress may not offer a suitable place to hide the equipment.

Since wireless microphones are actually small radio transmitters and receivers, they are susceptible to interference from other radio sources such as police radios, CB radios, and so on. It is very distracting, to say the least, if the transmission of the wedding vows is interrupted by a radio message from the local police dispatcher announcing a burglary in the neighborhood.

The final and perhaps greatest disadvantage of wireless microphones for most producers is that they can be expensive. A professional-quality wired lavaliere microphone can be bought for around $100; a serviceable wireless system (microphone, transmitter, and receiver) can easily cost 5 to 10 times as much.

Balanced and Unbalanced Lines

Whether your microphone system is wired or wireless, at some point it will be connected to the VCR with a cable. Two types of cables, or lines, are commonly used to carry the audio signal to the VCR. Professional, high-quality systems utilize cables that are called balanced lines. A **balanced line** is a cable that contains three wires. Two wires carry the signal, and the third acts as a shield to protect the other two from outside interference. **Unbalanced lines** contain two wires. The wire in the center of the cable carries the signal, and the other wire acts both as a grounded shield and as a signal lead. Unbalanced lines are cheaper to manufacture, but they are also significantly more susceptible than balanced lines to interference from electrical lines, radio and television transmitters, and so on.

You can easily tell whether your audio cables or VCR inputs and outputs are balanced or unbalanced by looking at the audio connectors. Three-pronged XLR (Cannon) connectors indicate that the line is balanced; mini-plugs, RCA/

phono connectors, and phone connectors indicate that it is unbalanced. Incidentally, connecting a balanced line to an unbalanced input causes the line to become unbalanced, and the effect of the shield will be lost. This does not affect the signal quality, but it may make it more susceptible to interference. Unbalanced lines, however, do *not* become balanced by connecting them to a balanced input.

RECORDING SOUND ON PORTABLE CAMCORDERS AND VIDEOCASSETTE RECORDERS

Inputs

Sound that is picked up in the field with a microphone is routed into the portable camcorder or VCR through the appropriate input. All portable VCRs have at least one audio input, and most have two. If your VCR has two inputs, each one corresponds to its own audio track, or channel. These will be labeled channel 1 and channel 2, or left and right.

Depending on the videotape format that you are working with, several different kinds of audio tracks may be available. Sound is recorded into linear, or longitudinal, tracks with one or more stationary audio heads. Many small-format systems have two linear sound tracks. There are no differences between these audio channels other than the fact that they occupy space on different places on the tape. They are equivalent in terms of size and the quality of the audio signal they are capable of recording.

Systems with high-fidelity sound record sound information along with the video information in the slanted video tracks on the tape. In these systems, the rotary video heads may also serve as the audio heads, or a separate rotary audio head may be used. Sound quality is significantly better than in linear track recording because the tape-to-head speed achieved by the rotating sound head is significantly better than what can be achieved with the stationary head(s) used to record sound in the linear track(s). In addition, some systems (most notably 8mm/Hi8) are capable of recording high-fidelity sound digitally through a process known as *pulse code modulation (PCM)*.

Input Level

It is important to know the kind of signal the input is capable of accepting. There are two different types of signals: microphone-level signals and line-level signals. A **microphone-level signal** is very weak because the electrical signal that the microphone produces is not amplified. **Line-level audio signals**, on the other hand, are amplified. They are considerably stronger than microphone-level signals. Line-level audio signals include the output from audiotape recorders, turntables, preamplifiers, and so on.

It is important that the level of the output signal be matched to the level of the input on the VCR when you connect audio sources to the VCR. Microphones should be connected to microphone-level inputs, and line-level outputs to line level inputs.

On professional-quality portable VCRs, audio input levels can often be switched from microphone level to line level. A small two-position switch near the input allows you to select the appropriate input level for your audio (see Figure 7–13).

Some VCRs have separate inputs for microphone-level sources and line-level sources. Microphone-level inputs accept an input from a microphone with no difficulty, but a pad must be used to connect a line-level source to a microphone-level input. A *pad* is a device that reduces the level of the signal from line level to microphone level. It is connected to the audio cable between the line-level source and the microphone-level input connector on the VCR.

If you want to feed a microphone-level source into a line-level input, small amplifiers to boost the microphone-level signal to line level are available. These are relatively inexpensive and they simply connect to the cable between the microphone and the line-level input connector.

Input from the Camera Microphone

The audio signal generated by a built-in camera microphone is automatically routed to the camcorder's VCR and recorded onto one of the audio channels available on the videotape. In systems with a separate camera and portable VCR, the camera microphone audio signal is carried from the camera to the VCR through

Figure 7–13   Switchable Microphone/Line VCR Input

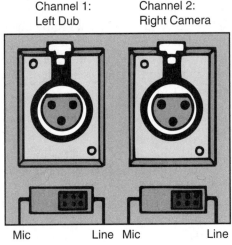

Channel 1:   Channel 2:
Left Dub   Right Camera

Mic   Line Mic   Line

the camera cable. In some systems, if an input from an external source is connected to the portable VCR in the same channel that has been allocated to the camera microphone, the external source will override the camera microphone, and the camera microphone input will not be recorded.

Automatic and Manual Gain Control

We have already discussed the gain control circuits on portable VCRs in some detail in Chapter 5. However, it is worth mentioning again here that the gain control—the control over the amplification of the signal—may be either automatic or manual. Most consumer and industrial-grade portable VCRs and camcorders contain an automatic gain control mechanism built into the audio circuitry of the VCR. Manual adjustment of audio source levels that are patched (connected) directly into the VCR is not possible on such machines.

Professional-quality camcorders and portable VCRs and many full-size VCRs contain manual gain control circuitry. Typically, there is a switch that allows you to choose either automatic or manual gain control. If manual gain control is chosen, a small potentiometer must be adjusted to bring the level up to the appropriate peak without overamplifying, and consequently distorting, the signal (see Figure 7–14).

Limiters

Many VCRs contain audio peak limiters. A **peak limiter** is an electronic device that prevents the audio level from exceeding 100 percent (0 db) on the volume unit (VU) meter scale. Usually, the limiter is controlled with a simple on/off switch.

Figure 7–14   VCR/Camcorder Audio-Level Controls

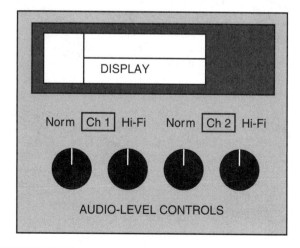

Limiters are useful if the sound in your recording situation is very unpredictable. If loud noises appear at random intervals, the limiter ensures that the recorded signal is kept within acceptable parameters. If the sound in the remote location contains predictable peaks, the recording level can be manually set with the limiter off, and the recorded signal should meet acceptable technical standards.

Connectors

As equipment becomes standardized, so do the connectors that carry the audio signals in and out of the VCR. Presently, however, a wide variety of connectors perform essentially similar functions (see Figure 7–15). Professional-quality machines utilize three-pronged XLR (Cannon) connectors for all audio inputs and outputs. These balanced connectors carry either line-level or microphone-level signals.

Microphone inputs on many VCRs often accept mini-plug connectors. These are unbalanced. Line-level inputs and outputs on consumer and industrial-grade equipment frequently utilize RCA/phono connectors, which are also unbalanced lines. Finally, some machines use phone connectors for microphone or line-level signals. Again, these are usually unbalanced lines.

If you are not working with professional-quality video equipment with standardized audio connectors, it is to your advantage to acquire a set of audio adapters that will enable you to adapt any type of microphone or cable to any type of input connector. Adapter kits are available from most audio-video supply houses, or you can simply go to a local electronics store and buy the ones you will need. The importance of making connections properly cannot be overemphasized.

Figure 7–15   Typical Audio Connectors

XLR (Cannon)
• Used for Microphone and Line-Level Signals
• Professional Quality
• Balanced Line

Mini-Plug
• Used Mainly for Microphone Inputs and Earphones
• Unbalanced Line

RCA/Phono
• Used Mainly for Line-Level Inputs and Outputs
• Unbalanced Line

Phone
• Used Mainly as a Headphone Connector or for Microphone or Line-Level Audio Signals
• Unbalanced Line

If you cannot get the audio signal into the VCR, you cannot record it. Well-prepared field producers are certain to have the connectors or adapters they will need to route the signal into the VCR being used.

MIXERS

As we mentioned above, most portable VCRs have two channels available for audio information. However, if you have more than two audio sources, or if you want to record a number of sources together onto one audio channel on the videotape, you will need to use an audio mixer.

An **audio mixer** is a device that combines a number of independent audio inputs by mixing them into one signal. For example, say you are recording an interview in which three or more people—each equipped with a microphone—are speaking. Each microphone could be fed into a mixer where the signals would be combined. The output of the mixer—a single channel—could then be recorded onto one audio channel of the videotape.

There are two different kinds of audio mixers: passive mixers and active mixers. *Passive mixers* simply combine a number of individual inputs into one output without amplifying the signal. Passive microphone mixers with two inputs and one output are extremely popular in video field production since the most typical field production situation involves the use of two microphone sources—usually an interviewer and a subject.

Active mixers give you control over the amplification of each of the audio sources. Each channel on the mixer has its own potentiometer as well as a potentiometer to control the *master gain*—the overall amplification of all the individual channels. Professional mixers are equipped with a VU meter so that levels can be set for the individual inputs as well as for the master gain (see Figure 7–16).

Depending on the type of portable mixer you are working with, you may have two channels (inputs), four channels (inputs), or more. Four channel mixers are the most common. They are capable of combining four different input signals into one output signal. The input signals may be microphone level (unamplified) or line level (amplified), as several of the inputs are switchable to either. In addition, the output level is also commonly switchable. It may be sent to the VCR as a microphone-level signal or a line-level signal.

Setting the Mixer Gain Levels

To use a portable mixer effectively, the gain levels for each of the input channels, as well as the master gain—the amplification for the combined signal of each of the individual channels—must be correctly set. Since overamplification of any signal increases the electronic noise inherent in the system, care should be taken to keep amplification levels within tolerable limits. A general rule of thumb to follow

Figure 7–16   Four-Channel Mixer (Shure M-67)

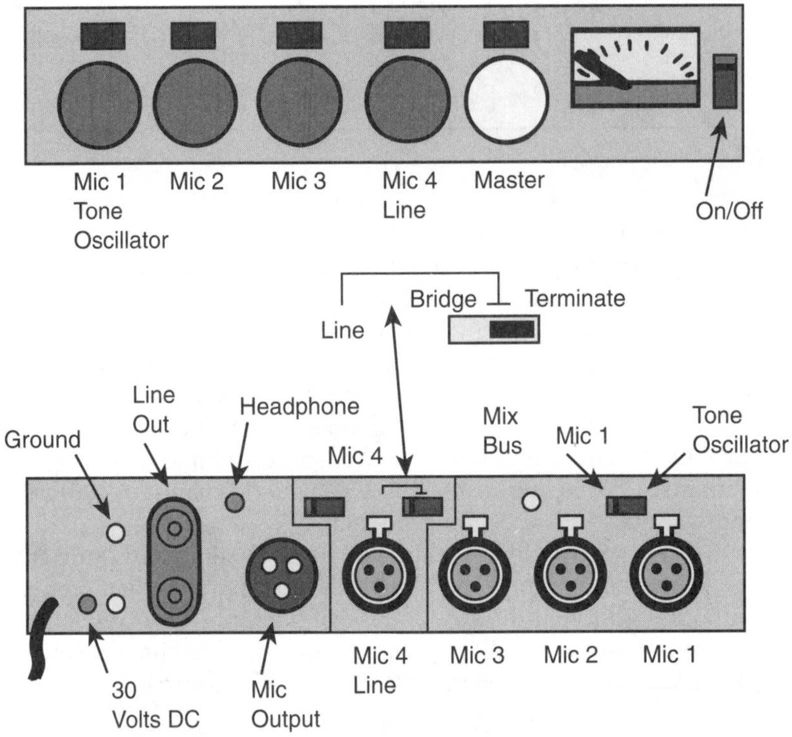

in setting levels is to keep the master gain control lower than the individual channel gain controls.

Using a Built-In Tone Generator.   If your portable mixer has a built-in tone oscillator, the channel and master gain levels can be easily and precisely set. First, make sure that all individual potentiometers and the master gain potentiometer are turned down to zero. This prevents them from creating unwanted electronic noises. Then, turn on the tone generator and turn up the potentiometer on the channel to which the generator is assigned approximately half way. Finally, turn up the master gain control until the needle on the VU meter reaches 100 percent. The mixer master gain level is now set.

Levels can now be set for each of the audio inputs. Turn off the tone generator and turn the channel potentiometer back to zero. Connect the appropriate input sources to the mixer, and set the level of each in turn by turning up the appropriate potentiometer until the VU meter shows an acceptable signal. Make a note of the setting for each channel. If an acceptable signal level cannot be obtained, you may need to increase the master gain. On the other hand, if all the sources are peaking in the red with their individual potentiometers at very low settings—1 or 2, for example—it may be necessary to turn down the level of the master gain.

If No Tone Generator Is Available. If no tone generator is available, you can experiment with level settings. Try a setting of 3 or 4 on the master gain, and then turn up one of the channel gain controls. If the VU meter peaks with the channel gain at an extremely low setting, then *decrease* the master gain level. If the VU meter peaks with the channel gain at an extremely high setting, then *increase* the master gain slightly. With a little experimentation, you will soon find the master gain setting that gives you the most control over the signal through the channel gain selector without overamplifying the signal or introducing spurious noise.

STANDARDIZED RECORDING PROCEDURES

Very few standardized recording procedures can be found for any aspect of field production. Most producers simply adopt systems that they are familiar with or that have worked for them in the past. Audio recording procedures are no different. However, a few suggestions for a standardized approach to sound recording are in order.

Where to Record Principal Audio

Perhaps the most important decision that needs to be made in the field with respect to sound is the decision about where (which channel) to record the principal audio. If your system only has one available audio channel, the choice is simple, but if you have two available audio channels and are using one or more external microphones or other external sound sources, it is more complex. Two factors should be considered:

1. Which channel is safe in terms of the track layout?
2. If time code is added to the tape later, onto which channel will it be added?

Safe Track. The safe track is the track that is located in the interior of the videotape. The unsafe track is the one closer to the edge. If you have a two-channel system, you will probably want to record the principal audio, usually the most important voice part of the program, on this safe track, and use the other track for additional audio—music, sound effects, other voice, and so on.

Time Code. Although SMPTE time code is described in considerable detail in Chapter 8, the importance of time code and its relation to the audio tracks needs to be mentioned here. Time code is an audio signal that is recorded onto the videotape to aid in computer editing. If you plan to edit using time code, you must know how your editing system will read the time code. Some systems are preset to read time code from only one of the two audio channels. It may be either channel 1 or channel 2, but in any case, it is probably not switchable. Therefore, you must record time code onto the channel that the editing equipment is set to read. If the time code editor reads time code off audio channel 1, then audio channel 1 should be left free for time code and all program audio must go onto channel 2. Similarly, if your system reads time code off channel 2, then channel 1 should be used for program audio. Familiarize yourself with the time code requirements of your editing system before you shoot any field tape to avoid the costly and time-consuming problem of switching audio and time code to opposite channels after they have been recorded onto the tape.

Count Down Stand-Ups and Voice-Overs

If you are recording a stand-up or a voice-over (VO) segment, you should identify it and count down to it. A **stand-up** is simply a shot in which the program talent, usually a reporter or the host of the show, talks directly into the camera at the remote location. Some identifying detail of the location is usually visible in the background. (Think, for example, of the traditional shot of a newscaster on the White House lawn.) A **voice-over**, on the other hand, is narration that is delivered by an off-camera announcer. The voice of the narrator is heard over the visuals but the narrator is not seen on camera.

If you are recording a stand-up to be used at the beginning of a news or documentary piece, you might simply face the camera and record the following: "Documentary introduction, take 1. Five, four, three . . . ." (Silently count: two, one, zero.) "Today at the State Capitol, legislators passed two bills that would severely censor cable television programming . . . ."

The countdown is useful to both the person on camera and the editor. If you will be speaking on tape, you can use it to pace your presentation. Always count off the first three seconds—"five, four, three." Remain silent for the rest of the countdown (two, one, zero) and then begin. This allows you to catch your breath and deliver the introduction without surprising the audio person, who has to set the levels. Count down at the same voice level that you plan to deliver the on-camera statement.

The countdown is also useful to the editor because it serves as a timing reference and cue for the beginning of your statement. In addition, should you happen to boom out the first few syllables, causing an audio-level problem that will need to be corrected during editing, the editor will know exactly where that point is on the tape. The editor can then decrease the level slightly for the first few syllables and increase it to the proper level for the rest of the segment.

Use a Slate

Identification **slates**—audio and video—should be used at the start of each tape. These should clearly indicate what follows on the tape. If you are shooting a fully scripted production, one in which each shot will be recorded individually, then each shot and each take of each shot should be slated. A production slate is a small board (often a chalkboard) that contains essential information about the production, such as the production title, date, shot number, take number, and so on. Sometimes, when a visual slate is not available, the slate information may simply be read into a microphone and recorded at the beginning of a shot. Such an audio-only slate is often used when recording stand-ups and voice-overs, as the essential slate information can be read by the talent immediately before the take.

By giving the take number on the slate, you will be able to easily identify the good take when you edit your raw tape. If four takes of the same introduction are recorded, and the first three were all disasters, you will know to fast forward to take number 4 when you edit. Without the slate, you will have to waste valuable editing time by listening to each of the four takes to find the correct one.

MONITORING SOUND

Volume Unit Meters

Field sound should be monitored for quality as it is being recorded. There are two ways to check the sound during the recording process. First, the audio levels should be monitored by watching the volume unit (VU) meters. They give you an accurate indication of the level, or strength, of the audio signal going into the recording deck. Since level problems are extremely difficult to correct later in the production process, care should be taken to record sound with good, consistent levels in the field. If the levels vary a lot from tape to tape, source to source, or location to location, the editor will later have to continually adjust the audio record level on the editing VCR to achieve a consistent level in the final edited tape. If audio levels on the field tapes are correctly and consistently recorded, the editor will not have to balance the levels in postproduction, and the overall sound quality and impact will be better.

Headphones

In addition to visually monitoring the levels on the VU meters, use **headphones** or an **earphone** to listen to the quality of the sound as it is recorded. Although headphones provide some information about the strength of the audio signal as it is being recorded, they are actually more important for other reasons.

Headphones tell you what the audio sounds like. Are you getting a clear recording? Is there any distortion in the recording? Are there any extraneous noises interfering with your audio? Are background noises overwhelming the important foreground sound? If you are using a mixer and mixing several inputs down to one channel, how does the mix sound? In an interview, can all the people on microphone be heard clearly? If you are recording a musical group with several instruments, how does the musical mix sound? Are the levels of each of the instruments correctly set in relation to each other? These questions cannot be answered by looking at a VU meter. They can be answered only by listening to the sound itself and by making a judgment based on what you hear.

Test Recording and Field Check

All field recording should include a test recording and field check of the recorded sound. If time permits, a test recording should be made before you travel to the field location. Record video and audio onto the VCR and then play it back. Problems that are apparent in this test recording are unlikely to disappear by the time the equipment reaches the field. It is better to delay or postpone a shoot while correcting an important audio problem than to labor all day in the field only to find out that your audio has a problem, or worse, is altogether missing from the field tapes.

In addition to making a test recording prior to the shoot and monitoring the sound with VU meters and headphones while the shoot is in progress, be sure to conduct periodic field checks of the audio and video quality of the tapes. A good time to check is when you are switching tapes (if time permits) or during breaks in the action. Rewind the recorded tape in the VCR slightly and play it back. Monitor sound quality through headphones and picture quality in the camera viewfinder or an external color monitor. Loss of picture or sound may be caused by a poor connection, clogged head, or something more serious. Again, it is better to identify the problem early than to spend the day recording only to find that your tapes are blank or that you have a serious technical problem that will prevent you from using them.

HINTS FOR RECORDING GOOD SOUND

Good field sound recording depends on several important variables, including correct microphone selection, correct microphone placement, and correct signal recording.

Microphone Selection

There is no such thing as the perfect, all-purpose microphone. All microphones are different, and selecting the proper microphone for field use depends on matching the microphone's characteristics with those of the recording situation.

Obviously, in choosing a microphone, you should consider how it will be used. First, consider what you are going to record—voice, music, and so on—and then identify the microphone that provides the frequency response best matching the characteristics of the sound source to be recorded. Next, consider the unique characteristics of field recording. Will you be able to use multiple microphones to selectively record each part of the audio? Or will one microphone be used to record everything? How will the microphone be mounted? Will it be hand held?

Frequency response, pickup pattern, size, durability, and ease of operation are all factors to consider when choosing a microphone for field recording.

Microphone Placement

Because of the great possibility of interference from ambient noise when microphones are placed at a distance, the most important principle of microphone placement in field production is to get the microphone as close as possible to the sound source, but not so close, of course, as to create distortion. Remember also that some microphones tend to emphasize low frequency sounds when placed too close to the sound source. When only one microphone is to be used for an on-camera interview, a hand-held shotgun may serve best. However, if you are able to attach a high-quality condenser lavaliere to each of the participants, you may be able to achieve excellent sound reproduction without the visual distraction of the hand-held microphone.

In some situations, such as a football game, it is not possible to get close to the sound source. It is common practice to attach wireless lavalieres to the referees, but the football players themselves present an audio pickup problem. Since microphones are fragile, they cannot be attached to the players. Pickup must be from a distance, and shotgun or *parabolic microphones* that reflect the incoming sound to the focal point of the parabola are most frequently used.

Close microphone placement may also be a problem if the nature of the production demands that the microphones not be seen on camera. If they cannot be hidden on the performers or the set, off-camera shotgun microphones will probably be used.

A general rule of thumb for microphone placement when two or more microphones are used simultaneously in close proximity is to observe a 3:1 ratio where the distance between microphones is at least three times greater than the distance between either microphone and the person who is using it. For example, if two or more people are seated at a table and each one is miked with an omnidirectional microphone on a desk stand, and the distance between each person and his or her microphone is one foot, the distance between the two microphones on the table should be at least three feet. This type of positioning reduces the tendency of the microphones to cancel each other out when both are being used at the same time.

Signal Recording

No matter how close the microphone is to the sound source or how well the microphone's response patterns match the characteristics of the sound source, the final recording will be only as good as you make it when you connect the inputs and adjust the recording level. Automatic gain control tends to overamplify the signal during periods of silence and then boom out the next loud sound. Manual gain control eliminates this problem, but care must be taken to correctly adjust the level. Adjust it too high and the signal will be noisy or distorted; adjust it too low and the signal will be weak and the quality poor.

SPECIAL PROBLEMS

Location Acoustics

Unlike the studio producer, who operates in a tightly controlled acoustical environment, very little control is afforded the remote producer. Therefore, much attention should be paid to the acoustics of the remote location when the initial survey of the remote location is conducted (see Chapter 12).

Sometimes problems caused by the acoustical properties of the location can be solved simply by the use of filters, or by changing the position of the person who is speaking and/or the type and location of the microphone.

Some microphones, and the standard four-channel mixers, contain **low-cut filters** that eliminate low frequency sounds, thereby eliminating the booming that occurs in large rooms. If the remote location has an extremely hollow, boom-like quality, a low-cut filter can improve the quality of the sound.

We all know that hard, polished surfaces such as glass reflect sound, whereas soft, textured surfaces such as cloth tend to absorb sound. The proximity of highly reflective surfaces can cause sound problems that are easily corrected. Consider an interview being conducted in front of the glass window of a local coffee shop. The coffee shop is located on a very busy street with an almost constant flow of car and truck traffic. If the shop proprietor stands in front of the window and the sound is picked up with a shotgun mounted on the camera (or held off camera), the traffic sounds reflected off the glass will probably overwhelm the sound of the proprietor's voice. Use of a lavaliere microphone will improve the sound pickup, but the traffic sounds (which now enter the microphone as direct, rather than reflected, sound) will probably still be too loud. If, however, a lavaliere is used and you change the positioning so that the proprietor's back is to the traffic, the proprietor's body will physically shield the lavaliere from the traffic sounds. Thus, the voice pickup will be considerably improved (see Figure 7–17).

Wind Noise

Wind noise is the most common problem encountered when recording outside. Even a light wind can sound like a hurricane when it passes over a microphone. For this reason, always use a wind screen on microphones when recording outside (see Figure 7–18). A **wind screen** is a foam cover placed over the microphone to screen out wind noise. Wind screens for most types of microphones are commercially available. If you cannot buy one, you can easily make one by

Figure 7–17   Adjusting to Location Acoustics

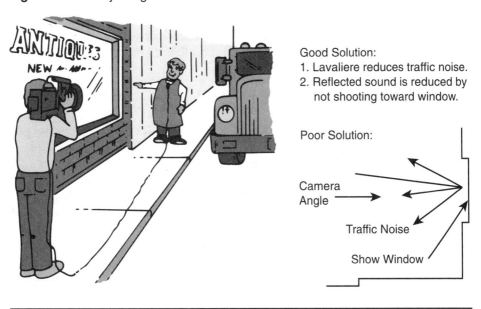

Good Solution:
1. Lavaliere reduces traffic noise.
2. Reflected sound is reduced by not shooting toward window.

Poor Solution:

Camera Angle

Traffic Noise

Show Window

Figure 7–18   Microphone Wind Screens

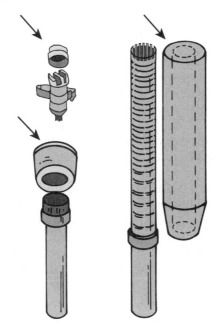

cutting a piece of porous polyurethane foam to the dimensions of the micro-phone.

Some microphones have built-in **pop** or **blast filters**. These filters protect against sound distortion caused by particularly strong blasts of breath when a microphone is placed very close to the subject's mouth. Pop filters also provide some protection against wind noise.

Ambient Noise

Ambient noise—unwanted background noise—is the scourge of field production. A shot of a tranquil suburban street with birds chirping in the background can eas-ily be destroyed if the local public works department selects your shooting day to bring out a jackhammer crew to remove part of the pavement on a nearby street. Freeway and airport noises often seem much louder when you watch your field tapes back in the editing facility than they did when you recorded a stand-up on a freeway overpass or near the airport passenger terminal.

The problem with ambient noise is that it is often unpredictable and uncon-trollable. You might be able to persuade the jackhammer crew to take a short work break while you get your shot, but you probably will not have much luck in con-trolling the freeway traffic or air traffic.

The most severe problems can be avoided by thoroughly surveying the loca-tion before the shoot and paying close attention to the sounds of the location. Correct selection and placement of microphones can also help to reduce the pickup of unwanted ambient noise.

Radio Frequency and Electrical Interference

Interference from electrical or radio frequency (RF) sources causes a consistent problem in location sound recording. Unbalanced lines may pick up outside elec-trical or **RF interference** that will be extremely difficult to remove from the final audio track. Balanced lines provide protection against this, but only if all the con-nections are solid. If the shield solder comes loose or if the cable has a break in it, signal quality may be adversely affected.

No cable, balanced or unbalanced, can withstand radio waves if it is placed too close to a transmitter. In effect, cables act like antennas. If you are in the line of sight of a radio or television transmitting tower or if you are extremely close to a microwave transmitter, your audio cable may pick up the sound of the radio sta-tion or the microwave transmission. Depending on the circumstances, the inter-ference may be louder than the wanted audio signal. The problem can sometimes be corrected by changing the position of the cables, but occasionally the problem is so severe that the only solution is to move to a new location that is further away or out of the line of sight of the offending RF source.

High-voltage electrical lines, electrical transformers, and motors may also interfere with the audio signal. Always try to keep audio cables away from such sources. Sometimes cables can be wrapped in black electrician's tape to provide insulation against electrical interference. Noise from motors, particularly if they run intermittently, is often more difficult to identify and control.

EQUALIZING AND FILTERING TO IMPROVE SOUND QUALITY

In extreme cases of interference, the audio on prerecorded field tapes can be manipulated to improve sound quality. Two common types of sound manipulation involve the use of filters or graphic equalizers. Audio **filters** allow you to cut out certain parts of the high or low end of the audio signal. The filter works by blocking out the parts of the signal above or below a specified cut-off frequency. For example, you could eliminate the high frequencies in a signal to create a bassy effect, or you could eliminate the low frequencies to give it a higher effect. **Notch filters** can be used to eliminate a particular range of frequencies in the signal. An obtrusive electrical hum, for example, might be isolated at 60 hertz. With the notch filter, you could eliminate this part of the signal and let the rest pass by.

Graphic equalizers are similar to filters but are somewhat more complex. Graphic equalizers break down the audio signal into a series of equally wide ranges of frequencies. The level (gain) of the signal can then be increased, decreased, or left unchanged in each of the intervals. By increasing the level of some of the intervals and decreasing the level of others, the overall quality of the sound can be changed.

Filters and equalizers can also be used to achieve a particular kind of production effect. For example, the tinny sound of an inexpensive portable radio can be achieved by using a low frequency filter to cut out the rich, low frequency part of the signal, allowing only the thin high frequencies to pass. A normal audio signal can thus be manipulated to make it sound like a radio, telephone, loudspeaker, and so on.

ADDING SOUND TO PRERECORDED VIDEOTAPE

So far, we have concentrated on discussing general aspects of sound and sound recording, particularly with respect to recording live sound on location. Indeed, this is probably the most common type of sound recording in video field production. However, another extremely important aspect of sound recording concerns adding sound to a prerecorded videotape. Perhaps you have recorded video onto a videotape and want to add background music. Or perhaps you want to add a voice-over (VO) narration to connect the visual sequences on the tape. Almost all video recording systems let you add new sound to the videotape in a number of ways.

Audio Dub

Most VCRs contain an *audio dub feature*. The audio dub control allows new sound to be added to one of the available audio channels. When the audio dub control is engaged, the audio circuitry for one of the audio channels goes into the record mode. An audio erase head erases the old audio signal from the designated channel, and the audio record head lays down the new audio signal. The new audio input signal can usually be either microphone level or line level, as long as it is connected to the proper audio input connector.

There are two complications with the audio dub feature. First, audio dubs can be made only onto longitudinal (linear) audio tracks. If your VCR or camcorder has high-fidelity sound that was recorded with the rotary video heads (or a special rotary audio head) along with the video information in the slanted tracks of video information on the videotape, you will not be able to make an audio dub into these tracks. Second, on VCRs or camcorders that do record audio information in two separate linear sound tracks, the audio dub feature may be designed to work in only one of the two channels. For example, on $3/4$" systems, an audio dub can be made only onto audio channel 1. (Incidentally, this is the reason why many producers using $3/4$" systems record their principal field audio on channel 2. If they want to add something to the audio track, they can add it quite easily by performing an audio dub onto channel 1.)

It is extremely important to monitor the sound level and quality when performing an audio dub. If background music is to be dubbed in, the music should not be so loud that it interferes with the quality of the voice on the other channel. The proper level can be set by watching the VU meters and by monitoring the sound with headphones. The quality of the mix can be monitored by listening to the mixed output of both audio channels. Simply set the audio monitor selector switch to mix (rather than to either channel 1 or 2), plug in the headphones, and listen. Adjust the level of the music so that it takes its proper place in the background, behind the voice.

Audio-Only Insert Edit

New audio information can also be added to either one of the two linear audio channels available in most tape formats by performing an audio-only insert edit. This is a form of electronic editing, and in order to accomplish this you will need to use a special editing VCR. This is discussed in greater detail in the next chapter.

Sound-on-Sound

Some portable VCRs, usually VHS format machines with a single audio channel, have an audio dub feature called sound-on-sound. The **sound-on-sound** feature allows new audio to be added to an existing audio signal. This is significantly different from the conventional audio dub function. Whereas audio dub erases the old signal and replaces it with a new one, the sound-on-sound feature does not erase the old signal. Rather, the old signal is recorded along with the new audio input. The old signal becomes the background sound (lower audio level) and the new signal becomes the foreground sound (higher audio level).

Although the sound-on-sound feature is useful, it does not afford as much control over the quality of the mix of the two signals because all the level setting is done automatically. However, this is still better than having no ability to add sound to a prerecorded tape.

PART TWO: SOUND AESTHETICS

Effective control of the sound portion of a program involves control of the aesthetics of sound as well as control of sound from a technical standpoint. Just as changes in lighting, camera position, and shot composition can affect the audience's perception of a scene, so can manipulation of the audio.

TYPES OF SOUND

Silent television productions are extremely rare. We have become so accustomed to the presence of sound within television programs that even a few seconds of silence seems out of the ordinary.

Sound, as we mentioned at the beginning of this chapter, is any audio element whose presence in the program is intended. Noise, on the other hand, is unwanted or unintended sound. Sound is used to enhance communication; noise interferes with communication. Four typical types of sound commonly found in most television productions are voice, natural sound, music, and sound effects.

Voice

Voice is probably the most common type of sound found in video field productions, since many remote productions are interviews. The two most common uses of voice are dialogue and narration. **Dialogue**, conversation between two or more people, may be scripted or unscripted. Scripted dialogue is found most often in a drama or simulation; unscripted dialogue is found most often in interviews.

Narration is another extremely common use of voice. Narration may be on camera or off camera. In either case, the narrator describes the situation at hand and generally serves to link together portions of the program for the viewer. When narration is given off camera, we usually see visuals on the screen that correspond to someone or something other than the narrator. Off-camera narration is referred to as **voice-over (VO)**. When the narrator (or any other person on camera) is shown while speaking, this is called **sound on tape (SOT)**.

Natural Sound

Natural sound is an extremely important component of video field production. One might argue that it is natural sound that distinguishes field production from studio production, since, strictly speaking, there is no natural sound (other than noise from the video equipment, studio personnel, and air conditioning!) in the studio. Natural sound is sometimes called *location sound*—it is the sound present in the location in which the action is taking place. For example, in an interview with a shipyard welder, the natural or location sound would be the sound produced by the workers and machinery in the shipyard, or the sound produced by the welding equipment itself. In a sequence on water-skiing, the natural sound would be the sound of the boat engines and the sound of the water against the boat's hull and the water-skis.

Natural sound adds an important dimension of detail to remote productions. Tape shot in the field that does not include natural sound seems flat and lifeless. You have all seen those weekend television sports programs, usually of fishing or hunting, in which a voice-over is used with silent footage of the sporting activity. Such a technique gives the program a distance and sense of unreality that is immediately noticeable. The viewer, consciously or unconsciously, is aware that something is missing. Something is indeed missing—the sounds one would hear if one were alongside the hunter. We expect to hear natural sound anytime we see a picture, since this is how we experience things visually and aurally in the real world.

Music

In contrast to the naturalness and reality of natural sound, music is one of the most unrealistic sound elements within a program. How many times in real life has music been present as a background to your activities? Yet, ironically, a program without music often seems as flat, lifeless, and unnatural as one constructed without natural sound! The reason that music seems so natural is that we have become conditioned to its presence within visual presentations. The use of music is an easily understood convention that viewers have come to expect. A car chase without music to heighten the drama would be unusual indeed!

The principal use of music is often to reinforce or create a mood, as in the heightened drama that results from the music in the car chase. Music can also be used to present important information about locale (place) or time. A desert without music is simply a desert. However, with the appropriate background music it can become the desert of the American West, the desert of ancient Asian nomads, or a lunar desert in a futuristic space adventure.

Music, like natural sound, is important because it adds another layer to the audiovisual mosaic. As more layers are added, the mosaic becomes more complex and consequently more interesting to the viewer. Music, then, can be used to add energy to a scene that might otherwise seem to be slow or lifeless.

Another common use of music is in television program themes. It is particularly noticeable and useful when used to introduce a program. While we would probably object to the use of background music during an interview with a leading head of state, we nonetheless readily accept it at the beginning of the news program that contains the interview. The reason for this is that music serves an important cueing function. It tells us when something new is about to happen. For this reason, it functions effectively to introduce a program, where it is used to catch the viewers' attention.

Music is used similarly as a punctuator within a program. Music introduced into a previously silent scene may tell us that something is about to happen or it may simply reinforce the situation as it has been presented.

Sound Effects

In studio television production, **sound effects** are often used to present the natural sounds of the location being depicted. The sounds of birds gently singing in the background during a scene supposedly taking place on a porch swing on a warm summer day will most certainly need to be added as a sound effect if the scene is staged in a studio. On the other hand, if the scene is shot on location these background sounds may actually be present on the location as natural, background sound.

Sound effects are widely used in both studio and remote production to suggest something that is happening off camera. Explosions, car wrecks, rocket launches, and other events of proportions that are difficult to stage can effectively be represented through the use of off-camera sound effects.

For a sound effect to be effective, it must be believable to the audience. Believability is achieved if the sound effect accurately represents the sound of the phenomenon in question. To do this, the sound effect must be characteristic of the phenomenon, and it must be presented at the proper volume and have the proper duration. A car crash sounds different from a bottle breaking, and the sound of the engine of a passenger car is different from the sound of the engine of a high-performance racer. To be effective, these and any other sound effects must accurately match the sound of the event depicted, or the effect will be comedic. Show a man talking and dub in the voice of a woman, or show a rabbit with its mouth moving and dub in the sound of a chicken, and the audience will almost certainly laugh.

SOUND PERSPECTIVE AND SOUND PRESENCE

Sound Perspective

Two important aesthetic variables commonly associated with sound are perspective and presence. **Sound perspective** refers to the way in which the perspective of the sound matches the perspective of the visuals related to that sound. A train in the distance appears to be small on screen, and the sound created by the train is faint. As the train gets closer, its image becomes larger and the sound becomes louder. This is the phenomenon of sound perspective.

Although this may seem straightforward and simple to achieve, in fact we often violate rules of absolute perspective in television production. In an interview, for example, when cutting from a long shot to a close-up, we seldom vary the perspective of the sound, although an absolute faithfulness to the principle would demand that we do so.

Problems with sound perspective frequently occur when shooting in the field. They usually result from the camera changing its perspective of a scene (by zooming in or out, for example) without a change in perspective of the sound picked up by the microphone. This occurs particularly if the microphone is attached to the camera or mounted in a fixed position. Tight shots look very different from wide shots, and we would expect the sound to be different if we strictly adhered to the rules of sound perspective. However, the microphone picks up sound in a consistent manner, whether it is attached to the subject or the camera.

Another problem with sound-visual perspective mismatches occurs when the sound source moves. One of our favorite examples of this occurs in a small-format student documentary. One shot records the movement of a car down a narrow country road toward the camera. At the beginning of the shot, the car is far off in the distance and the sound of its engine is almost inaudible. The lens then zooms in all the way, so that the car fills the screen. Yet, in reality, the car was still quite a distance from the camera, where the microphone was mounted. Consequently, the sound of the engine was still rather weak. The camera held the shot of the now empty road, but the car, now off camera, continued in fact to approach the camera position. Several seconds later the car actually passed the camera and the engine sound swelled to the full volume that was expected when the car's image had filled the screen. What had happened was that the sound had become detached from the visual and did not match the perspective change of the visual. The sound seemed to follow the car rather than to have been created by it.

Sound Presence

Nearby sounds are different from sounds far away. One obvious difference between the two is volume, as we have seen in the discussion of sound perspective. However, not only are nearby sounds louder than far away sounds but they also have a different sound quality. This difference in sound quality is called **sound presence**. Nearby sounds not only sound loud but they sound close. This difference in quality results from the fact that microphones respond differently to sounds that are close than to ones that are farther away. At close distances, microphones pick up subtle tonal qualities of the sound that are inaudible at greater distances.

The effect of sound presence, then, can be created by closely recording the sound source. A hand-held microphone held inches away from the speaker's mouth has a greater presence than a lavaliere held 15 inches away. And the lavaliere has a greater presence than a shotgun microphone located 15 feet away from the subject. Most television programs feature relatively close shots of speaking subjects, and it is important to capture as much of the sound presence of their speech as possible to facilitate the audience's perception of closeness.

CONSTRUCTING THE AUDIO PORTION OF A PROGRAM

Just as a series of technical decisions must be made about the type and placement of microphones to ensure high-quality sound pickup, so must a series of strategic decisions be made about the design of the audio portion of a program.

Narrator versus No Narrator

In any kind of documentary or informational program, basic decisions about the structure of the audio portion of the program center on the presence or absence of a narrator or host. Some documentarists prefer to let the story tell itself and are therefore resistant to the use of a narrator. Whether or not to use a narrator is a matter of both your personal preference and the goals of the program. A narrator might be an unnecessary intrusion into a program designed as an ethnographic study of people in a particular community. On the other hand, a program on the local pasta factory might be difficult to complete without a narrator to explain the technical elements of the factory's operation and to link together the program's various segments.

Narration serves many useful functions. It can quickly provide expositional details that might take considerable time to develop if left to emerge from the comments made by the participants in the program. Also, narration can effectively present technical information in nontechnical terms. Often, experts on a particular subject present information that is too detailed or complex. Narration is an effective way of providing transitions or bridges from one segment of the program to another. In addition, narration is often used to introduce speakers as they appear within a program. This is an effective and economical technique that eliminates the need for intrusive name superimpositions.

On-Camera and Off-Camera Questions

One of the first decisions that must be made when designing an interview-based program is whether the interviewer's questions will be incorporated into the final program. If the questions will be used, then the interviewer must be miked. Furthermore, if you plan to include the questions, then you must decide if the interviewer will appear on camera or if the questions will be asked from off camera.

Question Re-Asks. In a single-camera shoot, on-camera questions are typically recorded after the interview is completed. This technique is called shooting **question re-asks**. Two important factors must be considered when shooting question re-asks:

1. The questions must be re-asked accurately; they should be the same questions as originally asked.
2. The camera must be correctly positioned so that the question re-asks can be edited together properly with the rest of the original interview material.

If the interview questions are scripted, then the same script of questions can be used to shoot the question re-asks. If the interview questions are asked spontaneously (ad-libbed) rather than from a script, the production assistant (PA) should write down the questions as they are asked. If this is not possible, or if the PA is not sure of having accurately written down the questions, then the audio portion of the videotape should be reviewed to produce an accurate transcript of the questions. The question re-asks can then be shot using this transcript as a guide.

Question re-asks should be shot immediately after the interview is completed and in the same location in which the interview was recorded. Move the camera and shoot the interviewer from an angle complementary to the angle at which the interview was shot. Care should be taken to ensure that the questions will cut together with the answers in terms of the screen directions of interviewer and interviewee. Care should also be taken to guarantee that the backgrounds for the interviewer and interviewee are consistent. They need not be exactly the same, but enough background information should be given for the viewer to know that the questions were asked and answered in the same locale.

Another important reason for shooting question re-asks in the same location as the interview is to guarantee that the sound quality of the questions matches the sound quality of the answers. The presence of consistent ambient room noise is particularly important in determining that the sound quality matches.

In addition to shooting the question re-asks in the same location, many shooters make it a practice to record some additional **room tone**—wild sound of the ambient sound present in the room. If a question needs to be reconstructed, recorded, and inserted into the program later on, room tone can be dubbed in under the question so that it will not sound like the question was asked at a different time or in a different place. Room tone can be recorded directly onto videotape by letting the camera and VCR run for several minutes. If the camera has a good-quality microphone attached to it, this will usually provide an acceptable room tone recording. Remember to keep quiet on the site while recording room tone. It is good practice to record at least 30 seconds of room tone at each location to be used if needed in editing.

Natural Sound

Every attempt should be made to record as much natural sound as possible while shooting in the field. Natural sound should be recorded onto the videotape along with the visual material that corresponds to it. Even if the tape is merely being shot to be used as the background visuals for narration voice-over segments, the natural sound should still be recorded. A segment with natural sound under the voice-over is usually more effective than the same visual sequence with narration and no natural sound.

Music and Sound Effects

The need for music and/or sound effects should be assessed early in a program's production. Indeed, the selection of music or effects is just as important as the selection of individual **sound bites**, or voice segments, and visual sequences.

Aside from the legal questions regarding permission to use music (see Chapter 12), great care should be taken in the selection and use of previously recorded music. Probably the greatest problem with prerecorded music is the fact that it may be familiar to a large part of the audience and may have very unique associations for different audience members. The lilting instrumental signifying blissful romance to one person may have been popular at the time someone else was enduring a bitter divorce. It may therefore symbolize loss rather than fulfillment to that audience member. This is one of the principal arguments for the use of original music. Uniquely composed original music can exhibit the expressive characteristics called for by the production, and therefore will facilitate rather than inhibit communication.

When music plays a supportive or reinforcing function within a scene, care should be taken to match it to the visuals in terms of mood, location, and historical time. Just as ragtime piano music would most likely be inappropriate as background music for a solemn funeral scene, so would bagpipes be inappropriate as the background for an Italian wedding—unless one intends a comic effect. Electronically synthesized music would similarly fail to match the historical time of a scene supposedly taking place in medieval England.

One final caution about music concerns the use of music with lyrics. Instrumental music is usually more easily incorporated into a production than a song with lyrics, for the simple reason that the lyrics may provide unwanted, unnecessary information to the viewer. When music is used as background, lyrics often compete for the viewer's attention. Lyrics create an almost unsurmountable distraction to narration or dialogue. Furthermore, lyrics become even more distracting if the music fades out before the lyrics reach their conclusion. Music with lyrics should only be used if there is a precise reason for the inclusion of the lyrics—for example, if a particular song is being used for historical accuracy or if the lyrics reinforce or describe the visual action of the scene.

THE VISUAL IMPACT OF MICROPHONES

Obtrusive versus Unobtrusive

No discussion of the aesthetics of sound would be complete without mention of the visual impact of microphones. A microphone visible in a scene affects that scene. If characters in a drama all carried visible microphones, the illusion of the drama would be destroyed. For that reason, great care is taken to hide microphones in dramatic presentations. They are mounted on booms out of camera range, hidden in plants or on the set, or cleverly concealed on the actors themselves—all to preserve the illusion of reality that the drama intends to convey.

In an interview-based presentation, microphones seem to be a necessary evil. We accept their presence unquestioningly. However, some care should be taken if you want to achieve a documentary effect in which the recording crew and its technology are unobtrusive. For example, in an ethnographic production, the story tells itself: No narrator is used and the questions are not heard within the program. This illusion of objectivity should be supported through the relative invisibility of microphones.

Relatively unobtrusive lavaliere microphones can be used, or if the presence of any microphones will destroy the illusion, then a shotgun microphone held out of camera range may be most appropriate. The ENG-style intrusion of the microphone in someone's face is inappropriate in most circumstances other than on-the-street news interviews, and should be avoided.

Consistent Use of Microphone Types

If microphones are to be visible in various shots, then an attempt should be made to be consistent with respect to the types of microphones used. If lavalieres are used, then the same type of lavaliere should be used on all interview subjects. Similarly, if a hand-held microphone is used, the same type should be used consistently throughout the program. This is particularly important if an on-camera narrator does stand-ups throughout the piece. The same type of microphone should be used because it provides both visual and aural continuity. This is particularly important if various program segments will be edited together into a complete program. Consistent microphone use helps give the program unity, whereas inconsistent microphone use draws attention to differences in sound quality and will fragment the program.

SUMMARY

Although television is most often thought of as a visual medium, the sound or audio portion of the program is equally important. Video field producers are concerned with the use of sound in three different situations: location recording, adding sound to prerecorded videotapes, and sound manipulation during editing. In all cases, producers should strive for recordings with clear sound. Noise that interferes with the intended sound is a common problem in field recordings.

The two most important physical characteristics of sound are its intensity and pitch. These are identified as differences in amplitude and frequency of sound waves. Loudness is measured in decibels (db) and frequency in cycles per second, or hertz (Hz).

Location sound is picked up with a microphone, which changes the sound into electrical energy. Microphones vary with respect to their pickup pattern, type of construction, frequency response, and impedance. Common microphone pickup patterns include omnidirectional, cardioid, and supercardioid. Supercardioid microphones are also called shotgun microphones.

The most common types of microphones used in field production are dynamic microphones and condenser microphones. Of the condensers, the electret condensers are very popular. Ribbon microphones and crystal microphones are used less frequently in high-quality television field production.

Microphones should be matched to each recording situation with regard to their frequency response, and they should be positioned correctly for optimum sound pickup. Microphone impedance must also be considered. Most professional microphones and inputs are low impedance. High-impedance microphones are sometimes used in field production, but signal quality is noticeably affected if cable length exceeds 25 feet.

Camera-mounted microphones are often used in field production. These microphones may be built into the camera or they may be physically attached to the camera. The most significant advantage to their use is in the convenience they provide. Disadvantages center on the poor quality of sound pickup that often results from the distance between the microphone and the subject, and from their susceptibility to picking up camera noise and other nearby noises.

For these reasons, external microphones—microphones not built into or mounted on the field camera—are widely used in field production. The principal types of external microphones include hand-held microphones, lavaliere microphones, PZM microphones, shotgun microphones, contact microphones, and hanging microphones. External microphones may be placed on hard surfaces, mounted on stands or booms for convenience, or suspended on a fishpole to allow maximum mobility and unobtrusiveness when shooting a moving subject.

Field microphones may be wired or wireless. Wired microphones are connected directly to the VCR by audio cable. Wireless microphones, also called radio microphones, rely on a miniature transmitter to send the audio signal to a small receiver, which is then connected to the VCR.

Microphones and microphone cables may be balanced or unbalanced lines. Balanced lines are shielded from outside interference; unbalanced lines are not.

Sound that is picked up in the field with a microphone is routed into the portable VCR through the appropriate input. These input signals can either be weak unamplified microphone-level signals or stronger amplified line-level signals.

Depending on the videotape format, sound may be recorded in one more longitudinal audio tracks by the stationary audio heads, or high-fidelity sound may be recorded by the rotary heads along with the video signal in the slanted tracks of video information.

The recording level of the audio signal may be controlled manually or with the use of an automatic gain control device. In addition, some VCRs are equipped with peak limiters that protect against overmodulation.

Connections between audio sources and the inputs on the deck can be made only if the appropriate connectors and adapters are available.

When multiple audio inputs are used, an audio mixer may be employed to combine several signals into one. Both passive and active mixers are available. If an active mixer is used, the levels for each of the input channels as well as the master gain must be correctly set.

Standardized recording procedures for sound include deciding where to record the principal audio, recording a countdown for stand-ups and voice-overs, and slating all audio segments.

Sound can be monitored by looking at the VCR volume unit (VU) meters and by using headphones or earphones. It is good practice to make a test recording and check the sound prior to each recording session.

The quality of your sound recording can be improved by choosing the correct microphone for the situation at hand, by placing it properly, and by adjusting the record level properly.

Special problems in recording sound in the field include unpredictable location acoustics, wind noise, unwanted ambient background noise, and radio frequency (RF) and electrical interference. Problems with the audio portion of a program can be eliminated somewhat through the use of filters and equalizers.

There are a number of ways to add sound to prerecorded videotapes, including audio dubbing, audio insertion during editing, and recording sound-on-sound on VCRs equipped with this feature. Sound mixing can be accomplished without a mixer by using a microphone source in conjunction with a home stereo system.

Beyond technical considerations, there are a number of aesthetic considerations to the manipulation of sound in field production. The most common types of sound found in television include voice, music, natural sound, and sound effects. Sound perspective and sound presence are two important qualitative sound dimensions.

When planning a program, much thought should be given to the construction of the audio portion of the program. Factors to consider include whether or not to use a narrator, whether to ask interview questions on camera or off camera, maximizing the pickup of natural sound, and assessing the need for music and sound effects.

Finally, the visual impact of microphones used in the field should be considered. Microphones may be obtrusive or unobtrusive. In either case, it is important that microphone use be consistent to provide visual and aural continuity within the program.

8

Videotape Editing 1: Technical Factors

PHYSICAL AND ELECTRONIC EDITING

From a technical standpoint, there are two ways to edit: physically and electronically. We will examine physical editing first.

Physical Editing

Physical editing means that the film or videotape you are editing is actually cut and reconnected in a different order. You may be familiar with film editing. Motion picture film is composed of a number of still frames that appear to be moving when the film is projected onto a screen. If you take a piece of motion picture film and examine it closely, you will see that it is really just a series of still pictures, or frames (see Figure 8–1). Each frame is separated by a thin frame line. Film editing involves cutting the piece of film into its component shots, arranging them into the desired order, and then splicing (joining) the film together on the frame lines.

Splices are usually made with film cement or glue, although sometimes they are made with transparent splicing tape. The frame line is never seen when the film is projected because it is between frames (remember, the projector flashes on to show one frame, then flashes off as the next frame is pulled into place). Therefore, all correctly done film splices, or edits, are invisible.

Physical editing is technically simple to perform on film because each of the frames is visible and each is separated by a distinct frame line. Videotape, on the other hand, poses some problems. Since the signal on videotape is recorded magnetically, there are not any visible images or dividing lines to be seen. In addition, in film a clean edit is achieved by precisely lining up the film's sprocket holes. In video, the control track pulses, which act like sprocket holes in film, are invisible to the naked eye.

Despite these problems, physical editing of videotape is possible. Physical tape editing involves actually cutting the videotape and then splicing it back

Figure 8–1 Frames of Information on Film

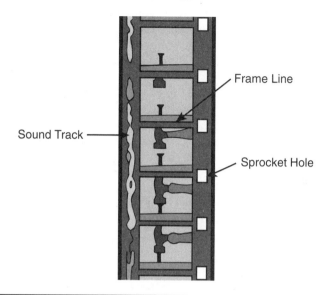

Frame Line

Sound Track

Sprocket Hole

together in the new sequence with splicing tape. To physically edit videotape, you need to see the video information and the control track pulses. Since the control track pulses must be equally spaced on the tape to ensure stable playback, you must maintain the precise spatial relationship between control track pulses when cutting and splicing the tape. Similarly, to edit cleanly, you have to join the end of one frame of video information to the beginning of the next frame. Sound impossible? Actually, it is not.

The magnetic information on the videotape can be made visible by using a special viewer that senses the magnetic impulses on the tape, or by painting a special solution onto the tape (see Figure 8–2). With one of these methods, you can actually see the areas of information on the tape. Then, using a precise splicing block to hold the tape and a very sharp razor blade to cut it, you can physically cut the tape and join it to the new segment.

Figure 8–2 Tracks of Magnetic Information on Videotape

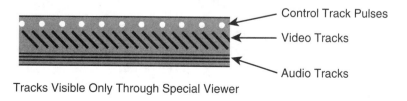

Control Track Pulses

Video Tracks

Audio Tracks

Tracks Visible Only Through Special Viewer

Before the advent of electronic editing, this type of physical editing was widely performed on 2" tape. The process was extremely delicate because the editor needed to identify the position of the video tracks, and then cut precisely in between the frames of video information. Since the distance between tracks on 2" tape is only 0.005 inch, and the cut had to be made precisely in the center of this area (in the guard band area), a good eye, a steady hand, and an extremely sharp razor blade were needed.

Although it was possible to physically edit 2" tape, helical scan tape presented some logistical problems. Since the information was arranged at a slant, the cut would have to be made at an angle rather than straight across, as in 2" tape. In addition, physically cutting tape in any format presents a significant problem to the video heads. They spin at high speed across the tape, and require a smooth and polished tape surface. Physical cuts in the tape produce rough spots that can potentially clog the heads with stray oxide particles, or even damage the heads through friction with the spliced joint. Clearly another way needed to be found to edit videotape.

Electronic Editing

The solution was electronic editing, which is now universally practiced with videotape editing. **Electronic editing** is simply a process of rerecording information into a new sequence. Two videotape machines are used: the playback VCR, or source VCR, which contains the original videotape; and the record VCR, or editing VCR, which contains a blank videotape (see Figure 8–3). Material from the source VCR is recorded onto the editing VCR in the desired sequence. After editing, the new edited version is on the editing VCR, and your original tape remains in its original form on the source VCR. You have made a copy of certain portions of the original, rearranged in a new order.

Figure 8–3   Diagram of a Simple Editing System

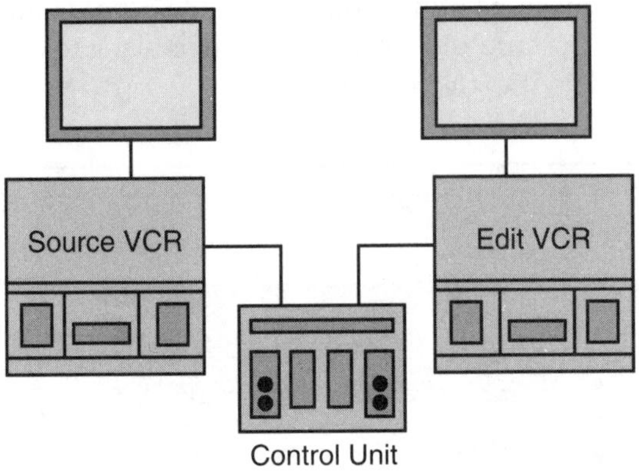

Although this sounds simple, electronic editing is complicated by the fact that the video signal can be reproduced only when the videotapes are already moving through the machines. Therefore, you need a system that can make an edit at a precise point while both the source VCR and the editing VCR are rolling. In this respect, making an edit can be compared to passing a baton during a relay race. As the runner with the baton approaches the baton pass area, the second runner, who will receive the baton, begins to run. When the baton actually passes hands, both runners are moving at full speed.

Editing Videocassette Recorders

To electronically edit, a special type of videocassette recorder—the **editing VCR**—is used (see Figure 8–4). An editing VCR accomplishes an edit by synchronizing the incoming signal from the source VCR with the signal on the editing master tape. The **editing master tape** is the tape in the editing VCR onto which the program material is being edited. For the edit to be accomplished cleanly, the editing VCR must begin recording a new field (track) of information at precisely the same instant that the source VCR plays back that field of information. In addition, the edit must be made in the vertical interval between frames of information on the videotape in the editing VCR (see Figure 8–5).

This synchronization is achieved in two ways. First, the editing VCR reads the incoming vertical sync pulses from the source VCR. This information is transmitted to the capstan servo, which adjusts the playback phase and speed of the editing VCR to correspond with the speed of the source VCR. This aligns the vertical interval of the video signal in the editing VCR with the vertical interval of the video signal on the source VCR (see Figure 8–5). When the video signals have been synchronized, the position of the video record heads in the editing VCR is adjusted by the head servo so that they precisely scan the tracks of information on the tape.

If this sounds complicated, it is! Editing VCRs are marvels of modern electrical and mechanical engineering. They are complicated, sensitive, and sometimes temperamental pieces of equipment, and deserve to be treated with respect.

Interformat Editing

For years it was standard practice to edit videotape onto the same tape format on which it was originally shot. For example, field tapes shot in $^3/_4$" format would almost always be edited to a $^3/_4$" master. However, given the proliferation of videotape formats and the advantages of some formats as field acquisition formats and others as editing formats, this is no longer always the case.

Since editing is an electronic process in which the signal from a source machine is rerecorded on the editing VCR, tapes that were recorded in the field in one format can be edited to master tapes in another format. This is known as *interformat editing*. For example, 8mm/Hi8mm and VHS/S-VHS have become popular field acquisition formats for many video field producers because the equipment is

Figure 8–4 (A) Hi8 Desktop Video Editing System (Sony (EVO-9700), (B) $\frac{1}{2}$" VHS/S-VHS Videocassette Editor (JVC BR-822U), (C) $\frac{3}{4}$" U-Matic SP Videocassette Editor (Sony VO-9850), (D) Betacam SP Videocassette Editor (Sony PVW-2800), (E) $\frac{1}{2}$" VHS/S-VHS Videocassette Editor (Panasonic AG-7750)

(A)

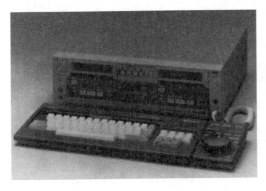

(B)

(C)

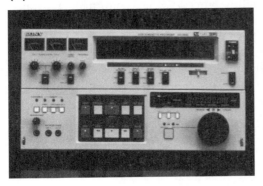

(D)

(E)

Figure 8–5   Synchronized Source and Editing VCR Signals

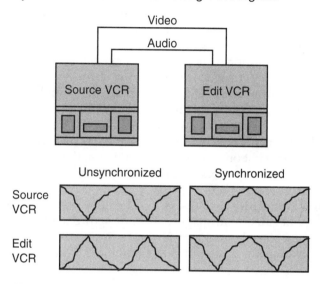

portable and relatively inexpensive. By using the appropriate format machine as the source deck in a compatible editing system, 8mm/Hi8mm or VHS/S-VHS field tapes can be edited to a master tape in a different format. It is not unusual to see editing systems with an 8mm/Hi8 or VHS/S-VHS source machine and a 3/4" (or other format) editing VCR. Extremely high-quality video can be produced by shooting on S-VHS or Hi8 and editing onto Betacam SP. Producers aiming for even higher quality might shoot field tapes in Betacam or M-II formats, and edit to 1" tape or one of the digital tape formats for their program master.

Tapes that have been shot in the field in one format can, of course, first be dubbed to another format for editing if the editing system format is different from the field recording format. However, you lose a full tape generation in the process. Interformat editing eliminates the intermediate dubbing step and thereby saves one generation, as well as the time it would take to dub the tapes.

ASSEMBLE AND INSERT EDITING

There are two different types of electronic editing: assemble editing and insert editing. The differences between the two can be understood in strategic terms as well as technical terms. That is, we can talk about assemble and insert editing in terms of how we approach editing, as well as how the edits are physically accomplished within the electronic editing VCR. We'll examine the strategic differences first.

Editing Strategy: Assemble versus Insert Editing

Videotape editors commonly talk about *assembling* a program or program segment. A literal definition of **assemble editing** might therefore simply be to join the parts together. And, indeed, that is what an assemble editing strategy is. When you assemble a program, new information is added to a tape shot by shot, or scene by scene, in proper sequence. Beginning at the beginning of the master editing tape, you lay down shot 1, then shot 2, then shot 3, and so on, until the program is complete. Or, perhaps you have already put together a number of different sequences or scenes, each of which contains a number of individual shots. You can assemble the final show out of these sequences by editing them together into the proper order. First one sequence is laid down, then another, and another, and so on, until all the sequences for the final program are assembled in a new order on the tape (see Figure 8–6).

Insert editing strategy is significantly different from assemble editing strategy because you insert a shot or sequence into a preexisting shot or sequence within the program. If you have already transferred shot 1 to the edit master and now want to put shot 2 into the middle of shot 1, leaving the begin-

Figure 8–6   Assemble and Insert Editing Strategy

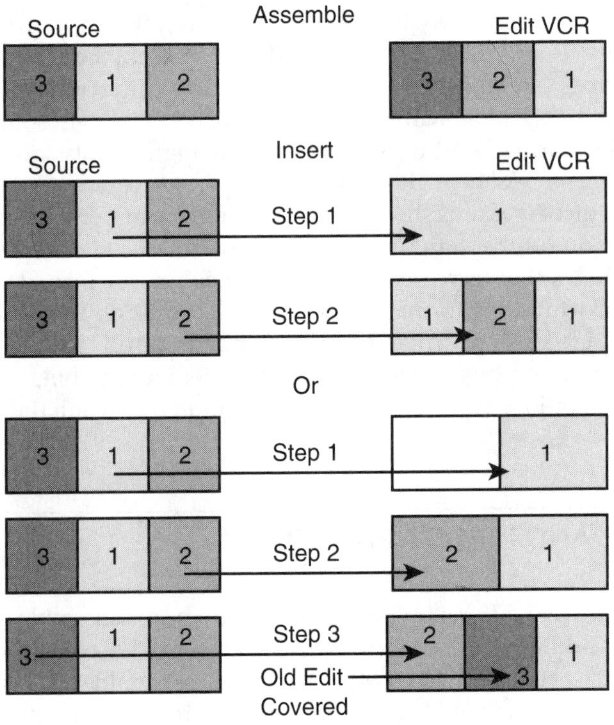

ning and end of shot 1 on the edit master, you are inserting shot 2 into shot 1 (see Figure 8–6).

Another use of the insert is to bridge a cut between two shots. Perhaps you have assembled shots 1 and 2 together, only to find that the transition point between the shots looks bad. Perhaps shot 1 shows the subject looking to the left side of the screen and shot 2 shows him looking to the right. The transition between shots creates an obvious and irritating transition—a jump cut—that should be eliminated. So, take shot 3, a long shot of the subject seen over the shoulder of the interviewer, and insert it at the transition point. This insert of the cut away acts as a bridge to eliminate the disturbing jump cut. Once again, you are inserting new material into a sequence that has already been recorded.

To summarize, laying down shots or scenes in a sequence one after the other is an assemble editing strategy Editing information into an already recorded shot or sequence, while leaving the head and tail (beginning and end) of the original shot or sequence intact, is an insert editing strategy.

Technical Differences: Assemble versus Insert Editing

Not only can we describe the differences between assemble and insert edits in terms of editing strategy but there are also some very large technical differences in the way assemble edits and insert edits are accomplished by the editing VCR. (The following discussion of the technical differences between assemble and insert editing describes those tape formats in which the control track signal has been recorded in a longitudinal track by a stationary head: VHS/S-VHS, $^{3}/_{4}$", Betacam/Betacam SP, and M-II. 8mm/Hi8 systems are slightly different and will be discussed separately at the end of this section.)

All high-quality editing recorders contain a control that designates the *editing mode* as assemble or insert. An assemble edit is the simplest type of edit, and in fact, when electronic editing was developed, many machines only had an assemble editing mode. Assemble editing adds new information on to the end of prerecorded information on another tape. An assemble edit can be used for *editing in* only. The assemble mode allows you to get a clean edit where the edit begins, but the only way to end an assemble edit is to shut off the machine. This causes the image to break up. An insert edit, on the other hand, is really two edits: one at the beginning of the insert and the other at the end. The edit is executed cleanly at both points.

Assemble and insert editing differ technically in how the new information is recorded on the editing VCR. Of particular importance is what happens to the control track on the edit master tape and how the old information on the edit master tape is erased. In the assemble mode, *new control track, audio, and video information is recorded onto the tape in the editing VCR*. In the insert mode, *the control track is left undisturbed, and only new audio and/or video information is laid down in place of the original information* (see Figure 8–7).

Whenever new information is added to a tape, the old information must be erased. The differences between assemble and insert editing result from the differ-

Figure 8–7   Assemble and Insert Editing—Technical Differences: (A) Assemble Editing, (B) Insert Editing

(A)   Assemble Edit

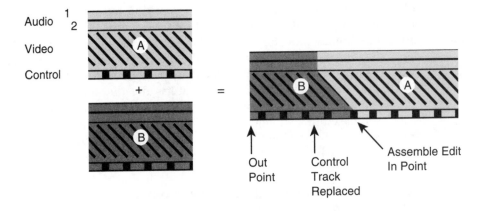

(B)   Insert Edit

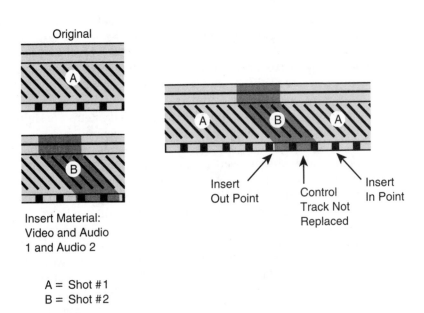

Insert Material:
Video and Audio
1 and Audio 2

A = Shot #1
B = Shot #2

ent ways in which the old information is erased. In the assemble mode, a stationary **erase head** erases the full width of information on the videotape before the new information is laid down by the spinning record heads. However, the use of the stationary erase head in the assemble mode creates a problem at the end of the edit, because the erase head completely erases the tape before it reaches the record heads. As a result, when the VCR stops at the end of an edit, there is a blank spot of tape between the erase head and record heads. This blank spot does not contain any audio, video, or control track information. For this reason, when you play back the tape, the beginning of the edit will be clean, but the picture will break up at the end of the shot. This occurs because both the control track and video information are missing.

No such problem occurs in the insert mode. The control track is not erased because the stationary erase head is not used in the insert mode. When a video insert is made, only the video information (not the control track) is erased by a pair of **flying erase heads** located immediately in front of the record heads. This allows erasing of precise frames of information without the gap between the erase and record heads found in the assemble mode. Audio inserts are accomplished by erasing only the tracks of linear audio information that are to be replaced by new information. In both the video and audio insert modes, the control track is not affected. The video flying erase head erases only those frames of information that are to be replaced by new information, but not the control track. Thus, continuous control track and video information are maintained, and the edit is clean at both the entry and exit points.

Please note: Audio-only inserts can be performed only when the audio information has been recorded into one or more longitudinal tracks of audio information. In videotape formats where high-fidelity sound information has been recorded in the slanted tracks of video information with rotary record heads, an audio-only insert cannot be performed without affecting the video information.

Assemble Editing Review

Let's briefly review what we know about assemble editing. An assemble edit involves the transfer of information from the source VCR to the editing VCR. Assemble editing strategy means that shots or sequences are added onto the tape in the editing VCR in the desired sequence. From a technical standpoint, assemble editing means that each time an edit is made, the editing VCR records new video, audio (both channels if on a two-channel VCR), and control track. Furthermore, an assemble edit is used for editing in only—that is, it adds new information to the end of other video information already present on the tape in the editing VCR. The beginning of the edit is stable, but the end of the shot will break up where the edit ends because control track and video information will be missing from the tape in the small space between the location of the stationary full-track erase head and the place where the video record heads hit the tape.

Approaching Assemble Editing

To perform an assemble edit, two VCRs are needed: the source VCR containing the original unedited material and the editing VCR containing the **edit master tape** (which is the tape onto which the edits will be made). Since assemble editing involves adding information to a tape in sequence, the tape in the editing VCR cannot be blank. It must have video information and control track on it for the edit to be made properly. If you already have some information recorded on the tape in the editing VCR, assemble editing is easily accomplished. You simply add new material to the end of the old material. But what do you do at the beginning of a program? How do you make the first edit of a program onto a blank tape?

To make the first edit in a program, it is customary to record some **video black** at the beginning of the edit master tape. Video black is a black video signal. It can be produced by a video switcher and sync generator, equipment typically found in a television studio or editing facility. Video black can also be produced simply by capping the lens of a video camera and recording the black picture. This provides a video signal and all the synchronizing pulses that the editing VCR needs to make an edit, since control track pulses are recorded whenever a video signal is recorded on a VCR.

If a video signal and control track are not present on the edit master tape, the first edit will be unstable. The editing VCR needs control track to regulate its playback speed. Also, without video information on the tape, there is no way to synchronize the movement of the video heads so that they begin recording the new tracks of video information at the correct place on the tape.

Overlapping Edits

When using assemble edits to construct a program, the technique of overlapping edits is employed. An **overlapping edit** is one in which the end of the last shot recorded on the editing VCR is erased and recorded over by the beginning of the next shot that is being transferred from the source VCR. This technique covers up the messy picture breakup that always comes at the end of an assemble edit.

Assume that you want to transfer seven seconds of shot 1 on the source VCR to the editing VCR. If you end the assemble edit precisely at the seven-second mark, the picture will break up, causing a problem in the program. The solution is to record more than the seven seconds you need. Then begin the next edit at the seven-second mark of shot 1 and erase the breakup after that point. Figure 8–8 illustrates this technique.

Whenever you are editing in the assemble mode, use this technique of overlapping edits. Always allow both the source and editing VCRs to roll several seconds beyond the planned end point of the edit, and then record the beginning of the next shot over this material (see Figure 8–8).

Problems with Assemble Editing

Each time an edit is made in the assemble mode, a new segment of control track is recorded. If the edit is not made in precisely the correct place, or if there are any irregularities in the signal on the source VCR (which is now being recorded onto the editing VCR), this will cause a momentary loss of stability in the final edited program. For this reason, most professional editing is done in the insert mode, even if the editor is simply recording the shots in sequence. Using the insert mode

Figure 8–8   Overlapping Edits

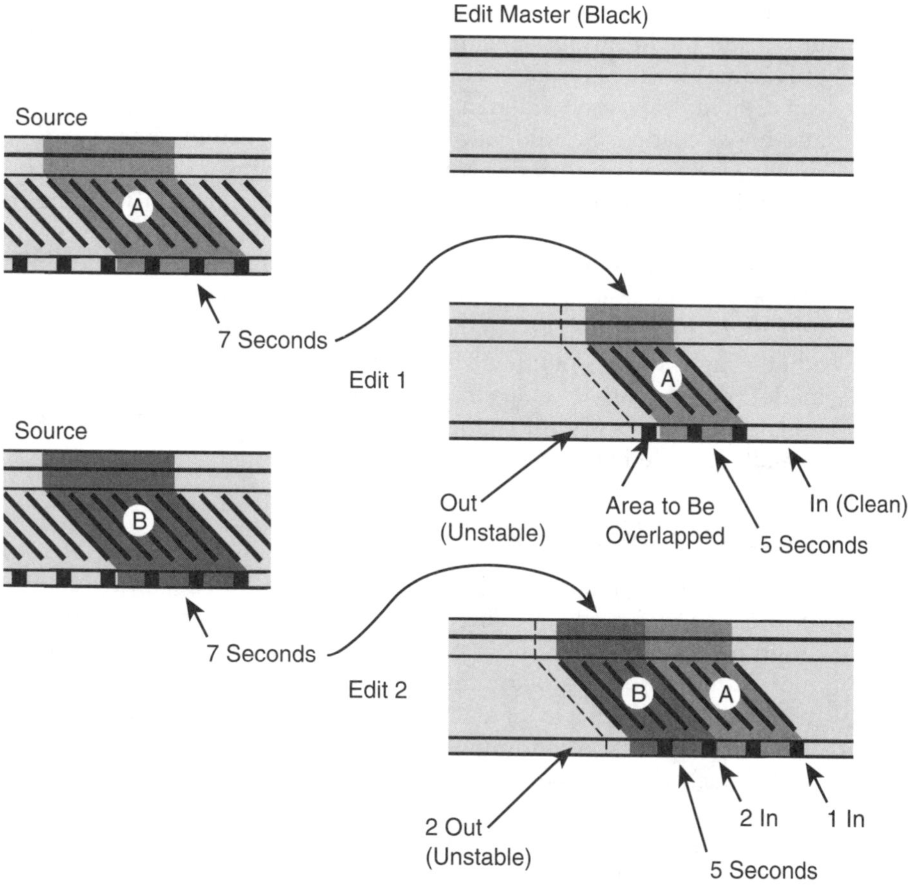

Edit Master (Black)

Source

A

7 Seconds

Edit 1

A

Out
(Unstable)

Area to Be
Overlapped

In (Clean)

5 Seconds

Source

B

7 Seconds

Edit 2

B   A

2 Out
(Unstable)

2 In   1 In

5 Seconds

guarantees a continuous, uninterrupted control track on the edited master tape, since control track information is never affected in the insert editing mode.

Insert Editing Review

Insert editing differs principally from assemble editing in that the edit master tape—the tape onto which you will edit—must already have a continuous control track. In the insert mode, the control track is not erased because the VCR's large stationary erase head is not activated. Rather, the insert mode uses the small flying erase heads, which are positioned immediately in front of the video record/playback heads. These flying erase heads erase only the tracks of video information that have previously been laid down on the tape. They do not affect the control track at all, and may be used in conjunction with or independent of the stationary audio erase heads. The result is that in the insert mode you can insert new video, linear channel 1 audio, linear channel 2 audio, or any combination of the three. You can do video-only edits, in which new video information is laid down and the linear audio channels are left undisturbed. Or you can do audio-only edits, in which the old video information is left undisturbed. In addition, you can combine video and audio insert edits. For example, you can insert new video and linear channel 1 audio onto the master tape, leaving linear audio channel 2 undisturbed. Or you can insert new video and linear channel 2 audio, leaving channel 1. Insert editing gives the editor incredible flexibility during the editing process.

In those videotape formats where video and high-fidelity audio are recorded together in the same slanted tracks of information on the tape, any video insert will affect the high-fidelity sound information as well. Similarly, any attempt to edit the high-fidelity sound will affect the video information. Audio inserts can be made independently of video inserts only if the tape format contains one or more longitudinal tracks of audio information or, as is the case with 8mm/Hi8 systems, digitally recorded PCM audio tracks.

Approaching Insert Editing

To edit in the insert mode, the tape you are editing onto must have continuous pre-recorded control track and video information for the entire length of the edited program. As explained, the control track is needed because new control track information is not recorded in the insert mode. Therefore, the master tape must have control track on it to regulate the tracking of the editing VCR. In addition, the control track must be continuous. If there are any breaks or interruptions in the control track, the edits will not be stable. The picture will break up wherever control track pulses are missing.

Therefore, before you can begin editing in the insert mode, you need to know the length of the finished program. You then need to record enough control track onto the edit master tape to safely cover the length of that program. Before you can begin editing a 10-minute program segment, you need to record at least 10 minutes of video black and control track onto the tape. It is always a good idea to lay down more control track and black than you think you will need. Then, if you slightly exceed the projected program length, you will still have some control track and video black to work with. To protect against running out of control track, most professional producers simply lay control track down along the entire length of the tape they are editing onto.

Video Black and Crystal Black

Sometimes you will hear videotape editors use the term *crystal black* to describe what we have been calling video black. **Crystal black** is simply a color black video signal recorded onto a videotape—usually for the entire length of the tape—when the tape will be used as an edit master tape. This color black video signal includes

color burst, the pulse that controls the phasing of the color signal and activates the color circuitry in a television receiver, as well as the horizontal and vertical sync pulses associated with the video signal.

When video black is recorded onto a tape, control track is automatically recorded as well, since the control track is triggered by the vertical sync pulses in the black video signal. Video black is usually recorded directly from a video switcher that has video black as one of its standard outputs. If a switcher with video black output is not available, a video camera that is turned on with the lens capped or aperture closed will produce a black video signal that can be used in editing.

At this point, we would like to emphasize that video black is different from having no video signal. A videotape with video black recorded onto it is not a blank tape. A blank tape contains *no* video signal, whereas video black is indeed a video signal.

You will remember from our discussion of basic video theory in Chapter 2 that video signals have luminance (picture brightness in black and white) and chrominance (color) and are held together by horizontal and vertical sync pulses. Video black is a black video signal—it has horizontal and vertical sync as well as color burst. If you look at video black on a monitor, you will see a stable, black screen. If you look at the signal on a waveform monitor, you will see that it does indeed produce a video waveform, and you will be able to identify the sync pulses and color burst in the waveform.

Blank tape, on the other hand, has nothing recorded on it. There is no video signal, sync, or color burst. When you play back a blank tape and look at it on a monitor, you will see snow or the screen will be black but the picture will jitter and roll. If you look at a waveform monitor, you will not see the characteristic video waveform because no signals are recorded on the tape.

Video black is used in the editing VCR because it provides a stable reference signal into which your new video and audio information can be laid. Since control track pulses are recorded as the black video signal is laid down, the editing VCR will have the information it needs to maintain stability throughout the program.

Some videotape editors prefer to lay down **color bars** instead of video black for the entire length of the tape. The reason for this is that occasionally, when editing, you may accidentally leave a small bit of space between the end of one edit and the beginning of the next. In the insert mode, the end of the edit is as clean as the beginning of an edit, and these mistakes are sometimes hard to see. If you are editing onto a tape with video black recorded onto it, you may not see the space between the shots when you play back the tape. But, if you are editing onto a tape with color bars on it, the space between shots will reveal an unerased segment of color bars that will jump out at you like a red flag at a bull in a bullring. You can then correct this error by redoing the edit to eliminate the gap between the shots.

Assembling in the Insert Mode

Although insert editing is most commonly thought of as the process of inserting new information into a prerecorded shot or sequence, it is also possible to assemble a program in the insert mode. You will recall from our discussion of assemble and insert editing that we distinguished between the *strategy* used in editing and the *technical processes* used to execute the strategy. This distinction is important because one frequently wants to put a program together shot by shot in sequence (assemble strategy) while using the technical process of insert editing.

You may wonder why anyone would want to do this. The answer, of course, lies in what we have already said with respect to the control track. In the assemble mode (technical process), the old control track is erased and new control track recorded with each edit. The problem with this process is that you have a good chance of winding up with a slightly irregular control track. Even slightly inaccurate timing of any edits, or inaccurate spacing of the edit master control track pulses, results in an unstable edit that may cause the picture to break up or roll. In a program with several hundred edits, the chances are good that at least one control track segment will be bad.

In the insert mode, however, the control track is not affected during the editing process. Therefore, assembling the program in the insert mode usually produces a higher-quality finished product. As in assemble editing, the process of overlapping edits is usually followed. While this is not necessary from a technical standpoint, since the output of the edit will be clean and stable, overlapping edits are used because most editing systems are not frame accurate. Recording more information than you need as you lay down each shot on the edit master is a safety measure that prevents a black space from appearing in the tape between shots, even if the next edit is a frame or two late (see Figure 8–9).

8mm/Hi8 Editing

As you will recall from the discussion in Chapter 4, in the 8mm/Hi8 videotape formats, all the critical signal information (audio, video, control signal) is recorded in the slanted tracks of information by the rotating video/audio heads. There is no stationary erase head to erase the tape, no stationary head to record control track, and no stationary head to record audio, since there are no linear audio tracks. Because all the recording and re-recording is accomplished with the rotary recording and flying erase heads, editing with 8mm/Hi8 more closely resembles insert editing in the other tape formats, but with some significant differences.

Because the audio, video, and control pulses are recorded in the same slanted tracks of information, whenever an assemble edit is made all of the audio and control signals are replaced as well. Insert edits, on the other hand, can be performed independently on the video, time code, and PCM (digital) audio channels. 8mm/Hi8 systems also contain one or two AFM (high-fidelity) audio tracks. Since these high-fidelity audio tracks are recorded at the same place on the tape as the video information (the video and audio signals are actually recorded in the same track but at different depths in the magnetic recording layer on the tape), audio inserts on the AFM audio tracks cannot be made independently of the video. Similarly, whenever a video insert is made, the AFM audio tracks are re-recorded as well. So, in order to achieve fully independent insert editing of video and audio, the PCM digital audio tracks, rather than the AFM high-fidelity tracks, should be used.

Figure 8–9   Assembling in the Insert Mode

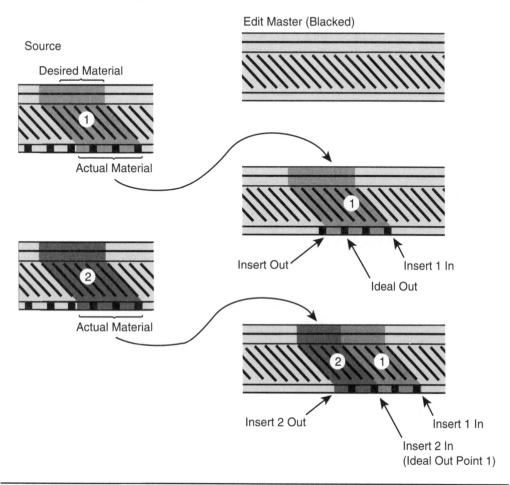

Wrong Field Edits

For an edit to be stable and clean, it must come at the appropriate point in the signal. The edit must be positioned correctly with respect to control track pulses and the tracks, or fields, of information on the videotape. However, in helical scan systems each frame of video information is composed of two separate fields, and each one of those fields is recorded in its own track of information on the tape. Thus, there is only a 50 percent chance that an edit will be made correctly. A correct edit must come at the end of the second field of information of a video frame in the editing VCR, and before the first field of information of the appropriate frame in the source VCR. A correct edit will look like this:

recorder field 1—recorder field 2—*edit point*—source field 1—source field 2

Edits that do not come between the end of the frame on the editing VCR and the beginning of the frame on the source VCR are called **wrong field edits**. Here are two examples of wrong field edits:

recorder field 1—*edit point*—source field 1—source field 2

and

recorder field 1—recorder field 2—*edit point*—source field 2

Wrong field edits are apparent because a curved black line will appear for an instant at the top of the frame (see Figure 8–10). There are two ways to solve the problem. The first method is to redo the edit until it is correct. It may take several attempts to correct the problem, but the odds are that sooner or later you will get it right. The second method is somewhat easier and more reliable. Many editing VCRs contain a frame servo control. Setting this control to the on position in the editing VCR guarantees that all edits are made at the correct place, thus eliminating wrong field edits. Since wrong field edits can cause problems with stability and color reproduction, this control on the editing VCR is extremely helpful.

EDITING SYSTEM COMPONENTS

As mentioned above, videotape editing is really a process of re-recording information; that is, it transfers information from one machine to another. Therefore, before you can edit, the videotapes in both the source and editing VCRs must be

Figure 8–10   Wrong Field Edit

Wrong Field
Interference

moving at the normal playback and recording speed. Not only do you have to identify the appropriate edit entry and exit points on the videotapes in each machine but you also have to allow adequate preroll time for the machines to stabilize and for the editing VCR to lock onto the incoming signal. In addition, your editing VCR must be capable of sensing precisely where one frame of video information ends and another begins. This is necessary to perform the edit cleanly in the space between the frames. Thus, a complete editing system (see Figure 8–11) must include the following components:

1. Playback (source) VCR, to play back the original, unedited videotape
2. Record (editing) VCR, capable of making a clean edit in the vertical interval between frames
3. Monitors for the source and editing VCRs, to allow you to see and hear the audio and video from each source
4. A system or device for controlling both VCRs, so that edit points can be found and edits precisely made by incorporating an adequate preroll time that allows the machines to stabilize and reach their edit points at the same time

Figure 8–11 Simple Editing System

Editing systems can be extremely simple or complex. The level of complexity of an editing system is usually determined by two factors: your editing needs and/or the amount of money you want to spend on the system.

Let's turn our attention now to the fourth point in the list: systems or devices that can be used to cue up the source and editing VCRs.

Cueing Systems

The process of locating editing points and then **backspacing** the machines several seconds to allow adequate preroll time—also called backtiming, prerolling, or cueing—is done with automatic editing control units that read control track pulses or SMPTE time code.

CONTROL TRACK EDITING

The most common type of edit cueing system is probably the type that relies on an *automatic edit control unit* to cue up the tape by counting the tape's control track pulses (see Figure 8–12). Commonly referred to as **control track editors**, these relatively inexpensive controllers are used in both broadcast and nonbroadcast production applications. Although they are sometimes criticized because they are not as accurate as SMPTE time code systems, they are considerably less expensive. In some applications, they also allow the editor to work faster. Simple control track edit controllers are widely used in many educational and institutional editing facilities.

Standard Controls

All control track editors contain a set of standard controls. First, the controller contains a set of player (source VCR) and recorder (editing VCR) controls for both of the machines in any of their normal operating modes: play, fast forward, rewind, stop, and so on. Usually, the left side of the edit control unit contains a full set of controls for the source VCR, and the right side contains all the controls for the editing VCR. The edit control unit, then, is simply a remote control device that can be used to control the playback and record functions of the machine (see Figure 8–13).

Since editing demands that precise frames of information be found at the edit points, the control units also typically contain a **joystick** or **search dial** that allows the editor to look at the image on either machine in a number of different modes: frame by frame, slow motion, normal motion, and fast motion. Through the use of the joystick or search dial, the tapes can be jogged forward or reverse with the videotape against the VCR heads. The picture and sound are displayed

Figure 8–12   Cuts-Only Edit Control Units: (A) Sony RM 450, (B) Panasonic AG A750

(A)

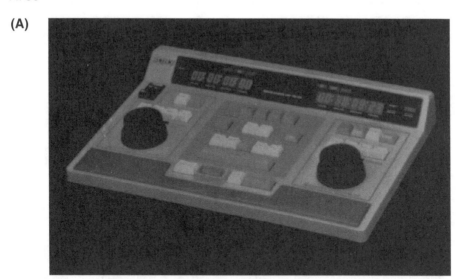

(B)

in the monitor, allowing you to select the precise frame to be edited. Joystick or search dials are usually provided for both the source and editing VCRs.

Most edit control units also contain a *digital time display* in hours, minutes, seconds, and frames for both the source and editing VCRs. This digital display works by reading the control track pulses on the tape. When you put a tape into a VCR and push the play button, a readout appears on the edit controller that

Figure 8–13   Functional Diagram of a Cuts-Only Edit Control Unit

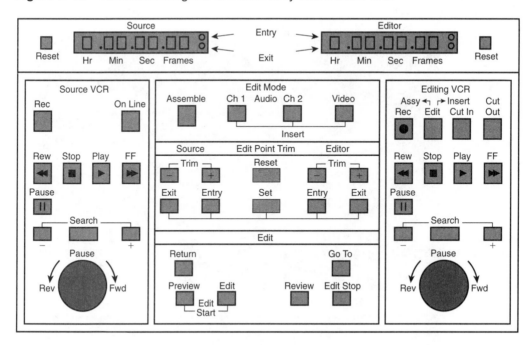

displays the location in the tape in digital time. In reality, the edit controller is not displaying clock time. Rather, it is translating control track pulses into a time readout. This may seem minor, but it is really a very important point. The control track editor does not use a clock to tell time. It simply counts control track pulses and then translates the count of those pulses into a time readout: 30 pulses equals one second; 1,800 pulses equals one minute; 108,000 pulses equals one hour; and so on.

It is important to remember that the time readout on the edit control unit is accurate only if the counter is reset to zero at the beginning of the tape, and if the tape has continuous control track on it. If the counter is reset to zero in the middle of a tape, the time readout will begin counting again from 0 hours, 0 minutes, 0 seconds, and 0 frames.

The time readout, then, must be treated carefully. If it is *not* reset to zero at the beginning of a tape, or if it *is* reset to zero in the middle of a tape, the readout will not be accurate.

The center part of the edit control unit contains the editing controls. The *edit mode* buttons are used to select either the assemble or insert edit modes. If the insert mode is selected, an additional group of buttons allows the operator to select video, audio 1, or audio 2 in any combination as the signals to be inserted. *Edit point* controls are used to enter the edit entry and exit points. In the assemble mode, an entry point must be entered for both the source and editing VCRs. In the insert mode, exit points need to be set in addition to the entry points. **Trim** controls allow you to add or subtract frames from the edit points after they have been entered into the control unit.

Also included among the editing controls are those that set up the performance of the edit once the edit points have been selected. The *preroll* control (sometimes called the *cue* control) backspaces each machine five seconds before the edit entry points to allow enough time for the machines to get up to speed and stabilize before the edit takes place. The *preview*, or *rehearse*, control allows you to preview an edit without actually recording it. Both machines will roll forward and do a practice edit that you can view on the monitor of the editing VCR; however, the editing VCR will not actually record the edit. If the edit meets with your approval, you can use the *perform edit* or *edit start* control to recue the machines and actually perform and record the edit.

Most edit control units also contain a *review* control. After the edit has been made, the control unit will stop both tapes and rewind the editing VCR to the exit point of the edit just completed. When the review control is depressed, the control unit rewinds the editing VCR to a point in front of the entry point of this edit. It then puts the machine into the play mode so the edit can be viewed at normal playing speed. You should always review each edit at normal speed and in slow motion after it has been recorded. Make sure that the edit achieves the desired aesthetic effect, and check it for technical accuracy and stability.

Setting the Edit Points

On control track edit control units, edit points are set by finding the precise frame on which the edit is to be made and then putting the machine into the pause mode at that point. The precise frame of the edit is found by using the joystick or search dial with the VCR operating in the search mode. Edit entry and exit points are then entered into the edit control unit by pressing the appropriate buttons to set the entry and exit points for the source and record VCRs.

On some systems, you can enter edit points *on the fly*, with the VCR in the play mode. When the editor sees the desired edit point (or hears it, if this is an audio edit), the editor pushes the edit entry control as the tape is playing. This enters the edit point into the system. The difficulty with entering the edit decisions on the fly is that accuracy depends on the speed of the editor's reaction. If the editor's reflexes are slow, the edit point may be off by a second or more. For this reason, the search mode is most often used to enter edit points by slow speed searching for the precise frame and then putting the machine into the still frame mode at the edit point.

Yet another option allows the editor to perform edits on the fly. Most editing VCRs and automatic edit control units contain a pair of buttons labeled *cut in* and *cut out*. If an input signal is being fed into the editing VCR (from a source VCR or other video source) and the cut-in button is depressed, an insert edit will be made. When the cut-out button is hit, the edit will end.

You should exercise great caution when editing in this manner. As with setting edit points on the fly, correct edit points depend on quick reflexes. Furthermore, since the cut-in button actually executes the edit (and consequently erases and records over the original material on the edit master tape), you will not have a chance to correct a wrong edit.

Backspacing

Once the edit entry and exit points have been entered into the control unit, the VCRs need to be cued to a point before the edit entry points so that both VCRs can be backspaced. The control of this process—also called backtiming, cueing, or prerolling— is one of the most important functions of the edit control unit, and it is in the way the VCRs are backspaced that the meaning of the term *control track editor* emerges.

When you give the edit control unit the command to backspace the tapes, they typically back up to a point five seconds before the edit point. However, the control track editors do this *not* by measuring time but rather by counting control track pulses. Since there are (or should be) 30 control track pulses per second, the control unit counts off the control track pulses from the beginning of the edit point. When it reaches 150 pulses (30 pulses per second × 5 seconds = 150), it stops the VCR, which is now cued. Similarly, when the command is given to perform the edit, the control track editor does not know where the edit point is in terms of the video or audio content of the picture. It simply counts off the 150 control track pulses again and makes the edit when it reaches pulse 150.

Perhaps the most common problem encountered with the control track edit units occurs when you attempt to cue a tape that lacks enough control track in advance of the edit point to allow the control unit to backspace the tape. *Tapes must always have at least 5 seconds of continuous video information and control track before the edit point. Just to be safe, it is better to have more than 5 seconds (10 seconds is good).*

Let's suppose that you are trying to cue up a tape on the source VCR. You find a point that is two seconds into a shot and identify that as the beginning of the edit—the edit entry point. You then attempt to cue the shot by giving the control unit the command to backspace the tape. The edit control unit begins to count control track pulses and counts back to the beginning of the shot: 2 seconds = 60 control track pulses. However, it needs 90 more control track pulses to properly cue up the shot. Unfortunately, your video ends at the two-second mark. The VCR, oblivious to the fact that there is no video beyond this point, will simply continue to rewind the tape until it reaches the next control track pulse or until it reaches the beginning of the tape.

If your VCR refuses to park the videotape in the cue mode, and rewinds the tape to the beginning, chances are great that there is not enough control track in front of the edit point. The VCR is fruitlessly searching for the place at which to stop. Again, it is for this reason that *all tapes must have at least 5 to 10 seconds of usable video and control track before each edit point on both VCRs.* Without it, the edit control unit cannot cue the shot for the edit.

Problems with Control Track Editing

All Control Track Pulses Look the Same. The main weakness in control track editing systems lies in the fact that all control track pulses look the same to the edit control unit, which is only capable of counting control track pulses when it cues the VCR. An error in counting will affect the amount of time the VCR is back-spaced, thereby affecting the accuracy of the edit.

For example, let's assume that one of your tapes is slightly wrinkled at the edge and that this wrinkle has destroyed one second of control track pulses (30 pulses). Let's assume further that these missing control track pulses come two seconds in front of the edit point. As the control unit counts back to 150, it will be at pulse 60 when it hits the spot where the pulses are missing. The tape will continue moving, but the control unit will not count pulse 61 until it gets to the next pulse. Since one second of pulses is missing, the control unit will count pulse 61 at the spot in the tape that should have produced pulse 91. When the control unit reaches pulse 150, it will stop the VCR. Instead of backspacing the tape five seconds, it will have backspaced it six seconds. But because its only time reference is through control track pulses, it has no way of knowing this.

If this error is made as the tape on the source VCR is cued, when the command to perform the edit is given and both VCRs are rolled, the edit will be made at a point one second off the planned spot on the source VCR. This is a considerable difference, especially if you are trying to edit between words or in other places where a difference of a few frames may be critical.

Accuracy. Control track editors are not **frame accurate**. That is, they seldom make the edit exactly on the planned frame. Most systems are only accurate within two to four frames on either side of the planned edit point. In many situations this is good enough, but in some it is not. Two factors contribute to the inaccuracy of these editing systems: problems with counting and system mechanics. Pulse counting tends to be more accurate when edits are of short duration, and less accurate when they are long. In a one-*second* insert, only 30 control track pulses need to be counted to mark the edit entry and exit points. On the other hand, in a one-*minute* insert, 1,800 pulses are counted and the chances of miscounting are magnified. If the pulses are not counted correctly, the edit points will be off the mark.

The other problem with the accuracy of control track editing systems lies in the mechanics of the machines. When the VCRs cue up a shot, they rewind five seconds and then pause the tape. However, the braking mechanism in the VCR is not always frame accurate. The VCR may overshoot the mark by two frames. However, since all control track pulses look the same, the control track editor will not know that the VCR is two frames off. When the perform edit command is given, it will simply count off 150 pulses—not 152—and will assume that it has reached the edit point correctly. For this reason, *the more times you preview or rehearse an edit, the greater the chance of the system making an error when it performs the edit.*

Some VCRs are more mechanically accurate than others. New VCRs are usually more accurate than old VCRs, and certainly well-maintained VCRs are better than abused ones. However, no matter how good the condition of your VCR and editing system, you will seldom be able to achieve frame accurate editing with a control track editing system.

Varying the Preroll Time

Most control track editing systems use a 5-second preroll. On some systems, preroll time can be decreased. If your machines stabilize quickly, you may be able to reduce the time to 4.5 or sometimes 3.5 seconds. By reducing the preroll time, you can edit with less control track at the head of each shot, and you can save a second or so every time you make an edit. This is not a lot of time if you do not do much editing, but it adds up quickly when you edit for eight hours a day, every day.

SETTING UP A CUTS-ONLY SYSTEM FOR EDITING

The previous sections of this chapter gave you a background in the basic technical elements of editing. To be able to diagnose problems when they occur, a good editor needs to understand what is happening within the system. You may not be able to fix the system if it is broken, but you should be able to figure out if a problem is really a problem or if it is the result of operator error. It is rather embarrassing to run to your maintenance or engineering staff because your machines will not cue up properly—only to find out that you forgot to record video black on your tape and thus the machine does not have any control track to cue to.

Cuts-Only System: Machine Setup

Most editing systems are very basic, consisting of two VCRs (source and editing), two monitors (one for each VCR), and an edit control unit. These simple systems are referred to as **cuts-only editing systems** because the only transition they allow the videotape editor to use is the cut. Dissolves, wipes, and other special effects require at least two source VCRs and a video switcher interface.

Figure 8–14 shows a schematic of a cuts-only editing system. Connecting the system is simple: Connect both VCRs to each other and to the control unit with a multipin cable; patch the video and audio output of each VCR into its own monitor; and connect everything to AC power. That's it! You can now insert your tapes and begin editing.

Figure 8–14   Cuts-Only Editing System Schematic

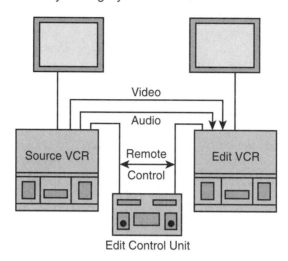

Edit Control Unit

Videotapes

You will need at least two videotapes to edit. One or more tapes will contain the original unedited material. These tapes will go into the source VCR as they are needed. You will also need one blank tape, which will become the **edit master tape** and will go into the editing VCR. If you plan to edit in the *insert mode*, this tape should contain video black and control track for the expected length of the program. If you plan to edit in the *assemble mode*, you will need some video black and control track at the beginning of the tape, so that the edit control unit can cue up for the first edit.

Source Videocassette Recorder Setup

Once the basic editing system is in place and you are ready to begin editing, you need to prepare the source and editing VCRs. First, turn on the power to all elements of the system and insert your original tape into the source VCR. Before you can begin to edit, several switches and meters need to be set in the proper position on the VCR.

Sync.   The sync switch tells the VCR what the source of vertical sync is for this machine. In most situations, you should set the sync switch on the playback VCR to the *internal* position. This means the VCR will be synchronized to an internal crystal oscillator with a frequency of 60 cycles per second. In large editing facilities, the source VCR may be operated in conjunction with **house sync** (sync supplied by an external sync generator to all the video equipment in a given facility), or a **time base corrector (TBC)**, an electronic device that improves the stability of the playback signal. In both of these situations, set the sync selector switch to the external position.

Tracking. Once you have selected the correct sync position, put the VCR into the play mode. When the image appears on the monitor and stabilizes, adjust the tracking control so that the needle reaches the maximum position on the tracking meter. If all of your tape was shot on the same VCR, you will not have to adjust tracking again. However, if you are using tapes that were recorded on a number of different machines, or if you notice the tracking meter wavering from the maximum position, you will have to readjust the tracking control. Some source VCRs have a tracking control but no tracking meter. In that case, adjust the tracking control until the picture in the monitor is clear and stable.

Input Signal Selector. Set the input signal selector for the input going into the VCR. The *TV* position is used to record audio and video signals from a television receiver; the *line* position is used to record audio and video signals from normal audio and video sources; and the *dub* position is used for dubbing or editing.

Counter. With sync and tracking set, and the VCR in the proper video mode, you can now rewind the tape and zero the counters on the edit control unit and the VCR. This will ensure that they both start counting from zero.

Editing Videocassette Recorder Setup

Once the source VCR is set, you can turn your attention to the editing VCR.

Sync. Set the sync selector switch on the editing VCR to the normal position, unless you have an external sync input from a house sync generator or a time base corrector. The normal setting allows the editing VCR to reference to incoming sync from the source VCR, thus making editing possible.

Tracking. The tracking level should be set with the tape in the play mode, just as tracking was set on the source VCR. If you are editing in the insert mode or the assemble mode, and have video black recorded on the entire tape (insert mode), or just on the head of the tape (assemble mode), you will only need to set your tracking level once. No adjustment should be made after this initial adjustment.

Input Signal Selector. This switch should be set either to the dub position or the line position, depending on your system.

Counter. Once you have set the sync, tracking, and input controls, stop and rewind the tape. Then zero the counter, as you did on the source VCR.

Record Levels. It is now time to set the record levels on the editing VCR. Video and audio levels can be set independently. Most machines allow you to set the levels on automatic gain control (AGC) or to adjust them manually. Most editors prefer to set the video level on AGC because video levels on field tapes tend not to vary greatly, since much of the initial level control during recording is automated by the camera and the VCR. On the other hand, since audio levels in field recording may vary greatly, it is typical to adjust the audio level manually.

Most audio and video meters on editing VCRs show audio and video levels when the machines are in the electronics to electronics, or *E to E mode*. Some machines go into this mode if the VCR is in the stop mode; others go into this mode if the record button is pressed while the machine is in the stop mode. In the E to E mode, the record circuits are engaged, and the output of the source VCR is looped through the editing VCR. This allows you to see the incoming audio and video levels on the editing VCR's meters, and to see and hear picture and sound on both the playback and record monitors.

Once the levels are set, press the stop button on the editing VCR to break the E to E loop. Then press stop and rewind on the source VCR. Make sure that all tape counters on both machines are reset to zero. You are now *almost* ready to edit.

Editing Leader

One last thing requires attention before you begin editing. Every edited master tape should have a standard **leader sequence** at the head of the tape before the beginning of the program. This standard leader serves a number of purposes. First, it provides protection for the beginning of the program. Remember, the first part of the videotape is the part grabbed by the mechanical arm in the VCR and wrapped around the head drum. This part of the tape is therefore subjected to considerable stress, and is occasionally damaged. Try to avoid using the first minute or so of tape for critical information—such as the beginning of your program! By placing identifying leader at the head of the tape, the beginning of your program will be protected from the machine's mechanical maw.

The other reasons for using standard leader are to identify the program on the tape and to give your engineering staff a way of checking the audio and video signal levels before the program starts. Finally, the leader provides a way to cue up a tape so that the beginning of a program can easily be found. There is nothing more frustrating than watching someone try to find a 30-second program that was recorded somewhere on a 60-minute tape without any identifying leader before it.

Unfortunately, there is no standard videotape leader. Commercial producers, independent producers, broadcasters, and corporate producers all use somewhat different leaders. However we have found the following leader sequence to be extremely useful:

Video black	10 seconds
Color bars with tone (0 db)	30 seconds
Slate (program identification)	10 seconds
Countdown leader	8 seconds
Black	2 seconds
Program start	

This leader sequence provides all the necessary advantages. It provides a 60-second buffer between the beginning of the videotape and the beginning of the program; it gives the engineering staff video and audio reference levels; and its countdown allows the tape to be accurately cued up for playback. No edited tape should be produced without this or other similar leader.

You can assemble your own leader by editing together the material you need in the proper sequence. Use the camera to record video black if you do not have a switcher with a video black output available. Color bar and tone generators are common fixtures in all studios and postproduction facilities. If you do not have access to them, you can improvise. Many cameras now have a color bar output, and some audio mixers have a tone oscillator. You can combine the two to create color bars with tone. You can make your own slate and record it, and if you do not have a prerecorded countdown leader you can easily make one by editing together one second segments of the numbers 10, 9, 8, 7, 6, 5, 4, 3. Leave two seconds of black at the end of the countdown before the program begins.

Editing Strategy

Setting Edit Entry Points. Try to set the edit entry points as accurately as possible. If you are editing to audio, try not to cut off the first part of the first word spoken by your subject. Sometimes it is better to start with a brief pause than to risk cutting off someone in the middle of a word.

Setting Edit Exit Points. If you are editing in the assemble mode (or if you are assembling a program in the insert mode), use the technique of overlapping edits. Let the edit continue past your planned exit point, and then cut off this unwanted material when you set the entry point for the next edit. This gives you a little breathing room for the next edit. It is better to have a little room after the shot than to cut it so closely that you have to cut the tail off the shot on the edit master tape when you make the next edit.

Avoid Overuse of the Pause Mode. It is a good idea *not* to leave either VCR in the cue/pause or preroll mode for any significant time while you are looking for the edit points on the tape in the other VCR. When a VCR is in the pause mode, the heads continue to hit the tape. This is what produces the still frame image on the monitor. Excessive use of the pause mode may wear out the tape in that spot. The oxides may wear off the tape, causing the image to look bad, or even causing the video heads to clog. Some machines automatically go into the stop mode if they are left in the pause mode for more than a few minutes.

An easy way to avoid leaving a tape in the pause mode for too long is to set the edit points on the source VCR before you set the edit points on the editing VCR. It usually takes longer to find the edit points on the source VCR because you may have a number of takes of each shot, or perhaps a number of tapes from which to draw your material. On the editing VCR, however, the next edit is almost always made immediately after the last one on the tape, so it does not take very long to find the entry point.

Performing an Assemble Edit

Once the VCRs are set up, the tapes are tracked to a maximum, and your record levels are set on the editing VCR, you are ready to begin editing. To do this, you must follow these steps:

1. Select the assemble editing mode on the edit control unit.
2. Find the edit entry point on the source VCR, and enter this into the edit control unit.
3. Find the edit entry point on the editing VCR, and enter this into the edit control unit.
4. Cue the tapes, allowing the edit control unit to backspace them to the preroll point five seconds before the edit point.
5. Preview the edit. Watch the editing VCR's monitor to see if the edit takes place at the correct spot. Also, listen closely to the audio. Does it sound correct? Is the level correct? If the preview is satisfactory, continue to step 6. If the preview is not satisfactory, reset the edit point that is causing the problem.
6. Recue the tapes to the preroll point.
7. Perform the edit. Allow the editing VCR to record several seconds more information than you actually need.
8. Stop the source VCR.
9. Stop the editing VCR and review the edit.
10. If the edit is satisfactory, continue on to the next edit. If it is not satisfactory, redo the exit.

Performing an Insert Edit

The following steps detail how to perform an insert edit:

1. Select the *insert editing mode* on the edit control unit, and select the type of insert you want to make (video, audio 1, or audio 2).
2. Locate the critical out point of the edit. Is it on the tape in the source VCR? Or is it on the tape on the editing VCR? Enter the edit entry and exit points for the critical tape. Enter the edit entry point on the other tape.
3. Cue both VCRs.
4. Preview the edit.
5. Recue the tapes.

6. Perform the edit.

7. Stop both VCRs and review the edit.

Getting More Complex: Manipulating Audio

If all you want to do is transfer material from the source VCR to the editing VCR, then the simple editing system and procedures described above will suffice. However, most editors want to do a little more with their material in the editing process. Most frequently, they also want to manipulate the audio.

Every simple editing system should contain at least a simple *audio patch bay* or switch that allows the editor to manipulate the audio as it flows from the source VCR to the editing VCR. A simple device that allows you to send the source VCR's channel 1 to either channel 1 or 2 on the editing VCR, and the source VCR's channel 2 to either channel 1 or 2 on the editing VCR, is essential. Although it is possible to reach behind the VCRs and simply repatch the audio inputs when you need to redirect the audio signals, an *outboard patch panel* can save a lot of wear and tear on the VCR's cables and connectors (see Figure 8–15).

The next step up in complexity with respect to audio manipulation is having the ability to incorporate additional audio sources into your edited program. You will often need to add narration, music, and/or sound effects to the edited program. How can you do this? One way is to patch the additional audio sources directly into the editing VCR. Most machines have inputs for microphones, or line-level inputs for audiotape recorders and turntables. However, with direct patching into the editing VCR, it is very difficult to lay down the information accurately at the edit point. If you do not manually activate the record circuits and cue the audio to roll at the right time, you are out of luck.

A much better way to deal with the problem is to record the audio information that needs to be dubbed into the program on another videocassette. New or additional audio information can easily be integrated into a program if it can be controlled and cued in the same way that videocassettes can be controlled and cued. For this reason, it is a good idea to keep several video cassettes on hand with video black and control track. If you need to add music to a program and you have it on audiotape, transfer it first to the appropriate audio channel of one of the videocassettes with the video black and control track. With the audio information recorded onto a videotape, it can now be cued by using the edit control unit.

New audio information can be added to the edit master tape by doing an audio-only insert into the appropriate linear audio channel on the editing VCR. Voice-overs can be added in the same way. Record the voice-over onto a videocassette that has been blacked, and then insert this cassette into the source VCR. All cueing can then be done with the edit control unit.

If multiple audio sources are going to be used during editing, an audio mixer should be incorporated into the editing system. The audio mixer can be placed into the audio line between the source and editing VCRs. Additional audio inputs

Figure 8–15 (A) Schematic Diagram: Audio Mixer and Patch Bay, (B) Eight Channel Audio Mixer (Sony MXP-290)

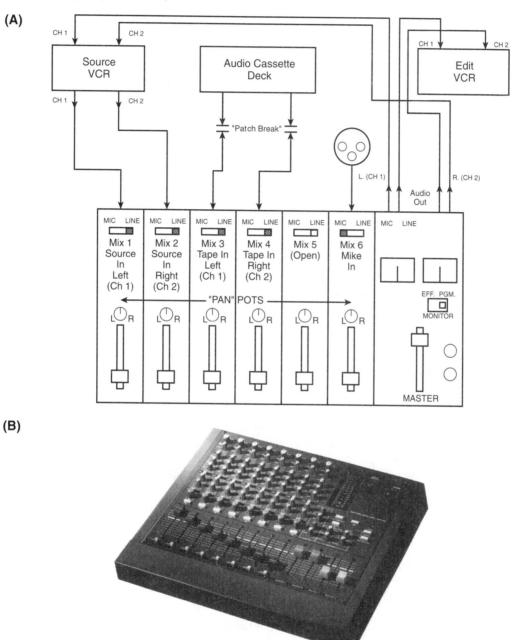

can be patched into the system through the mixer. Figure 8–15 illustrates a simple audio patch system that provides considerable flexibility in working with audio during editing.

Monitoring Audio While Editing

One aspect of audio that is frequently overlooked in the editing process is the quality of the audio speakers used to monitor in the program audio. Many editing systems contain only the audio speakers in the video monitors for the source and record decks. These speakers are usually of very poor quality, and more often than not they mask the way the audio recording actually sounds.

For this reason, you should use a pair of good-quality audio speakers (one for each channel) to monitor the audio while editing. Bookshelf-sized loudspeakers do the job well, as do some of the high-quality mini-speakers that have become available in the last few years. These should be used in conjunction with the normal television monitor audio speakers. The high-quality speakers let you hear things that may not be apparent on the television monitor speaker, whereas the television monitor speaker lets you hear the audio the way it will most likely be heard when the program is received at home and viewed on a conventional television.

If you are editing in a very noisy area, use headphones to monitor audio. This way you can hear the program audio without distraction from outside noise.

A/B ROLL EDITING

Editing systems that consist of one source VCR and one editing VCR are called single-source editing systems, or cuts-only editing systems. In contrast with these simple single-source cuts-only editing systems, **A/B roll editing** systems utilize two source VCRs and one editing VCR. A/B roll systems are somewhat more complicated than single-source cuts-only systems and are used for three reasons:

1. To allow the videotape editor to perform multiple source transition effects, such as dissolves and wipes
2. To allow precise control of additional audio sources
3. To key titles

Checkerboard Assembly

A/B roll editing takes its name from the technique of A/B rolling in film production. To make splices between shots invisible, or to dissolve from one shot to another, shots are arranged on rolls of film in checkerboard fashion. Shot 1 is put onto the A roll, and an equivalent length of black leader is placed on the B roll.

Shot 2 is placed on the B roll, and a corresponding length of black leader is placed onto the A roll. Shot 3 goes onto the A roll, with black leader on the B roll. This alternating checkerboard pattern is completed for the length of the film. If only two rolls of film are used, it is called A/B rolling. If more rolls are used to build more complex effects, it may become A/B/C rolling, and so on (see Figure 8–16).

When the A and B rolls are sent to the laboratory for final assembly, the transitions are put into the film. To cut from shot 1 to shot 2, the last frame of film of the A roll (shot 1) must match the beginning of the first frame of shot 2 on the B roll. (The black leader is invisible and does not affect the quality of the picture.) Shot 1 and shot 2 are overlapped for the desired length of a dissolve. When the film is processed in the printer in the lab, the B roll is faded in as the A roll is faded out, creating the dissolve effect.

It is possible to assemble A and B rolls of videotape with black leader in between each of the shots, roll both VCRs simultaneously through a switcher, and perform the dissolves manually with the dissolve lever. However, for the dissolves to occur at the proper place, the tapes must roll in perfect synchronization.

Automatic A/B Roll Edit Control Units

Automatic A/B roll edit control units with built-in dissolve capability offer an alternative to the checkerboard method of creating dissolves (see Figure 8–17). These control units also often perform simple wipes and key in titles. Automatic A/B roll edit control units control two different source VCRs along with the editing VCR. After all the tapes have been cued, a dissolve (or wipe) is performed as follows.

First, the control unit rolls source A and the editing VCR. An edit is made at the first edit point, so that source A is now being recorded onto the editing VCR. At the appropriate cue point, source B is rolled. At the dissolve point, the edit control unit automatically brings up the video and/or audio level of source B as it simultaneously fades out the video from source A. During the transition, the two video sources appear superimposed. When the dissolve is complete, source A automatically stops. Source B continues to record onto the editing VCR until the edit out point of the shot is reached.

Figure 8–16   Checkerboard Assembly (Film or Video)

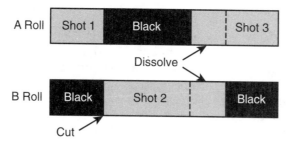

Figure 8–17   Sony BVE-600 A/B Roll Edit Control Unit

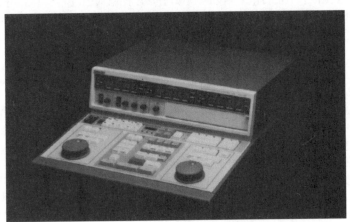

Matched Frame Editing

If the next desired transition is a straight cut, this can be performed as a normal edit between the appropriate source and editing VCRs. If, however, the next transition is a dissolve or wipe back to source A, then the technique of matched frame editing is used.

A **matched frame edit** is an invisible edit made in the last shot laid down on the editing VCR. In a matched frame edit, a single shot is broken into two individual shots. A part of the shot is laid down onto the editing VCR. The matched frame edit then joins the part of the shot on the editing VCR with the rest of the shot, which is supplied by the source VCR. The two "parts" of the shot are perfectly joined, so the edit is completely invisible. Indeed, the shot appears to be perfectly continuous.

The matched frame edit allows you to dissolve back to the other source machine. Once the matched frame edit has been made, the other source machine can be rolled, and the next dissolve can be executed (see Figure 8–18).

A/B Roll Audio Editing

A/B roll audio editing is often used to mix several audio sources. Consider this very simple example. Source A contains the principal video with sound on tape, to which you want to add background music. Source B contains a videocassette with music recorded onto the appropriate audio channel. Both sources can be controlled by the edit control unit, and the music on source B can be introduced at the correct time by the control unit.

Of course, music can instead be added by playing it back directly from an audiotape recorder or turntable. However, the A/B roll audio editing system

Figure 8–18   Matched Frame Editing

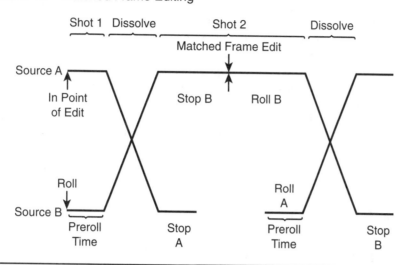

allows all sources to originate on videotape and thereby provides much more precise cueing and recording.

Keying

Some A/B roll automatic edit control units contain a *keyer*, thus eliminating the need to use a switcher for keys. The A/B roll control unit can be used to easily control the points at which keyed letters are introduced and deleted. It also controls the way in which the letters are introduced: They can be cut in (abruptly appearing at full intensity on the screen); faded in; wiped in; or introduced as a **wipe-key**, a combination of a wipe and a key. The edit control unit usually lets the operator determine the speed at which keys are faded or wiped into the picture.

SMPTE TIME CODE EDITING

The most sophisticated editing systems utilize Society of Motion Picture and Television Engineers (SMPTE) time code. **SMPTE time code** is an identification system in which each frame of video information is give a unique code number that identifies it in terms of hours, minutes, seconds, and frames. The first frame of video information is coded 00:00:00:01 (0 hours, 0 minutes, 0 seconds, and 01 frame). A frame of information 10 minutes into the tape would be coded 00:10:00:00 (0 hours, 10 minutes, 0 seconds, and 0 frames), and so on.

SMPTE time code has a number of advantages over systems that lack time code, and it has become an important part of video production. Unlike other kinds of tape counters, which may vary from machine to machine and can be reset to zero by pressing the reset switch on the VCR, SMPTE time code becomes a permanent part of the tape. This provides an accurate and precise time reference for any frame of video information and allows you to find a particular point in a tape on any VCR that is capable of reading time code information.

Because of its accuracy, SMPTE time code is widely used in videotape editing. Entry and exit points for each shot can be logged in terms of their time code numbers, and a complete list of all of the shots that will comprise the program can be compiled. The edited master tape can then be assembled by referring to the time code numbers for each of the shots. If a mistake is made during the editing process, or if it is necessary to change the length of a shot or its order within the program, these modifications can be made much more quickly and with greater accuracy than with control track systems.[1]

Types of Time Code and Where It Is Recorded

Time code information is recorded as digital electronic information on the videotape. It can be recorded during field production or it can be added to videotapes that have already been recorded without it.

There are two basic types of time code: longitudinal time code (LTC) and vertical interval time code (VITC). **Longitudinal time code** is typically recorded by a stationary head in one of the longitudinal audio tracks on the videotape or in a special cue or address track that is found on some professional-quality VCRs. The VCR needs to be equipped with special heads and amplifiers in order to accurately record and play back longitudinal time code. On many small-format VCRs, only one of the longitudinal audio tracks is capable of recording time code. By activating a special time code switch, the audio circuitry is converted to record and read the time code signal.

Since longitudinal time code is recorded in its own track, it can be recorded at the same time the video information is recorded or it can be added to a tape after the video has been recorded. This latter method of adding time code to a prerecorded tape is known as **poststriping**.

Vertical interval time code is recorded by the rotating video heads in one of the video tracks during the blanking interval between the fields of video information. Unlike longitudinal time code, which can be recorded at the same time the original video is recorded or added to a tape afterwards, VITC is recorded as part of the video signal on one of the video tracks and it must be recorded at the same time the video information is recorded.

The advantage to recording the time code in the vertical interval or the *address track* is that it leaves both audio channels free for audio production. If the time code is added in one of the audio channels after the video has been recorded, only one audio channel is available for audio production because the other contains time code information.

As with many other elements of video field recording, there is no standard for where to record the time code information. Some editing systems demand that it be recorded in audio channel 1; others require audio channel 2. Most will work with the time code recorded in the vertical interval and some will be able to handle a mixture of time code locations. For example, time code is often recorded on the edit master tape in the vertical interval when the video black is recorded. Field tapes, however, might include a mixture of time code recorded in the vertical interval and in one of the audio channels. Most sophisticated systems can read time code from any of these locations.

It is always a good idea to check your editing system's time code requirements before you decide where to record the time code on your tapes. There is nothing more frustrating than recording the time code in audio channel 2 and then finding out that your control unit or VCR only reads time code in channel 1. Planning is of the utmost importance here. If you record the time code in the wrong audio channel for your editing system, you should **ping-pong** the time code and audio information by making a dub of the tape and rerecording the time code and audio on the correct channels. Time code that had originally been recorded on channel 2, for example, would wind up on channel 1 in the dub, whereas the audio originally recorded on channel 1 would be rerecorded on channel 2. The problem with this procedure is that you lose a generation in your tape. Instead of editing from a first-generation original, your original now is a second-generation tape. This means that the edit master tape will be a third-generation tape instead of a second-generation tape, and some quality loss may be apparent.

Drop Frame and Nondrop Frame Time Code

Normally, time code numbers are generated to match the 30 frames per second scanning rate of the video system. This is **nondrop frame time code**. However, the frame rate for the American NTSC color standard is actually closer to 29.97 frames per second. In order to correct for this discrepancy—which is equivalent to 3.6 seconds or 108 frames per hour—some time code generators are capable of generating **drop frame time code**. Drop frame time code generators drop (do not generate) two frames of time code information per minute each minute of the hour with the exception of the tenth minute of each hour. To look at this another way, 2 frames are dropped during 54 of the minutes in each hour ($2 \times 54 = 108$ frames/hour).

In many editing situations where time code is used, nondrop frame time code provides sufficient accuracy. However, if absolute precision in the timing of a segment is necessary, particularly if it is a long program meant for broadcast distribution, dropframe time code should be used.

Generating and Recording Time Code

The **time code generator** is the device that produces the time code information. Some time code generators are portable (they are built into some portable VCRs, or can be attached to them; see Figure 8–19). Others are mounted in studio equipment racks and are not portable.

There are two different kinds of time codes: time of day time code and dedicated time code. **Time of day time code** is referenced to a 24-hour clock and runs continuously, day and night. At midnight, the time code reads 00:00:00:00; at noon, it reads 12:00:00:00; and so on. Time of day code is often found in large production houses where a central time code generator feeds the time code simultaneously to all the VCRs in each of the studios, thus eliminating the need for each machine to have its own time code generator.

A more common type of time code found in video field production is called dedicated time code. **Dedicated time code** means that a particular VCR has its own time code generator. Dedicated time code is also called *zero start time code*, because the time code generator can be set to start counting at 00:00:00:00 at the beginning of each tape. Typically, dedicated time code generators can be used in one of two modes: free run or record run.

In the **free-run** mode, the time code generator begins producing time code when the power to the VCR is turned on, and continues until the power is turned off. Time code is produced as long as the VCR power remains on, although the VCR must be in the record mode for it to record the time code. When the time code

Figure 8–19   Portable Time Code Generator (Future Video TCG-2000)

generator is in the **record-run** mode, time code is produced only when the VCR is in the record mode. The following example illustrates the difference between these two modes.

Suppose that after recording an opening shot, the VCR is placed in the pause mode while the next shot is being set up. The time code at the end of the opening shot is 00:02:00:00, indicating that the first shot was two minutes long. In the record-run mode, the time code generator will stop producing time code until the next shot is recorded. The time code for that shot will begin with the next frame: 00:02:00:01. In the free-run mode, the next time code number recorded will reflect the amount of time that has elapsed between shots. If the crew took a 10-minute coffee break between shots 1 and 2, the time code at the beginning of shot 2 will be 00:12:00:01. In the record-run mode, the time code will be 00:02:00:01.

The most common mode used on portable VCRs is record run. This produces time code with no gaps in it. Time code on a 20-minute mini-cassette begins at 00:00:00:00 and ends at 00:20:00:00 if exactly 20 minutes of tape are used.

One nice feature on many portable time code generators is that the hour digit can be manually preset. Many field producers identify their field tapes by presetting the time code hour to correspond with the number of the tape. Field tape 1 begins with 01:00:00:00, tape 2 begins with 02:00:00:00, and so on.

This technique can only be used if you are working with a videotape format with field recording capacity of less than one hour (for example, $^3/_4$" or VHS/S-VHS mini-cassettes, both with 20 minutes of recording capacity), since recording time in excess of one hour will cause the preset hour digit to advance, thereby rendering the indexing function useless.

If preset hour digits are used to identify the field tapes, the time code generator should only be operated in the record-run mode. Since it is common practice to pause between recorded shots, a 20- or even a 60-minute cassette seldom is filled in that amount of clock time. Indeed, 20 to 60 minutes of actual recording may well represent a day's work. In the free-run mode, on the other hand, a shooting session that lasts more than an hour will wipe out the preset digit, even if that session produced less than an hour of recorded information.

Displaying the Time Code

Since time code is recorded as electronic information, it is invisible when it is recorded onto a videotape. This is true both for time code recorded in one of the audio channels as well as for time code recorded in the vertical interval. However, if the time code is recorded on either one of the two audio channels, you can listen to it as the tape is played back by monitoring the appropriate audio channel. The time code is very loud; it makes a noise like a piece of metal being held against the spokes of a rapidly spinning bicycle wheel.

Now, you may ask, if the time code is invisible and sounds like the noise made by the spokes of a bicycle wheel, what good is it in editing? Good question. To use the time code to make editing decisions, you need to be able to see it. Two options—a time code reader and a time code character generator-inserter—are available.

A **time code reader** is a device that displays the time code as a visual digital readout in hours, minutes, seconds, and frames. The time code reader may be a piece of rack-mounted equipment that is positioned near the VCR providing the time code being read. Time code readers are also built into some control units and some VCRs. If the time code output of the VCR is connected to a time code reader, the reader displays the time code information as the tape is played.

A **time code character generator-inserter** works like the time code reader in that it displays the time code as a digital readout. It also goes one step further by converting the readout into video information that can then be inserted into the picture on a monitor, or be rerecorded with the video information on another videotape. The character generator-inserter makes the time code numbers appear in a black window within the picture. High-quality character generator-inserters can vary the size of both the window and time code numbers, and the position of their placement within the frame. Time code is often displayed at the bottom of the frame as editing decisions are being made. It is visible to the editor, who needs it to make editing decisions, but it does not interfere with the editor's view of the principal picture information in the frame (see Figure 8–20).

Figure 8–20   Television Frame with Time Code Inserted

Window Dubs

A common step in the process of editing with time code involves making a window dub. A time code **window dub** is a copy of the original unedited videotape that is made by using the time code character generator-inserter to insert the time code into the picture. Making a window dub leaves you with two videotapes: (1) the original, with the time code information invisibly recorded as audio information in either the vertical interval, cue, or address tracks or one of the audio channels; and (2) a copy of the original tape, with the time code window visually inserted into the picture (see Figure 8–21).

Making Edit Decisions

With a window dub of all your unedited material, all editing decisions can easily be made with the use of a simple playback VCR and a monitor. As you view the window dub, the time code numbers will be displayed on the screen along with the picture. When an edit point is found, place the VCR in the pause/still mode. This freezes the frame and gives you a still picture along with a still frame display of the time code for that precise frame of video information. You can then write down the time code numbers and prepare an **edit decision list**, or **EDL**, for the entire program, without tying up the editing system itself. Specify the in and out points for each shot in terms of their time code numbers on your list (see Figure 8–22). This

Figure 8–21 Window Dub Schematic

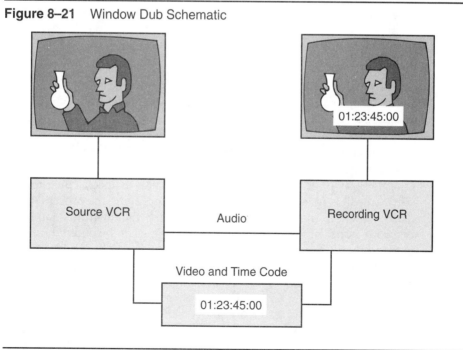

Figure 8–22 Edit List with Time Code

Edit#	Tape Reel	Audio/Video	Cut/Dissolve	Transition Length	Source In	Source Out	Record In	Record Out	Time Code	Type
001	AX	V12	C		00:00:00:00	00:01:00:00	01:31:00:00	01:32:00:00	NN	R
002	AX	V	C		00:00:00:00	00:00:13:04	01:32:15:00	01:32:28:04	NN	R
003	01	A1	C		00:00:28:10	00:01:58:20	01:32:26:20	01:33:57:00	NN	R
004	BL	V	C		00:00:00:00	00:00:00:00	01:32:27:00	01:32:27:00	NN	R
004	02	V	D	075	00:04:01:27	00:04:08:21	01:32:27:00	01:32:33:24	DN	
005	02	V	C		00:04:04:17	00:04:04:17	01:32:29:28	01:32:29:28	NN	R
005	01	V	D	090	00:08:19:02	00:08:33:08	01:32:29:28	01:32:44:04	DN	
006	01	V	C		00:08:29:14	00:08:29:14	01:32:40:10	01:32:40:10	DN	R
006	02	V	D	065	00:03:59:13	00:04:22:24	01:32:40:10	01:33:03:21	NN	
007	03	V	C		00:01:52:16	00:02:01:04	01:32:52:28	01:33:01:16	NN	R
008	03	V	C		00:01:52:02	00:01:59:23	01:32:52:28	01:33:00:19	NN	R
009	03	V	C		00:01:52:15	00:02:02:22	01:32:52:13	01:33:02:20	NN	R
010	02	V	C		00:04:18:21	00:04:18:21	01:32:59:18	01:32:59:18	NN	R
011	03	V	C		00:47:08:00	00:47:20:11	01:32:59:18	01:33:11:29	NN	
012	02	V	C		00:04:18:21	00:04:18:21	01:32:59:18	01:32:59:18	NN	
013	03	V	C		00:47:08:00	00:47:20:11	01:32:59:18	01:33:11:29	NN	
014	03	V	C		00:47:12:10	00:47:12:10	01:33:03:28	01:33:03:28	NN	R
015	02	V	C		00:07:25:28	00:07:34:24	01:33:03:28	01:33:12:24	NN	
016	01	A1	C		00:00:28:10	00:01:16:09	01:32:26:20	01:33:14:19	NN	R
017	BL	A1	C		00:00:00:00	00:00:46:11	01:33:14:05	01:34:00:16	NN	R
018	02	V2	C		00:07:32:13	00:07:32:29	01:33:10:13	01:33:10:29	NN	R
018	03	V2	D	040	01:50:02:09	01:50:31:17	01:33:10:29	01:33:40:07	NN	
019	01	V	C		00:46:22:07	00:46:26:07	01:33:16:03	01:33:20:03	DN	
020	02	V	C		00:01:15:03	00:01:21:08	01:33:19:25	01:33:26:00	NN	R
021	01	V	C		00:47:35:16	00:47:49:16	01:33:24:22	01:33:38:22	DN	R
022	01	V	C		00:50:57:25	00:51:07:06	01:33:35:19	01:33:44:28	DN	R

information can then be entered into the keyboard of the edit control unit when it is time to actually perform the edits.

Not only does SMPTE time code allow you to specify the precise frame at which an edit is to begin and/or end, thus simplifying the process of editing, but it also speeds up the process of finding specific shots within a tape. The precise time code numbers for a particular video frame can be entered into the control unit, and the VCR will then fast forward or rewind to the precise frame number specified in the command. This eliminates a time-consuming visual search for information with the joystick or search dial controls on a control track editor unit.

The edit list using time code numbers makes editing easier and more precise than control track editing. If a program needs to be reedited, new time code numbers reflecting the changes to be made are entered into the system (or edited within the system). Many systems have the capability to **ripple** changes throughout an edit decision list. For example, a change in a shot early in a program (lengthening, shortening, or deleting) will affect the entry and exit points of all subsequent edits on the edit master tape. In a computer-aided time code system, such changes in the edit list are easily made by the computer by adding or subtracting the appropriate number of frames to each of the subsequent shots in the list. In a control track editing system, no such edit list exists. A change in one edit means that you will have to redo all other edits by finding the appropriate cues for each shot: dialogue, visuals, and so on. In addition, since even some of the most simple SMPTE edit control units allow an edit list to be entered, the videotape editor can push a *perform edit* control or an *automatic assemble* button and leave the room as the machines automatically make each of the edits. In a control track system, the videotape editor would have to relocate and perform each edit.

8mm Time Code

Some 8mm and Hi8 format VCRs and camcorders include their own time code systems, called **8mm time code** on industrial/professional equipment or **RC (rewritable consumer) time code** on consumer-quality equipment. These time code systems are incompatible with each other but allow for precise editing on those editing systems that are capable of reading them.

The higher-quality 8mm time code functions much in the same way as the SMPTE time code: It can be transferred from one tape format to another; it can be added to a tape after it has been recorded; it can be used to generate window dubs; and, with the addition of the appropriate accessory interface, it can be converted into SMPTE time code when 8mm tapes are dubbed to another format.

Time Code Edit Control Units

The feature that distinguishes a time code edit control unit from a control track edit control unit is the keyboard (see Figure 8–23). All time code control units contain a *numerical keyboard* into which the time code numbers for edit points are entered. Depending on the complexity of the control unit, it may accept the edits one at a time or it may be capable of storing an edit list and then executing the edits automatically when the list has been made final. Computer-controlled time code editing systems often have extensive memory for edit lists, and often can accept, remember, and execute hundreds of edit decisions.

A number of different kinds of time code editing systems are in use. The simplest system is a cuts-only system, in which the time code controller can control one playback machine and one recorder. This system provides time code accuracy at a very simple level of operation. The next level of complexity is found in the controllers that can control two source machines simultaneously with the recorder. Multiple source machines are necessary if any kind of transition other than a cut is desired. For example, a dissolve or a wipe requires the use of two playback machines. One tape is dissolved to the other, and the transition is recorded onto the editing VCR. Some edit controllers in this group achieve the special effect tran-

Figure 8–23 Time Code Editing Controllers: (A) Ampex ACE 25 Video Editing System, (B) Sony BVE 910 Editing Controller, (C) Panasonic AG-A800 Editing Controller

(A)

(B)

(C)

sition within the control unit itself. Others require that the two VCRs be run through a special effects generator in a video switcher and that the transition (wipe, dissolve, and so on) be manually made in the switcher (see Figure 8–24).

The most complex type of time code editing system has several playback machines, a recorder, and a switcher, which are all controlled by a computer. With this type of system, all edit commands are entered into the computer. The computer then cues up the playback machines and the recorder, rolls the tapes, and controls the execution of any special effect transitions that have been programmed into the system (see Figure 8–25).

On Line, Off Line, and the End of the Line

Two terms frequently used to describe editing that we have not yet discussed are *on line* and *off line*. These terms primarily describe two different editing stages when the final edit will be done on a computer editing system.

Editing that is done **on line** refers to editing the final program, usually on high-quality VCRs. Since rental costs for on-line editing time are fairly high, most producers make all of their editing decisions on paper before they go into the editing suite. In many cases, a rough cut of a program will be made from the window dubs on a cuts-only editing system, often using VHS format tapes and machines. This **off-line** editing is considerably cheaper than experimenting with edits on line, and gives the production personnel the opportunity to see what the program

Figure 8–24   Video Switcher/Editing System Schematic

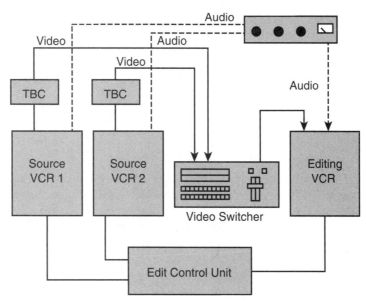

Figure 8–25   On-Line Editing Suite—Realtime Video, San Francisco, CA

will basically look like. When all the final editing decisions have been made, the edit list and the original tapes can then be taken to the on-line editing system. There, the final program assembly is done.

If you have read this chapter through from the beginning, by now you may be suffering from a little information overload. We'll talk more about other components of the production system that can be utilized in the editing process in Chapter 10. However, for now, this is the end of the line for the discussion in this chapter.

SUMMARY

From a technical standpoint, videotape may be edited physically or electronically. Physical editing means that the videotape is actually cut and then reconnected in a different order. Electronic editing is simply a process of re-recording information into a new sequence. All professional videotape editing is done electronically and requires the use of a special electronic editing VCR.

There are two different types of electronic editing: assemble editing and insert editing. Insert and assemble editing can be viewed both as editing strategies as well as technically different types of editing. Assemble editing strategy means that shots or sequences are added onto the tape one after the other in the desired sequence. Insert editing strategy means that a shot is inserted into another shot or sequence.

From a technical standpoint, new video, audio, and control track are recorded each time an assemble edit is made. Insert editing requires that the edit master tape have a continuous, prerecorded control track. This control track is not disturbed during editing.

Two VCRs are needed to edit: a source VCR and an editing VCR. The technique of overlapping edits is used whenever assemble editing is being performed. The major problem associated with assemble editing is that the control track is more likely to contain irregularities than if editing was performed in the insert mode.

To edit in the insert mode, a tape with continuous control track must be prepared. This is done by recording video black onto the tape.

A recommended approach to editing is to use an assemble editing strategy but to execute all the edits in the insert mode.

The principal components of any editing system include the playback or source VCR, the record or editing VCR, video and audio monitors for both VCRs, and an edit control unit to cue both machines to their precise edit points.

The most common type of edit cueing system utilizes automatic edit control units that cue up the tapes by counting control track pulses. These are commonly referred to as control track editors. The control units have a number of standard controls, including remote controls for both the source and editing VCRs, a joystick or search dial, a time display, and edit mode and edit point controls. Editing is accomplished by first finding and setting the edit points. The control unit then backspaces the tapes approximately five seconds and executes the edit upon command. On some systems, backspace or preroll time can be varied to save time while editing. The major problem associated with control track editors is their lack of frame accuracy.

Most control track editing systems are cuts-only systems and are fairly simple to set up. Controls on the VCRs must be properly set and source and editing videotapes are necessary. An editing leader sequence should always be recorded at the head of the tape before the beginning of the edited program.

The videotape editor should have a strategy for editing. Edit entry and exit points must be known and set. Overuse of the pause mode should be avoided, as it may damage the videotapes. Audio may also be manipulated during the editing process and should be carefully monitored while editing.

A/B roll editing systems utilize two source VCRs and one editing VCR. A/B roll editing makes it possible to dissolve from tape to tape and to manipulate audio more effectively while editing. In addition, some A/B roll edit units can perform wipes and keys. Automatic A/B roll edit control units with built-in dissolve capability eliminate the need for the checkerboard type of assembly that characterizes film editing.

The most sophisticated editing systems are SMPTE time code editing systems. There are two basic types of time code: longitudinal time code (LTC) and vertical interval time code (VITC). Longitudinal time code is usually recorded in one of the linear audio tracks or in a special cue track; vertical interval time code is recorded by the rotating video heads in one of the video tracks during the blanking interval between the fields of video information.

Time code edit control units contain a numerical keyboard that is used to enter the time code for each of the edit points. This time code is produced by the time code generator and is recorded directly onto the videotape. To see the time code, a time code reader or character generator-inserter is needed. Window dubs are frequently made to simplify the process of making editing decisions. These window dubs are often used to make editing decisions off line. In time code editing, the final edit is frequently made with a computer-assisted editing system. The process of making the final edit is known as on-line editing.

ENDNOTE

1. For a thorough technical discussion of time code, see "SMPTE/EBU Longitudinal & Vertical Time Code (The Time Code Book)," EECO Computer Controls for Video Production, EECO Incorporated, Santa Ana, CA, 1982.

9

Videotape Editing 2: Aesthetic Factors

Editing is an invisible art. When it is done well, it is hardly noticed—yet almost every visual message in television and film has been edited.

If we define *editing* as the process of selecting and ordering shots, we can identify two kinds of editing in television: editing done during a program's production and editing done after the program has been videotaped. This latter type of editing is called *postproduction editing*.

Television directors have always had the ability to choose and order the shots within a program. Until the advent of postproduction editing, these decisions were made live, as the program was being taped or broadcast. The signals from several television cameras were simultaneously fed into a video switcher, and their pictures were displayed on monitors in a control room. The director would look at the monitors and call for the shots desired. This type of production is still widely done. Shot selections in most live news broadcasts, sports telecasts, and even many soap operas are still made by a director in a control room who calls the shots as the program unfolds.

Videotape editing in postproduction eliminates the need for making editing decisions while a live program is in progress. Production personnel can concentrate on getting the information they need onto tape, without worrying about the arrangement of the shots until after they have finished taping the program. In addition, where video switching is often tied to events in one locale, postproduction editing allows gathering of material for a program from different locations over a longer time.

Postproduction editing, simply referred to as editing from here on, is extensively used in video production. Many programs that look live—such as interviews and variety shows—have been edited in postproduction, long after the initial material was taped.

Editing is the process of arranging individual shots or sequences into an appropriate order. The appropriate order is determined by the information the editor wants to communicate and the impact the editor wants to achieve with the material. The process of editing includes making a series of aesthetic judgments, through which the editor decides how the piece should look, and performing a series of technical operations to carry out the editing decisions. This chapter focuses on the aesthetic elements involved in editing.

ROLE OF THE EDITOR

The videotape editor is potentially one of the most creative members of the production team. No single-camera production shot with postproduction editing in mind would ever appear on a television screen without the services of a competent videotape editor. However, the importance of the editor to the production team depends on both the role and the amount of creative freedom given to that editor. In video production, two broad categories of editors are typically found: the autonomous creative editor, who makes the principal editing decisions, and the subordinate technical editor, who carries out editing decisions made by someone else (see Figure 9–1).

Figure 9–1   The Video Editor at Work in the Editing Suite

The Creative Editor

The autonomous **creative editor** is an individual with significant responsibility for making and executing editing decisions. The creative editor must understand both the aesthetic principles of editing as well as how to operate the video editing equipment. Working in a variety of production situations, the creative editor may be given a brief story outline and a dozen cassettes of field tapes from which to edit a story segment that conforms to the general conventions of the program. Here, the editor has an incredible amount of creative freedom. Decisions about the use of music, sound effects, sound bites, shot sequences, and even the structure of the segment may be left to the editor's discretion. However, the segment or program producer or director usually retains veto power.

At the other end of the spectrum, the creative editor may edit material for a program that was shot from a full script. In this situation, the editor's role is to make the raw material conform to the script. Even within this process, the editor has considerable creative freedom. The editor works with multiple takes, from similar or different angles, of a number of individual shots. Although the basic structure and dialogue of the scene is given in the script, the editor can significantly influence the shape and impact of the scene by selecting the particular shots and takes that work best.

The Technical Editor

The subordinate **technical editor** is usually (but not always) primarily a technician or engineer who is thoroughly familiar with the operation of the editing system from a technical standpoint. The technical editor executes editing decisions made by someone else.

Many video production companies do not own production equipment of their own, choosing instead to rent or lease production equipment and facilities from companies that specialize in providing these services. This is often the case with videotape editing equipment. Since editing systems vary in complexity and flexibility from one facility to the next, when a suite of videotape editing equipment is rented at a postproduction facility, a videotape editor is usually provided from the staff of the postproduction facility to operate the equipment in an efficient, cost-effective manner. Creative control of editing decisions is retained by the producer or director of the program, and the technical editor performs the edits as they have been determined by the individuals with creative control over the program.

It would be grossly unfair to say that technical editors understand only the technical process of editing, and not the aesthetics of editing. In reality, most technical editors know what edits together well and what does not. The principal difference between creative and technical editors lies in the location of creative control over editing decisions. The autonomous creative editor has such control, whereas the subordinate technical editor usually does not. However, most good subordinate technical editors make suggestions about the aesthetics of the edit and, for that reason, they too are partners in the creative editing process.

In many production situations, one individual performs both of these editing functions. Indeed, in many small video production companies and in video production units located in educational institutions, corporations, cable television, and sometimes even broadcast television, one person may produce, direct, and shoot the entire production as well as edit it! Therefore, it is extremely important to understand both the aesthetic and the technical aspects of videotape editing, and how to plan and execute a production reflecting both of these areas of concern.

TYPES OF EDITING

There are two general techniques, or styles, of editing. One is continuity editing; the other is dynamic, or complexity, editing. These two terms represent somewhat of an oversimplification of many ways that editing can be approached. Editing is seldom solely one technique or the other. In most cases, it is a combination of the two techniques. However, these two terms, *continuity editing* and *dynamic editing*, provide a useful place to begin talking about different kinds of editing.

CONTINUITY EDITING

The goal of **continuity editing** is to smoothly move the action along without any discontinuous jumps in time or place. It is easier to perform continuity editing of visual sequences if the material has been shot with postproduction editing in mind. (You may want to review the guidelines for shooting to edit in Chapter 3.)

However, even if the field tape has not been shot according to the rules, there are a number of guidelines that the editor can follow to achieve continuity in editing. Four of the more important guidelines are discussed here.

Establish and Maintain Screen Position

Establishing Shots. The use of the **establishing shot** is an important feature of continuity editing because it identifies the location and the position of the people in the shot in relation to their environment. Once a scene has been set up through an establishing shot, many of the other principles of continuity editing follow logically.

Cut In and Cut Out. By their nature, establishing shots tend to be medium or long shots. As we have mentioned with respect to composition, these shots often do not have the dynamism or energy of the close-up shot. Once a scene has been established, it is standard editing technique to then **cut in** to a close-up of some detail of that scene. The interview that begins with an over-the-shoulder 2-shot of the interviewer and subject is frequently followed by a cut in to the close-up of the

Figure 9–2 Establishing Shot, Cut-In, and Cut-Out Sequence

 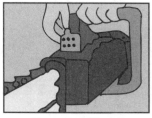 

| Establishing Shot | Close-Up of Detail | Wide Shot of Action |

subject. In a demonstration of a product or machine, the establishing shot may present a shot of the object and the person with the object. The cut in presents important details not visible in the longer shot.

Conversely, once the cut in establishes the important detail, it is frequently necessary to **cut out** again to the wider shot, particularly if action is about to take place. A shot sequence utilizing the techniques of the establishing shot, cut in, and cut out is shown in Figure 9–2.

When cutting in to a tighter shot from a wide shot, objects and people should maintain their same relative place in the frame. Someone who is on the left side of the frame in the wide shot should remain on that side of the frame, or in the neutral center of the frame, when you cut into a medium close-up. The cut in should not cause the person to flip to the other side of the frame (see Figure 9–3).

Jump Cuts and Matched Cuts. Jump cuts and matched cuts violate the conventions of continuity editing because they destroy the invisible, or seamless, quality of the editing. A **jump cut** occurs when something is removed from the middle of

Figure 9–3 Screen Position Reversal

2-Shot   Medium Close-Up

Figure 9–4 Jump Cut in the OK Corral

Cowboy and Horse Cowboy Walks to Horse Cowboy Mounts Horse

Jump Cut

Shot 1   Shot 2

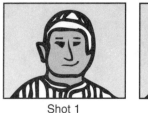

Cowboy and Horse   Cowboy Is on Horse

a shot and the two remaining end pieces are joined together. If the size and position of the subject is not exactly the same, the cut from the beginning shot to the end shot will cause the subject to appear to jump in the frame. For example, imagine a wide shot of a corral that begins with a cowboy leaning against a fence on the left side of the frame (see Figure 9–4). After several seconds, the cowboy walks across the corral and mounts a horse on the right side of the frame. If the middle part of the shot—the part in which the cowboy walks across the corral—is removed, and the beginning and end parts of the shot are joined together, the cowboy will instantly jump from his position against the fence to his position in the saddle. This is an extreme example of a jump cut.

Matched cuts are similar to jump cuts. A **matched cut** is a cut from one shot to another that is similar in terms of angle of view and camera position. When the

Figure 9–5 Matched Cut

Shot 1   Shot 2

two shots are joined together, the effect is of a jump or change in the screen position of the people and objects in the shots (see Figure 9–5).

Avoid jump cuts and matched cuts because they are visible and obtrusive. They look like editing mistakes because they violate the spatial continuity of the subject in the frame. When the subject jumps or moves from one part of the frame to another without any motivation, continuity is lost.

Use Eyelines to Establish the Direction of View and Position of the Target Object

An **eyeline** is simply a line created by your eyes when you look at a **target object**. If you look up into the sky at a bird, the bird is the target object and the eyeline is the imaginary line between your eyes and the bird. Look down at your feet and a similar eyeline is created between your eyes and their target.

Eyelines and the position of the target object are very important in creating continuity. A close-up of someone looking up, followed by a close-up of a bird, makes sense (see Figure 9–6). The same close-up of a person looking up, followed by a shot of the subject's feet, does not.

Eyelines are formed between people when they talk, and they can be used to create continuity when the conversation is edited. This type of continuity editing is facilitated if the original material has been shot utilizing **complementary angles**. A simple scene with two people illustrates the point, which can be applied to interviews as well. Assume that an establishing shot has been recorded. Figure 9–7 shows the establishing shot as the editor sees it on tape. Close-up details of each of the people in the shot have been recorded using complementary angles—one looks to the right side of the screen, the other looks to the left side of the screen. When the establishing shot and two close-ups are edited together, the shot sequence reveals the two people talking to each other.

Violating the rule of complementary angles produces a discontinuous, if not comedic, effect. Figure 9–8 uses the same characters, but in this sequence, they are facing the same angle on camera. These two shots cannot be edited to make it look

---

Figure 9–6   Eyelines Establish Position of Target Object

Eyeline

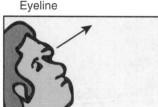 

Figure 9–7   Sequence Using Complementary Angles

Establishing Shot   Two Medium Close-Ups Shot at Complementary Angles

like the two people are talking to each other because the people in the shots are not in the target positions created by their eyelines.

Maintain Continuity in the Direction of Action

Perhaps nothing is more important to maintaining the continuity of action than maintaining **directional continuity**. Characters or objects moving in one shot should continue to move in the same general direction in a subsequent shot. A cut in to a close-up of a football player running toward the goal should show that player running in the same general direction as in the long shot. If the direction of the runner is reversed in editing, continuity will be lost. This may confuse the audience (see Figure 9–9). This principle also applies when taping activities other than sports.

Mismatches in directional continuity are most apparent when a strong horizontal movement in one direction is immediately followed by another movement in the opposite direction, as in the example of the football player. If the editor needs to use such discontinuous shots, they should be bridged by a neutral shot in which the action moves directly toward or away from the camera. Figure

Figure 9–8   Violating the Rule of Complementary Angles

Establishing Shot   Two Medium Close-Ups <u>Not</u> Shot
                           at Complementary Angles

Figure 9–9   Discontinuous Action Sequence

Long Shot   Medium Shot

9–10 shows a sequence in which such a shot is used to bridge the shots in the football sequence.

Directional continuity will be apparent in the raw footage if the videographer has paid attention to the 180-degree rule and the principal action axis when shooting the original field tapes (see Chapter 3).

Use Shot Content to Motivate Cuts

In continuity editing, each edit or cut is usually motivated. That is, there should be a reason for making an edit. The two principal motivators of cuts are dialogue and action.

Much editing is motivated by what is said. For example, a question demands an answer, and each line of dialogue in a dramatic scene must be met with another. In these situations, the editor's task is to cut the material together so that what is said makes sense and so that the visual and aural sequence flows smoothly. The rhythm of the editing should match the rhythm of what is being said in the scene. To do this, edits are usually made at the natural breaks in the dialogue.

Figure 9–10   Bridging Discontinuous Action with a Neutral Shot

Action Moves to the Left   Action Moves toward Camera   Action Moves to the Right

Long Shot   Neutral Shot   Medium Shot

Figure 9–11   Cutting on Action

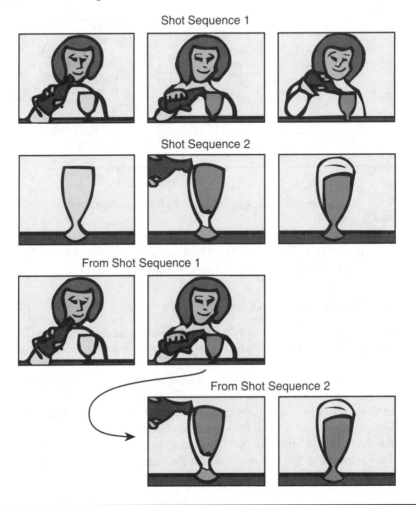

The other great motivation for a cut is action. Indeed, one of the cardinal rules of cutting is to cut on action. Look at the sequence in Figure 9–11. This sequence contains two different shots of someone pouring a glass of beer. Shot 1 is a medium shot, whereas shot 2 is a close-up of the glass. Both shots cover the same general action. What is the best time to cut from the medium shot to the close-up of the glass? The answer is to cut on the action as the bottle is moved to the glass. The editor needs to match the edit point carefully on the two shots. Since the action is repeated in both shots, it must be edited in such a way that no duplication of action is visible. The sequence should look as if it is happening in real time.

As this example demonstrates, it is easier to cut on action if the editor has several shots repeating the action from different angles. A good field producer makes certain that this material has been shot.

DYNAMIC EDITING

Dynamic editing differs from continuity editing in two important ways. It tends to be a bit more complex in structure and it frequently utilizes visual material to create an impact rather than simply to convey literal meaning. Dynamic editing, then, is more *affective* than continuity editing. This is not to say that continuity editing must be listless or boring, or that dynamic editing cannot be used to convey a literal message. The differences between the two are often differences of degree rather than of substance.

Editing to Maximize Impact

Dynamic editing attempts to maximize a scene's impact rather than simply to link together individual shots into an understandable sequence. The selection of shots for use in dynamic editing, therefore, is somewhat different than in continuity editing. Dynamic shot selection frequently includes shots that exaggerate or intensify the event rather than simply reproduce it. Extremely tight shots or shots from peculiar angles are frequently incorporated into dynamic shot sequences to intensify a scene's impact.

Manipulating the Time Line

Dynamic editing frequently is discontinuous in time. That is, rather than concentrating on one action as it moves forward in time (a technique typical of continuity editing), dynamic editing can use **parallel cutting**—cutting between two actions occurring at the same time in different locations or between events happening at different times. The dynamic editor might intercut frames of past or future events to create the effect of a **flashback** or a **flashforward**.

Editing Rhythm

Continuity editing is usually motivated by the rhythm of the event (either the action of the participants or the dialogue of the characters); dynamic editing is more likely to depend on an external factor for its motivation and consequent rhythm. Two common techniques include editing to music and timed cuts.

In its most common form, **editing to music** involves editing together a series of related or unrelated images to some rhythmic or melodic element in a piece of music. In the most clichéd type of editing to music, the editing matches a regular rhythmic beat and does not deviate from it. Editing that uses various musical components—the melody or a strong musical crescendo, for example—to motivate the edits is more energetic and interesting.

A **timed cut** is one in which shot length is determined by time rather than content. You can edit together a sequence of shots that are each two seconds in length, or you can use shot length like a music measure to compose a sequence with a rhythm based on the length of the shots.

TRANSITIONS

For most video producers with simple editing systems, the cut is the only visual transition possible from shot to shot. The most frequently used transition in television and film, the **cut** is an instantaneous change from one shot to another. It approximates the effect achieved by blinking, without leaving a blank or black space between shots.

For the producer with access to a video switcher, or something other than a cuts-only editing system, a number of other transitions are available.

A **fade** is a gradual transition from black to an image or from an image to black. Fades are usually used at the beginning and end of a program; thus we have the terms *fade in* and *fade out*. However, fades are also used within a program. A fade signals a break in continuity of the visual message. Fades are used to insulate the program material from a commercial, to signal to the audience that an event or episode has ended, that time has passed, and so on.

The **dissolve** is similar to the fade except it involves two visual sources. One gradually fades out as the other fades in, and the two sources overlap during the transition. The effect is one image changing into another. Dissolves, once widely used to signal passage of time, now are more often used to show the relationship between images, particularly structurally related images. A dissolve from a photograph of a young man to another photograph of the same man in old age not only clearly shows the passage of time but it also represents the metamorphosis of one image into another.

A **wipe** is a transition in which one screen image is replaced by another. The second image cuts a hard- or soft-edged pattern into the frame as the transition takes place. The wipe pattern is selected and preset by pressing the appropriate button on a video switcher. Most video switchers are equipped with a standard array of wipe patterns: circles, squares, diagonals, diamonds, and so on.

Once extremely popular in television commercials, but seldom used in news or dramatic productions, wipes have now largely been replaced by **digital video effects**. Digital video effects are made possible by digital processing equipment, which digitizes and processes the video signal. Common digital effects include **page push** and **page pull** (the picture appears to be pushed or pulled off the screen by another), **page turn** (this looks like the page of a book or magazine turning), and a host of three-dimensional effects that transform the image into a sphere, the side of a cube, and so on.

Other common digital video effects include **image compression** and **expansion**, which result from stretching or squeezing the horizontal and vertical dimensions of the picture. Through image compression, a full frame image can be reduced to any size and positioned anywhere in the frame. Similarly, through expansion, a reduced image located in a section of the frame can increase in size until it fills the frame.

Digital video effects are often used as transitions. Once, only state-of-the-art production houses and television studios had the sophisticated video switchers with the processing equipment necessary for these effects. But with the increasing convergence of computer and video technology, many of these special effects are now available in cost-effective desktop video systems.

Camera-Generated Transition Elements

Despite the availability of this wide range of transition devices in many sophisticated editing systems, much videotape editing is accomplished on rather simple systems that allow only cuts for transitions. The creative challenge, then, becomes to plan for transitions during the shooting process so that effective and interesting transitions can be achieved even with the cuts-only limitation.

For example, the effect of a dissolve can be approximated by cutting on shots that are out of focus. As you are shooting what will be the first shot in your edited sequence, roll the image out of focus and record this. Begin shooting the second shot in the sequence with the image out of focus and then bring it in to focus. If the focus rolls are timed well and the edit is made at the point where shot 1 ends (out of focus) and shot 2 begins (out of focus), the edit will be relatively invisible and the edited sequence will provide an effect similar to a dissolve. Similarly, fades can be achieved by using the camera iris to fade shots in or out when they are originally recorded. Many consumer camcorders contain a fade-in/fade-out control that accomplishes this electronically.

Camera movement can also be preplanned to accentuate the editing process by controlling the speed and direction of pans, tilts, and zooms during the field production phase of the program. Shots can then be cut together in which camera movement continues in the same direction and at the same speed from one shot to the next, or sequences can be constructed in which the direction of camera movement reverses from one shot to the next.

SOUND IN EDITING

Sound is one of the most important components of videotape editing. From a technical standpoint, control over sound is essential to avoid distortion and make a clear recording. From an aesthetic standpoint, sound plays an important role in influencing the mood and pace of the edited piece, and subsequently the audience's response to the program. Control of sound during the editing process involves a number of different steps, including sound selection, sequencing, layering, and processing.

Sound Selection

The most basic decision to be made about sound while editing is deciding which sound segments to include and which not to include. The editor must first choose from the material available on the unedited videotapes, and then must decide what material needs to be added. Additional material may include narration, music, or sound effects.

If the unedited material is interview based, the editor will need to identify those sections of the interview with the most impact and/or those that concisely present the speaker's point of view. These segments are called **sound bites** when they are edited into the program.

A narrator can link together these sound bites. Narration will then need to be written and recorded for these transition segments. When the narrator is heard, but not seen, on screen, this is called a **voice-over (VO)**. If the narrator is seen on screen while speaking, this is referred to as **sound on tape (SOT)**.

Music, voice, or sound effects recorded onto the audio channel of a separate videocassette—known as tracks—can later be edited into the program master tape. The process of recording these sound tracks is known as **laying down tracks**. Most editors always have several video cassettes available with crystal black to use for tracks (see Chapter 8). These videotapes have video black recorded onto them and both audio tracks are available for recording music, voice, or sound effects. When the editor cues up the cassette for editing, the sound tracks can be heard without visual distractions, as the video portion of the tape is black.

Sound Sequencing

Once the principal sound segments have been selected, the editor must put them into the proper sequence. No matter what the purpose of the segment is, some kind of order is needed. In an instructional or dramatic program, the presentation of the basic material may follow a rigid structure that is geared to maximize the learning or dramatic impact of the program. In an experimental production, sound sequence may be determined by other concerns. In both types of productions, however, basic decisions need to be made about the order of presentation.

In addition to determining the sequence of the sound segments, the editor must also determine the kind of transitions that will be used between them. When editing voice, the most common transition is a straight cut. When one audio segment ends, the next one begins, leaving a natural pause between segments. In other kinds of audio sequences, segues or crossfades may be used.

A **segue** (seg way) from one sound to another is a transition in which the first sound gradually fades out. When the sound has faded out completely, the next sound is gradually faded in. There is a slight space between the two sounds but no overlap. In a **crossfade**, the first sound fades out but the second sound fades in before the first one fades out completely. This results in a slight overlap of the two sounds.

An edit that simultaneously affects both audio and video is known as a **both edit**—that is, both audio and video are edited at the same time. Most dialogue and interview editing is of this type. An on-camera SOT introduction from the field news reporter that is immediately followed by a SOT statement from a county official under arrest for corruption is an example of a both edit. One picture and its corresponding sound are immediately replaced by another picture and its corresponding sound.

Another sound editing technique is the **split edit**. In the split edit, an edit is made first on sound (or picture) and then is followed by the edit to the corresponding picture (or sound). Two separate edits—one on audio, the other on picture—are made, and one follows the other in time.

Consider a sequence in which an on-camera news field reporter, standing outside the local federal building, announces that a noisy protest by tax resisters is going on inside. Instead of cutting from the reporter to the video and audio of the protesters inside, the editor can first cut in the sound of the protesters under the shot of the newscaster giving the introduction. Then the editor can follow with the video of the demonstrators after the introduction is complete. In an interior scene in which a distraught father is waiting for word from the police about the condition of his missing daughter, we see the father glancing nervously out the window. An audio-only edit can introduce the sound of the police car approaching at high speed, followed by a video edit to the patrol car itself, with the sound in sync as it grinds to a halt in front of the house.

Sound Layering

The sound portion of a program can include several sound sources heard simultaneously. When voice-over narration is used, the voice is usually heard over both a picture and some kind of background sound. A more complex example of sound layering might include hearing voice-over, natural sound, and music simultaneously in the same shot. The editor, therefore, must not only select the appropriate sound sources but must layer or **mix** them together appropriately.

The relative strength of each of the sounds layered together is usually determined by its importance in the scene or sequence. The editor must correctly mix them so that their relative volume matches their importance. A voice-over should not be overwhelmed by the natural sound or music that is supposed to be in the background. On the other hand, in a highly dramatic scene, the music may well come to the foreground as it overwhelms the background and other sounds in the scene.

Sound layering, then, involves determining which sounds should be heard in the foreground, as background, or in between. It also involves achieving the proper layering effect through volume manipulation when mixing the sound in the editing process.

Sound Processing

Sound quality is also frequently manipulated during the editing process. Filters and graphic equalizers are widely employed to either correct a problem in the field audio or to manipulate an audio source to achieve a particular effect. The editor must consider all the available sound sources and determine whether manipulation of the sound quality is needed. If there are inconsistencies in the quality of the voice recordings on various field tapes, a graphic equalizer should be used to achieve maximum consistency.

SUMMARY

Editing is the process of arranging individual shots or sequences into an appropriate order. Videotape editing is done in postproduction.

The videotape editor is potentially one of the most creative members of the production team. There are two types of editors: the autonomous creative editor, who has significant responsibility for making and executing editing decisions; and the subordinate technical editor, who executes the editing decisions made by someone else.

The two general techniques, or styles, of editing are continuity editing and dynamic editing. The goal of continuity editing is to smoothly move the action along without any discontinuous jumps in time and place. Important guidelines to follow include:

1. Establish and maintain screen position.
2. Use eyelines to establish the direction of view and the position of the target object.
3. Establish and maintain continuity in the direction of the action.
4. Use shot content to motivate cuts.

Dynamic editing attempts to maximize the impact of a scene rather than to simply link together the shots into an understandable sequence. Important components of dynamic editing include dynamic shot selection, manipulation of the time line, and manipulation of the editing rhythm.

Transitions link one shot to the next. The cut is the most frequently used transition in video production. Other transitions include fades, dissolves, wipes, and various digital video effects.

Sound is one of the most important components in videotape editing. The creative editor is concerned with sound selection, sound sequencing, sound layering or mixing, and sound processing.

10

Additional Production System Components

There is an increasing tendency to incorporate various kinds of studio-based production sources into programs or program segments that originate in the field. Producers increasingly want to incorporate titles, special effects, and film into their productions. These other materials are added in postproduction. Video field producers are increasingly finding that while a production may originate in the field, it often reaches its conclusion in an editing suite that is significantly more complex than a cuts-only editing system. In this chapter, we will examine some of the basic editing system add-ons such as the video switcher, character generator, film chain, and basic signal processing equipment, including the time base corrector and video processing amplifier.

THE VIDEO SWITCHER

The **video switcher** is a production device that allows the editor to combine or manipulate different video sources (see Figure 10–1). Its function parallels that of an audio mixer. A number of different video sources can be fed into the switcher, and the editor can select the source or combination of sources that will be fed out of the switcher to the recorder.

Distribution Switchers

Two types of video switchers are commonly found in video facilities: distribution switchers and production switchers. A *distribution*, or *routing*, switcher is a routing device for video signals. A number of different, nonsynchronous sources are fed into the switcher. By pressing the appropriate button on the switcher, you can feed one of these sources out of the switcher to its destination, where it is displayed. Because they are used to switch from one nonsynchronous source to another, distribution switchers generally do not produce clean transitions from source to

Figure 10–1 Video Switchers: (A) JVC KM-2000U, (B) Grass Valley 100, (C) Ampex Vista, (D) Panasonic WJ-MX50 Digital Audio Video Mixer

(A)

(B)

Figure 10–1 Video Switchers: (A) JVC KM-2000U, (B) Grass Valley 100, (C) Ampex Vista, (D) Panasonic WJ-MX50 Digital Audio Video Mixer *Continued*

(C)

(D)

source. The picture may break up or roll, reflecting a momentary loss of stability. For example, in a large postproduction facility several VCRs might all be connected to a distribution switcher, and the output of the switcher might be connected to one high-quality monitor for viewing the output of any one of the VCRs, thus saving the expense of multiple monitors. By pressing each of the buttons on the switcher, the output of each of the VCRs can be viewed in turn on the monitor. Since each VCR is running independently, they can be considered to be nonsynchronous with each other. Each time a button is pressed on the switcher, a new picture will appear on the monitor, but the picture will roll momentarily as the switching transition is made.

Production Switchers

Production switchers are used in the actual process of video production. They differ from distribution switchers in a very fundamental way: When a switch is made from one source to another on a production switcher, there is a clean cut from source to source. The picture remains stable, without a break up, or **glitch**, in the picture.

Production switchers are able to make this clean switch for two reasons. First, all video sources fed into it are synchronized. Second, the switch from one source to another is made during the vertical interval of the picture, which means that, in effect, a switch is similar to an edit.

For the switch to be made cleanly, all incoming video signals must be synchronized. Therefore, all camera sources are simultaneously driven by an **external sync generator**. The horizontal and vertical drive pulses supplied to each camera cause each of the cameras to scan synchronously. As a result, each camera is at exactly the same scanning point as that of the other cameras at all times. The cameras also all reach the end of the frame at the same time, so the switch from one source to another can take place in the vertical interval.

Videotape recorders present a special problem because they are nonsynchronous sources. That is, the signal that a VCR puts out already has its own horizontal and vertical sync, which is not in sync with the cameras and other sources driven by the sync generator. A **time base corrector (TBC)** corrects this problem. The time base corrector compares the sync pulses of the incoming signal from the VCR with the sync pulses from the sync generator. It then corrects the VCR's signal so that it is synchronized with all the other video sources.

Video switchers were originally designed for use in live, multiple-camera television studio productions where they are still widely used today. The switcher allows the director to select the camera shot that is to go out live to be broadcast or recorded. Several cameras simultaneously feed pictures to the switcher. The **director** sits in a control room, where each camera shot is visible on its own monitor. The director calls out the camera shot—usually by the number assigned to the camera—that is to go out on line. The switcher operator, called the **technical director**, then quickly punches it up on the video switcher to make the switch.

The video switchers used in postproduction are the same ones used in multiple-camera television production. Usually the only difference is the kinds of sources fed into the switcher. Instead of switching between a series of live cameras, the postproduction editor who utilizes a switcher usually chooses from a variety of sources on videotape, film, or originated by an electronic character generator. In some cases, live cameras may also be fed into the switcher, but this is rare (unless the camera is being used to generate titles or other graphics from a studio camera card). Figure 10–2 presents a schematic diagram of the way in which a video switcher can be integrated into an editing system.

In a very complex system, the various system components—the videotape recorders, character generator, and the switcher itself—are controlled by a computer interfaced to the different components.

Operational Characteristics of the Switcher

Each video source fed into the switcher (camera, VCRs, character generator, film chain, and so on) is assigned to a button on the switcher. These buttons are arranged in rows across the switcher, and each row is called a **buss**. Most switchers contain a number of busses. Each of the sources is arranged in the same order in each buss.

Three kinds of busses are typically found on video switchers: program, preview, and mix/effects (see Figure 10–3). Decisions about which video source (or sources) will go out **on line** are made in the *program buss*. When you depress the button corresponding to a particular video source, that source becomes the switcher's output. If the switcher is connected to the editing VCR, the signal will go to that

Figure 10–2 Editing System with a Video Switcher

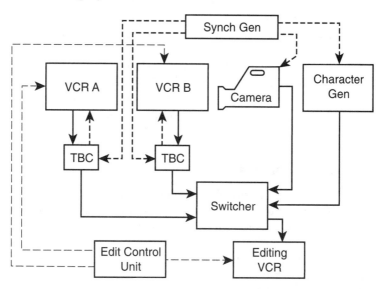

Figure 10–3   Switcher: Mix, Preview, and Program Busses

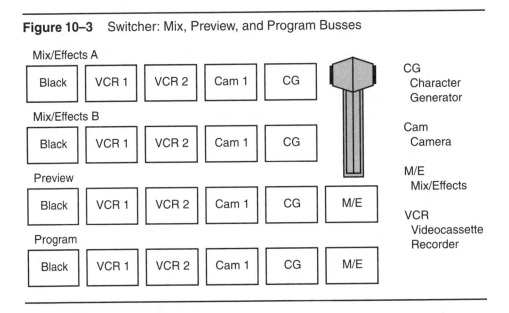

machine. In a live television broadcast, the signal goes to the transmitter and is broadcast live. The output of the program buss can be seen on the *line monitor*.

The output of the *preview buss* is usually connected to a special *preview monitor*, which allows production personnel to see the source before it goes out on line. This buss works completely independently of the program and mix/effects busses, and the preview buss is typically used to preview or rehearse a special effect before it is sent out on line through the program buss.

Special effects are performed through *mix/effects* busses. Superimpositions, fades, wipes, and keys are varieties of special effects commonly found on video switchers.

Inexpensive switchers usually have one program buss, one preview buss, and one mix/effects buss. More expensive switchers are more versatile, and may have three or four pairs of busses that can be assigned to one of the different switcher buss functions (program, preview, or mix/effects). No matter how the switcher is organized, operation is relatively the same.

Switcher Transitions

A typical switcher can do four types of transitions: cut, fade, dissolve, and wipe. To cut from one shot to another, you simply depress the appropriate button. For example, if source 1 is on line, you depress the button for source 2 in the program buss to cut to source 2.

Fades and superimpositions are a bit more complex. A **fade** is a gradual transition from a source to black or from black to a source. To achieve a fade, the effect must be set up in one of the mix/effects (M/E) busses. To fade from black to a source, you punch up black in the mix/effects A buss. Then you punch the source you want to fade to on the mix/effects B buss. You select which buss (A or B) goes out on line with the **fader bar** at the end of the busses. If it is moved to the A position, M/E A will go out. When it is moved to the M/E B position, the switcher output gradually changes from A to B (see Figure 10–4).

A dissolve is executed in the same way as a fade, except it involves a gradual transition from one video source to another rather than to black. Punch source 1 on M/E A and source 2 on M/E B. With the fader bar in the A position, source 1 goes out on line. When the bar is moved to the B position, A gradually fades out and B fades in. When the fader bar is positioned in between A and B, both sources appear **superimposed** over each other on the line monitor. The intensity of each source can be adjusted by moving the fader bar. As it is moved toward A, source 1 becomes stronger and brighter. As it is moved toward B, source 2 becomes stronger and brighter (see Figure 10–5).

Wipes are performed by presetting the wipe pattern and then selecting the wipe sources. Most switchers have a number of wipe patterns—how many depends on how complex the switcher is (see Figure 10–6).

Figure 10–4 How to Perform a Fade

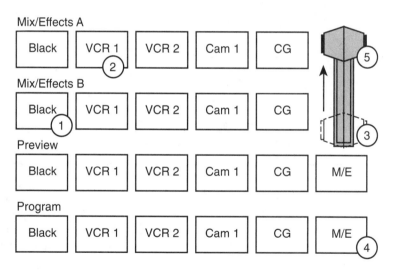

```
START: PROGRAM ON BLACK
PRESET: ① MIX/EFFECTS B ON BLACK
        ② MIX/EFFECTS A ON VCR 1
        ③ FADER BAR ON MIX/EFFECTS B
EXECUTE:
        ④ M/E ON PROGRAM
        ⑤ MOVE FADER BAR TO MIX/EFFECTS A
```

Figure 10–5   How to Perform a Superimposition or Dissolve

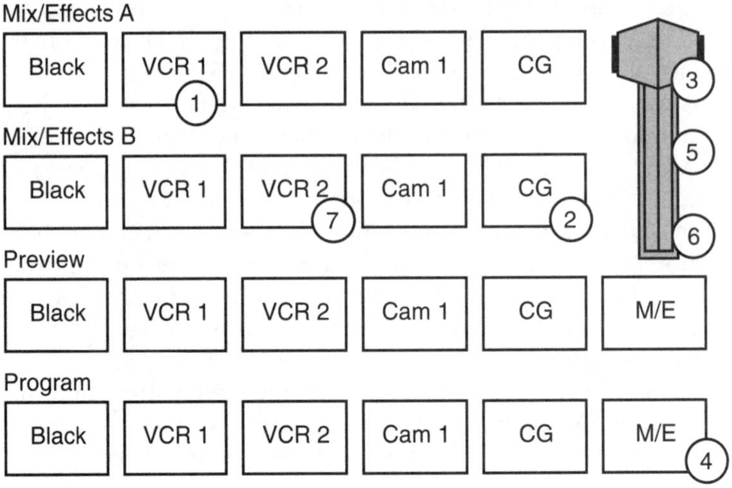

Mix/Effects A

| Black | VCR 1 ① | VCR 2 | Cam 1 | CG |

Mix/Effects B

| Black | VCR 1 | VCR 2 ⑦ | Cam 1 | CG ② |

Preview

| Black | VCR 1 | VCR 2 | Cam 1 | CG | M/E |

Program

| Black | VCR 1 | VCR 2 | Cam 1 | CG | M/E ④ |

(fader bar markers ③ ⑤ ⑥ at right)

SUPERIMPOSITION
  (ASSUME *PROGRAM* IS ON *VCR 1*)
  PRESET:
      ① *VCR 1* ON *MIX/EFFECTS A*
      ② *CG* ON *MIX/EFFECTS B*
      ③ *FADER BAR* ON *MIX/EFFECTS A*
  EXECUTE:
      ④ *M/E* ON *PROGRAM*
      ⑤ *MOVE FADER BAR* MIDWAY BETWEEN *MIX/EFF A* AND *MIX/EFF B*
DISSOLVE
      MOVE *FADER BAR* THROUGH ⑤ TO ⑥. TO DISSOLVE FROM *VCR 1* TO
SUBSTITUTE ⑦ (*VCR 2*) FOR ②. ABBREVIATIONS AS IN FIGURE 10–3.

The wipe is set up in much the same way as a dissolve. Punch up source 1 on M/E A and source 2 on M/E B. Select the wipe pattern by depressing the button with the wipe pattern that you want to use. The wipe is now controlled with the fader bar. As the bar is moved from M/E A to M/E B, the wipe pattern will move through the picture and reveal the shot on source 2 (M/E B).

Wipes are frequently used to achieve a split screen effect. A **split screen** is simply a horizontal wipe that has been stopped at the halfway point (see Figure 10–7).

There are many variations on the basic wipe. The speed at which the wipe is executed can be controlled by varying the speed at which the bars are moved. On computer-controlled editing systems with a switcher interface, wipe speed (as well as dissolve or fade speed) is commonly set by programming the length of the wipe into the computer in terms of seconds or frames. A two-second wipe has a duration of 60 frames, and so on.

Figure 10–6 Wipe Patterns

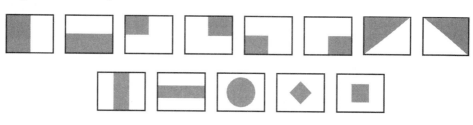

The definition of the edge of the wipe can also be controlled. Most switchers allow the operator to select either a *hard-edge* wipe or a *soft-edge* wipe. In addition, the position of certain wipes on the screen, usually circles or diamonds, can be changed by using the **joystick**, sometimes called the *wipe positioner*. This allows the operator to move the wipe pattern up, down, and around on the screen.

We should note here that when you are setting up a wipe, fade, or dissolve, it does not matter which mix/effects buss you start out in. You can wipe (face or dissolve) from M/E A to M/E B or from M/E B to M/E A.

Keying

In postproduction, a video switcher is often used to insert titles over the tape during editing. Two common methods of inserting titles are keys and mattes.

A **key** (like a wipe and a matte) is an electronic switch from one video source to another. With respect to titles, the most common sources of the key are either a

Figure 10–7 Split Screen Wipe

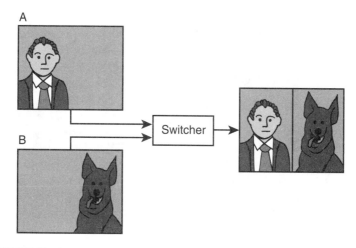

character generator or a camera shooting a title card. In either case, the lettering is the keyed source. Another video source—usually videotape in one of the source VCRs—serves as the background (see Figure 10–8).

Through keying, the lettering can be electronically cut into the background picture. The **clipper**, a small control on the switcher, regulates the point at which the electronic insertion of the lettering takes place. You can adjust the clipper so that the brightest frequencies of light trigger the electronic switch and the dark background of the source with the lettering is completely eliminated. Only the letters will then appear over the other picture (see Figure 10–8). For this reason, lettering to be keyed in over a background is usually composed of white letters on a black background. The white letters are cut into the other picture, and the black background behind the letters disappears. Since the key is triggered by the brightness of the letters, this type of key is also called a *luminance key*.

Internal and External Key. Switchers equipped with an *internal keyer* can use any video source on the switcher as the signal to be keyed over the background picture. Switchers with an *external keyer* require that one source be directly wired into the keyer. As a result, only that one source (usually a character generator or a camera used only to shoot graphic cards) can be used as the key source.

Matte

Another effect commonly used for titling is the **matte**, sometimes referred to as a *matte key*. A matte involves the use of three separate video sources: lettering, background picture, and another source to fill in the letters. Typically the letters are first cut into the background using the clipper to adjust the clarity of the key. Then the let-

---

Figure 10–8   Key

Character Generator

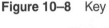

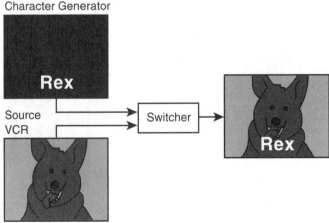

Source
VCR

Switcher

---

ters are filled in with another source. Although any video source could be used, the source used most often is the **colorizer** or a color background generator. The colorizer simply generates a color video signal. By adjusting the hue, saturation, and luminance controls (found on either the colorizer or the switcher as part of the matte controls), the letters can be filled in with any color the colorizer can generate.

Matting in color is a simple way to make lettering more visible; sometimes white letters are not visible if they are keyed in over a white or very bright background. The addition of color can make the lettering stand out from the background source.

Downstream Key and Matte

On some switchers, a key or matte can be set up only by using one of the mix/effects busses. The source to be keyed or matted is set up in one buss—M/E A, for example. Then the background is punched up in M/E B. When that group of M/E busses is punched up on line the key or matte effect appears.

Another type of switcher design incorporates what is known as a downstream keyer. A **downstream keyer** introduces the matte or key effect over the line output of the switcher, leaving the mix/effect buss or busses free to perform other effects. For example, if you have a switcher with one pair of mix/effects busses and a downstream keyer, you can set up a split screen effect in M/E A and M/E B, and then add titles with the downstream keyer. Without the downstream keyer you would have to set up your effects one at a time. You could perform a split screen, or key titles over a background picture, but you could not perform both effects at the same time. The downstream keyer, then, simply provides more flexibility to the switcher and allows you to achieve more effects (see Figure 10–9).

Chroma Key

Another special effect that is part of the key and matte family of effects is the **chroma key**, also called a *chroma key matte*. Actually, a chroma key is more of a matte than a key. As with a key and a matte, one video source is used to cut an outline into a background source. Then, like a matte, the outline is filled in with a third source.

A chroma key differs from a luminance key in the way in which the background is subtracted from the source to be keyed. In a chroma key, the background is subtracted by eliminating a particular color. In a simple key or matte, it is subtracted on the basis of brightness. The typical chroma key background color is blue, although any other color can be used. (Blue is used most often because skin tones have less blue in them than any other primary color.) Place a newscaster in front of a blue background, engage the chroma key effect, and the blue background disappears. The newscaster can then be made to appear over any desired background (see Figure 10–10).

Chroma keys are frequently used in television newscasts during the presentation of weather information. In one typical application, a remote video camera is positioned outside the station to provide a live or taped view of a particular locale.

Figure 10–9   Split Screen Wipe with Downstream Key

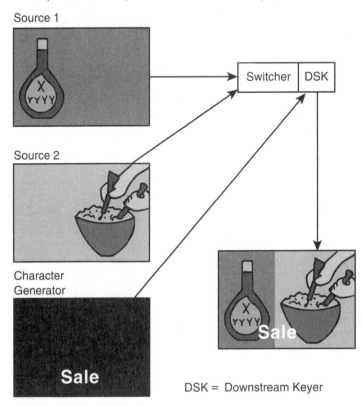

DSK = Downstream Keyer

The weathercaster remains in the studio and stands in front of the chroma key background. When the two sources are combined, the weathercaster appears to be standing in front of the image produced by the background camera or tape source. Another very common application of chroma key in the presentation of weather data electronically places the weathercaster in front of a computer-generated map or perhaps even a video image gathered from a weather satellite.

Chroma keys can just as easily be applied to lettering. Generate white (or any other color) letters on a blue background with a character generator. Use the chroma keyer to subtract the blue background and the letter will appear over the video source of your choice.

As with a matte, a chroma key also gives you control over how the keyed source will be filled in. When the newscaster is chroma keyed in over a background, the camera shooting the newscaster is typically used to fill in the picture. One could just as easily fill in the outline of the newscaster with another source: color from a background generator, video supplied by a different camera, a videotape, or a film chain. This would, however, make for a most unusual newscast.

Figure 10–10   Chroma Key

Blue or Green Background

RGB and Encoded Chroma Key. The video producer should be aware of the differences between the two major types of chroma keyers—the red-green-blue (RGB) chroma keyer and encoded signal chroma keyer. An *RGB chroma keyer* can only be used if the source to be keyed is not encoded. That is, it must have the color signal in the form of separate red, green, and blue channels of chrominance. While many professional-quality cameras can produce unencoded RBG signals, most consumer-quality camcorders are equipped only with an encoded output—one in which the luminance and chrominance are encoded together. If such a camcorder is being used as the chroma key source, an *encoded signal chroma keyer* must be used. It accepts the signal as the basis for the chroma key, whereas the RGB chroma keyer does not. This is a concern only with respect to the keyed source. An encoded signal can be used with an RGB chroma keyer if the encoded signal is the base or background picture, and not the keyed source.

CHARACTER GENERATORS

When on-screen lettering is needed, an electronic character generator is used. Most character generators contain three parts: keyboard, screen, and memory system (see Figure 10–11).

Figure 10–11   Character Generators: (A) Character Generator System Components, (B) Ampex ALEX Character Generator System, (C) Generating Titles with a Character Generator for a Video Production

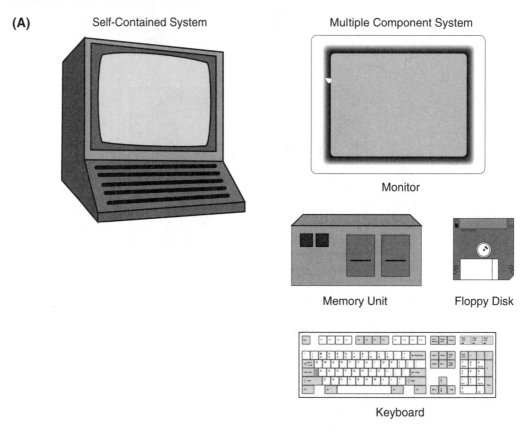

(A)   Self-Contained System   Multiple Component System

Monitor

Memory Unit   Floppy Disk

Keyboard

The character generator keyboard is a standard typewriter keyboard, offering the full range of alphabetical and numerical symbols. Information typed in appears on the screen—a television monitor. The keyboard contains a number of controls that affect the lettering display. Sophisticated character generators contain a number of lettering styles or fonts. In addition, they can vary character sizes from extremely small to rather large. You can adjust the color of the background on which the letters appear, as well as the color and edges or borders of the letters themselves. Some character generators produce white-, black-, and colored-edged letters in hard, soft, outline, or shadow modes. The choices are mind boggling.

The keyboard also contains controls for positioning and displaying the letters. Centering is a common function, as is flashing. In the flashing mode, individual letters, words, or lines of information can be programmed to flash on and off. Some keyboards also provide control over the movement of the lettering: They can be

Figure 10–11 Character Generators: (A) Character Generator System Components, (B) Ampex ALEX Character Generator System, (C) Generating Titles with a Character Generator for a Video Production *Continued*

(B)

(C)

programmed to *roll* (move vertically through the frame) or to *crawl* (move horizontally across the frame).

The information that is typed into the character generator is stored in its memory system. Simple systems store a few pages of information in internal memory. These memory systems tend to be *volatile;* that is, they are erased when the power is turned off. More sophisticated systems store information on magnetic floppy disks—small flexible disks like those used to store information from personal computers. *Magnetic floppy disk* systems are the most versatile, offering a large amount of storage with fast access for text editing.

Information from a character generator is typically introduced into the editing system through a video switcher. The character generator is treated just like any other video source. It is usually assigned to a button on the switcher, where it can be punched up by itself or used as the lettering source for a key or matte. In addition, some automatic edit control units are capable of accepting the output from a character generator as a key source.

Some character generators are able to **gen-lock** to an incoming video signal; that is, synchronize the video signal produced by the character generator with the incoming signal from the VCR. The video output from a VCR is fed into the character generator. The video output of the character generator (which now is a combination of both sources with the lettering from the character generator in the foreground and the picture information from the VCR in the background) can then be fed to another VCR to record the combined signal, or it can be fed to an editing VCR and edited directly into a program as it is being assembled.

The technique of gen-locking a graphics generator to an incoming video signal from a VCR has been widely adopted by video producers who use inexpensive personal computers with graphics capabilities to generate video images and/or modify recorded video images with their computers. A whole new field of production, sometimes called **desktop video** (the parallel to desktop publishing), has emerged out of the fusion of personal computers and video. More information on the video production uses of personal computers is presented later in this chapter and in Chapter 11.

TRANSFERRING FILM AND SLIDES TO TAPE

Film Chain

Video producers often find that they need to incorporate material that was originally shot on film into their productions. Many organizations that sell stock footage, for example, provide their material on 16mm film. Home video producers may want to transfer their old 16mm or 8mm home movies to videotape.

There are several ways to integrate film into a television production. Professional producers typically have the film transferred to videotape. To do this, a special film chain or **telecine** (*tele*vision and *cine*ma) is needed. The film chain consists of a special film projector that shoots the image directly into a television camera.

What makes the system special is the need to convert the film, with a projection rate of 24 frames per second, into the television projection standard of 30 frames per second. This is accomplished by projecting each odd-numbered frame of film twice, and each even-numbered frame three times. Since one second of film consists of 24 frames, then by using this system, the 12 odd-numbered frames are flashed on 24 times (2×12). The 12 even-numbered frames are then flashed on 36 times (3×12). Thus, in one second, the television camera sees 60 flashes of film.

This, of course, corresponds with the 60 field per second scanning rate of the television system.

Two types of film chain scanning systems are currently used. The most common type uses a modified television camera equipped with conventional pickup tubes or CCDs. This type of system is frequently found in television stations and at photographic processing houses catering to home video producers. The film image is projected directly onto the face of the image sensor(s). A much higher-quality transfer of the film image to video is achieved with the use of a **flying spot scanner**. These systems used an electron beam that scans the film image and converts it directly into a video signal. The resulting transfer does not suffer from the lagging, and image and color distortions that often accompany conventional telecine system transfers.

Telecine Camera Lens Attachments

A variety of **telecine attachments** are available for the video producer to purchase and use. The attachment screws into the camera in place of the lens. Film or slide projectors can then be attached to the converter and the camera output can be recorded directly onto videotape. Although these systems do not correct for timing differences between the film and television scanning systems, they nevertheless deliver a reasonably bright image to the camera (see Figure 10–12).

Other Lens Attachments

Slides may be transferred to video by using a simple slide holder that attaches directly to the end of the lens. Slides can be transferred directly to videotape by

Figure 10–12   Telecine Lens Attachment

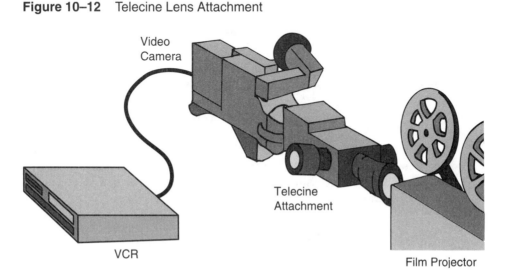

Video Camera

Telecine Attachment

VCR

Film Projector

inserting them into the holder, setting the lens to the macro position, and pointing the camera at a bright, diffused light source. Some cameras also have a *polarity reversal switch*, which changes a positive image into a negative image. When the polarity of the camera is reversed, the camera normally produces an image that looks like a photographic negative. If, on the other hand, the polarity is reversed and a photographic negative is inserted into the slide holder, the camera produces a positive image. Photographic negatives, then, can easily be converted to positive video images.

Screen or Wall Projection

When all else fails, there is always screen or wall projection. A film image—moving or still—can be projected onto a screen or a wall. This image can then be recorded by the camera. Two problems commonly occur with this method of transfer. If the projected image is a film, the video image will tend to flicker. This happens because the film projection rate does not match the camera scanning rate. This also explains the somewhat complicated conversion methods found in the telecine units, as described above.

The second problem concerns the overall brightness of the image. The projected image should be small and intense. Move the projector close to the wall or screen so that the maximum amount of light is reflected back to the camera. As the image becomes larger because of zooming out the projector lens or moving the projector farther away from the projection surface, the image's intensity decreases. It may not provide enough light for the camera to produce an acceptable picture. The problem is in finding the right relationship between the projector, projection surface, and video camera.

SIGNAL PROCESSING

In simple editing systems utilizing a single-source VCR and an editing VCR, the output of the source VCR is commonly fed directly to the input of the editing VCR. However, whenever a video signal is recorded, a certain amount of signal degradation takes place. Both the stability and the quality of the signal (how the picture looks) may be affected. For these and other reasons, several different kinds of signal processing devices are routinely used during postproduction. The most common types of signal processing units include time base correctors, video processing amplifiers, and dropout compensators.

Time Base Correctors

A **time base corrector (TBC)** is used to correct timing errors in the signal that is played back from the videotape recorder. All VCRs introduce errors into the time base of recorded material. The *time base* refers to the rate at which individual lines, fields, and frames of video information are reproduced. As you know from our earlier discussion, each of these components of the video signal should take place in a precise amount of time: A line lasts 63.4 microseconds, a field has a duration of one-sixtieth of a second, and a frame lasts one-thirtieth of a second. Deviations from this model are called deviations in the time base of the signal. Portable VCRs are notorious for producing a video signal that deviates from the standard.

The function of the time base corrector is to correct the video signal with respect to timing. The VCR's output is fed into the time base corrector, where it is digitized, analyzed, and corrected. The time base corrector's output is a broadcast-quality signal in terms of its timing.

A time base corrector must be used in conjunction with any VCR if you plan to broadcast a tape. Similarly, if you want to transfer the material from one tape format to another, the VCR output should first be processed through a time base corrector to guarantee the ultimate stability of the dub. A time base corrector must also be used if the output from a VCR is going to be connected to a video switcher or if several VCRs are going to be used in an A/B roll editing system (more on this in a moment). The time base corrector stabilizes the video signal from the VCR(s) and synchronizes it with the other video sources in the system.

This is done by routing the VCR's output signal into the time base corrector which converts it into a digital signal and stores it line by line. Then, the time base corrector compares the horizontal sync pulses from the sync generator with the sync pulses on the tape. It brings the tape into sync with the standard established by the sync generator by reading out each line of information at the correct time. This ensures that each line of video coming from the VCR through the time base corrector begins and ends in time with the horizontal sync pulses supplied by the sync generator (see Figure 10–13).

Figure 10–13   Signal Timing Corrected by a Time Base Corrector

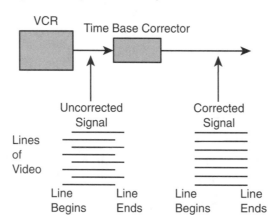

Time base correctors are often described with respect to their *window*, which indicates how many lines of information it is able to store at a given time. A time base corrector with a 2-line window can store and correct only 2 lines of information at a time, whereas a time base corrector with a 16-line window can store 16 lines of information. Time base correctors that can store a full frame of information are called full-frame time base correctors, or **frame synchronizers**. These are the most sophisticated and expensive time base correctors.

We should mention two things that time base correctors will not do: They will not correct the timing of a signal that is grossly out of whack nor will they improve picture quality.

Processing Amplifiers

Time base correctors are commonly used to improve playback signal stability; improvements in signal quality are made with a video **processing amplifier**, or **proc amp**. Proc amps, or color correctors as they are sometimes called, are used to correct both the quality of the color in the signal as well as the quality of the sync and color burst signals. With a proc amp, adjustments can be made in the overall video level (gain) and setup level (pedestal), as well as in the quality of the color itself in terms of luminance, hue, and saturation.

As with time base correctors, there are limits to the amount of color correction possible with a proc amp. If the signal was originally recorded with gross errors resulting from camera malfunction or some other severe problems, the proc amp will probably not help.

Dropout Compensators

Another common type of signal processing equipment is the **dropout compensator (DOC)**. The dropout compensator is used to correct signal-quality problems caused by the loss of particles of the oxide coating from the surface of the tape. When dropouts are detected in a line of video information, information from the previous line is repeated to fill in the hole. Dropout compensators are frequently built into other video components. For example, time base correctors frequently have built-in dropout compensators, as do many VCRs.

THE PERSONAL COMPUTER IN DESKTOP VIDEO PRODUCTION

In no area in the field of video production have more dramatic changes recently been made than in the emergence of the personal computer (PC) as a video production tool. Of course, computers have long been used in television and video production. The advanced time code editing systems discussed in the previous chapter use a computer to log edit decisions and control VCRs and other production equipment during the on-line editing systems. Word-processing software packages designed to emulate standard video script formats have long been available, and the computer has widely been used by video producers for a number of ancillary production organization tasks such as budgeting, tape logging, facilities and equipment scheduling, and so on.

Recently, however, a number of software packages and hardware accessories have been developed that enable the personal computer to be used even more directly to perform a number of tasks that previously could be done only by expensive pieces of dedicated video hardware. **Software** is a computer program, usually available for purchase on magnetic floppy disks, that contains a set of commands for the computer that allow it to perform a specified set of tasks, such as word processing, generation of video graphics for titles and graphs, video editing, and so on. Computer hardware and software manufacturers have now begun to refer to their systems as "video workstations" and "video production suites." The convergence of the computer with video production has given rise to a new term that describes the fusion of these two technologies: **desktop video (DTV)** (see Figure 10–14). Some of the capabilities of these systems are described here.

Figure 10–14 Commodore AMIGA Computer Running NewTek Video Toaster Video Switcher Program

Components of Desktop Video Systems

The two essential components of any desktop video system are a personal computer, equipped with appropriate software, and a video component capable of sending a video signal into a computer. This may be a VCR, a video camera, a still video recorder, a video disc player, and so on. In addition, an interface that converts the incoming video signal into a digital signal that the computer can understand is usually a necessity. Similarly, if at the end of the process the producer wants to record the video signal on a conventional VCR, an output device is necessary to convert the digitized computer signal back into an NTSC video signal. A number of video input/output (I/O) boards are available from a variety of manufacturers.

If VCRs are to be used as the input sources, a time base corrector will be needed for each source machine. Once only available as an expensive piece of video hardware, plug-in TBC cards are available for many computers at a fraction of what they used to cost (see Figure 10–15).

Finally, if the computer is going to be used to control the playback and recording functions of one or more VCRs, the appropriate interfaces for the computer and the particular model VCRs used in the system must be obtained.

The advantage of desktop video production systems is that they can be expanded and upgraded by adding on additional memory capabilities to the

Figure 10–15 Computer Plug-In Card (Future Video Edit Controller and Time Code Reader)

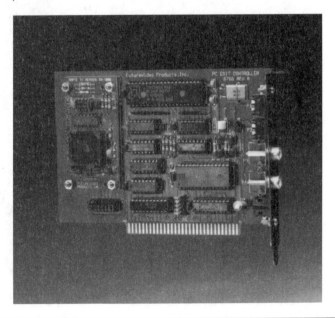

Figure 10–16   Video Toaster Switcher Screen Display

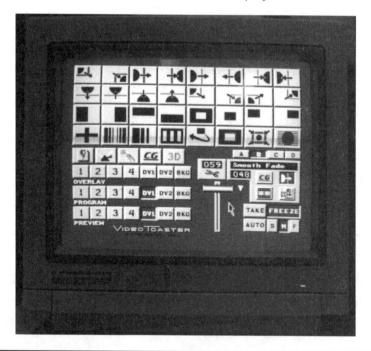

computer (usually in form of magnetic hard-disk drives), by taking advantage of updated versions of the computer software that controls the various video production functions, and by obtaining additional peripheral video equipment.

Today's desktop video production systems can be used to perform a number of functions that previously could be done only on very expensive pieces of single-function video production hardware.

Video Switching. The computer can function as a video switcher with separate inputs for various video sources. A full range of transitions (cut, fade, dissolve, wipe) are typically available (see Figure 10–16).

Keying. In combination with graphics software, text can be keyed over video. Chroma key and luminance key systems are available.

Digital Video Effects. A full range of digital effects are available.

Still Store. This feature is used to create freeze frames of video in the computer, which can then be manipulated with special effects.

Video Graphics. A full range of graphics programs are available, including character generation, two- and three-dimensional graphics and animation, and video paint systems that allow the graphic artist to modify or "paint" video images. These are described in more detail in the next chapter.

Audio Production. Hardware and software are available to allow the computer to function as a multiple input audio mixer. They can be used to do audio mixing independent from video production or in conjunction with video editing software (see Figure 10–17).

Video Editing. The computer can be used in a variety of editing operations, such as off-line editing, as an on-line edit controller, and for nonlinear editing. These are described in more detail next.

Figure 10–17   SunRize Studio 16 Audio Editing System Computer Screen Display

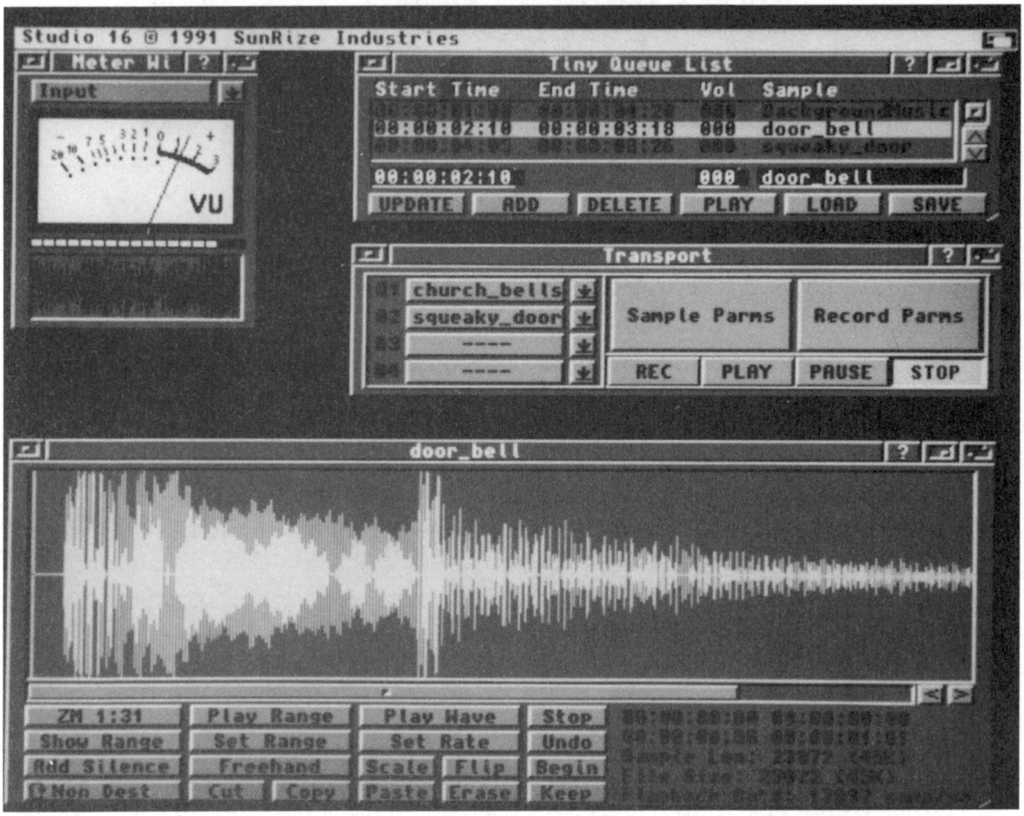

The Personal Computer and Video Editing

The personal computer can be used to facilitate videotape editing in a number of ways. At the simplest level, a number of software programs are available to allow the producer to make logs of field footage and final edit decision lists. These edit decision lists then can be transferred to a computer floppy disk and used to control the on-line system that performs the final edit. Or, with the appropriate machine interfaces, the same PC on which the logs and EDLs were created may control source and editing VCRs to perform the actual tape assembly.

A number of recently developed video editing software programs take advantage of the computer's ability to display pictures as well as time code numbers (see Figure 10–18). In these systems, the unedited videotape is converted into digital information and stored within the computer on hard-disk drives. Editing decisions can be made by referring to the time code numbers for each shot (if available) or simply by viewing the video display on the computer screen and identifying appropriate entry and exit points. Once individual shots are identified, the information is stored in the data base, often with a picture of the first frame of the shot. One system calls this a *picture icon*, or *picon*. These icons can then be used to build a storyboard of the finished production (see Figure 10–19).

Another advantage of transferring the videotape field footage to the computer's hard drive is that it allows for random access to the information. That is, unlike tape-based systems where you must view each shot in sequence or search through the tape in fast forward or reverse for the shot you have selected, information

Figure 10–18   OZ Video Editing System Screen Display

Figure 10–19   Matrox Personal Producer Screen Displays: (A) Video Clip Editor, (B) Clip Collection, (C) Storyboard

(A)

(B)

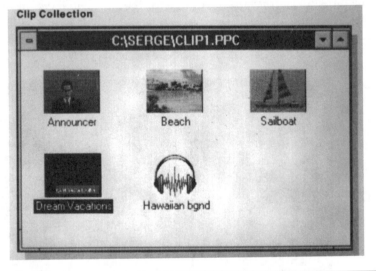

recorded on the disk can be accessed immediately—much in the same way that a compact disc (CD) player can go directly to any song on a CD almost instantly.

The ability to have random access to the video and audio information on the disk, and to edit it through a cut-and-paste process very similar to the way text is

Figure 10–19   Matrox Personal Producer Screen Displays: (A) Video Clip Editor, (B) Clip Collection, (C) Storyboard   *Continued*

(C)

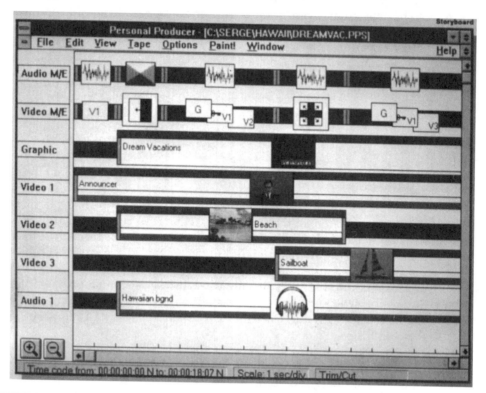

edited in a word processor, is sometimes referred to as **nonlinear editing**. Thus, when building your program or sequence within the computer, not only can you organize your shots in a shot-by-shot assembled sequence as you would in traditional editing (what we referred to in Chapter 8 as assemble editing strategy) but you can also change the order in which shots appear in the segment by cutting and pasting them into the appropriate place in the program's timeline (see Figure 10–19C). This allows you to easily change the sequence of shots in your program and to insert new material between existing shots. Unlike insert editing in linear tape-based systems, which erases the old material under the newly inserted material, in nonlinear editing the inserted material can actually be inserted between two shots. This is a feature lacking on tape-based systems, and one that videotape editors have long hoped for.

Because it still takes an extraordinary amount of computer disc space to store full motion color video with sound, many of the available desktop video editing systems function only as off-line editors. Field footage is imported into the computer where editing decisions are made, taking advantage of the random access and cut-and-paste features of the computer. Rough cuts of the segment can be viewed on the computer screen, typically as a less than full frame image. Once editing decisions have been made and the edit decision list has been finalized, the EDL can be transferred to disc or the computer can be used as an edit controller to control the source and edit VCRs. Depending on the complexity of the system, it may be able to perform transitions as well as add titles and digital effects.

The most sophisticated nonlinear systems are capable of *printing to tape*. That is, the edits are performed within the computer and the program is output from the computer as full screen video, in real time, in full motion with color and sound.

SUMMARY

Many producers need to integrate special effects, titles, or film into their productions.

Most editing effects require the use of postproduction facilities that are considerably more complex than a cuts-only editing system. A common component of such a system is the video switcher—a production device that allows the editor to combine or manipulate different video sources. There are two types of video switchers. Distribution switchers are used only as routing devices for video signals, whereas production switchers are used during the actual production process. Production switchers typically contain three types of busses: program, preview, and mix/effects. A typical switcher can do four types of transitions: cut, fade, dissolve, and wipe.

Switchers are also used to key titles over tape during editing or to achieve matte and chroma key effects. Switchers equipped with downstream key and matte are among the most flexible switchers.

Electronic character generators are widely used to produce titles for video production. These devices usually contain a keyboard, screen, and memory unit to store graphic information.

To transfer film to videotape, a special film chain or telecine is needed. Film conversion can be achieved inexpensively with the use of a telecine lens attachment if a large telecine unit is not available. Some consumer cameras contain lens attachments that hold slides or negatives in front of the camera so that they can be recorded onto videotape. An unprofessional but nonetheless effective method of transferring film or slides to videotape involves projecting the film image onto a screen or wall and recording it with the video camera.

Several forms of signal processing may be used to improve the stability and quality of the video signal. Time base correctors correct timing errors in the signal that is played back from a VCR. Processing amplifiers are used to correct color quality, as well as sync and color burst. Dropout compensators correct problems caused by dropouts in the tape.

The personal computer is finding increasing use as a video production tool, and the fusion of computers and video has created a new type of production called desktop video. Desktop video systems include a computer, peripheral video equipment, interfaces between computers and VCRs, video input/output boards, and appropriate software to allow the computer to perform video production functions. Nonlinear video editing provides random access to audio and video information stored within the computer, and greatly facilitates the process of editing.

11

Graphics and Design

INTRODUCTION

The graphic materials selected or created for use on television convey important information to the viewer. The term **graphic materials** describes a spectrum of visual materials ranging from whole settings, in which action is staged, to the simplest of captions identifying a speaker. Their content and their style—the manner in which they present that content—each contribute to the viewer's understanding of the message. In skilled hands, graphic materials generate a supporting mood or atmosphere much like that associated with the use of background music. In other hands, the effect may be distracting to the purpose and function of the program.

A relatively simple set of principles is central to the creation of effective graphics, regardless of whether the program is produced in the most lavishly equipped studio or in the austere circumstances characteristic of single-camera field production. Obviously, techniques for these contrasting situations will vary as resources allow. Even the seemingly endless array of computer-generated graphics will fail to help a program achieve its purpose if the principles of unity and clarity are ignored (see Figure 11–1).

Unity

For a program to be effective, all graphic materials must act together in support of the major theme or purpose of the program. Each element must be coordinated with the others if **unity** of effect is to be achieved. Failure to coordinate elements results in a distraction—the worst sin the graphic artist can commit—that causes the viewer to focus on some unique quality of the graphic, rather than on achieving the goal of viewing the program. The following series of numbers, for example, obviously lacks unity of expression:

one, two, three, IV, fünf, six, 7, ocho

Figure 11–1 Generating Television Graphics with a Computer

Use of these numbers to identify points made in a public health meeting or a corporation's marketing goals would be dysfunctional. In a comedy program, however, it might provide effective visual support to the proceedings.

Unity of expression includes control of all aesthetic and expositional factors that enrich the presentation of the message, story, or personality around which the program is designed. Camera angles, lighting, editing techniques, and sound (each considered in separate chapters) also contribute to this overall expression and must be considered if unity is to be achieved.

Clarity

The concept of *clarity* involves both simplicity of expression and the visibility of the graphic elements or characters themselves. Obviously, the display of a full page of newsprint on a television screen means that each word will be too small to be legible. While the news stories may be selected on the basis of their importance to the program, their graphic presentation in a single shot is incompetent. The principle of clarity has been violated. Functional and practical factors in the preparation of television graphics must be considered if clarity is to be preserved.

AESTHETIC FACTORS

Space—The Third Dimension

The television picture is sprayed onto the face of the cathode ray tube. It is a two-dimensional display in a three-dimensional world. In addition to being flat, the picture is small and does not overwhelm the viewer with scale in the manner of the motion picture. The television viewer—unlike a member of a film, dance, or theater audience—is not a part of the medium. The medium of television is the screen; it does not include other participants who share a viewing or listening space and whose responses influence each other; the space does not flex with the movement of dancers or actors.

Television viewers need not move their heads, thus changing their perspective, to keep up with the action. Eye movement from one part of the screen to another is the viewer's only option. The director controls everything else by moving the camera and cutting from one shot to another.

In order to engage the attention of the viewer and to hold it, the television director must provide a picture that not only identifies the objects and locations necessary to the story but expresses a relationship between those physical elements and the significance and emotional tone of the story to the viewer. The camera takes the place of the viewer and the director moves that camera as the viewer would have to be moved through the action-on-location in order to appreciate the story. The television director takes special care to emphasize the third dimension—the depth of each scene—as a means of simulating the spatial relationships the viewer would notice if the scene was visited in person.

There are several common techniques for suggesting this depth in a picture: Objects in the foreground overlap objects understood to be behind them, the size of objects diminishes as the distance from the viewer increases, objects close to the viewer seem to move faster than do objects in the distance, and objects in the distance often appear to be darker than similar objects close to the viewer (see Figure 11–2). In film and studio television production, these techniques can be applied by constructing whatever illusion is desired. In field television production, however, the camera must be positioned in a real-world location so as to enhance the feeling of three dimensions without faking anything.

Positioning the camera so that objects in the scene overlap each other begins the illusion of three dimensions. Adjusting the height of the camera above, below, or at eye level further manipulates the illusion by calling attention to descending or ascending diagonals, the speed of movement, and diminishing size factors. Assuming the subjects of the video coverage are in the foreground, increasing the light intensity of the foreground well over that of the background also adds to the effect. The illusion is complete when the subjects move *through* the scene; that is, move from behind to a position in front of objects rather than merely stand in front of them in a static manner.

The generation of this three-dimensional quality results in a more dynamic picture because the viewer is reminded of personal experience with spatial relationships and can use this experience to "feel" the scene being televised.

Figure 11–2   Illusion of Three Dimensions

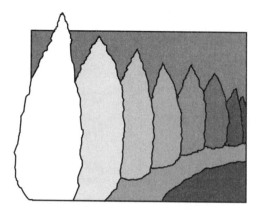

Visual Composition

Traditionally, consideration of the aesthetic elements of pictures has revolved around the rules of composition. These include attention to balance, mass, movement of the eye through the composition, and use of color. These rules are based on experience with paintings—essentially still images—hanging in galleries.

In contrast, television provides a sound-supported moving image in a story line context in which to judge the factors of visual composition. Rather than standing as a complete statement, each television picture continues what preceded it and introduces what follows. Action flows through each frame and is accelerated, arrested, or focused for the next. To some extent, visual composition serves as a kind of punctuation in the flow of the story. An asymmetrical composition might accelerate audience attention into the next picture, whereas a symmetrical composition might serve to conclude the thought. For example, a conversation between two people can seem fraught with meaning when staged as a series of extreme close-ups of single faces at opposite sides of the screen. A lingering 2-shot in which the people are centered on the screen can express resolution of the conflict and signal the end of the drama. This applies to the use of scenic and graphic materials, as well as to the presentation of actors and action.

There are no lasting "rules of composition" because story context and audience expectations constantly change. "Rules" reflect current practices and change as audiences become too familiar with them and they lose their effectiveness. One such practice was called the *rule of thirds* because the screen area was divided into three equal parts both horizontally and vertically (see Figure 11–3). The four points located one-third of the distance from the four parts of the frame are considered to be the optimum location for objects and persons of importance to the story. In practice, this type of composition offers an unobstructed view of the objects or persons central to the story but with a relatively neutral treatment. No particular tension, movement, or progression of the story is suggested by this composition.

Figure 11–3   Rule of Thirds

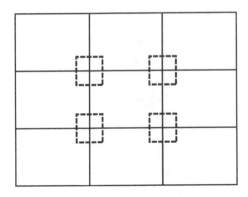

The 3 × 4 aspect ratio of television provides a lazy rectangular frame in which to compose the picture. Directors have learned to create more dynamic frames with the television screen's boundaries by using silhouettes, doorways, scenic devices, or crowds of people in the extreme foreground (see Figure 11–4).

Aesthetic factors also include attention to the values and expectations of the audience. Taste and experience are important to the audience's appreciation of the significance of each picture to the whole. To communicate with the audience, the producer/director must use visual as well as aural terms that the audience

Figure 11–4   Creating a Frame within a Frame

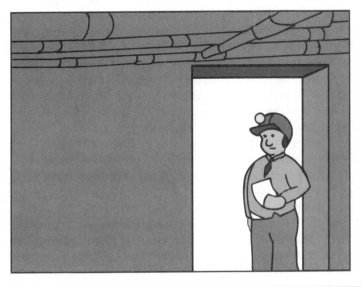

can understand. Highly stylized settings and graphics in a program designed for a culturally disenfranchised audience might appear only as pretentious trappings rather than communicating sophisticated relationships between ideas. Graphic materials are used to make the point of the program easier to understand. Those with a purely decorative function should be discarded.

Style

The style of a television presentation can take many forms. Photographic realism (naturalism) is one style. Selective realism, symbolism, and expressionism are others from an endless list of abstractions of style familiar to artists, dramatists, musicians, and literary and film critics. On the surface, it might seem that the very use of cameras in video production would reduce the choice to photographic realism, but this is not so.

An examination of popular programs reveals that although a form of selective realism dominates, dance and music programs feature a range of abstract expressions. Even the most conservative of journalistic programs is selective in its video presentation in that extraneous background details are most often conveniently out of focus. If everything in the field of view were in equal focus, the audience might not know what to look at. The camera may not lie, but it does not often tell all the truth!

Once the question of basic style is answered for the program, attention can be given to the design and preparation of graphic elements that will reinforce its expression. Graphics should be compatible with settings and costumes. For example, lettering for program graphics should seem to belong with the lab coats and architectural details of a modern hospital; use of an Old English alphabet to identify modern surgical procedures would distract the audience. All lettering, regardless of source, must match the other visual elements of the production.

Form, Texture, and Color

Beyond consideration of style, graphic materials must contribute to the general visual character of the program through control of form, texture, and color. This is most evident in the use of transparent elements in production, but applies equally to the use of opaque cards or scenic elements.

A scene shot through the glass door of a law office would feature the lettering on the door, which identifies the firm as well as a view of the furnishings of the office itself. The style and form of the lettering on the door would tell us something about the quality of the firm—how it viewed itself and wanted others to understand it. Being painted on glass, the texture of the letters would stand in sharp contrast with the softer edges of the leather furniture within. To avoid being obscured by the small details of the arrangement of books on a wall, the letters are simple and black so that the highest possible contrast is achieved. Attention is shifted to the details of the interior of the office by rolling the focus of the camera from the lettering on the door in the foreground to the office wall in the background (see Figure 11–5).

Figure 11–5   Foreground and Background Focus

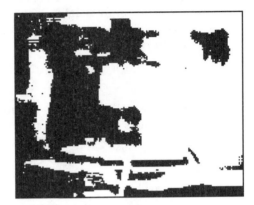

Each style of lettering has its own personality that must match the context in which it is used. That context includes the emotional tone of both the program and the target audience. This personality has no relationship to the traditional classifications of lettering and typeface. The television producer must select lettering that fits the mood of the program and that remains legible on the screen. This means that letters composed of very thin lines (a problem with the weak resolution of the television picture) and decorated with serifs (often a problem with the requirements of the interlace scanning system) are often deemed unsuitable, even though they are attractive in print (see Figure 11–6).

Foreground and background detail must be coordinated. The more detail in the background, the simpler the foreground graphic materials must be. The more detail in the foreground, the simpler (or more out of focus) the background must be (see Figure 11–7).

Much attention has been given to the choice of *colors* in graphic materials, especially with those associated with theater, advertising, and marketing. A trip through the supermarket confirms the popular notion that certain colors are linked with definable emotional responses. Reds and yellows are considered warm, greens and blues are cool, and dark colors are somber. Audiences know this code and generate expectations accordingly.

Inspection of advertising and packaging techniques also reveals that printed detail is reduced and selected words are expanded (or coined) to create a general impression—an emotional response linked with the product—rather than a specific meaning. Symbols replace paragraphs. These same symbols come to identify whole companies and appear on corporate letterheads and on buildings. The field television producer is quick to use these graphic materials because of the associations the audience has already established with them. Producers develop such symbols to use as reinforcing agents, often in graphic form, in their programs.

Figure 11–6 Typical Fonts

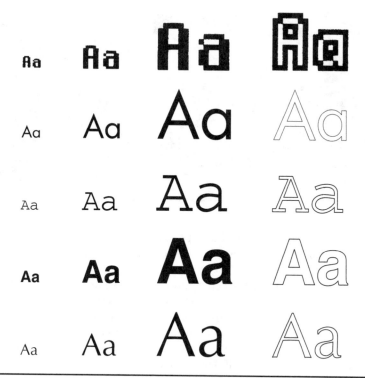

Generally, recognizable symbols are used to open, provide transitions, and close popular television programs. Batman's bat figure in a yellow circle and *L.A. Law*'s license plate have proved to be effective graphics. Each reflects a salient element of the story or the story teller, enhances audience anticipation of what is to follow, or summarizes a major story element.

The element of brightness is important in generating effective graphic materials. Paints are opaque and can reflect only so much light. The lighter the color, the more light that can be reflected back to the camera and the brighter the graphic will appear. In comparison with the electronic effects possible in the studio, camera cards seem to lack life and sparkle no matter how light and bright the colors. The use of translucent materials illuminated from behind provides some welcome variation and allows the field producer to work beyond the conventional brightness levels.

The standard **light table** can be used to present luminescent graphics. Titles, credits, and prepared or live illustrations can be created using plain tracing paper and a felt-tip pen. If the audience is to see someone draw a picture, draw guidelines with a hard pencil so the artist can see the lines but the audience cannot. Color control is possible through the use of theatrical gels behind the

Figure 11–7   Relationship between Foreground Lettering and Background Detail

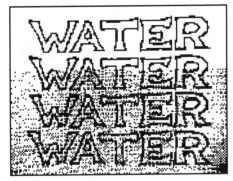

glass. Large versions of the light table can be constructed to provide a flexible production device for the display of small objects, x-ray plates, or even blueprints.

The development of computer graphics has given the video field producer a capacity for visual expression once reserved for major studios and postproduction houses. Graphic support to camera video generated by special computer programs naturally features a luminescence component (brightness) as well as control of focus, image dimension and color, and ease of preparation *if* such graphics are transferred electronically directly to videotape. The luminescent quality is lost if the graphic is first printed on paper and then transferred to videotape via a camera. If photographic realism is desired in a color graphic, it may be better to use a camera to transfer an image to videotape because not all computer programs and equipment have sufficient color and brightness capacity for that effect.

Although the visibility of objects and lettering is most often created through the use of contrasting colors, attention must be given to the relative brightness of those colors. This is particularly important if the video will be viewed on a black and white television receiver. Many **gray scale** charts (a sequence of tints and tones, ranging from white at one extreme to black at the other) are available to the producer and arguments abound over just how many shades of gray (expressions

Figure 11–8   Gray Scale

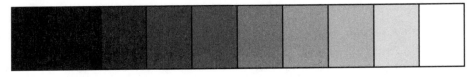

of brightness) can be identified on the television screen (see Figure 11–8). As a rule of thumb, reduce the scale to 10 shades and maintain at least a 2-shade separation between adjacent objects. Objects and graphics thus treated are visible because they are differentiated by both color and brightness. Adding texture and focus contrasts heighten the effect. Contrast viewing glasses, which reduce a scene to a black and white image, are a useful tool for determining relative brightness, particularly when comparison with a gray scale chart is not possible.

Television producers use program titles to attract attention, establish a mood, generate interest, and inform viewers. Common sense and consideration of the target audience's experience must guide the aesthetic decisions. Keeping all elements stylistically similar creates a visual harmony that supports the general theme or tone of the presentation in a systematic way.

EXPOSITIONAL FACTORS

Specifics of time and place can be communicated by means other than words. San Francisco's Golden Gate Bridge, the Eiffel Tower in Paris, the Colosseum in Rome, and the Egyptian pyramids are immediately recognizable and need no further identification. Similarly, clothing and automobiles and the representation of certain types of music serve to place a program at a particular time in history. Graphic materials can be designed to function in the same way, adding selected information to a program without actually stating it.

Location

The location chosen for field production provides its own elements. Street signs, company logos, government agency plaques, monuments, or even the view from the location can serve to orient the viewer. Orienting the viewer is the purpose of all expositional detail. Lettering styles identified with specific eras are commonly used: Liquid crystal display-style numbers suggest the computer age, block serifs on capital letters suggest the Old West, and letters formed from sticks suggest an even earlier West (see Figure 11–9).

Architectural Designs

Architectural details are a chief source of expositional information. Field producers are in a much better position in regard to using such details to enrich their presentations than are their studio cousins. Floors and ceilings provide special opportunities to add visual detail to the field production. High angle shots can be used to frame action with a chandelier against the background of a marble floor. A camera placed on such a floor can reflect its special texture in support of the sharp sounds of approaching footsteps.

Figure 11–9   Expositional Detail in Lettering

FUNCTIONAL AND PRACTICAL FACTORS

Once the creative decisions have been made, attention can be focused on less excit-ing, but equally important, factors: ease of preparation and operation of graphic materials, their cost, and their most effective presentation. Aspect ratio, size, tex-ture, brightness, and clarity are central to the construction of television graphics.

Aspect Ratio and Size

Regardless of its size, the television screen is a rectangle with an **aspect ratio** of three units tall to four units wide. Graphic materials meant to fill the screen must maintain that 3:4 proportion (see Figure 11–10).

The matter of size is not as simple. Graphics can be made in almost any size, but they will never appear to the viewer any larger than the screen used in the viewing situation. A 16-foot graphic will appear to be no larger than the standard 11" × 14" camera card. Why 11" × 14"? That size represents an efficient division of the readily available poster materials (22" × 28"). Since 11" × 14" is not exactly a 3:4 ratio, care must be taken to use only that portion that fits into the 3:4 rectangle. During the era of poster-board camera cards, graphic artists worked in a "real size" environment because the home television screens were about the same size as the cards. In the present computer era, the home viewer sees an image four or more times as large as that with which the artist works.

The major problem related to size is the tendency to put more information on a large graphic than the viewer can see clearly at a normal distance from the tele-vision screen. This concept of audience distance from the television screen is important; the home viewer sits 6 to 8 feet from the screen, whereas the student in a classroom might be more than 30 feet from the screen and forced to view the

Figure 11–10   Television Screen Aspect Ratio

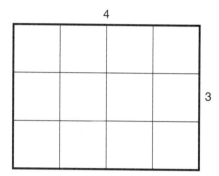

screen from less than an optimum angle. For this reason, we suggest that all planning for graphics be done on a 2″ scratch pad. There is no room on such a small
piece of paper to include more than the viewer can see on the television screen.
Though not absolutely necessary, this technique works well.

The 2″ horizontal dimension for planning materials has another use. A rectangular opening 2″ wide and 1.5″ high cut into a piece of black cardboard can
serve like a viewfinder if used with one eye and held at arm's length. If you can
read an illustration, caption, or commercial logo on the side of a building through
this frame, the audience will also be able to read the material if it is placed on the
screen the way it appears in the frame. This open frame can be used to check the
clarity of camera cards, photographs, and other graphic materials.

Many field production clients request graphics based on apparent experience
with magazine illustrations. Full-page advertisements or corporate statements
seem to be about the size of the television screen, but unlike television, they are
viewed from a distance of 18 inches! The full pages of print found in magazines
cannot be read on television. It is useful to test the magazine illustration by viewing it through the 2″ frame. Most often, the one-page illustration contains too
much information for effective presentation on the screen.

Essential Area

When preparing graphics for television, it is not enough to leave a margin around
the edges for the sake of neatness. Due to edge distortion aggravated by the production and transmission processes, about 10 percent of the horizontal dimension
of the picture must be left clear at each side, and 10 percent of the vertical dimension must remain vacant at the top and the bottom of the picture. The remaining
space on the graphic is termed the **essential area**. By the time the picture reaches
the viewer, this area will fill the screen (see Figure 11–11). In most field production
situations, the camera operator can adjust the field of view to preserve the pictorial material for the viewer.

Figure 11–11   Television Screen Essential Area

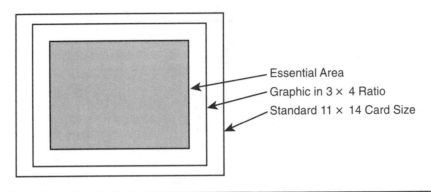

Essential Area
Graphic in 3 × 4 Ratio
Standard 11 × 14 Card Size

Style

Much has been written over the years about the amount and size of the lettering that can be used in a single graphic. All the formulas are calculated to preserve the clarity of expression with state-of-the-art television equipment. Rather than depending on such mechanical aids and remembering to allow for varying color and brightness contrasts and varying line widths, the field producer is better served by the 2" note pad and an experienced squint. Why squint? Because that draws attention to the basic masses of color that comprise the graphic. Bold, simple arrangements communicate more directly and effectively than chaotic, cluttered, and overly verbal displays. Squint through the 2" frame or at a 2" sketch and note the dominant impression the graphic creates. If it is positive and contributes to the general effect desired, produce it. If it calls attention to itself or tells a different story, discard it and try again. While they are not presented in any particular context, the illustrations in Figure 11–12 represent the range of expressions the producer should consider.

The most effective letters are no less than one-tenth of the total graphic in height, and spaced so that the words formed are clear. When possible, letters and words should be designed to express something of their meaning by their very

Figure 11–12   Graphic Clarity, Clutter, and Style

shape (see Figure 11–13). As with most novelties, this technique should be used sparingly and saved for special emphasis. Again, keep the lines forming the letters thick enough to be seen easily. The resolution limitations of the television system destroy illustrations crafted with too fine a line.

Various lettering kits and computer fonts are available to television producers. Press-on letters and the like are neat, relatively easy to apply, and not terribly expensive. Fonts featured in the popular computer programs provide greater variety of style and size. The style or personality of all the available letters, however, may not seem right for the peacock exhibit or to sell the current favorite in lipsticks, so it may still be necessary to create what is desired.

Texture

In addition to aspect ratio, graphic size, essential area, and basic color, style and size of lettering, the **surface texture** of camera cards may cause production problems. Glossy photographs provide the best example of materials requiring special treatment to avoid creating distracting glare. The solution involves arranging the card, camera, and illumination source so that light reflected from the shiny surface of the photograph is not reflected directly into the lens. The photograph must be flat for this technique to work properly. The same principle applies when shooting through a glass door (see Figure 11–14).

Keystoning

If the camera card or photograph is not displayed perpendicular to the camera axis, another complication may arise: **keystoning**. This form of visual distortion is

Figure 11–13 Expressive Lettering

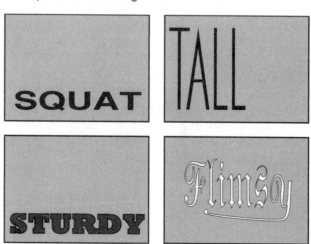

Figure 11–14   Avoiding Surface Reflection

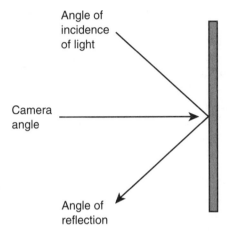

caused by placing one edge of the graphic closer to the camera than the opposite edge. The closer edge then appears to be larger because it fills a greater portion of the camera's field of view. This is especially troublesome when printed material is involved, unless, of course, distortion is desired for reasons of a specific story (see Figure 11–15).

Gobos

A variation of the camera card called a **gobo** can serve as a foreground frame for action. In its simplest form, it is a silhouette that places the action in a particular context. Gates, wreaths, keyholes, and leafless branches are easily and most frequently used.

Figure 11–15   Keystoning

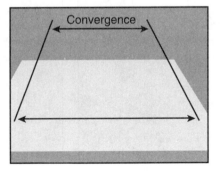

A more complex variation features printed or pictorial detail that is the focus of attention until the action in the background becomes important. Zooming in to that action or rolling the focus serves as the transition from the graphic to the action. Such gobos may contain clear acetate or fine gauze to which letters are affixed (see Figure 11–16). The use of acetate introduces the same glare problems which plague users of glossy photographs.

Computer graphic techniques have displaced the use of two-dimensional gobos in all but the most severely time-constrained circumstances (see Figure 11–17). In-camera titling programs can be used during recording to identify locations, time, sponsor, or other such information if the lettering style does not pose an aesthetic problem. More elaborate computer graphic elements can be integrated into the video during postproduction as time and resources allow. Elaborate three-dimensional effects produced by computers are regularly used in feature films and "high-end" video production and are increasingly available to video field producers who have access to computer-based graphics workstations.

Figure 11–16   Gobos

Letters on Acetate

Three-Dimensional Model on a Post

Two-Dimensional Photo Cutout

Figure 11–17   Computer-Generated Title and Background

 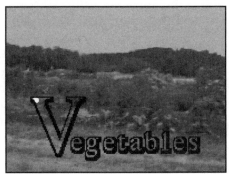

The next step in complexity involves the construction of three-dimensional detail—built-up door frames or stone walls, for example. These are simpler and less expensive than real scenery, but are cumbersome and extend production schedules.

The longer the gobo remains on the screen, the more noticeable its lack of real detail. The more elaborate three-dimensional quality requires more attention to maintaining a unity of perspective from the gobo to the scene of the live action. If such complex gobos are to move with the camera—an automobile, boat, or aircraft window from which the action is viewed, for example—they should be fastened to the camera with a *shoe* that attaches to the camera tripod head, or some other means must be devised to steady them.

Use of Location Material

The special character of a field location can be conveyed to an audience through the use of readily identifiable local materials in the preparation of graphics. As is true with most novelties, it is better to use such displays sparingly so that they don't become too cute and distract attention from the purpose of the program. Titles can be formed in the sand at the beach and simulated wave action (augmented by a portable pump and off-camera hoses) can be used as a transition device. Perhaps the effect would be better if a sand castle or program symbol was allowed to wash away gradually while serving as a background to titles added in postproduction.

Three-dimensional graphic materials used behind electronically inserted titles seem more effective if some movement is introduced. Allow a breeze to ruffle the leaves on a branch slightly; or place a figurine on a turntable and rotate it very slowly to reveal a separate expression for each title, while maintaining progress toward a climactic visual statement.

Such special expressions are best handled with some subtlety. Remember, their purpose is to create a mood appropriate to the remainder of the program.

Beginning a program with Dickens's opening lines, "It was the best of times, it was the worst of times," spelled out on the beach in abalone shells might evoke a mirthful response among the less devoted in the audience. Such irreverence is contagious; do not trigger it lightly.

Special Graphic Effects

The use of mirrors, light tables, gobos, turntables, fans, water tanks, and shadow boxes has expanded graphics well beyond the use of simple camera cards. In an age dominated by electronically animated graphics, it may seem passé to include attention to mechanical animation techniques. There is no reason, however, for even the most technologically sophisticated among us to be unprepared to work effectively in the preproduction and production phases of a project; the most heroic efforts during postproduction will not make up for failure to videotape program elements needed in the editing process. Computer graphics will not substitute effectively for shots of wildlife, falling water, billowing smoke, or location footage. Within the program materials gathered, electronic manipulation and image generation provided by computers increases the producer's capability to deliver a message or tell a story.

INCORPORATING TITLES AND ELECTRONIC GRAPHICS INTO A PROGRAM

Largely through the use of titles generated by electronic character generators, most television viewers have become conditioned to the appearance of titles within television programs. We see them at every significant point of a program. For example, they appear at the beginning of every program, often superimposed over the background visuals. The names of significant people within a program are commonly superimposed over the person during the program. At the end of each program, the familiar credit roll appears.

In a sense, titles are the mark of a professional production. However, the inclusion of titles within a program often presents a significant problem for the video field producer. Most titles are **superimposed** or **keyed** over a background picture (see Chapter 10 for a more detailed discussion of these terms). When a title is superimposed, the letters have a transparent quality; when they are keyed, they are opaque. In either case, the appearance of these effects indicates that two video sources are being combined—the titles and the background picture. To accomplish this combination, a **video switcher** is needed. Both video sources—titles and background picture—are fed into the switcher and are combined there. The switcher output is recorded, and what you see at that point is the desired titling effect.

The preferred way of titling is to add the titles as the program is being assembled. In this method, titles are added during the editing process. The source VCR feeds the program material into a video switcher that combines the program and title signals. The switcher output is fed into the edit VCR, which records the composite signal on a separate videotape. If a title is to be added, it is superimposed or keyed in the switcher. If no title is to be added, the source signal is fed directly through the switcher to the editing VCR without adding titles (see Figure 11–18). This method of titling is complex and demands access to some very sophisticated equipment.

If a production switcher and character generator are not available, and if the titles and credits need not be keyed or superimposed over program video, a separate videotape of titles and credits recorded by a camera from cards or a computer printer can be inserted like any other video. If no video editing equipment is available, such opening and closing information (and even print graphics) can be included in the program by using the backspace feature in the camcorder to hide the spaces between "takes."

In this age of the personal computer and desktop publishing, other simple ways to create titles and credits exist. Through the use of a laser printer, such graphics can be prepared for the camera and inserted into the program via video editing. If a "frame grabber" and time-base corrector can be added to the computer, the video signal can be manipulated more directly.

The Personal Computer as a Video Graphics Generator

Until digital VTRs are standard throughout the video industry, the integration of the video and computer images will be both complex and incomplete. As it now stands, the video analog system is not compatible with the digital system used in computers. The means by which color is specified and the image is scanned are different. A bewildering array of devices exists to bridge the gap partially. No one tool that solves all of the problems is likely to be available for some time to the video field producer.

A number of personal computers, when equipped with the appropriate hardware to properly interface their output to a videotape recorder and when

---

Figure 11–18   Titling through a Video Switcher

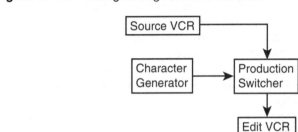

used in conjunction with the appropriate software programs, can be employed to produce graphics for television. *Character generator software programs* enable the personal computer to function as a television character generator. Different styles, sizes, and colors of letters can be generated and stored in the computer. *Drawing programs* enable the personal computer to be used to generate line drawings. *Paint programs* allow the artist to use the computer to manipulate the color and texture components of an image. Simple *animation programs* allow the artist to add horizontal and vertical movement to two-dimensional computer-generated images. Sophisticated manipulation of three-dimensional images is somewhat beyond the capability of most low-cost computer animation systems, but with the advances that are now being made in the technology even this is available to the desktop video producer.

With the addition of a video camera and a digitizing unit, camera-generated video images can be input into the computer and manipulated with the appropriate software programs. Similar manipulation of frames of information on videotape can be accomplished with the use of a frame grabber (see Figure 11–19).

Most low-cost personal computers used as television character generators use the RGB method of color generation. Different proportions of red, green, and blue are mixed to create the range of colors (over 4,000) available. These colors are identified individually in terms of their specific hue, intensity, and saturation. *Hue* is the RGB mix, *intensity* is the strength of the electronic signals representing the RGB mix as it is displayed on the monitor, and *saturation* is the amount of "white" that is added to the hue. In this context, "white" is itself an RGB mix and its presence acts to dilute a hue. A highly saturated hue has little "white" in the mix, whereas a less saturated hue includes a measure of this "white" RGB mix which turns red to pink, blue to light blue, and so on.

This RGB signal generated by the computer is not necessarily compatible with video monitors. Most video monitors use an encoded NTSC "composite" signal rather than RGB. Differences in vertical lines scanned, scanning frequency, and the interlace scanning system, itself, also create video resolution problems. The interlace system of scanning was developed to eliminate flicker in the television picture. The computer graphic image, however, contains such fine detail (some

Figure 11–19 Titling through a Computer

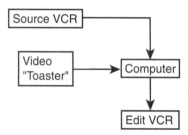

horizontal lines may be only one pixel wide) that the interlace scanning system of television *creates* flicker because the detail appears only on alternate fields.

The color encoding process used by the personal computer is more accurate than the signal encoding process developed (almost 40 years ago!) for broadcasting and scheduled to be used until the entire broadcast television system becomes digital (around the year 2005). Consequently, signal degradation of computer graphics is common when they are transferred to videotape. The major improvement in computer graphic color capability in recent years has been the replacement of the 4-bit system by the 24-bit board. With this, the range of colors available went from 16 to over 16 million if both hue and gray scale values are considered. This range of "colors" is considered to be necessary to the high degree of photo-realism that has been generated for feature film and network-level television.

Several devices have been developed to convert the sequentially scanned computer RGB signal to the slower, interlaced RGB NTSC video signal. The most inexpensive device converts digital pixel information of the computer to the analog RGB video signal and thus to the NTSC signal of television. Broadcast quality devices are the most expensive of these converters because they preserve the digital detail in the conversion rather than sacrifice it in a lowest-common-denominator fashion.

Although the computer graphics systems are capable of 4,000 colors, most consumer models can use only 8 colors in a given display (or "page") because of the immense RAM (memory or data storage capacity) required to describe the precise mix of each color. Rapid development of this technology followed. The "Targa+" era features videographic adapters with NTSC and Y/C inputs and outputs, internal keying, 640 × 480 resolution, and it retails for as little as $500. In contrast, the television system can produce millions of colors without such page or frame restrictions. Television's lack of edge resolution contrasts with its greater color capacity—if the range and quality of the colors can survive the process of converting them from computer-generated images. The graphics coprocessors used in the broadcast industry surmount these processing barriers but are priced beyond the range of most video field producers.

Several manufacturers have designed inexpensive computers that function well as video graphics generators. One popular example is Commodore's AMIGA®, which sells for under $3,000 and is used often in cable access centers and schools. As with most such inexpensive production equipment, it can provide three basic alphabet fonts in three predetermined sizes almost immediately and with relative ease.

The images generated by the AMIGA can be recorded on videotape or viewed on a composite monitor while being viewed on an RGB monitor since the console features both RGB and video "ports" (output connectors). The analog RGB monitor can display a full range of colors, so it is generally preferred over the digital RGB monitor (the type commonly used with the IBM PC), which can offer only 16 colors. Even allowing for signal degradation in the computer-to-VCR conversion process, videotape storage of the graphics is most often superior to the other

Figure 11–20   Computer Jaggies

two methods of image transfer available to the television producer: photographing the monitor screen or videographing the printed image. This computer is capable of generating a relatively high resolution image in which *jaggies* (the stairstep effect in diagonal lines or edges on the screen) are barely visible (see Figure 11–20). However since the computer has limited memory capacity with which to work, this high resolution acts to reduce the number of graphics that can be produced at one sitting.

An increasing number of software programs are available for the AMIGA and other personal computers for the production of television graphics. While special characters for foreign alphabets or science symbols can be constructed individually, three ready-made fonts, each containing upper- and lower-case characters in three sizes, are generally used for television. They are transferred from a disk to internal RAM to generate the desired text. Once the font is selected and loaded into the memory, characters can be stretched, italicized, edged, underlined, and colored. Once titles or credits have been assembled, they can be scrolled up, down, left, right, or diagonally.

The assembled text can be placed over contrasting backgrounds. This background can consist of a plain or abstract image generated from within the computer, or it can be a low-resolution version of a picture supplied directly to the computer by a video camera or television set. To do this, a framegrabber is plugged into the expansion bus on the computer console. This device contains an NTSC jack for outside video input. Using this accessory, the AMIGA can be used to freeze background images, alter colors, or generate MTV-type effects. The addition of a gen-lock board allows the mixing of sound and picture between television equipment or laser discs and the computer.

It must be noted that the less expensive home-type computers need special accessories and software programs to produce original graphics that meet broadcast television expectations.

In addition to alphabets, geometric forms can be generated and manipulated. Squares, rectangles, triangles, circles, and ovals can frame text or stand as objects themselves. These objects can be animated and coordinated with internally generated electronic music. Sophisticated and complex graphic displays require great amounts of time and energy to produce. Students are advised not to hold their breath while preparing original three-dimensional animations on a computer.

Termed "a studio in a box," NewTek's Video Toaster (registered trademark) originally provided manipulation of broadcast-quality images via the AMIGA.

Subsequently, versions were developed for IBM-PC and Macintosh computer users. The Toaster contains a computer videoboard that permits gen-locking, multifont and motion choices, dual-frame buffing, framegrabbing, still storing, and three-dimensional modeling with animation. A time base corrector is a necessary accessory. The AMIGA/Toaster combination makes available good-quality color, resolution, and two- and three-dimensional animation, although not necessarily all at once (see Figure 11–21).

Figure 11–21   Creating Video Graphics with the Video Toaster: (A) Video Toaster Workstation, (B) Creating a Three-Dimensional Image, (C) Manipulating Digitized Video with a Paint Program, (D) Creating a Program Title

(A)

(B)

(C)

(D)

Titling in the Camera

Many video cameras and camcorders have simple character generators built into them. These devices generate titles within the camera at the moment of recording. There are a number of problems with these systems. First, the size, font style, and color of the letters may not be what is wanted. Second, a very limited amount of information can be generated and keyed over the picture, usually only several lines of a dozen or so characters each. Finally, once the titles are recorded, there is no way to remove them. Overall, we think the disadvantages outweigh the advantages associated with the use of these systems.

SUMMARY

Regardless of the form of graphic materials or the materials from which they are made, there is no substitute for refined taste. Understated elegance serves the purposes of a program better than a sloppily executed collection of tacky tricks. Consequently, the field producer must take special steps to generate images that tell the story in the most direct manner possible. The personality of each visual element used in the production must contribute to a clearer understanding of the message—the point of the program. To accomplish this, a range of factors must be considered: aesthetic, expositional, functional, and practical. Once the design has been chosen, attention shifts to its execution and manipulation in the production.

Realistically, graphic support to most video field productions will be largely two-dimensional in the immediate future, if only for reasons of cost and time constraints. Computer programs provide the means of titling and labeling video and preparing a variety of frames, charts, graphs, and pointers to clarify and enrich a presentation. Equipment is increasingly available from many manufacturers that bridges part of the gap between video and computer systems. Ultimately, the adoption of a universal digital video system by all manufacturers and broadcasters will solve this compatibility problem.

The inclusion of titles within a tape, either as title inserts that are edited onto the beginning or end of a tape, or as superimposed or keyed titles that are recorded over background video, provides a set of strategic problems for the video field producer. To find the simplest and most economical way to title a program, these problems must be addressed thoroughly during production planning. In the last analysis, good graphic materials make a strong positive contribution to the success of the program and avoid generating distractions of any kind.

12

Production Planning

Without a doubt, the key to success in field production lies in adequate production planning. The remote producer is at the mercy of the location and the people in the production, and does not have the same kind of controlled situation as the studio television producer. Therefore, it is imperative that all elements of the production be as carefully planned as possible. This is not to suggest that such planning ensures that the production will go off without a hitch. If there is one thing that can be guaranteed in field production, it is that the unexpected will happen—and you must be able to cope with it.

Nevertheless, producers who carefully plan out the course of their productions undoubtedly have greater success in the field than those who do not plan. In fact, the planning part of the production often involves more time and energy than the actual production time in the field.

STAGES AND TYPES OF PRODUCTIONS

Three Stages of Production

All productions can be broken down into three stages: preproduction, production, and postproduction. The **preproduction** stage is crucial to a production's success because it is in this stage that the initial idea for the subject is developed and the production mechanism put into motion. Thorough preproduction planning ensures that the actual production phase goes smoothly. The **production** phase of a field production is the actual shooting time for the program. Finally, the **postproduction** phase involves the editing and packaging of the production. Once again, anticipating and solving problems through thorough planning in the preproduction and production stages will make the postproduction process easier.

Too many times we have heard field producers say, "We'll fix it in postproduction." While this is sometimes possible, more often than not major problems that are not corrected in preproduction or production will haunt a production.

Some problems can be solved, others cannot. The place to anticipate and solve problems is in preproduction, not postproduction.

Adequate planning is an important part of all three production stages. A comprehensive map of the program plan must be communicated clearly to all members of the production group for the overall program design and production to be executed efficiently and smoothly. This is in large part accomplished through production planning. All major decisions about a production should be made on paper before the camera is uncapped and the tape rolled.

Independent versus Client-Based Production

The production planning process is influenced by the nature of the production. An *independent production* is one in which the producer is responsible for the development of the program idea and does not have to report to another agency or individual for consultation or approval. This type of production operates somewhat differently from a *client-based production*—one in which the producer has been hired to carry out someone else's program idea.

Video producers find themselves in many different production situations. In the commercial arena, the producer most often executes production ideas developed by others. In the area of independent documentary production, the producer most often develops an idea and carries it through the production process. However, in many cases, the producer must report to a grant-giving agency to obtain the funds necessary for the production. The in-house corporate television producer may have to report to an executive producer or department head to win approval for production projects but may then be given significant autonomy to develop and execute the production idea.

PREPRODUCTION PLANNING

Getting and Developing a Program Idea

Whether a television program is developed to communicate an idea about a political issue, to attempt to persuade the audience to buy a particular brand of deodorant, to convey information about changes in corporate policy to employees, or to entertain through the presentation of a dramatic, comedic, or musical extravaganza, the program idea is at the heart of the production. No program can proceed without a basic idea governing its organization and production. Both the media experimentalist, who breaks narrative and aesthetic conventions of media structure in order to challenge the audience to focus on new relations between visual and aural images, and the instructional television producer, who uses the medium to clearly and unambiguously teach a subject to a target audience, make a series of initial decisions about the design of their respective programs.

In the early stages of program development, the program idea contains at least several components. Central to the idea is the concept of the program's subject. What does the program producer want to communicate? Evaluating the target audience gives the producer important information about the medium best suited for transmitting the idea, and the way in which the subject can best be treated in that medium to effectively communicate the program idea to the audience. So, in the initial planning stages of a program, we come full circle to concerns that were raised in the first chapter of this book: The idea for a program can only be moved to effective actualization through thorough consideration of the elements of subject, medium, treatment, and audience.

For the independent producer, or the student who is required to complete a program for a television production course, getting the idea may be the hardest part of the production process. For the in-house producer or educational media specialist, ideas may be generated by resource people with expertise in particular content areas. The producer's role, then, is to adapt the content to the particular requirements of the medium and audience by applying the proper treatment to its development.

Program Conceptualization and Design

No matter what the source of the idea for a program or program segment, the video field producer should follow a method for the development and execution of the program idea. At least four areas should be addressed in the initial stages of program design and conceptualization: subject, treatment, visual potential, and feasibility.

Subject

Preliminary planning should consider the subject from at least two perspectives: content and structure. Analysis of the content of the subject identifies the important information to be conveyed in the piece—what is to be communicated and why this information is important and/or appealing to the audience.

Information about the subject and audience can be gathered by conducting basic research on the subject and audience. For many years, U.S. broadcasters were required to ascertain the needs of their community through systematic research and interviews with community leaders, and then broadcast programming designed to meet those needs. The staffs of many ongoing program series include one or more researchers, whose job it is to identify subjects of interest to their audience. In news operations, assignment editors determine which of the day's stories have the greatest importance and/or potential interest to the viewing audience, and then assign their production to the various ENG production teams.

Initial program planning should also consider the structure of the presentation. At the very least, you should make some preliminary plans as to the organization of the material. Aristotle's observation that all drama contains a beginning, a middle, and an end is just as useful to television producers as it is to theatrical dramatists. Indeed, concepts of dramatic structure are as indispensable to the producers of television news, documentaries, and commercials as they are to the producers of televised drama.

Program Format/Treatment of the Subject

Once the subject has been identified, a decision needs to be made about how the program idea will be presented. Not only does a program format have to be identified but decisions need to be made about the way in which the subject will be treated within the chosen format. For example, concern about the uncontrolled proliferation of nuclear weapons might lead one producer to produce a documentary on the medical consequences of a nuclear holocaust, while another producer might develop a campaign of issue-oriented public service announcements (PSAs) to be distributed to local television stations.

The documentary approach, for example, can rely on the testimony of experts, focus on victims or survivors of previous nuclear disasters, or combine the two. The public service announcements can focus on one issue or many, perhaps using so-called commercial production techniques.

Visual Potential

While developing a production idea, some thought must be given to the visual potential of the subject. In many ways, this is a two-edged sword. Concern with those subjects having greater visual potential over those with less visual potential has led to some serious, justified criticism of television. Subjects with more visual potential often seem to be those that receive coverage, while those with less visual potential are ignored.

In evaluating the visual potential of the subject, the producer should consider not only whether one subject has more visual potential than another but also *how* the visual potential of any subject can be maximized. On the surface, a discussion of the failing economy might seem to have less visual potential than a magazine segment on trained chimpanzees who parachute from airplanes on skis and slalom down a mountain ski course. But this may only be because the producer has not thought out the visual potential of the piece on economics. At the very least, discussion of economic theory could be supplemented with visual material on the subject: computer-generated graphics, or perhaps three-dimensional models to convey information about various concepts, or support the discussion with relevant visual material. Interviews or profiles of real people suffering the consequences of the economic problems can be integrated into the program. For example, a discussion of rising interest rates need not focus only on the statements of a mortgage banker sitting in an office. It might also include shots of construction sites and lumber mills to provide external, visual information about the issues being discussed.

Even if additional visual material is not going to be used in the story, the visual potential of the basic interview with the banker should be considered. The interview location, camera position, shot selection, and lighting can all be manipulated to maximize the visual potential of the interview.

Feasibility

No program proposal is worth developing if it is not feasible. A documentary based on the lifestyle of the members of the local Zen Buddhist bakery might seem intriguing. But the likelihood of ever producing a piece is slim if the local Buddhists are cloistered, have taken a vow of silence, refuse to allow interviews, and prohibit cameras from entering their premises. Preliminary decisions about the feasibility of the program should focus on the field producer's ability to get access to the subject, as well as the availability of resources to support the production. Production resources include *financial support* (an adequate budget to pay for the production), *personnel* (paid or unpaid production personnel to execute the production), and *equipment and facilities*.

Formal Program Proposal and Shooting Schedule

Once the preproduction planning has been completed, you will be able to develop a formal program proposal. The amount of detail contained in the proposal will vary, depending on your production situation. A proposal for submittal to an agency as part of an application for a development or production grant will be more detailed than one developed for an in-house production or an independent production not dependent on outside funds.

Depending on your particular situation, your formal program proposal will contain some combination (and perhaps all) of the following elements.

Treatment. A narrative description of the idea for the project should be presented to convey the essential idea behind the project, as well as its importance and need.

Outline of Major Elements. This section should present an outline of the major elements of the program. If your proposal is for an entertainment or documentary program, this section identifies the program's most important parts. If you are producing an educational program, this section will outline your major goals or objectives, perhaps in the form of a list of what is to be learned from the program.

List of Locations and Setups. A list of locations and setups is extremely important, because it will give you an idea of how you will need to budget your production time. A *location* is a general area where shooting will take place, whereas the *setup* describes specific shooting areas at the more general location. For example, one might schedule a location shoot at the local airport. At that location, specific setups might be needed at the ticket area, baggage area, and maintenance area.

Outline of Proposed Shooting Schedule. The shooting schedule outline presents a realistic estimate of how each production day will be spent. The outline should include a breakdown of the amount of time each segment is expected to take to shoot, as well as the more mundane elements such as time for travel, equipment setup, and breaks for the crew.

Figure 12–1 presents a proposal for a remote segment from the PBS series, *Over Easy*. Notice how the four elements listed are developed and presented in this proposal.

Comments on Technical Feasibility. You should address any questions about access to the location, crowd control, or access to power and/or adequate light. If a remote survey has been completed, this can provide answers to the most important questions about the use of the proposed remote locations.

Script. A script is an important part of any production. If your program will be completely scripted, then a copy of the script or an excerpt from it should be included in the proposal. If your program is a documentary or is based on interviews, you will not have a complete script. Instead, present an outline of the major components of the program. (We'll talk more about scripts later in this chapter.)

Evaluation. Programs produced with particular goals in mind need to be evaluated for effectiveness. The proposal form, therefore, should contain a description of the method that you plan to use to evaluate the effectiveness of the program. Evaluation of program effectiveness can take many forms. You can simply propose to report the number of copies of the tape that you sell, provide an estimate of the number of people who see the program, or provide the number of broadcast stations or cable systems that carry it. If your program has specific learning objectives as its goal, you may want to test your audience to see how much of the information conveyed by the program they retain. Again, the extent to which this element is contained within the formal program proposal depends on the goals of the program itself.

Budget. Many program proposals include an estimate of the budget for the program. The budget should be a realistic estimate of all the costs associated with the production. Video producers find themselves in a variety of production situations with respect to budgeting. For example, a home video producer or a student in a university production course may find that the only cost associated with a production is the cost of videotape. The independent producer, on the other hand, may have to rent a considerable amount of equipment for the field shoot and rent editing facilities for postproduction editing. The field producer working within a television station might not have any responsibility at all for developing budgets, since all production costs may be carried as part of the normal operating expenses of the station.

How, then, does one go about developing a budget? As we have stated, the budget should present a realistic assessment of the costs associated with the production.

Figure 12–1 *Over Easy* Segment Proposal

KQED, INC.
500 EIGHTH ST.
SAN FRANCISCO, CA 94103

Wednesday, August 2   Jim Langton
                         Disneyland   Al Miller - contact
                                         (213) 555-8805 or
                                       (714) 555-4456

6:30 AM	Call
6:30-7:30	Travel
7:30-8:30	Set-up Interview w/ Jim (Street Car in Town Square)
8:30-8:45	Break
8:45-9:30	Shoot Interview with Jim
9:30-10:00	Shoot from inside trolley
10:00-11:00	Shoot off trolley

                1. Scene with Gary
                2. Jim changing horses
                3. Jim enters Main Street & greets Ralph
                4. LS trolley car drives off

11:00-11:30	Lunch
11:30-12:00	Set-up for Parade (Town Square)
12:00-1:00	Shoot Mickey Mouse Parade
1:00-1:30	Set-up Exterior Disneyland (Entrance to Park)
1:30-1:45	Shoot Exterior Disneyland
1:45-3:00	Wrap and Travel

Four set-ups

1. Jim Interview in Town Square by train
2. Main Street
3. Parade in Town Square
4. Disneyland Entrance

366

Figure 12–1 *Over Easy* Segment Proposal *Continued*

```
Jim Langton
(213) 555-1196
Disneyland
```

Jim Langton at 62 is a rough and tough rodeo cowboy who for the last 15 years has worked as a driver of a horse drawn street car on "Main Street, USA" in Disneyland. Although Jim still ropes calfs in small rodeo contests on the weekends, his fulltime job is at Disneyland. For Jim the job puts him in contact with two of his favorite things: horses and people. Jim talks about the older people who come to Disneyland, and what it's like to relate to them as well as the younger ones. Sometimes the job can be difficult - "It's like being a P.R. man all day long," he says. Jim enjoys being around the younger employees and adds, "I'm not exactly a spring chicken no more." Seven months ago Jim lost his thumb in a calf roping accident and was in the hospital for the first time in his life. Several years ago he divorced his wife who was also a rodeo cowgirl, and moved to California. Two years ago she committed suicide when she found out she had cancer. Today, Jim lives alone but retains a close relationship with his daughter and 95-year-old father-in-law. Jim has lived an active life and is just reaching the stage of realizing that he too is growing old. He is just beginning to face the fact that he's got to prepare for his old age.

Elements
_____

1. Second career
2. Living alone
3. Divorced late in life
4. Intergenerational

Focus
_____

1. How he feels about his job at Disneyland - the stress and the joy
2. His interrelations with the other younger employees and the tourists, young and old
3. His marriage and divorce
4. How he feels about living alone and preparing for his old age

Developing the budget, then, depends on your particular production situation. The cost of producing an hour of prime-time dramatic television for distribution on one of the commercial networks may exceed $1,000,000. Although only a few video producers work in this budget range, even nonbroadcast productions produced to professional specifications may be relatively expensive.

Figure 12–2 presents a budget estimate for five sales training modules to be produced for a corporate client. The total running time of the project was 90 minutes, and the project was produced using professional equipment ($\frac{1}{2}$″ Betacam recorded in the field edited onto a 1″ master tape) and professional talent. The total budget estimate for this project, including a 10 percent contingency estimate, was $77,241, well within the $1,000 per minute of finished video product that many producers give as a ballpark estimate of cost for corporate productions in our area as this book goes to press.

Many producers of small-scale productions find that their budget needs are significantly more modest than those listed in the previous example. A 30-minute independent documentary, a tape documenting the accomplishments of a community organization, or an edited videotape of a wedding ceremony can often be produced on a shoestring budget and delivered for a few thousand dollars or less.

Figure 12–3 shows the actual production costs for a small-scale production that resulted in the completion of a 20-minute videotape produced and edited in the S-VHS format for a municipal government client. The principal production equipment (camcorder, lights, microphones, etc.) was supplied by the university department in which the students who produced the program were enrolled. Members of the production crew were not paid for their time, thereby eliminating personnel expenses completely. Minor additional expenses included videotape, rental charges for editing time, and miscellaneous supplies. The total cost of the production was $514.

Scripts

Because the types of programs that video field producers work with are quite varied, a number of different script formats and scripting strategies are used.

Story Outline Script. In most electronic news gathering (ENG) situations, and in many other production situations as well (such as television magazine segments), a formal script probably will not be developed. Because time is of the essence in such productions, it is more likely that a story outline will be developed The **story outline** is a list of the major elements that will be used in the story. Usually, it specifies the locations to be used, the essential visual material to be recorded at the various locations, and the subjects of any interview segments. Occasionally, specific recommendations for shots, particularly transition shots and opening or closing shots, are specified (see Figure 12–4).

Sometimes the story outline is not written but is instead presented orally by the segment producer to the production crew. This type of production planning (or lack of it) is not recommended for the beginning producer. Professional crews are

Figure 12–2   Large-Scale Production Budget

PRODUCTION BUDGET						
CLIENT :		XXXXXXXX				
PROJECT TITLE :		Sales Training--5 video modules				
DATE OF THIS BUDGET :		2/7/89				
SPECIFICATIONS :		- Total completed running time : 90 minutes (5 separate modules)				
		- 4 days production on a stage (1 pre-light, 3 shooting)				
		- 4 sets, as described in bidding specifications				
		- Professional talent :				
		- On camera spokesperson (2 days)				
		- 4 additional talent (5 talent working days total)				
		- Broadcast quality production standards (Betacam shoot, 1" edit master)				
CLIENT WILL PROVIDE :		- Animated treatment of logo, on tape				
SUMMARY OF COSTS		ESTIMATE		COST	ACTUAL	
PRE-PRODUCTION						
Personnel & Script	A	$9,730.21			0.00	
Equipment & FAX	B	$100.00			0.00	
PRODUCTION						
Personnel	C	$7,451.22			0.00	
Equipment & FAX	D	$11,305.00			0.00	
Talent	E	$3,920.82			0.00	
Narr. & Music	F	$650.00			0.00	
Graphics	G	$985.00			0.00	
POST PRODUCTION						
Personnel	H	$4,440.68			0.00	
Facilities	I	$15,405.00			0.00	
MISCELLANEOUS	J	$3,006.60			0.00	
Grand sub-total		$56,995			0.00	
*amount taxable			$23,410			
Tax		$1,521.65			0.00	
Production Fee		$11,703.24			0.00	
		----------			----------	
GRAND TOTAL		$70,219			0.00	
Contingency 10%		$7,022				
(TOTAL INCLUDING CONTINGENCY		$77,241)				

Continued

Figure 12–2 Large-Scale Production Budget   *Continued*

	UNIT	DESCP.	COST	ESTIMATE	UNIT	COST	ACTUAL	
PRE-PRODUCTION								
Personnel								
Writer		script	$0	$0				
Director--Prep	5	day	$450	$2,250				
Director--Casting	2	day	$450	$900				
Director--Set	1	day	$450	$450				
Prod. Asst.	1	day	$125	$125				
(subject to insurance)		125						
Workers Comp. Ins.		4.17%		$5				
			----------	----------			----------	
	A		SUB TOTAL	$3,730			0.00	
Casting								
FAX	1	day	100	$100				
supplies		day		$0				
		day		$0				
			----------	----------			----------	
	B		SUB TOTAL	$100			0.00	
*Taxable			100					
PRODUCTION								
Personnel								
Director	4	day	$450	$1,800				
Camera Operator--prep	1	day	$300	$300				
Camera Operator--shoot	3	day	$300	$900				
Tape Op/Sound	3	day	$250	$750				
Lighting Director--prep	1	day	$275	$275				
Lighting Director--shoot	3	day	$275	$825				
Grip--prep	1	day	$225	$225				
Grip--shoot	3	day	$250	$750				
Utility	1	day	$150	$150				
Script Supervisor	2	day	$200	$400				
Prod. Asst.	4	day	$125	$500				
Prompter Operator	incl	day	$0	$0				
Make-up	2	day	$175	$350				
(subject to insurance)		5425						
Workers Comp. Ins.		4.17%		$226				
			----------	----------			----------	
	C		SUB TOTAL	$7,451			0.00	

Figure 12–2 Large-Scale Production Budget *Continued*

Equipment & FAX							
Cam pak 3/4"		day		$0			
Cam pak Betacam	3	day	$700	$2,100			
Crew mileage		miles		$0			
Camera Dolly *	3	day	$150	$450			
Teleprompter *	3	day	$425	$1,275			
Stage electrical & grip	4	day	$300	$1,200			
videotape stock *	25	casste	$15	$375			
wireless mike *		unit	$75	$0			
crew meals *	30	meals	$12	$360			
stage rental-prep *	1	day	$640	$640			
stage rental-shoot *	3	day	$640	$1,920			
stage expendables				$100			
Stage paint				$500			
props				$100			
Set design/rental *		bid		$2,285			
	D		SUB TOTAL	$11,305		0.00	
*Taxable				7305			
Talent							
On-Cam Spoksprsn	1	day	$580	$580		0.00	
On-Cam Spoksprsn	1	second day	$319	$319			
Speaking Roles	5	day	$319	$1,595			
Non-speaking Roles		day		$0			
Voice-Over Narrator		day		$0			
sub total				$2,494			
benefits & payrolling		53%		$1,322			
Wardrobe	7	fees	$15	$105			
	E		SUB TOTAL	$3,921		0.00	
Narr. Recording							
Studio *		hour	$70	$0			
Audio tape stock *		reel	$25	$0			
Music							
Search time *		hour	$80	$0			
Royalties	10	drop	$65	$650			
Original Music				$0			
Tape stock *		reel	$50	$0			
	F		SUB TOTAL	$650		0.00	
*Taxable				0			

Continued

Figure 12–2 Large-Scale Production Budget *Continued*

Graphics						
Paint box	2 hours		$275	$550		
tranfer	hours			$50		
Stock	2.0		$80	$160		
lunch						
Director	0.5 day		$450	$225		
G		SUB TOTAL	$985			0.00
*Taxable			600			
POST-PRODUCTION						
Personnel						
Director--off line	3 day		$400	$1,200		
Director--on line	4 day		$400	$1,600		
Editor	7 day		$225	$1,575		
(subject to insurance)		1575				
Workers Comp. Ins.		4.17%		$66		
H		SUB TOTAL	$4,441			0.00
Facilities						
Window dubs*	25 casste.		$14	$350		
Dub Stock*	25 casste.		4	$100		
Transfer*	2 hour		$75	$150		
Off-line suite*	7 day	flat		$900		
Off-L Stock*	4 casste.		$45	$180		
On-line B-Cam">1"*	38 hour		$225	$8,550		
On-line 1"-Cam">1"*	8 hour		$295	$2,360		
ATR in post	3 hour		$45	$135		
Character gen*	7 hour		$60	$420		
Add. 1" machine*	6 hour		$100	$600		
ADO *	3 hour		$250	$750		
On-line stock*	100 minute			$300		
Audio sweetening*	3 hour		$120	$360		
Sweetening Stock*	minute			$0		
Preview dubs*	2 casste.		$125	$250		
I		SUB TOTAL	$15,405			0.00
*Taxable			15405			
MISCELLANEOUS						
Insurance @ 4%		4%	70,165	$2,807		
COPY				$100		
Shipping/Messngr				$100		
J		SUB TOTAL	$3,007			0.00

Figure 12–3   Small-Scale Production Budget

Production Expenses
Drug Diversion Video Program (20 Minutes)

Blank videocassettes	$102.00
7 S-VHS tapes for production and editing	
2 VHS tapes for client copies	
Photocopies (talent release forms)	2.00
Food for extras	13.00
Photography	37.00
Black and white film, processing and prints	
Posterboard to mount prints	
Editing facilities rental	360.00
20 hours of S-VHS editing @ $18.00 per hour	
Total:	$514.00

---

able to utilize this shorthand method of production planning principally because they are used to working together as a team, and most importantly, because they understand the conventions of television. That is, they all know what they need to get onto videotape in order to gather enough material for the story to hold together. Without even having a script, the camera operator knows what needs to be shot, and may even stage multiple takes of a particular shot or sequence that will be important to the overall story. The producer may have a list of questions, or an outline of subject matter to be treated in an interview.

In the ENG situation, an on-camera stand-up introduction and close are usually recorded on location. In other kinds of EFP, such introductory and summary statements, are most often added to the production later as a voice-over by the principal talent. In both types of productions, the videotape editor has responsibility for viewing the tape and making the primary editorial decisions about which shots to use, what order to use them in, and how much of the primary interview material to include in the segment. Figure 12–4 presents an example of a story outline written by a field producer for the videotape editor.

Storyboard. A **storyboard** is a visualization of the principal visual material in a film or television production. In developing a storyboard, the principal frames of visual information that correspond to the written script are drawn and arranged in sequence with the script. Storyboards have long been used in the production of television commercials and spot announcements. Because these announcements are short, the visual parts of the program can be drawn in considerable detail. Storyboards are also used extensively in feature film production; they allow the director to see what the film will look like before it is shot. In some cases, directors

Figure 12–4 *Evening Magazine* Story Outline

WESTINGHOUSE BROADCASTING COMPANY □ 855 BATTERY STREET □ SAN FRANCISCO, CA 94111 □ (415) 765-8832

OUTLINE FOR FALL FASHION

OPEN: Vis of Japan from the old stories that we did lasting about (:10) seconds before going to the V/O. The vis after that should follow the copy.

V/O #1 - To find this year's hot fashion look we'll have to direct our sights to the east, to Japan. A land where art and beauty merge with life and a country determined enough to ride to world dominance atop a transistor. This year fashion is TURNING JAPANESE! (:15)

TRANSITION: To hot fashion show vis and music for (:10).

V/O #2 - Fashion is all about what's new and the Japanese look is certainly that. From the one size fits all concept to exotic textiles, what some have come to call the BAG LADY look is this fall's hot fashion ticket. It is a blend of working class cottons and the Japanese ethic of form and function. (:15)

BITE: (Beth Trier #3 4:23) "Right now they are what is hot, the trend. Therefore stores, retailers are picking up on it and making a lot of fuss about it...can comprehend it, we're not sure." (:15)

VIS: For Beth's I.D. use a shot of her from the fashion show.

V/O #3 - Beth Trier of the San Francisco Chronicle doesn't feel that the Japanese look is just another trend, but rather an influence on fashion that will have an impact. (:08)

BITE: (Beth Trier #3 5:00) "The whole concept of dressing according to the Japanese...Taking a garment shaped like a box... fabric taken away from everyday concepts." (:30 cut down if it drags)

TRANSITION: To the art museum and vis of Issey Miyake...limping around. (:10)

V/O #4 - One of the most influential of the Japanese designers is Issey Miyake. Not a household word and probably will never be one, but his fashions adorn the likes of David Bowie, Grace Jones and Diana Ross. In design circles Miyake is equally noted for his art along with his fashion designs. (:10)

Figure 12–4   *Evening Magazine* Story Outline   *Continued*

WESTINGHOUSE BROADCASTING COMPANY □ 855 BATTERY STREET □ SAN FRANCISCO, CA 94111 □ (415) 765-8632

BITE: (Issey #1 13:25) "When I see all the beautiful tradition...
that is probably living inside me." (:30)

V/O #5 - What has brought Miyake to San Francisco is an exhibition
of his art called "Bodyworks" which is a computerized
environmental show that highlights many of his art to wear
pieces. But what people are waiting to see are the
clothes. (:10)

TRANSITION: To the rehearsal music montage with the models and
action. (:10)

TRT: 2:55

V/O #6 - Tonight the hottest ticket in town is the Issey Miyake
fashion show and it's a packed house at I. Magnin. The
show begins with a display of his ready to wear fashions
called Plantation. To model these garments Miyake chose
real people, and it's interesting to note the designs
only come in one size. (:15)

VIS: Music up and pictures for about (:30).

V/O #7 - Then it was time for Miyake to reveal his Fall Fashions
to a waiting crowd. (:03)

VIS: Of the fashion show for as long as it'll hold up (:40)?

V/O #8 - (This is the end my friend) Now think what you may, all
I know is they were all shocked and amused by the mini-
skirt. And the Leisure Suit was universally hated, but
both are still around. Even though you may not rush out
and buy a Miyake, one thing Beth Trier did say was the
most lasting impact of Japanese clothes will be their
creative use of natural fabrics. (:20)

O/C: (Rich #2 8:40) "Wool, silk, linen, all natural fibers for
an all natural guy. (Freeze video)

THE END!

Courtesy of Matt Chan, KPIX-TV, San Francisco.

even make preliminary decisions about shot choices and the arrangements of visual sequences on the basis of the still frames in the storyboards. Storyboards are also used extensively in the development stages of animated features.

The treatment of the content of a program is reflected in the storyboard. Producers are expected to present such storyboards to clients or potential backers as the primary means of "pitching" the proposed production. Often, commercial clients expect to consider several treatments before commissioning a production. The storyboard need not include each shot that will be used in the final product, but it must include the major visual elements that establish the scope and tone of the production. The storyboard is arranged in proper sequence so that the progression of the narrative is clear and the integration of sound and picture can be considered in practical terms.

The storyboard is a working document subject to change as the production design evolves. It reflects the vision and discipline of the producer and often allows the production crew to anticipate problems and prepare solutions before shooting begins. Experienced videographers understand essential differences between static drawings and the sound-supported-moving-image-in-a-story-context of television. They do not allow the substitution of pretty pictures for a useful sequence of sketches that identify the physical elements important to the story and illustrate the manner in which those elements are to be presented in the execution of the production.

The development of a full script and storyboard is probably the best exercise the beginning video producer can undertake to plan out a production's visual sequences. You can use a number of different storyboard formats. In the professional arena, storyboards such as the ones shown in Figures 12–5 and 12–6 are common. The individual frames of the storyboard are arranged across the page, with the principal audio information written below.

An alternative way of arranging storyboard information is shown in Figure 12–7. In this example, the storyboard information is drawn on the left side of the page, the center of the page contains the video information, and the audio information is on the right side of the page. This is a convenient, economical way of laying out picture and sound information.

Full Script. Many single-camera productions are shot from a full script. In many ways, the use of a full script (and storyboard) creates the best of all possible production situations. Preparation of the full script and storyboard saves a great deal of time in the production and postproduction stages. Any program that is prepared for a client should be fully scripted. All educational/instructional programs and dramatic programs are fully scripted. Even many interview-based documentaries utilize very detailed shooting scripts. Although you may not know exactly what the interviewees will say, you can predict their general position and roughly how they will answer your questions. The script can therefore describe in detail the program's organization, the questions to be asked, and the predicted answers. This will serve as the initial shooting guide. Modifications in the script can be made after the field material has been shot to bring it into line with what was actually said in the interview.

Figure 12–5   Public Service Announcement Storyboard

Americans for Fair Elections

:30 "Check-off"

This is Eric Sevaried. Since I began covering politics, campaign costs have skyrocketed. More and more people are wondering: does money talk louder than votes? It doesn't have to. There's something you can do:

Check this box on your tax return. That'll keep our presidential elections financed publicly and not by special interest groups.

It won't increase your tax or lower your refund. So it doesn't cost you a cent.

Remember, check the "yes" box for fair elections.

:10 "Check-off"

I'm Eric Sevaried. If you think that in politics, money talks louder than votes.

Check this box on your tax return.

It doesn't cost you a cent--and it buys fair elections.

Courtesy of Public Media Center, San Francisco.

Figure 12–6   Commercial Storyboard

U.S. NAVY

Title: "This is David"
Comm'l No.: QUAQ-2013

Public Service Advertising

Time: 30 Seconds
Commercial Produced by BBDO/NY

For additional info please contact: Navy Recruiting Command, 4015 Wilson Blvd., Arlington, VA 22203 (703) 696-4777

Music up and under throughout
AVO: This is David.

DAVID: Oh, hi.

AVO: This is what David's done.

David went to college.

Sorry, Annapolis.

David taught himself to play piano,

the sax,

even the bagpipes. Well, maybe not the bagpipes.

David was NBA Rookie-of-the-Year.

He's also been to the Olympics...twice!

David even became a Naval Officer.

David's sure done a lot. But do you know

one thing David's never done?
DAVID: Drugs.

AVO: David doesn't do drugs.

Maybe that's why he's done so much.
DAVID: Hmmmmmmm.

Courtesy of Navy Recruiting Command, Arlington, VA.

378

Figure 12–7 Script and Storyboard—Haight Ashbury Switchboard

30 SECOND PUBLIC SERVICE ANNOUNCEMENT
SUBJECT: HAIGHT-ASHBURY SWITCHBOARD

Storyboard	Video	Audio
	LS OF EMPTY BEACH SCENE SAVE FOR ONE SOLITARY FIGURE IN THE DISTANCE	NATURAL BEACHY SOUNDS OF WAVES, WIND AND SO ON
	CUT TO MS OF TALENT ON BEACH. TALENT HAS A DEPRESSED, CONTEMPLATIVE LOOK ON HER FACE	
	MS OF TALENT PICKING UP PORTABLE RADIO TO HER SIDE AND TURNING IT ON	CLICKING SOUND AND MUSIC UP (WITH POOR SQUEAKY AM RADIO QUALITY)
	SLOW ZOOM OUT FROM MS TO LS	MUSIC UNDER TO HALF VOLUME VO: Are you sad, lonely or confused? Surprise. We all are at times of our life. Some of us just hide it better than others.
	CONTINUE SLOW ZOOM FROM LS TO XLS OF TALENT ON BEACH	VO: If you would like to quit hiding and share your feelings with someone, call us at the Haight-Ashbury Switchboard at 555-6211. We still care.
	CUT TO BLACK	FADE OUT MUSIC

Courtesy of Jack Banks.

Although there are a number of different kinds of full-script styles or formats in use, the two-column split page format is one of the most widely used and one of the most useful to beginning video producers. In this script format, information about the program's video is contained in the left column and information about the program's audio is contained in the right column (see Figure 12–8).

The full script will contain sufficient detail to answer most production questions. Location and shot angle are specified. This, in turn, may suggest lens focal length, depth of field, and light requirements of the shot. The audio associated with the shot is also included because it is important to the duration of the shot and, if music is identified, to the rhythm of the shot, and the speed of camera movement or movement of objects within the frame.

The full script is central to the calculation of the production budget. The production calendar is generated from the full script, as are equipment, location, audio, light, costume, and property requirements. These, in turn, lead to rental, transportation, food, insurance, and salary calculations (and profit, too, for that matter).

The split-script format lends itself particularly well to the *script breakdown*. In the script breakdown, each shot is given a number (if you have not already done so in writing the original version of the script), a shot list is compiled, and then—by considering the shot list and the availability of shooting locations and any actors/actresses (talent) who may be involved in the production—a daily shooting plan for the production is constructed. Figure 12–9 presents an example of a shot list, and Figure 12–10 presents the plan for one day's shooting schedule on this production.

Preinterview

An extremely important part of the preproduction planning process is the preinterview. The **preinterview** is simply an interview scheduled before the production date with the program's subject. Preinterviews can be extremely important to both the segment producer and the interviewee. From the producer's perspective, a preinterview establishes contact with a subject and gives the producer initial permission to actually produce the piece. In terms of program design, the preinterview is an important point at which to gain familiarity with the subject in terms of the person and the content of the piece. The preinterview may well tell you what is important about the topic being investigated. This serves at least three functions: It provides initial information about the structure and content of the piece; it suggests possibilities for visual material to be incorporated into the piece; and it may suggest possibilities for interviews with other people or visits to other sites to gather additional information relevant to the program.

Often the people who are the subjects of video field productions have not been on television before. For example, a magazine program that focuses on unusual people or unique local characters is likely to identify as subjects for segments people who have little experience on camera. The preinterview serves an important function for such subjects in that it allows them to establish rapport

---

Figure 12–8   Full Script in Split-Script Format with Numbered Shots

VIDEO SCRIPT

Title: "BRANCH PRODUCTION MANAGEMENT CASE STUDY"
Draft: FINAL

Note: Throughout the program, we hear natural background sounds appropriate to the scene. When we are focusing on people, at times we hear them speak under the narrator's voice. We may understand a word or phrase here and there, but what they say is not important to the content of the program unless it is detailed in quotes.

VIDEO	AUDIO
Super Title: "Case Study: Part I: The Players"	
Fade Up On: 1. Exterior: Front of Branch seen from street. Signage is clearly visible. We hear street sounds.	NARRATOR (Male Voice, VO): Welcome to the Longtree Branch of XXXXXXXXXXXX Bank. We're located in a medium-sized California suburb.
Dissolve to: 2. Interior: WS (wide shot) of lobby. We see customers in line.	We serve a mix of customers with a variety of banking needs. Everyone from seniors to college students, merchants to manufacturers, middle class families to professionals.
Cut to Pan of: 3. A TELLER crossing the lobby and approaching EDITH FARNSWORTH at her desk on the platform. There are pictures of her grandchildren behind the desk. The TELLER has a question for EDIE.	Edith Farnsworth, or Edie as she likes to be called, is our Branch Manager. Edie's been with the bank for twenty years and is proud to have risen to the Branch Manager position.
4. Another angle of EDIE. She is distracted from her conversation	

Continued

Figure 12–8   Full Script in Split-Script Format with Numbered Shorts   *Continued*

by something she notices in the branch (we do not see what it is).	She likes to be aware of everything that is going on in the branch and is always very busy.
5. MS of DOROTHEA HALL. Pull back to reveal EDIE conferring with her over a piece of business. They are standing somewhere behind the teller windows. EDIE nods, smiles at Dorothea, then exits frame.	Dorothea Hall is our Customer Service Representative. She and Edie have worked together since they first came to the bank as tellers.
Cut to:	
6. DOROTHEA on phone. Hangs up and goes back to working on the daily report.	Dorothea handles customer concerns and problem phone calls referred by the tellers.
7. CU of DOROTHEA's face as she works.	She also compiles detailed daily reports for Edie.
8. GEORGE BEALES at the merchant window. He greets an approaching customer as if they know each other well.	George Beales, our Purchase Merchant Teller, knows his customers well and enjoys working with them. He has been with the bank for six years and aspires to the job of Branch Manager.

Courtesy of Robert Tat Video Communications and Wells Fargo Bank, Retail Staff Development.

with the producer and/or other production personnel. This puts them at ease for the interview, particularly if a rough outline of the interview topics is discussed.

There is no set way to approach the preinterview. Some producers are content to make the initial preinterview contacts with the subject over the telephone, whereas others prefer an in-person visit. In either situation, it is essential that the producer take accurate notes on the discussion. Some producers prefer to use an unobtrusive audiocassette recorder to tape the preinterview discussion.

When deciding whether or not to conduct a preinterview, several factors should be taken into account. Since the preinterview often entails a visit to the

Figure 12–9 Shot List

SHOT LIST:
Drug Diversion Program

Shot	Camera Angle	Description	Location
1	LS	Probation officer giving instructions with people in background	Conference Room
2	MS	Probation officer	
3	CU	Officer giving instructions	
4	MS	Probation officer talking/holding agreement	
4A	Zoom to CU	Zoom in to CU of agreement	
5	MS	Probation officer explains program to David	
6	MS	David paying fee	Front Office
7	MS	David turning in proof of completion	
8	MS	Probation officer talks about program	Probation Office
9	CU	Probation officer	
10	CU	Sign on courtroom doors	Courtroom
11	LS	Dolly into courtroom	
12	LS	Judge refers David to diversion program	
13	MS	Courtroom activity	
14	MS	Judge	
15	CU	Judge	
16	MS	David's reaction (over the shoulder)	
17	CU	David	

remote location, preinterviews are somewhat time consuming. This illustrates a major advantage to the telephone preinterview—it eliminates travel time and may be more efficient for the producer who is pressed for time. On the other hand, the producer who travels to the interview site can also conduct an on-site remote survey to gather information about the location.

Perhaps the greatest danger in the preinterview is that it may cause a loss of spontaneity in the actual interview. Few news producers who are conducting an investigative report would want their subjects to have the opportunity to rehearse their answers. Similarly, even in noninvestigative reports, subjects who appear to be reciting rehearsed answers to questions often lose credibility or destroy the credibility of the segment itself. The remote producer, then, must walk a careful line in conducting the preinterview. Important information about the subject should be gathered, and the subject should be put at ease, but this should not destroy the spontaneity of the interview, its personal nature, or the sense of discovery that makes an on-camera interview come alive.

Figure 12–10   Shooting Schedule

SHOOTING SCHEDULE:
City and County of San Francisco
Adult Probation Department
Drug Diversion Program

Date: Friday, April 7
Location: Hall of Justice
             880 Bryant St., Room 200
Contacts: Christina Marina 555-1718
             Jimmy Lee 555-5717

Time	Activity/Shot
8:00 AM	Arrive and set up—Conference Room

9:30   Call: David and Probation Officer
Probation Officer explains program procedure
    1   LS with people in background
    2   MS Probation Officer giving instructions
    3   CU Giving instructions
    4   MS Probation officer talking/holding agreement
    4A Zoom in to CU on agreement
    5   MS Probation officer explains program to David

11:30   Set up—Probation Office

12:00   Call: David and Probation Officer
Probation Officer explains the rules
    8   MS Probation Officer talks about program
    9   CU Probation Officer talks about program

12:45   Shot of paying cash (near office)
    6   MS David paying fee
    7   MS David turning in proof of completion

1:00   Lunch Break

2:00   Set up—Court Room

3:00   Call: David and Judge Gross
Dolly Shot
    11 LS Dolly into the courtroom

3:30   Shots in courtroom
    10 CU Sign outside courtroom
    12 LS Judge refers David to diversion program
    13 MS Courtroom activity
    14 MS Judge
    15 CU Judge
    16 MS David's reaction (over the shoulder)
    17 CU David

4:30   Strike equipment and leave

Remote Surveys

Television producers working in the controlled environment of the studio know that they will always have adequate light for the production, adequate power for the equipment, and an acoustic environment that is insulated from unwanted, exterior noise. The video field producer has no such guarantees. Location production presents the production crew with an incredible array of variables that seldom concern the studio producer.

Every location is unique, so field producers adopt one of two strategies to deal with the peculiarities of different locations. You can bring along every piece of remote equipment imaginable, so that any production situation can be dealt with, or you can visit the remote location in advance of the production date to determine the location's characteristics and the production strategies and equipment needed to shoot in that location. If you are fortunate enough to have a production van equipped with a wide array of power, audio, and lighting equipment, you are operating at a considerable advantage over the field producer who must order and budget each piece of equipment individually.

Most field producers rely heavily on the **remote survey**—a technical and aesthetic assessment of a remote location—to provide important information about the location in which the shoot will take place.

Technical Factors. Any remote survey should gather data on at least three important technical factors: lighting, power, and sound. The available light in a location setting is extremely important. The remote survey should indicate what the nature of the available light is and whether there is enough of it to meet the camera's baselight requirements. If the light is not adequate, then external lights or reflectors will be needed. If external lights are used, then the availability of power may be critical. Not only will it be needed for the camera and the VCR but power may also be needed to run the lights if adequate batteries are not available.

The location should also be assessed for sound characteristics. You need to know what kind of microphones and how many of each are necessary.

Legal and Safety Factors. Also of primary importance with respect to the remote survey are certain legal and safety factors. The production crew should be able to operate safely in the remote location. The remote survey, therefore, should carefully identify any potential hazards on the location and determine whether the presence of the remote crew will create hazards. For example, consider a sequence that is to be shot on the floor of a warehouse where there is significant activity by forklifts moving pallets of merchandise within the production area. This should be duly noted in the remote survey. Will the crew be in the area in which the machines are operating? What will you do about the AC power lines? Will they interfere with the movement of the equipment?

Perhaps you plan to shoot a segment inside an elevator. How will you ensure that the elevator remains on the floor on which you are shooting? Will this present a problem to people in other parts of the building who might need the elevator to get from one part of the building to another?

Particularly in large buildings or industrial locations, it is always advisable to discuss the nature of the production with the maintenance or plant supervisor or the building supervisor. The supervisor will know about potential dangers that exist on the location and safety regulations that are in effect, and may be able to help you solve technical problems with the location.

Aesthetic Factors. The remote survey should also note any relevant aesthetic factors apparent at the location. For example, the technical survey may indicate that sufficient light exists on location, but it may not be the kind of light needed for the production. Similarly, notes on the visual character of the remote location may serve to identify important architectural features that should be included (or excluded) from the production. Particular attention should also be paid to the sound environment. An interview scheduled in a house that is near the runway of a large, busy airport presents a challenging, if not impossible, situation for the audio person. A house next to a school playground may have appeared to be a suitable location for an interview if the remote survey was conducted while all the children were in class. However, if several hundred children are loudly playing in the playground during the remote shoot, it will be difficult to obtain a good audio recording.

Access to the Location. Your remote survey should also include information about access to the location. A primary concern is to obtain permission to shoot on the proposed location. If the property is private, permission from the owner should be obtained, preferably in writing. If the property is publicly owned, you will need to obtain permission from the appropriate agency. For example, in San Francisco, New York, and other large cities, permission must be obtained from the municipal government to shoot anywhere within the city. If you set up a camera and a tripod on a sidewalk, you must have the approval of the city agency that regulates these matters. If you are shooting a profit-making production, you may have to pay for the right to shoot and obtain an insurance policy that protects the city from damage suits in the event someone is injured during the production. If your project is nonprofit, the use fee and insurance requirements may be waived (see Appendix 3). Appendix 3 presents an example of a shooting permit required in San Francisco.

Permission to shoot in local, state, or national parks usually involves submitting the appropriate application. See Appendix 4 for an example of a permission form needed to shoot in one national park.

Similarly, if you are shooting in a public facility, you will need to obtain the permission from the appropriate agency. To shoot in the local airport, railway station, or on a city-owned bus, permission must first be granted by the supervising agency.

Conducting the Remote Survey

It is never possible to anticipate all the problems that may arise on a location shoot. However, it is certainly better to conduct a remote survey and anticipate some of them than to skip the survey and go to the location totally unaware.

Several guidelines can be used to help you conduct a good remote survey.

Survey When Conditions Are Similar to the Shoot. Try to survey the location at the same time of day and day of the week that you plan to do the actual shoot. If you plan to shoot on a weekend morning, survey the site on a weekend morning. This is primarily important in providing accurate information about the available light, but it is also important for other reasons. Traffic patterns and people patterns differ significantly from day to day (and certainly from weekday to weekend day) in many locations.

Bring a Viewer, Tape Measure, and Checklist. Bring a viewer or Polaroid® camera, a tape measure, and a survey checklist with you (see Figure 12–11). Director's viewers, which enable you to see a location the way the camera will see it, are available from equipment supply houses. The viewer lets you look at the site and determine how it will look on camera. Also consider bringing along an instant camera. While the field of view produced by a Polaroid camera may not be equivalent to the field of view produced by your video camera, it will nevertheless show you the location in a frame. It is also extremely useful in providing a photographic record of the location.

A tape measure is particularly useful. Measure the dimensions of any rooms that you expect to shoot in. Measure the distances between rows of objects that are important to the shoot. For example, you may want to dolly the camera between rows of bottles of aging wine in a winery, but you will only be able to do this if the distance between the rows of bottles is greater than the spread of the tripod dolly.

Make Parking Arrangements. Where will you park? If you are transporting a significant amount of equipment, you will need to be able to park your vehicle near the remote location. Is parking readily available? Will you need special permission to park near the shooting site?

Consider Crowd Control. If you are shooting outside, how will you control the inevitable crowd of onlookers who will appear as soon as you set up the camera and lights? Even in the smallest, amateur, nonprofit production, the appearance of a camera is sure to draw comments from passersby. Anticipate this and take steps to control the situation. For example, in the skid row section of San Francisco, field producers who shoot in that area have worked out an uneasy truce with local inhabitants. The production budgets usually contain a small fund used to pay off bystanders. A dollar or so will buy assurance that no one will jump in front of the camera when the tape is rolling.

Figure 12–11   Remote Survey Form

REMOTE SURVEY FORM

Production Title _____ Length_____
Location _____
Contact at Location _____ Phone # _____
Survey Day and Date_____ Time_____
Production Day and Date_____ . Time_____
Producer _____ Director _____
Camera _____ Production Assistant _____
Other Crew _____

Remote Survey Equipment:
    ☐ Incident Light Meter ☐ Paper and Pencils
    ☐ Tape Measure   ☐ Polaroid Camera

NOTES

Interior	Exterior
Lighting	Audio
AC Power	Legal

Arrange for Food for Cast and Crew. You will need to provide food if your shoot lasts more than a few hours. The need for your cast and crew to eat should be seen as an essential part of the production and production planning rather than as a sign of weakness among crew members and cast. Is food readily available at the location, or will other arrangements need to be made?

Arrange for Bathroom Facilities. Bathroom facilities may seem to be far from the lofty ideals embodied in your program but they are essential.

Releases and Related Legal Issues

The television producer working for a television station or production house often has access to the legal department of the station or production center. On the other hand, many independent producers often work without the benefit of such readily available legal advice. Amateur, student, and independent producers may find that legal advice on production matters is available free or at low cost from their local media arts or community access organization. In any event, there are a number of areas of legal concern that are of extreme importance to all video field producers.

Talent Releases. Perhaps the most important factor to be considered is the need for the field producer to obtain releases from those individuals who appear on videotape or from those individuals whose voices are used in a tape. To use someone's image or voice in a production, you must obtain a **talent release**, which is a standard agreement signed by the subject giving permission for such use to the program producer or production agency (see Figure 12–12).

In documentary productions and other nonfiction programs or program segments (for example, magazine segments), talent releases are obtained from anyone who is interviewed, as well as anyone who can readily be identified in the picture, even if they do not speak. On remote locations, it is a good idea to warn people when videotaping begins, so that they can get out of the camera's field of view if they don't want to be recorded.

Figure 12–12   Talent Release

TALENT/LABOR RELEASE
Broadcast Communication Arts Department
San Francisco State University

I, (print name) _____, hereby assign to the Broadcast Communication Arts Department, San Francisco State University, all rights in and to any photographs, motion pictures, video tapes and/or audio recordings taken in the production of

_____ at any time.

I hereby authorize the Broadcast Communication Arts Department, San Francisco State University, to reproduce, copy, exhibit, publish, or distribute any and all such photographs, pictures, video tapes and/or audio tapes.

I understand and agree that the Broadcast Communication Arts Department, San Francisco State University, will be held free and clear of any responsibility or claim for personal liability during the production of

_____

I certify that I am over the age of twenty-one (21).

_____   _____
signed   witness

_____   _____
address   parent/guardian (if under age of 21)

_____   _____
phone

_____
date   place

For a fully scripted program using paid (or unpaid) actors and actresses, you should secure the appropriate talent releases well in advance of the production date. If the actors and actresses are paid for their services and sign contracts, the allowable uses of the performance will be specified in the contract. For unpaid talent, particularly in documentary programs or interview-based magazine segments, the talent release is usually obtained on the day of the taping. It is usually the responsibility of the producer to obtain the signed release.

Professional actors and actresses are familiar with contracts and releases. Nonprofessionals, who are frequently the people featured in student productions, are usually completely unfamiliar with releases. Therefore, it is extremely important that the producer, or someone else on the production staff, clearly explain what rights are conveyed to the production group when the release is signed.

There is little agreement as to whether it is better to obtain the release before an interview is recorded or after it. Obtaining the release prior to recording the interview is certainly preferable from the production team's standpoint. Why waste time recording an interview only to be refused permission to use it in the end? On the other hand, many interviewees are extremely nervous about granting the interview, and being confronted with a decision about signing a release before the taping may cause them to refuse to participate. For such subjects, it may be better to wait until after the taping is finished, and then obtain the signed release.

Many subjects are nervous about how their image and voice will be used. Most producers and editors are ethical people who want to use the best of what was obtained in an interview, not the worst. A simple assurance from the producer about the intention to use the good material will often put a subject at ease with respect to signing the release. If your production is noncommercial or educational in nature, this should also be stressed when asking the subject to sign the release.

Shooting in public places presents a unique situation with respect to obtaining releases from individuals in a crowd. Generally, the producer in such a situation is protected by the public nature of the area. However, it is always a good idea to make an announcement that the area is about to be videotaped or, if possible, to post signs with a similar announcement, so that anyone who doesn't want to appear in the production will have the opportunity to get out of the camera's field of view.

Video producers should also be aware of the special conditions that apply to the use of members of the American Federation of Television and Radio Actors (AFTRA) or the Screen Actors' Guild (SAG) in their productions. AFTRA and SAG members are bound by the contracts of their respective unions, and if such union members are used in productions, specific rules apply to their working conditions and salaries. If you are working on a low budget, nonprofit production, the unions will often grant waivers that allow you to use union members without paying the standard union wages. Waiver forms are available from the local office of the appropriate union.

Location Releases. As discussed earlier, location releases are sometimes necessary. Releases are often needed to shoot on city streets; in city, state, and national parks;

and in public buildings such as government buildings, airports, and so on. The need for such location releases almost always extends to student producers, just as it applies to broadcast television producers. In many situations, however, the student producer can obtain a waiver of the use fee usually associated with the release.

Location Safety. Field producers should also pay particular attention to the safety requirements in effect at any remote location. Depending on your location, a number of different state or local safety codes may apply. The Occupational Safety and Health Act (OSHA) is a federal law that requires the states to set up safety regulations for employee protection. You should be familiar with local OSHA requirements and abide by them. If you are shooting in a factory, mine, or other industrial area, the plant supervisor can usually give you information about any OSHA requirements that apply.

Use of Copyrighted Music, Film, or Tape. Just as a release must be obtained from each person who appears in your production, so must permission be obtained if you plan to use any copyrighted material in your production. Violation of copyright with respect to music is very common but, nevertheless, illegal. Recorded music may *not* be used in a production unless permission is obtained from the copyright holder for its use. Similarly, any material that is broadcast or cablecast is almost always protected by copyright. It is illegal to tape something off the air and then incorporate it into your program. Permission must first be granted by the copyright holder. Troublesome and expensive legal hassles can be avoided if permission to use copyrighted material is granted before you use it in your program.

Stock Footage, Sound Effects, and Music. Many large cities have sound and visual image (tape and film) libraries that supply material to producers for a fee. Stock tape and film footage is typically available, as are sound effects and music. For example, old newsreel footage is available for a fee from Movie-Tone News in Los Angeles. The National Geographic Society in Washington, D.C., has an extensive collection of stock footage of wildlife, which is also available for a fee. The National Archives in Washington, D.C., has millions of feet of old newsreels and government film, all of which is in the public domain. No royalties have to be paid to use this film, but the Archives charges a minimal fee to search for and transfer the material to videotape.

If you are looking for a particular type of stock footage or sound, chances are good that you will be able to locate it and that rights to the material can be bought for a modest fee, depending on your intended use. The rights to copyrighted material cost more if you plan to use it in a widely distributed commercial production than if you plan to use it in a noncommercial program with a much smaller target audience.

Obtaining Original Music

One way to avoid the problems associated with obtaining permission to use copyrighted music in your production is to have someone compose original music for you. At first, it may seem more difficult to obtain original music than to simply write for permission to use already written music. In reality, this is not always the case.

Many professional and semiprofessional musicians, as well as many music students, will jump at the chance to write an original musical score, particularly if it is going to be used in a program that will be shown to a large audience. In most cases, music composed specifically for a program will work better than already written music. Make sure that you obtain a release to use the music in your program, just as you would obtain a release for the appearance of talent in your program.

PRODUCTION PLANNING

In many respects, while the actual process of shooting in the field is the focal point of the production, it is a rather insignificant part of the production process. While this may seem like a paradox, given the amount of time we have spent describing production techniques, there is an element of truth to the statement. Preproduction planning and postproduction almost always take more time and energy than the actual time and energy spent on production itself. Weeks of preproduction planning may precede a one- or two-day shoot, and the material recorded during those two days may take another week or two to edit. Story or program conceptualization and development, script preparation, design of the storyboard, and coordination of all the preproduction elements require a considerable investment of time and creative energy. Alfred Hitchcock, the great film director, once commented that for him the most creative part of making a film was in visualizing the story and planning how he would shoot it. The actual process of filming the story was a technical exercise in which he merely tried to capture on film what he had already committed to paper.[1]

Admittedly, very few producers and directors possess Hitchcock's skill in transferring to film or tape the ideas that had been planned out on paper. Indeed, if there is one given in visual production, it is that the finished product will differ from the planned product. Production in general, and the process of field production in particular, has a unique dynamic in which things that appear to work on paper often do not work in production; and things that do not look good on paper sometimes seem to come alive in the actual production Nevertheless, the initial planning and visualization of the production process are indispensable to the completion of the project.

From the standpoint of production planning and organization, three critical factors emerge during field production itself:

1. Equipment needs for a shoot must be identified and satisfied.
2. Crew assignments must be clearly delineated and responsibility must be delegated to the appropriate crew members.

3. The material that is shot must conform to the script or script outline, and the shoot must proceed efficiently.

Equipment Needs

The remote survey will tell a field producer precisely how much equipment is needed for a shoot. If a remote survey has not been conducted, then it is always wise to bring a little more equipment than you think you might need, particularly with respect to peripheral production equipment such as lights, microphones, cables, and so on.

In any case, a remote production equipment checklist serves as a guide to your available equipment and should be filled out when the remote survey has been completed. Figure 12–13 presents an example of a typical checklist that should suffice for most producers involved in simple to intermediate-level shoots.

Crew Assignments

The size of the crew and the responsibilities of the crew members vary with the type of production. An ENG crew, for example, may very well consist of two people: the camera operator and the on-camera talent. The camera operator, or shooter, has responsibility for operating the camcorder and thus principal responsibility for recording acceptable picture and sound. The on-camera talent, usually the segment or story producer, has responsibility for conveying the details of the story outline to the shooter, suggesting needed visuals, conducting required interviews, providing the on-camera stand-up introduction (or *intro*) and summary (or *extro*), and writing and delivering any additional voice-over narration. A more elaborate ENG crew might include an additional crew person who takes responsibility for sound recording.

In simple EFP shoots, characterized by those in which magazine segments are built out of on-location interview material, a three-person crew is often used. The producer has responsibility for story design and execution. The camera operator has responsibility for shooting the segments and for making sure that enough material is recorded to facilitate editing of the piece. The shooter, therefore, must make decisions about camera position, lens angle, zoom activity, and retakes of significant material. Although the field producer has the ultimate responsibility for planning the segment, the shooter has significant autonomy in shooting the visual material. A good shooter must be flexible, alert, and have a good eye for the visual potential of the scene, and must also keep in mind the requirements of the editor and the editing process. This is necessary to obtain material that will make the piece visually interesting and coherent.

The production assistant (PA) in an EFP shoot serves a number of important functions. The PA takes responsibility for setting up any needed lighting instruments and microphones, functions as sound recordist, particularly if a fishpole-type microphone is used, and labels and labeling tapes as they are shot. The PA is often called on to set up and strike equipment and to make sure that an adequate supply

Figure 12–13   Remote Production Equipment Checklist

REMOTE PRODUCTION EQUIPMENT CHECKLIST

VIDEO
- ☐ Camera
- ☐ Camera Cable Extension
- ☐ Portable VCR
- ☐ Videotape
- ☐ Tripod
- ☐ Tripod Dolly
- ☐ Lens Filters
- ☐ Shoulder Brace
- ☐ Monopod

LIGHTING
- ☐ Light Meter
- ☐ Spotlights
- ☐ Broadlights
- ☐ Softlights
- ☐ Light Stands
- ☐ Replacement Lamps
- ☐ Barn Doors
- ☐ Scrims
- ☐ Dichroic Filter
- ☐ Gels
- ☐ Lighting Kit

LEGAL
- ☐ Talent Release Forms
- ☐ Location Permits

MONITORING
- ☐ Color Video Monitor
- ☐ Headphones
- ☐ Audio Cables
- ☐ Video Cables

AUDIO
- ☐ Microphones
- ☐ Microphone Connectors/Adapters
- ☐ Wind Screens
- ☐ Audio Cables
- ☐ Audio Mixers
- ☐ Headphones
- ☐ Microphone Batteries

POWER
- ☐ Batteries
    - Camera
    - VCR
    - Battery Belt and Cable
- ☐ VCR AC Adapter
- ☐ Camera AC Adapter
- ☐ 2-Prong to 3-Prong Adapter
- ☐ Extension Cords
- ☐ 15 Amp Fuses

OTHER
- ☐ Pocket Knife
- ☐ Gaffer's Tape
- ☐ Black Tape (Electrician's)
- ☐ Face Powder
- ☐ Props
- ☐ Set Dressing
- ☐ Clothing and Costumes
- ☐ _____
- ☐ _____
- ☐ _____

NOTES:

Production Title _____

Production Date and Time_____

of charged batteries is available. In addition, he or she is often responsible for driving the crew to and from the location. If the producer has primary responsibility for story design and the shooter primary responsibility for visualization, the PA has the responsibility for making sure that the shoot goes smoothly in a technical sense.

Many, if not most, EFP crews that shoot magazine-type material also use on-camera talent. Most often this is *not* the segment producer, and in this regard, magazine EFP differs significantly from ENG shooting. The questions the on-camera talent asks are developed through consultation with the producer, who has significant responsibility for directing the questions and producing the actual content of the piece.

These two types of production situations are fairly simple ones. In some production situations, the field production crew can be extremely large. For example, in the production of a dramatic script (whether it is artistic, theatrical, or instructional in orientation), the crew will most likely consist of a producer, director, camera operator, lighting director and assistants, audio director and assistants, talent, make-up crew, set designers and/or properties coordinators, and maybe even a stuntperson or two. In these full-scale productions, the director becomes the field production person with primary responsibility for coordinating all elements of the production. The director is responsible for visualizing the script and blocking (staging) the action and for communicating these decisions to the appropriate cast and crew members.

Regardless of whether the production has a designated director, or if the producer or camera operator acts as the director, the director's role in the field is an important one. The director must delegate responsibility for performing production tasks to the various crew members, must have a clear idea of how the individual shots in the production will look, and must communicate that to the camera operator. The director must also analyze the shooting situation in order to direct the sequence in which shots or segments are recorded.

With respect to the last point, the goal is to make certain that the most important things are shot first. The ENG crew covering a disaster in progress has to make quick decisions in the field with respect to what to shoot and in which order to shoot it. The magazine EFP producer has to decide on the order in which interviews and supplementary visual material will be recorded and how much time to allocate to shooting each element. The director of the dramatic script needs to break down the script into its component parts and decide how best to make use of the actors, actresses, and various locations.

Labeling Tapes in the Field

Just as thorough preproduction planning creates a record or plan of what is supposed to happen during production, tape labeling and logging creates a record of what happens during production. The importance of identifying individual tapes and their content is critical, particularly when you consider that a 30-minute program shot in $^1/_2$" S-VHS-C format with a 10:1 **shooting ratio** (one in which 10 times as much tape is shot as is finally used in the program) produces at least 15 mini-cassettes of material (300 minutes of unedited footage = 15 cassettes of 20 minutes each). Clearly, some way needs to be found to unambiguously label and identify material. These suggestions should help you keep track of the content of your field tapes.

Label Field Tapes as They Are Shot.   Each tape should be labeled in the field as it is used. This is usually the duty of the PA. The most common method of labeling is simply to affix an adhesive label to the cassette box with the tape number and a brief description of the content, such as tape 1—parachuting chimps. If an adequate number of tapes are available, you might want to record different interviews or shots from different locations on separate tapes. Each segment can then be clearly identified when it is time to edit the piece. This also eliminates the danger of accidentally recording over and erasing a different segment. Also, if a field tape should be lost or destroyed, only one segment of material will be lost rather than a number of segments.

As field tapes are recorded and labeled, the record safety device should be removed or engaged to prevent accidental erasure.

Slate Tapes.   It is common practice to slate the head of each tape for identification purposes. The **slate** simply records onto the tape information about the content of the upcoming material. This is extremely useful, particularly if the tape and its box should become separated.

If the content of the tape will be an interview, it is good practice simply to ask the person who is the subject of the interview to face the camera and state his or her name and occupation (or other relevant data). This will then serve to identify the person on the tape to the production personnel (and the editor, in particular). Another advantage of this type of identification is that it provides you with the correct pronunciation of the subject's name. For example, the readers of this book probably have little difficulty with the pronunciation of *Sherriffs*, but our guess is that the pronunciation of *Compesi* provides a significant problem for many of you.*
Since the narration that will be added to a piece may well contain a reference to the name of the subject, correct pronunciation is essential.

Another method of slating involves the use of a formal production slate that is held in front of the camera at the beginning of the tape and at the beginning of each shot. An example of a production slate is shown in Figure 12–14. The slate should contain the essential information about the production. It is common to include the title of the production and names of the director, producer, and camera operator; the date; the shot and take number; and any other relevant notes. This kind of formal slate is typically used only when the production being videotaped is fully scripted. Since individual shots within the script need to be staged and recorded, the slate serves as a simple and consistent way to identify the shots on tape. If multiple takes of a particular shot are recorded, the good take can be identified from the bad takes by referring to the take number.

*Pronunciation key: *Sherriffs* is pronounced the same as the plural of *sheriff*, as in: "The criminals were arrested by two sherriffs after the holdup." *Compesi* is another story. It sounds like: *come peá see*.

Figure 12–14   Production Slate

Program Title			Date Time
P/D	Camera	Sound	Talent/ Subject
Shot #		Take #	
Notes			

POSTPRODUCTION PLANNING

Logging the Tapes

A **tape log** or field footage log is a list and description of every shot on the tape. When a program is fully scripted, tapes are usually logged in the field as they are recorded. This provides an instant record of what was shot and which takes were good and bad. At the end of the day, the director can compare the log with the script and check to see that all the necessary material was recorded.

In many types of field production, including most ENG and interview-based EFP productions, the tape log is not done in the field. Rather, tape logging is done in postproduction by the videotape editor. The editor must look at all the videotape anyway, and the process of tape logging therefore serves two functions: First, it allows the editor to see all the material shot in the field and to create a log. Second, it allows the editor to make initial judgments about the material in terms of what is good and bad, or what works and doesn't work. The process of logging, then, is often the initial step taken by the videotape editor in determining the basic structure and content of the edited program (see Figure 12–15).

Logging is more easily and accurately completed for videotapes that are encoded with SMPTE time code. However, tape logs can also be prepared for programs without time code. Make sure the counter on the VCR is set to zero and the tape is rewound to the beginning. Then simply note the reel number of the tape and the counter numbers for each shot or sequence on the tape. A more accurate log can be prepared by using a stopwatch to time the length of each segment.

Figure 12–15   Tape Log (Field Footage Log)

Boy Meets Girl
Raw Footage Log

From	To	Shot	Description	Quality	Use?
Shoot # one - dream sequence.					
0:00:00	0:00:31	LS & Pan	Alex walks up the street toward cafe. Walks inside.	Fair	
0:00:34	0:00:58	LS & Pan	Alex walking to cafe door. Stops briefly to look over at sign. Does not enter cafe.	Fair	
0:01:06	0:01:30	LS & Pan	Alex walking into cafe.	Fair	
0:01:33	0:01:43	MS	Writing on cafe window: "Kaffe Kreuzberg"	Good	
0:02:01	0:02:26	LS & Pan	Alex walking into cafe.	Good	
0:02:52	0:03:19	LS & Pan	From inside cafe. Alex walks in through door and takes a seat.	Fair	
0:03:19	0:03:43	LS & Pan	Same as above.	Good	
0:03:54	0:04:18	LS & Pan	Same as above. Shot on auto iris - no detail in face.	Poor	
0:04:31	0:04:42	LS	Carol walks into cafe looking at camera, and walks past camera.	Fair	
0:05:02	0:05:13	LS	Same as above, but Carol walks slower.	Good	
0:05:16	0:05:23	MCU	Carol standing inside cafe door. She then walks toward camera looking at camera.	Good	
0:05:24	0:05:38	MCU	Same as above, except Carol smiles.	Good	
0:05:39	0:06:02	LS	Lori standing inside cafe door. She's looking away then looks directly at camera. (Then discussion to clarify her movements for next shot.	Good	
0:06:10	0:06:17	LS	Lori walks into cafe, looks at the camera with disdain then walks toward it and past it.	Good	
0:06:20	0:06:28	CU	Lori looks at camera dryly then walks out of the frame.	Fair	
0:06:37	0:06:39	CU	Lori looks at camera, rolls her eyes, then walks out of the frame.	Good	
0:06:42	0:06:52	LS	Jerry walks into cafe, looks at camera, stops, smiles, then walks out of the frame.	Fair	
0:06:56	0:07:05	LS	Same as above.	Fair	
0:07:06	0:07:14	LS	Same as above.	Fair	
0:07:15	0:07:26	CU	Jerry looking straight at the camera. He smiles and winks.	Fair	

If time permits, it is a good idea to type the videotape logs. This is particularly important if the tapes contain lengthy interviews and decisions are to be made jointly by the production crew about what to include or exclude from the program. Typed transcripts of interviews and tape logs make all the basic program information available to all members of the production crew.

An increasing number of personal computer software programs for tape logging are also available. Individual shots are logged by shot and take numbers, time code (in and out), shot angle (CU, LS, MC, etc.), and a brief narrative description. Many of these software programs allow the video producer to take advantage of the data-base management capabilities of the computer. In some systems, the user can ask the computer to identify all the shots in the list that were taken from a similar angle (all CUs, for example) or all shots in which a particular word or character's name appears in the description (all shots of Jane, all shots of the giant pumpkin, etc.). Separate lists of these shots can be compiled and saved. If the editor needs a close-up, a shot of Jane, or a shot of the giant pumpkin, the available choices can easily be reviewed from the newly composed lists.

Rough Cut

Once all the tape has been logged, the editing process can begin. The first step in the process is to develop a preliminary editing script. An **editing script** is a written plan for editing a production and consists of a list of all of the shots to be used, a brief description of each one, and a notation of the in and out point (the beginning and end) of each shot.

Particularly in programs built around interviews, the first edit is usually cut to match the audio segment of the interviews, since that conveys the meaning of the piece. If montages are to introduce the piece or bridge segments, they should be identified in the script as well. The preliminary editing script, then, provides a rough guide to what the final program will look like. The edit of the program that is made from the preliminary editing script is called the **rough cut**. The rough cut is the equivalent of the workprint in film. It provides a rough template of the final program. If your production was fully scripted to begin with, you may be able to write the editing information (shot number, in and out point) directly onto your script. If your program was unscripted or semi-scripted, you may find that a standardized edit worksheet is a handy way to keep track of your editing information (see Figure 12–16).

When making a rough cut of an interview-based program, don't worry about bad edits or jump cuts from one audio segment to another. Edit to achieve sense in what is said. The rough cut can then be viewed to see if it conveys the essential meaning that is desired and if it adheres to your time limitations. The position of various sequences can then be considered. You may want to cut out some and add others or lengthen some or shorten others.

You will also want to make a preliminary judgment about the pace of the program or program segment. Does it flow? Does it drag along? If it seems slow, then you will need to find ways to pick up the pace. Perhaps sequences can be shortened or bridges built between sequences. Perhaps music can be added under certain segments, or long interview segments can be replaced with tighter voice-over narration by the announcer. Through decisions such as these, the rough cut will be modified and the final editing script produced.

Figure 12–16   Edit Worksheet

Edit List
Show Title: Love Makes a Family

Edit #	Tape #	Time In	Time Out	Video/ Audio	Description
1.	5	05:29:30:10	05:32:27:05	Audio	MUSIC
2.	CG #1	1 sec fade up; hold 4 sec; 1 sec dissolve to next shot.			
3.	1	01:17:30:13	01:17:43:15	V&A	audio lead in: dissolve from CG at 01:17:31:21
4.	1	01:23:55:10	01:24:00:00	V&A	2-shot women
5.	3	03:26:18:20	03:26:27:21	V&A	MCU black woman
6.	3	03:29:28:02	03:29:38:15	V&A	MS Asian man
7.	3	03:20:03:21	03:20:15:29	V&A	CU single mom
8.	4	04:30:50:16	04:31:04:19	V&A	MCU Cara

FADE TO BLACK
MUSIC UP

9.	CG "Love Makes a Family" FADE UP OVER BLACK, then FADE TO BLACK				
10.	2	02:14:09:26	02:14:15:03	Audio	Marisa's VO
11.	10	10:38:41:03	10:38:46:05	Video	photo, FADE UP over previous audio cut FROM BLACK then FADE TO BLACK
12.	CG "Co-Parenting" FADE UP FROM BLACK, then FADE TO BLACK, FADE MUSIC OUT				
13.	2	02:17:37:00	02:18:29:21	V&A (split)	audio under CG video in at 02:17:39:13

Final Edit

The final editing script will incorporate the changes suggested after watching the rough cut and modifying the preliminary editing script. The final edited version of the program should fulfill the goals set out in the initial program treatment. The essential meaning of the piece should be efficiently and effectively conveyed through the medium of television. Particular attention should be paid to visualization and sound. Finally, the program should conform to the limits placed on its length. If you plan to distribute your program through traditional broadcast channels, it should conform to broadcast standards for length. A 32-minute documentary will not be aired uncut, even if it reveals the ultimate truth about the meaning of existence. At the very least, it will need to be trimmed to 28:30, and if commercials are to be inserted, it will have to be cut even further.

Client Consultation

If your production was produced for a client, you may need client approval of the final cut. In such situations, the client will probably have been involved throughout the production process, and most certainly should see the rough cut so that you can receive some feedback at that time.

Copyright

We have previously discussed copyright with respect to obtaining permission to use material that has been copyrighted by someone else. However, as a producer of a complete program, you may decide that you want to protect your rights to the program you have produced. This is particularly important if you believe that your program has commercial potential or if you want to control its distribution and display. To obtain a copyright, you must apply to the U.S. Copyright Office in Washington, D.C. The address is: Copyright Office, Library of Congress, Washington, D.C., 20559. Complete the appropriate application form (the one used for programs produced on videotape is form PA—performing arts). Then send the form, a small filing fee, and a copy of your videotape to the Copyright Office.

If you produced the program independently, you will be considered the author and owner of the program. If you produced it for someone else (for example, the company you work for or a client who hired you), your program will be considered a *work made for hire*, and your employer or client will own the copyright. If you are a student at a college or university, you should check on your institution's policy with regard to copyright. Many schools stipulate that they be named the copyright owner for any programs produced using their facilities.

The length of time that the copyright remains in effect depends on the status of the owner. If you are the program's author, the copyright term is for the length of your life and 50 years after your death. If your program was made for hire, the copyright will usually protect it for 75 years.

Distribution

No discussion of production planning is complete without at least some mention of the area of distribution. For the home video producer or the student working on a class project, the issue of distribution is relatively simple: You assemble a captive audience (friends, family, classmates, or instructor), put the videotape into a playback VCR, and then observe their response. Similarly, the employee of a broadcast or cable station is usually not overly concerned about distribution—the program or segment is completed and then aired as part of an individual program or series.

For the independent producer, however, the area of distribution is critical. We all make television programs to be seen, and in many cases we hope that they will be seen by rather large audiences. The problem of distribution, then, is one of maximizing the exposure of the program to its target audience.

In recent years, the opportunities for distribution of visual materials have opened up somewhat. Whereas only a few years ago the options were limited, the proliferation of VCRs in education and industry, the expansion of the cable television industry, and access to public broadcasting and public access cable television have given independent producers a number of realistic alternatives for distribution. In addition, the large number of video festivals and competitions throughout the country also provides a significant number of outlets for visual materials.

The type of distribution you desire depends quite clearly on the program's content and target audience. Producers of educational materials might find a receptive market among public broadcasters or any one of the educational program distribution services. Documentary producers have traditionally had a rough time earning back the cost of their investment, but nonetheless have a number of distribution options. Video festivals, public broadcasting, subscription cable systems, and individual sales to libraries and other organizations all provide potential outlets and sources of revenue. A program on cancer, for example, might be attractive not only to a number of broadcast or cable outlets but also to local (or national) cancer societies or other health agencies. Individual hospitals might be interested in the program if it could be used for counseling or providing basic information to patients.

Clearly you need to accurately assess the market potential of your program in its initial stages of development. If a widespread sales campaign is contemplated, then promotional material and a list of potential buyers should be developed. An independent producer can rent out or sell tapes and can distribute them independently (self-distribution) or through an established distribution service.

SUMMARY

The key to success in field production lies in adequate production planning. The three stages of production and production planning are preproduction, production, and postproduction.

Principal components of preproduction include developing a program idea, conceptualizing and designing the program, conducting preinterviews of subjects when appropriate, conducting a remote survey of the field location, developing a formal program proposal and shooting schedule, gathering the necessary releases for both talent and locations, obtaining music, and developing a script.

During the production phase, equipment needs must be specified and filled, crew assignments must be made, the field shoot must be organized, and the necessary footage must be shot. All tapes should be clearly labeled as they are shot in the field.

The initial step in postproduction is logging the tapes. A rough cut provides a template of the final program, which can then be polished in the final edit. If the program is being produced for a client, you should consult with the client to obtain approval for the final cut. A copyright may be obtained to protect your rights to the program. The final step in the process involves distribution of the tape so that it will be seen by your intended audience.

ENDNOTE

1. Crawley, Budge; Markle, Fletcher; and Pratley, Gerald, "I Wish I Didn't Have to Shoot the Picture: An Interview with Alfred Hilchcock," in Albert H. LaValley (Ed.). *Focus on Hitchcock*. Englewood Cliffs, NJ: Prentice Hall, 1972, pp. 22–27.

APPENDIX 1

Production Projects

This appendix includes nine production projects designed to sharpen your production skills. The projects are arranged by type and complexity and focus on a range of production styles. Purposeful writing, careful attention to light, camera, and microphone problems, and crisp editing are important to each project; the tasks become more complex as you work down the list. The first three projects can be relatively simple sound-and-picture statements; the second group, "News" and "Instructional," can require more attention to crafting a message to be used by an intended audience in a specific way; the final group, "Magazine Feature," "Ballet Mechanique," "Historic Minute," and "Music Video" demand the most sophisticated control of the tools of production.

As you work on each of these projects, we suggest that you follow the guidelines for production planning and development that were discussed in Chapter 12. In addition, we suggest that you collect the following material as you produce these projects:

1. *Production log* (Keep a log of all time spent on the project. Make daily entries to update the log while your project is in progress. Include all your planning material in your log. Also keep track of important phone numbers, names of contacts, meeting dates and times, and so on.)

2. *Script and storyboard*

3. *Remote survey form*

4. *Tape logs*

5. *Editing scripts*

6. *Release forms*

Use a notebook or looseleaf binder to organize all the planning materials for your project.

PROJECT 1: PERSONAL STATEMENT

Video has often been characterized as a personal medium. Your first project is to write and record a 60-second personal video statement. Write a script and draw a storyboard for your statement so that someone else can act as camera operator and you can deliver the on-camera statement. Consider the following guidelines as you develop your project.

Subject. Make a statement about something that is important to you. This can be something that has affected you personally or an issue about which you have strong personal feelings. For example, one extremely effective personal video statement was made by a young man with severe speech anxiety. Whenever he was asked to give a speech or make a presentation, he became so nervous that he could barely talk. In his personal video statement, he described his speech anxiety and how nervous he was making the presentation! As the camera slowly zoomed in to a close-up, his nervousness became apparent. However, after viewing the tape himself, he felt much more confident about his oral presentation style. Although he had been nervous, his presentation was nevertheless quite effective.

In the San Francisco Bay area, a number of local television stations broadcast free speech messages. These are 60-second messages in which people speak out on topics that concern them. The nuclear freeze movement, U.S. military policy, and local political, social, and economic issues have all been topics of recent messages.

Structure. Deliver your statement without interruption. Your personal statement should be recorded in a single 60-second session. Do not plan to edit your statement. Try to use the camera effectively with respect to composition, zooming, panning, and so on.

Audience. Identify the projected audience for this statement. The message can be aimed at friends, family, or a general audience.

Length. Sixty seconds.

Editing. None.

PROJECT 2: VIDEO POSTCARD

All too often, the medium of television is reduced to "radio with pictures." This project is calculated to reverse that trend in that emphasis is on capturing the essence of a place in one continuing picture. Music, sound effects, dialogue, or narration should augment the video, not dominate it. In addition, video editing is limited to the provision of clean opening from and closing to black.

By effective placement and movement of the camera, control of focus, and field of view, you will convey the frantic pace of traffic on a city street, the authority of a public building, the serenity of a pond at sunrise, the chill of winter on the plains, or whatever gives your part of the world its character. You will establish a mood in which many messages or stories could be set.

Subject. Design a video statement that describes the central character of a place in or near your community.

Structure. Design your statement as a single continuing shot.

Length. Twenty to thirty seconds.

Audience. Identify a specific target audience appropriate to the mood and style of your visual statement.

Editing. None, except to provide black at the opening and closing of the statement.

PROJECT 3: PUBLIC SERVICE ANNOUNCEMENT

Public service announcements (PSAs) are a standard feature of commercial broadcast schedules. A PSA is

> any announcement (including network) for which no charge is made and which promotes programs, activities or services of federal, state, or local governments (e.g., recruiting, sales of bonds, etc.) and other announcements regarded as serving community interests, excluding time signals, routine weather announcements and promotional announcements.[1]

Although many PSAs are indeed noncontroversial, some organizations, like the Public Media Center in San Francisco, use the PSA format to develop short, spot messages on controversial issues of public importance. (You can write to them at 25 Scotland Street, San Francisco, CA, 94133 for their very useful handbook, *Strategies for Access to Public Service Advertising*.)

Subject. Design a PSA on the topic of your choice. You can produce a PSA for a local organization or you can design one that is issue oriented.

Structure. Design your PSA with editing in mind. You may want to include shots of a spokesperson for an organization, people involved with a particular group, or other visuals that identify the organization or issue to which your message is directed. Remember that most PSAs attempt to mobilize people to action—they provide an address or phone number that viewers can contact for more information. Therefore, you should include a graphic that provides an address or phone number that viewers can contact to get more information about the organization or issue featured in your PSA.

Audience. Adults in your community.

Length. Thirty or sixty seconds.

Editing. Continuity and dynamic.

PROJECT 4: NEWS

The on-the-scene field news report is a staple of television news. Design and produce a self-contained news report—one that is complete in itself.

Subject. News report of a local event, issue, or person.

Structure. The report should contain an introduction and close delivered by the reporter. These may be given on-camera or off-camera as a voice-over. Consider including the following elements in the news story:

1. On-camera stand-up delivered by the news reporter.
2. Sound-on-tape interview with the subject of the story, an expert on the topic, a witness to the event, and so on.
3. Visuals of the event, issue, or person.
4. Voice-over narration over the visuals. Try to achieve a good mix between the level of the voice-over and the natural sound that accompanies the visuals.

Length. Approximately two minutes.

Audience. Most news programs are targeted at adult audiences. You can produce your news spot for an adult audience or you might want to try to produce one aimed at children or adolescents. In any event, specify the characteristics of your target audience.

Editing. Continuity.

PROJECT 5: INSTRUCTIONAL

An instructional program is designed to teach someone something. Is there something that you know about or know how to do that would make an interesting subject for an instructional segment? Perhaps you are an excellent cook or a good mechanic. Consider teaching someone how to make a pizza or how to change the oil in an automobile. A demonstration of a mechanical device is often a good subject for an instructional segment because it has great visual potential.

Subject. An instructional program segment that will teach the audience something new.

Structure. You may want to appear on camera as the expert or the teacher or you may want to present the bulk of the spoken part of the program with an off-camera voice-over. If you choose the latter option, remember to record and maintain the natural sound on the visuals.

Audience. Identify a specific target audience for your tape. This is very important because you must structure your instructional program to appeal to your audience.

Length. Two minutes.

Editing. Continuity.

PROJECT 6: MAGAZINE FEATURE

The television magazine feature has gained immense popularity in recent years. Magazine features differ somewhat from traditional news field reports. Their subject matter is usually considered softer than that of news pieces—that is, they tend to be a mix of information and entertainment. Magazine features are also usually longer than typical news stories and often attempt to enhance the presentation of information with interesting editing and music. Their purpose is to tell a story in an interesting manner.

Subject. Focus your magazine feature on an interesting person in your community or on someone who has an interesting job or hobby. If you decide to profile an interesting place or event, try to identify a spokesperson whom you can interview.

Structure. Magazine features usually include segments of interviews with the subject of the piece, off-camera voice-overs from the segment reporter or host, generous amounts of music (for mood, pace, and transitions), and innovative editing. Try to build at least one transition segment into your magazine piece that is an edited montage of music and pictures.

Length. Five minutes.

Audience. General adult.

Editing. Continuity and dynamic.

PROJECT 7: BALLET MECHANIQUE

As our society becomes increasingly industrialized and we become more familiar with machine-produced goods, we are able to recognize and appreciate nuances of style in the process of mass production. In the precise repetition of a production sequence, machines can take on a personality or seem to exhibit human qualities, just as people's daily routines seem to take on a mechanical aspect. Our human relationship with the machines of mass production for a mass society can be explored as either a positive or negative experience.

Subject. Explore a mechanical process in a manner that both explains it and suggests a parallel with our human condition.

Structure. Use music, sound, and editing to express an attitude toward the mechanical process that is the subject of your video. While following the actual sequence of events, build toward a climax in much the same way drama and music are structured.

Length. Two to three minutes.

Audience. General adult.

Editing. Continuity and dynamic.

PROJECT 8: HISTORIC MINUTE

Using appropriate graphic materials and sound support, describe a person or an event of special significance to your community. Focus on the contribution your subject made to the progress of our society or on the progress of which it is a measure.

Subject. Person or event of historic importance.

Structure. Strong narrative supported by an edited montage of photos, graphic materials, videotaped action scenes, sound effects, and music, as appropriate.

Length. One minute.

Audience. General adult.

Editing. Continuity and dynamic.

PROJECT 9: MUSIC VIDEO

Music video segments representing a range of musical styles and target audiences are visible at almost any time of day on most cable television systems in the United States. MTV (Music Television) VH-1 (Video Hits 1), the Disney Channel, and The Nashville Network (TNN) are four cable television channels that regularly feature music video segments. Many music videos are produced as promotional pieces for new musical artists or new songs recorded by established performers. Some music videos—particularly those targeted at children and featured on the Disney Channel or as segments within the PBS television series, *Sesame Street*—are designed to teach something to their audience as well as entertain them.

Subject. Identify a local band or performer (singer or musician) to serve as the performing talent for your music video.

Structure. All music videos combine a soundtrack of the musical performance with appropriate visual images. Some music videos focus exclusively on the musical artist(s) in performance of their work, other music videos dramatize the narrative found in the lyrics of the song, and still others combine elements of the musical performance with images dramatizing the song. Determine which approach best suits the performer and performance you have chosen to present.

Length. Approximately three minutes. Music video production can be fairly complex. You will do best to limit the length of your music video segment.

Audience. Identify the specific target audience for your tape. This may be determined by the type of music represented in the selected performance.

Editing. Continuity and dynamic.

ENDNOTE

1. *Code of Federal Regulations 73.18101*. Washington, D.C.: U.S. Government Printing Office, 1983, pp. 355–356.

Measurement of Light Intensity

The science of photometry, the measurement of the intensity of light, preceded the use of the electric light. An open flame was used in the early experiments; thus, light intensity is universally expressed in units of candlepower. Simply stated, a **footcandle** represents the amount of light radiated from an **international candle** that reaches a point one foot from the theoretical center of the flame. The term *footcandle* is used to describe the minimum light level required for camera operations, as well as the power or intensity of light produced by lighting instruments.

Footcandles can be expressed in terms of **lumens** per square foot. The amount of light generated by the candle flame is expressed in lumens (which means "light" in Latin). It is the accumulation of light radiated in *all* directions from the flame. A *sphere* with a radius of 1 foot represents all the points of light created by a flame in the center of that sphere. There are 12.57 square feet on the surface of a sphere with a radius of 1 foot (sphere surface = $4\pi r^2$), and each square foot receives the same amount of light from the flame. Hence, at a distance of 1 foot, the candle produces a total of 12.57 lumens—one for each square foot of surface area. This terminology is used to rate lamps (light bulbs in common terms). The capacity of reflectors to capture a portion of the light produced by a lamp and focus it back through the center point toward the subject is also expressed in lumens.

Another term, **lux**, is used to indicate the basic illumination requirements of a camera. Simply stated, a lux substitutes *one meter* for the one foot used to calculate footcandles. One lux equals one lumen per square meter; one footcandle is one lumen per square foot. There are about 10 lux per footcandle because of the inverse square law, which describes the amount that the intensity of light decreases as the distance from the light source increases. We can use the formula $4\pi r^2$ to see the increase in a sphere's surface area in relation to an increase in the radius of that sphere:

    1-foot radius = 12.57 square feet of surface
    2-foot radius = 50.27 square feet of surface
    3-foot radius = 113.10 square feet of surface

Therefore, the light reaching the surface of the sphere with a radius of 2 feet is spread over four times the area of that on a sphere with a radius of 1 foot. The light intensity at any point is one-fourth that of the sphere with one half the radius.

A sphere with a 3-foot radius contains nine times the surface area of a sphere with a 1-foot radius. The light intensity at any point on that larger sphere is one-ninth that of the smaller sphere.

One meter equals about three feet and three inches; therefore, a lux is about one-tenth of a footcandle.

Television producers rely on the inverse square law when they position lighting instruments relative to a person being videotaped. Since dimmers are seldom available in the field, the producer can move a light short distances toward or away from the subject to produce relatively significant increases or decreases in the intensity of the light falling on the subject. Doubling the distance reduces the intensity on the subject by one-fourth; halving the distance creates four times the light intensity.

Remember, the inverse square law applies only to light with a point source (the center of the candle flame or the filament in an incandescent lamp). There is no point source to calculate from a fluorescent tube close to and larger than an object illuminated by it because the illumination literally comes from everywhere.

No discussion of the measurement of light intensity would be complete without consideration of the *cosine law of incident light*. This law concerns the intensity of light on a surface when all parts of that surface are *not* equidistant from the light source. The effect of this law is seen in film and television as shading on surfaces that are not perpendicular to the beam of light. This shading contributes to the illusion of a three-dimensional picture on your television screen. Briefly, just as the light produced by the candle in a sphere has to cover greater areas as the radius increases (and, consequently, illuminates any point within that expanded sphere to a lesser extent), the light from a point source is spread over a larger surface as that surface is tilted away from the perpendicular, and becomes less intense

---

Figure A2–1   Cosine Law of Incident Light

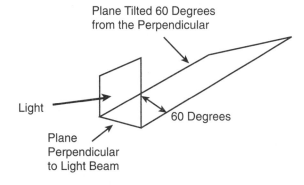

in direct ratio to the angle of tilt. Stated another way, the brightness of the perpendicular plane is multiplied by the cosine of the angle of tilt to determine the brightness of the tilted plane. *Discipuli, picturum spectate* (Students, look at the picture) (see Figure A2–1 on page 413).

At 60 degrees of tilt, the tilted plane is twice the size of the perpendicular plane. Therefore, the light energy radiated from the point source will have to cover twice the area and will appear less intense than it would on the smaller perpendicular plane. The ratio of intensities is found in the cosine of the angle of tilt, hence the term *cosine law of incident light*.[1]

ENDNOTE

1. Sturrock, Walter, and Staley, K. A., *Fundamentals of Lights and Lighting*. General Electric Bulletin LD-2, January 1956, pp. 5–6.

Guidelines and Information for Filming in San Francisco

1. Filming in San Francisco will be arranged through the Film Office, which will make referrals to departments and other jurisdictions (Police Department, Recreation and Park Department, Muni Railway, G.G.N.R.A., Airport, Bridges, Department of Public Works, the Presidio, Coast Guard, Fire Department, etc.) in order to arrange orderly filming in compliance with the law.

2. A certificate of insurance will be filed in the Film Office prior to filming, endorsed to the City and County of San Francisco (see Use Agreement for detailed information).

3. A permit fee to the San Francisco Film Office of $100 to $300 for each day of filming will be expected from each film company, except for non-profit and student productions.

   $100.00 Video, Travel, Documentary, Still Photography, Industrial, Other

   $200.00 Commercials

   $300.00 Television series and movies/Feature films

4. Uniformed police officers, working voluntary duty on an overtime basis only, will be assigned to motion picture details when the Office of The Chief deems it advisable for public safety and convenience. The number of officers assigned will be determined by the Police Department Coordinating Unit, depending

on the extent of filming and other factors. (As of January 1991, the Police rate is approximately $50.00 per hour.) A deposit for police services will be required in advance. (See Police guidelines.)

5. San Francisco Police Department vehicles, uniforms, insignia, and equipment will not be made available for use by film companies. Filming on departmental property must have express written approval of the Chief of Police.

6. San Francisco streets must be posted for parking or filming 24 hours prior to call time. See Police Department guidelines or contact Film Office for further information.

7. Residential areas can be used for filming only between the hours of 7 a.m. and 10 p.m. Night shooting between the hours of 10 p.m. and 7 a.m. is restricted without the prior express joint written approval of the Film Office and the Police Department. Commercial areas may be restricted between the hours of 6:30 and 9:30 a.m. and 3:30 and 6:30 p.m., due to rush hour traffic. Otherwise, commercial areas are available for filming. Industrial areas can be used for filming 24 hours a day, with care given not to affect the work activities in the area.

8. Companies are requested to provide the Film Office and the Police Department with copies of shooting scripts and location schedules, so that potential traffic and parking problems can be anticipated and avoided.

9. A film company, **no later** than 24 hours before shooting in a residential neighborhood, must notify in writing, the residents in the area as to the company, shooting times, and the name, address, and phone numbers of the companies' local office or representative. Prior to filming, the Film Office must be notified that this information has been distributed.

10. Meals shall not be eaten on public right-of-way.

11. All production vehicles shall be visibly identified (including equipment rental vehicles) with the name of the production company. Such identification is to

be placed in the windshield of each vehicle while on location.

12. The production company shall not interfere with the normal activities of a neighborhood. Filming crews and equipment should not interfere with street sweeping or refuse collection. No littering is permitted and must be cleaned up completely when leaving the location. The public must not be deprived egress or ingress to private or public property.

Appendix 3 courtesy of Lorrae Rominger, Director, San Francisco Film and Video Arts Commission.

IDENTIFICATION AND LOCATION INFORMATION

Date _____

1. Company Name: _____
2. Address: _____

   _____

   _____ Telephone: _____
3. Local address (production office or hotel)

   _____
4. Representative and title _____
5. Type of production:

   ___Feature Film   ___Documentary/
   ___T.V. Series/Movie/Pilot   Educational
   ___T.V. Commercial   ___Corporate/Industrial
   ___Print   ___Video
                                  ___Other (specify) _____

                                  _____
6. Title or Product _____
7. Producer _____
8. Director _____
9. Production Manager _____
10. Location Manager _____
11. Name Talent _____
12. Number in cast _____ Number in crew _____
13. Police Services required? _____
14. City services requested other than Police.

    ___Department of   ___Water Department
       Public Works   ___Health Department
    ___Fire Department   ___Airport
    ___Municipal Railway   ___City Hall
    ___Port Commission   ___Performing Arts (Davies
    ___Recreation & Park   Symphony, Opera House,
       Department   Herbst Theatre)
    ___Other (specify)

    _____

APPENDIX 4

U.S. Department of the Interior/ National Park Service Location Release

United States Department of the Interior

NATIONAL PARK SERVICE
GOLDEN GATE NATIONAL RECREATION AREA
FORT MASON, SAN FRANCISCO, CALIFORNIA 94123

IN REPLY REFER TO:

L30(GGNRA) SHORT-TERM PERMIT Date August 8, 1983

Permission is granted to Kathlyn Halvorsen

to use Ocean Beach, south of the Cliff House

for Student filming project (for a broadcasting class), 3-4 people, one camera and

one video recorder. Will simulate a 60 second Public Service Announcement.

during the period of 9:00 a.m. to 12:00 noon, August 13, 1983.

These directions are to be followed:
1. Maintain good order and proper decorum.
2. Use non-amplified music only.
3. Place all litter in supplied containers.
4. Leave the area in the same condition in which it was found.
5. Comply with any instructions from official personnel.

The United States will be held harmless for any injuries or property damage or loss occurring. In the interest of public health, public safety, or general welfare, the General Superintendent may cancel this permit at his discretion. The General Superintendent will require the permittee to pay for the repair or replacement of any park property damaged as a result of the activity.

ACCEPTED AND AGREED TO THIS APPROVED

8 day of August 19 83

by: Kathlyn Halvorsen For John H. Davis, General Superintendent
(signature)

Name: Kathlyn Halvorsen 8/8/83
Date

Address: 999 Font St.
Street

San Francisco, CA. 94132
City State

Telephone: 555-7477

Courtesy of Kathlyn Halvorsen.

Glossary

A/B Roll: Technique of rolling two source VCRs (the A machine and B machine) simultaneously while editing in order to perform special audio or video effects.

Above Eye-Level Camera Position: The camera is placed higher than the subject and shoots down at it.

AC Adapter: A device used to convert alternating current (AC) to direct current (DC). Most portable video equipment requires the use of an AC adapter to convert regular household current into DC.

Additive Primary Colors: Red, green, and blue are the additive primary colors of light. A color separation system based on these primary colors operates in all color television cameras.

Aesthetic Factors: Production variables and the ways in which they can be manipulated to affect audience response to the televised message.

Alternating Current (AC): The type of electrical power supplied to households in the United States and Canada.

Ambient Noise: Unwanted background sound.

Amplitude: The height of a wave. With respect to sound, amplitude determines the intensity or loudness of the sound.

Analog Signal: A signal that is continuously proportional or analogous to the input.

Aperture: The size of the iris opening of the lens, usually calibrated in f-stops.

Aperture Ring: A device that controls the size of the iris opening (aperture) of the lens.

Arc: Semicircular movement of the camera and its support around a scene.

Aspect Ratio: The relationship of the height of the television screen to the width of the screen, expressed as a ratio of 3:4.

Assemble Edit: (1) An edit in which new control track, audio, and video information is recorded onto the tape in the editing VCR. (2) The process of adding new information to a tape shot by shot, or scene by scene, in sequence.

At Eye-Level Camera Position: Camera and subject are at the same height; the camera does not look up or down at the subject.

Audio: The sound portion of a television program.

Audio In: Line-level audio input; where the audio signal is fed into a piece of equipment.

Audio Mixer: Equipment that combines a number of independent audio inputs into one output signal.

Audio Out: Line-level audio output; where the audio signal comes out of a piece of equipment.

Automatic Aperture: Electronic device that automatically sets the lens iris for correct exposure in the available light.

Automatic Aperture Lock: Locks in an aperture setting after it has been calculated by the automatic aperture control.

Automatic Backspace Editing: Automatic feature on many portable VCRs that produces clean transitions from one shot to the next when trigger is pulled in the record mode.

Automatic Focus (Auto Focus): Automatic focusing device on some cameras; operates by emitting a beam of infrared light or ultrasound.

Automatic Gain Control (AGC): Electronic device that automatically adjusts the amplification of an audio or video signal.

Automatic Track Finding (ATF): Signal that automatically adjusts tracking on 8mm/Hi8 VCRs, eliminating the need for manual tracking controls.

Azimuth Recording: Recording process used in Beta and VHS format recorders in which the gap of the video head is angled several degrees off the perpendicular line in the video track. This eliminates the need for guard bands, thus allowing more video information to be recorded onto the tape.

Back Light: Hard, focused light above and behind the subject used to separate the subject from the background by outlining the subject with a thin line of bright light.

Background Light: Light that falls on the background of a scene, often used to create mood or indicate time of day.

Backpack: Lightweight frame (sometimes an actual backpack frame) used by a cameraperson to carry a portable VCR.

Backspacing: Rewinding a videotape several seconds from the edit point in order to allow the machine to reach stable playing speed in time for the edit. Also called *backtiming, prerolling,* or *cueing.*

Balance: The distribution of the mass created by people or objects in the frame. These masses may be distributed evenly (symmetrical balance) or unevenly (asymmetrical balance).

Balanced Line: Professional-quality audio cable or connector with two signal leads and a shield that protects the signal from outside interference.

Barn Doors: Metal flaps that can be attached to spotlights to control the way in which the light is thrown onto a scene.

Base Illumination: Omnidirectional (or nondirectional) baselight that illuminates without creating shadows.

Baselight: The amount, or intensity, of light required to make a scene visible to the television camera.

Beam: Electron beam. The stream of electrons emitted by the electron gun in a camera pickup tube that scans the target and helps to create the video signal.

Below Eye-Level Camera Position: The camera is placed lower than the subject and shoots up at it.

Beta (Betamax): Once popular $1/2''$ consumer videocassette format developed by Sony Corporation.

Betacam: Professional-quality $1/2''$ videotape recording format developed by Sony Corporation.

Bidirectional: A microphone pickup pattern that is sensitive to sound coming in from the front or back of the microphone but not the sides. Characteristic of ribbon, or velocity, microphones.

Black Balance: Adjustment of the camera's black level or pedestal level.

Blanking Pulse: The signal at the end of each line (horizontal blanking) and field (vertical blanking) of the video signal that turns off the electron beam.

Blast Filter: Filter built into some microphones. Protects against sound distortion caused by strong blasts of breath when a microphone is placed too close to the subject's mouth. Also called a *pop filter.*

Blocking Diagram: A plan that indicates the position and movement of people and equipment in a production.

BNC Connector: A bayonet-type twist-lock connector used as a video connector on almost all professional equipment.

Boom: An extendable pole on a tripod base, sometimes wheeled, by which the microphone is suspended close to the action.

Both Edit: An edit that simultaneously affects both audio and video.

Bounce Light: Illuminating an object indirectly by reflecting light onto the object from a wall, floor, or ceiling.

Brightness: The range of values from black to white in the television picture. In color television, brightness is called *luminance.*

Broadcast: Transmission of radio and television signals through the air. Video and/or audio signals are transmitted from an antenna through the use of a carrier signal.

Broadcast Quality: (1) Technical standards set by the Federal Communications Commission for broadcast television signals. (2) Program content and production values of broadcastable material.

Bulk Eraser: A powerful electromagnet used to erase video or audiotapes.

Burn In: Damage to the photoconductive surface of the camera pickup tube due to overexposure to extremely bright light.

Buss: A row of buttons corresponding to different video inputs on a video switcher.

Cablecast: Transmission of radio and television signals via a wire or cable. Receivers must be connected to the cable to receive the signal.

Camcorder: A one-piece video recording system in which the camera and

videocassette recorder are combined into one easily carried unit.

Camera Control Unit (CCU): Electronic circuitry that regulates the way in which the camera produces the video signal.

Camera Light: A light mounted directly onto a video camera, often battery powered.

Camera Microphone: A microphone built into or attached to a portable video camera.

Camera Setup: Adjustment of the electronic parameters of the camera to provide accurate recording. Includes registration, white balance, black balance, and gain.

Capstan: A rotating shaft driven by the motor of the videotape or audiotape recorder that pulls the tape through the machine.

Capstan Servo: A servomechanism that adjusts the playback speed of a videotape by reading the control track pulses on the tape.

Cardioid: A heart-shaped microphone pickup pattern characterized by sensitivity to sound in the front but less sensitivity to the sides and rear.

Cassette: A plastic device that holds videotape or audiotape. The tape moves from the feed reel to the take-up reel inside the cassette when playing or recording. Cassette systems are self-threading, eliminating the need to manually thread the tape around the record and playback heads.

Center of Interest: The most important part of a picture in terms of the visual interest it generates.

Character Generator: Electronic device used to generate electronic lettering for use in video productions. Usually contains a keyboard, screen, and memory system for information storage.

Charge-Coupled Device (CCD): A camera pickup device that uses silicon chips instead of the conventional vacuum tube to generate the video signal. CCDs eliminate the problems of lag, comet tailing, and burn in.

Chroma Key: A special matte effect in which a particular colored area is eliminated from one shot and filled in with new video information from another source.

Chrominance: The color part of the color signal, composed of hue and saturation. The three chrominance channels in the color signal are red, green, and blue.

Click Stop: F-stop settings that click into place at each successive f-stop setting.

Clipper: A control on a video switcher used to adjust the level of a key.

Close-Up (CU): A tight shot that fills the screen with an object or the head of a subject.

Color Bars: Standard display of yellow, cyan, green, magenta, red, and blue bars used as a color reference by television engineers.

Color Burst: A 3.58 megahertz control pulse that controls the phasing of the color signal and ensures that the color information is kept in proper synchronization.

Color Encoder: Electronic component within a television camera that combines the individual chrominance and luminance channels into the color signal.

Color Lock: A playback control on color VCRs used to adjust the phase of the color signal.

Color Temperature: Variations in the quality of what appears to be white light, measured in degrees kelvin (°K). Standard television lights operate at 3,200 degrees kelvin. Light with a higher color temperature appears bluish; light with a lower color temperature appears reddish.

Colorizer: Electronic component of a video switcher used to generate color, often for the purpose of coloring letters. Also called a *color background generator*.

Comet Tail: A type of lag caused when a camera pickup tube is overstimulated by a light or a point of reflected light, creating an effect that looks like the tail of a comet trailing behind a bright point of light.

Compact Disc (CD): High-quality audio storage medium in which recorded information is read and reproduced via a laser beam.

Compatibility: The capability of a particular VCR to play back a particular videotape. Compatibility is determined by the size and the format of the videotape recording and the size and the format of the playback machine.

Complementary Angles: A shooting technique in which the eyeline of one person looking to the right side of the screen is balanced by the eyeline of another person looking to the left side. Each person becomes the target object of the other's eyeline.

Component Recording: High-quality video recording process in which luminance and chrominance information are recorded in separate tracks on the videotape.

Composite Signal: A video signal that includes both video information and sync.

Condenser Microphone: A high-quality microphone that uses an electric capacitor to generate the audio signal. Requires either AC or battery power to operate.

Confidence Heads: Video playback heads positioned immediately behind the principal recording heads that allow the recording to be monitored through a playback monitor as it is being recorded. Used to check the quality of a recording while the production is in progress.

Contact Microphone: A microphone attached directly to an object for sound pickup.

Continuity Editing: Editing of dialogue or

action without discontinuous jumps in time or place.

Contrast Range: The range or ratio between the darkest and brightest part of an image. Most portable color cameras function within a maximum contrast range of 30:1 or 40:1. Also called *contrast ratio*.

Control Track: A series of electronic impulses recorded directly onto the videotape in their own track that regulate the playback timing of the system. Small format helical scan systems have 30 control track pulses per second.

Control Track Editor: An automatic edit control unit that backtimes the videotape and executes edits by counting control track pulses on the tape.

Creative Editor: An individual with significant responsibility for making and executing editing decisions. Understands the aesthetic principles of editing as well as how to operate the video editing equipment.

Crossfade: A sound transition similar to a visual dissolve. As one sound fades out, the next one fades in, with slight overlap of the two sounds during the transition.

Cross-Keying: Use of two key lights to illuminate two subjects from reverse angles.

Crystal Black: See *Video Black*.

Cut: A straight edit from one audio or video source to another, resulting in an instantaneous change. The most common transition in television and film editing.

Cut Away: A cut to a shot that is related to the main action or separate from it. In an interview, cut aways include reaction shots of the interviewer and shots of people, places, or things referred to in the interview.

Cut In: A cut to a close-up detail of a shot or scene.

Cut Out: A cut to a wide or establishing shot after a close-up.

Cuts-Only Editing System: An editing system in which the only transition possible between shots is a cut. The most common type of small format videotape editing system.

Cutting On Action: The technique of using action as the motivation for a cut from one shot to another.

Cycles Per Second (cps): Standard unit of measure for the frequency of a wave. Also called *hertz (Hz)*.

Decibel (db): A standard unit, or ratio, of measure for gauging the relative intensity of a sound.

Dedicated Time Code: Individual time code produced by a time code generator that is assigned to one VCR. Can be stopped and started. Also called *zero start time code*.

Deflection Coils: Parts of the camera pickup tube that control horizontal and vertical movement of the electron beam by varying the magnetic field within the tube.

Degrees Kelvin (°K): A measure of the quality of light or the degree of whiteness of light. The hotter the filament, the whiter the light radiated from it.

Depth of Field: The portion of a scene in front of the camera that is in focus. Measured from the point in focus closest to the camera to the point in focus farthest from the camera.

Desk Stand: Small microphone mount used to support a microphone on a desk or table in front of someone who is speaking.

Desktop Video: Video production that utilizes relatively inexpensive personal computers with graphics capabilities to generate video images and/or modify or edit recorded video images.

Dew Lamp: Warning light to indicate when moisture or condensation has formed on the head drum.

Dialogue: Conversation between two or more people.

Dichroic Filters: Filters that allow only certain frequencies of light to pass. Often used to adjust the color temperature of light sources.

Dichroic Mirrors: Color-sensitive mirrors that reflect certain colors and allow others to pass through. Used to split incoming light into its red, blue, and green components in some three-tube color cameras.

Digital Signal: A signal in which the input is converted into bits of information that can be stored as numerical data.

Digital Video Effects (DVE): Special effects made possible by signal processing equipment that digitizes and processes the video signal. Image compression and expansion are common types of digital effects.

Diffuser: See *Scrim.*

Dimmer: A device that changes the intensity of a light by varying the voltage supplied to the lighting instrument.

DIN Connector: A type of connector. A four-pin DIN connector is often used to connect an external battery to a VCR. Abbreviation for Deutsche-Industrie-Norm.

Direct Current (DC): The type of current supplied by batteries. Most portable video systems require a 12-volt DC power source.

Directional Continuity: Characters or objects that are moving in one shot continue to move in the same general direction in a subsequent shot. An element of continuity editing.

Directional Light: Focused light coming from a particular direction, creating areas of light and shadow on the subject.

Dissolve: A gradual transition in which one visual source slowly fades out while another slowly fades in, and the two sources overlap during the transition.

Dolly (In or Out): Actual movement of the camera and its support toward or away from the scene.

Downstream Keyer: A device on a video

switcher that introduces a key or matte over the line output, leaving the mix/effects busses free to perform other effects.

Dropout Compensator (DOC): An electronic device that detects the loss of information on a videotape caused by oxide dropouts and corrects the problem by replacing the lost information with information from the line that immediately preceded it.

Dropouts: Loss of particles of oxide coating from the surface of a videotape. Adversely affects picture quality and stability.

Dub: (1) A copy of a video or audiotape. (2) To transfer video or audio information from one tape to another.

Dulling Spray: Any one of several liquid-form commercial products that are sprayed on objects to reduce surface reflection or glare.

Dynamic Editing: Editing technique that utilizes visual material to create an impact rather than simply to convey literal meaning or achieve continuity of action. More affective and complex than continuity editing. Also called *complexity editing.*

Dynamic Microphone: A rugged, professional-quality microphone widely used in field production.

E to E: Electronics to electronics. Method of monitoring a signal that is being fed into a VCR.

Ear Shot: Any medium close-up or close-up shot that shows the subject in profile, rather than from the front, and in which the ear is in the center of the picture.

Earphone: A small device that fits into an ear. Used to monitor audio.

Earspeaker: Small audio speaker built into the side of a video camera or camcorder that allows the camera operator to hear the sound input directly without the use of headphones or an earphone.

Edit Decision List (EDL): See *Edit List.*

Edit List: A list of all the edits for a program. Specifies all the edit in points and out points, often with reference to SMPTE time code. Also called *edit decision list.*

Edit Master Tape: The videotape onto which editing will be done.

Editing: The process of arranging individual shots or sequences into an appropriate order.

Editing to Music: Editing that is motivated by a melodic or rhythmic element (the beat) in a piece of music.

Editing Script: A written plan for editing a program. Consists of a brief description of each shot, including its in (entry) and out (exit) points.

Editing VCR: Videocassette recorder equipped with special electronic circuitry that enables it to edit the video signal. Can record and play back videotapes.

Eight-Pin Connector: A rectangular connector with eight pins that connects a VCR to a monitor/receiver.

Electret Condenser: Small battery-powered condenser microphone.

Electron Gun: (1) In a camera pickup tube, a device located at the rear of the tube that emits a stream of electrons, which scans the target. (2) In a television monitor or receiver, a device that emits a beam of electrons, which hits the phosphorescent surface of the picture tube and makes the television image visible.

Electronic Cinematography (EC): The use of electronic television cameras in place of film cameras. EC cameras look like 35mm film cameras and accept similar lenses.

Electronic Editing: A process of rerecording information into a new sequence by using one or more playback (source) VCRs and one editing (record) VCR.

Electronic Field Production (EFP): Video production that takes place in a location outside of a television studio. Usually refers to single-camera productions shot to be edited in postproduction.

Electronic News Gathering (ENG): The use of electronic video equipment for reporting news from field locations. Also called *electronic journalism.*

Electronic Viewfinder: A small television monitor mounted on a television camera that reproduces the scene the camera is shooting. The camera operator looks at the electronic viewfinder to cover the action.

Encoded Color Signal: The full NTSC color video signal, including chrominance, luminance, and synchronizing information.

EP: See *SLP/EP.*

Erase Head: A head that erases information from a tape so that new information can be recorded in its place.

Essential Area: The central, usable area of a television graphic.

Establishing Shot: An overall wide angle view of a scene, usually a long shot. Shows the relationship of the parts to each other and to the scene as a whole.

External Microphone: Any microphone not built into or mounted onto the field camera.

External Sync: Sync pulses generated by a source other than the camera, usually a sync generator.

Extreme Close-Up (ECU): The tightest shot possible on a person or object. Also called a *tight close-up (TCU).*

Extreme Long Shot (XLS): A very wide angle, panoramic shot of the elements of a scene.

Eyeline: A line created by the eyes when someone looks at a target object. Eyelines and the position of the target object are very important in creating continuity through editing.

Eyepiece Viewfinder: The most common

type of viewfinder found on portable video cameras. Allows the camera operator's (videographer's) eye to be placed firmly against the camera.

Eyeroom: See *Noseroom.*

Fade: A gradual transition from black to an image or sound (fade up) or from an image or sound to black (fade down or fade out).

Fader Bar: Device on a video switcher that controls the output of the mix/effects buss. Used to perform fades, dissolves, and wipes.

F-connector: A video connector frequently used on coaxial cables carrying an RF signal, such as a cable TV connection, or the RF output from a VCR.

Feedback: (1) Electronic distortion caused when a live microphone is placed near a speaker that is reproducing its output, or when a video camera shoots into its own monitor. Audio feedback is audible as a loud screech; video feedback appears as an undulating pattern of light and color. (2) That part of the communication process in which audience responses to the production are transmitted to the producers.

Field: One-half (262.5 lines) of a television frame.

Field Production: See *Electronic Field Production.*

Fill Light: (1) Nondirectional light, set at one-half to three-fourths of the intensity of the key and positioned opposite it. Used to fill in, but not eliminate completely, the shadows created on the subject by the key light. (2) Any light used to fill in shadows.

Film-Style Lighting: Lighting technique in which the lighting setup is changed each time the camera position is changed. Lighting done shot by shot.

Filter: A device used to eliminate certain frequencies of light or sound.

Filter Wheel: A component built into many portable cameras that is used to correct the color temperature of incoming light.

Fishpole: A hand-held telescoping metal rod widely used as a microphone support in field production.

Flag: An opaque card with a handle that is used to control the way in which light falls on a scene.

Flagging: Bending at the top of a picture that is caused by incorrect tape tension. Can be corrected by adjusting the skew control on the VCR.

Flashback: Insertion into a sequence of a shot or scene that took place in the past, prior to the main action.

Flashforward: Insertion into a sequence of a shot or scene that takes place in the future, after the main action.

Floodlight: Also called *broadlight.* Produces a wide beam of relatively soft, unfocused light.

Floor Stand: Telescoping stand used to support a light or microphone.

Fluid Head: High-quality tripod head that allows extremely smooth camera movement (panning and tilting).

Flying Erase Head: An erase head positioned in front of the video record head that allows precise frames of information to be erased. Makes insert editing possible.

Flying Spot Scanner: High-quality film-to-tape transfer system that uses an electron beam to scan the film image and convert it into a video signal.

Focal Length: The distance from the optical center of the lens to the point where the image is in focus (the face of the pickup tube or CCD). The angle of view of a lens is determined by its focal length.

Focus: Sharp detail in the important parts of the image. Pictures may be in focus or out of focus.

Focus Ring: A device that controls the distance between lens elements, thereby allowing the lens to focus on objects at different distances from the camera. Located at the far end of the lens on portable video cameras.

Footcandle (fc): A measure of the intensity of light.

Format: The way in which audio, video, and control track information is laid down onto a videotape. Popular portable video formats include 8mm/Hi8mm, VHS/S-VHS, ¾" U-Matic, and the professional ½" formats: Betacam and M-II.

Frame: One of the basic units of the video signal. There are 30 frames per second in the American NTSC system.

Frame Accuracy: The ability of an editing system to make an edit exactly on the planned frame. Most small format editing systems are *not* frame accurate.

Frame Synchronizer: A time base corrector that is capable of storing a full frame of video information. Often used to synchronize nonsynchronous remote signals to other synchronous signals in a television station or production house. Also widely used to produce television graphics.

Framing: The placement of people or objects within the television frame.

Free-Run: Operating mode of a time code generator in which time code is continuously produced while generator's power is on.

Frequency: The number of times a wave repeats itself in a given period of time. Usually measured in cycles per second (hertz). The frequency of a sound wave determines its pitch.

Frequency Response: The ability of any video or audio component to accurately reproduce a wide range of frequencies.

Friction Head: Inexpensive tripod head that gives fair control over camera movement.

F-Stop: A standard calibration of the size of the aperture opening of a lens.

Gain: Control of the amplification or level of an audio or video signal. May be automatic or manual.

Gain Boost: Special switch on some cameras that dramatically boosts the amplification of the video signal. Used most often in low-light situations to improve color reproduction. Tends to make the picture look noisy.

Gamma: A measure of the camera's ability to reproduce the tonal gradations of a scene.

Gap: The small space between the two sides of a video recording head.

Gel: Plastic or polyester filter, sometimes called *color media*, used to change the color or color temperature of a light source. Short for *gelatin*.

Generation: The relationship of a dubbed copy of a tape to the original. The original is a first-generation tape; the first copy made from the original is a second-generation tape; and so on. Signal quality decreases with each new generation.

Gen-lock: Synchronization of one piece of video equipment to an incoming video signal from another piece of equipment.

Glitch: A momentary problem in the video signal. Often caused by a loss of stability or dropouts in the tape.

Gobo: A foreground graphic that creates a frame for the action.

Graphic Equalizer: Audio component that allows the level of various ranges of frequencies within the signal to be manipulated in order to shape the overall quality of the sound.

Graphic Materials: Any visual materials. Ranges from whole settings in which action is staged to simple captions identifying speakers.

Graphics: Printed, drawn, photographed, or electronically generated graphic material incorporated into a production.

Gray Scale: A test pattern of 7 to 10 shades of gray, which correspond to the brightness range that the television system is capable of reproducing.

Guard Bands: Blank area between tracks of video or audio information on tape.

Halogen-Metal-Iodide (HMI) Lights: A highly efficient professional light instrument that produces light matching the color temperature of daylight.

Hanging Microphone: A microphone hung above a scene for sound pickup.

Head: A small electromagnet used to record a video or audio signal onto magnetic tape or to play back the signal from tape.

Head Clog: Clogging of the gap in the video or audio head caused by excessive oxide dropouts from the tape.

Head Drum: Metal cylinder inside a VCR around which the tape is wrapped to bring it into contact with the video heads.

Head Drum Servo: A servomechanism that adjusts the position of the video heads spinning in the head drum so that they rotate in phase with the tracks of video information on the videotape.

Headphones: Device used for monitoring audio. Consists of two small speakers attached to a flexible band that is worn on the head, positioning the speakers over the listener's ears.

Headroom: The distance within the television frame between the top of the subject's head and the top edge of the frame.

Helical Scan: Tracks of video information laid down at an angle on the tape. Characteristic of small format VCRs. Also called *slant track recording*.

Hertz (Hz): See *Cycles Per Second*.

High-Definition Television (HDTV): Television recording and transmission system that features improved resolution resulting from an increase in the number of horizontal scanning lines (1125 lines versus conventional 525) and a wider aspect ratio (9:16 versus conventional 3:4) than the traditional NTSC broadcast standards.

High Impedance: Equipment rated up to 20,000 ohms. Also called *high Z*.

Horizontal Resolution: See *Resolution*.

Hot Spots: Overexposed portions of a picture; bright, glowing spots in which color and detail are lost.

House Sync: Sync supplied by a sync generator to all the video equipment in a given facility.

Hue: A recognizable color: red, blue, green, and so on.

Image Compression: Digital video effect that squeezes the horizontal and/or vertical dimensions of the picture, thereby reducing it in size within the frame.

Image Expansion: Digital video effect that stretches the horizontal and/or vertical dimensions of the picture, causing it to grow larger within the frame.

Image Orthicon: High-quality camera pickup tube, usually found in large format black and white equipment. Now largely obsolete.

Impedance (Z): The amount of resistance in a circuit, measured in ohms (Ω). Audio equipment may be high impedance or low impedance.

Incandescent Lamp: Light bulbs that are similar in construction to common household bulbs. They have a tungsten filament within an evacuated glass bulb.

Inches per Second (ips): Measure of the speed at which video and audiotape move.

Incident Light: The light radiating directly from a source or sources that falls on an object or scene.

Input Overload Distortion: Distortion of the audio signal caused by placing the microphone too close to the sound source. Characteristic of condenser microphones.

Insert Edit: (1) An edit in which new audio

or video information is recorded onto the tape in the editing VCR, leaving the control track undisturbed. (2) The process of inserting a shot or sequence into a preexisting sequence.

Interformat Editing: Videotape editing in which the source tape is edited onto a master tape of a different format.

Interlaced Scanning: The process by which the electron beam scans each frame of the television picture. First one field of odd lines is scanned, then one field of even lines is scanned. Also called *2:1 interlaced scanning.*

Internal Sync: Sync pulses generated within a camera.

International Candle: The light given off by the flame of a sperm candle $7/8''$ in diameter burning at the rate of 7.776 grams per hour, or its equivalent.

Inverse Square Rule: A method of calculating the intensity of light falling on a scene from a given instrument. Reducing the distance between the source instrument and the scene by one half produces four times as much light on the scene.

Iris: The circular diaphragm composed of overlapping leaves that can be manipulated to create a hole of variable size in its center which controls the amount of light passing through the lens. May be controlled manually or automatically.

Jack: Female receptacle for a pin-type audio connector.

Joystick: A stick-like control on an edit control unit that can be used to move the tapes forward or reverse in a number of different modes: frame by frame, slow motion, normal motion, or fast motion. Performs the same function as a search dial. On a video switcher, a joystick is often used as the wipe positioner, which allows selected wipe patterns to be moved up or down on the screen.

Jump Cut: A discontinuous transition from one shot to another caused by a differ-

ence in the size and position of the subject in the two shots. Jump cuts often occur when the middle of a shot is removed and the two remaining pieces are joined together, as in editing dialogue.

Kelvinometer: A color temperature meter, used to measure the color temperature of light.

Key: Special effect used in tilting in which one video source (usually the keyed graphics) appears as opaque letters over the background video.

Key Light: The brightest light on the scene. Establishes the form of the subject by providing bright illumination and producing shadows on the subject.

Keystoning: Distortion of visual material caused when a graphic (or object) is not displayed perpendicular to the camera axis.

Kinescope: Film recording of a television broadcast made by focusing a film camera on a television screen.

Lag: A smearing effect visible in the picture when the camera or subject moves. Often caused by improper or inadequate lighting. Also called *vidicon lag.*

Large Format: Video equipment that is large and not portable. Tape width is 2'' or 1''; VTRs and cameras are very large.

Lavaliere Microphone: A small microphone pinned onto someone or hung around the subject's neck with a string.

Laying Down Tracks: The process of recording music, voice, or sound effects onto the audio channel of a videocassette so they can later be edited onto the edit master tape.

Leader Sequence: Information that identifies a program, usually recorded at the beginning of a videotape.

Lens: The optical component of a camera. Collects incoming light and focuses it on the camera image sensor.

Lens Cap: A protective cap that can be

attached to the end of the lens barrel when the camera is not in operation.

Lens Flare: Optical distortion of a picture caused when a light shines directly into the camera lens. Can be prevented by changing the position of the light or camera, or shielding the lens with a lens hood.

Lens Hood: A rubber extension at the front of a lens that works like a visor to prevent unwanted light from hitting the lens and causing lens flare.

Level: The strength of an audio or video signal.

Light Meter: A device used to measure the light on a scene. Incident light meters measure the amount of light falling on the scene; reflected light meters measure the amount of light reflected off the scene.

Light Table: A box, usually built into the top of a table, with a glass top and a light inside. Used to provide illumination for graphics, slides, photographs, or other visual material.

Lighting Plot: A plan that indicates the type and position of each of the lighting instruments in a scene or shot.

Line: The smallest unit of a television frame. In the United States and Canada, each television frame is composed of 525 lines of information.

Line-Level Audio Signal: An amplified audio signal considerably stronger than a microphone level signal. A line-level audio signal is 1 volt.

Long Shot (LS): A shot from a wide angle that shows the relationship between actors or actresses and their setting. Often used as an establishing shot.

Low-Cut Filter: An audio filter that eliminates low frequency sounds from the audio signal.

Low Impedance: Equipment rated at 600 ohms or below. Characteristic of most professional microphones. Also called *low* Z.

LP: Long-play (four-hour) mode on VHS machines.

Lumen: A unit of measure of the flow of light.

Luminance: See *Brightness*.

Lux: A unit of illumination.

M-II: Professional-quality $\frac{1}{2}$" videotape recording format developed by Matsushita Corporation.

Macro Lens: A lens used for extreme close-ups. Many portable cameras have a built-in macro lens that is activated by a macro lever.

Macro Lever: Lever on the barrel of the lens that activates the macro lens.

Manual Gain Control: Manual control of the amplification of an audio or video signal. See also *Automatic Gain Control*.

Matched Cut: A cut from one shot to a shot that is too similar in terms of angle of view and camera position. Similar to a jump cut.

Matched Frame Edit: An edit between two adjacent frames of video information in the same shot.

Matte: Special video effect that combines three separate sources. Often used to add color to titles in a video production.

Medium Close-Up (MCU): A head and shoulders shot that ends at the chest of the subject. One of the most frequently used shots in television.

Medium Shot (MS): A shot from a medium angle of view, often used to show the relationship between people in a shot or scene.

Microphone: A transducer that changes sound waves into electrical energy.

Microphone Level Signal: Unamplified output of a microphone; a very weak signal usually measured in millivolts.

Mini-Cassette: A videocassette in a small tape housing designed to be used with a portable VCR or camcorder.

Mini-Plug: A small, single-pin unbalanced

plug frequently used as a microphone and earphone connector.

Mix: The technique of combining several simultaneous sound sources in such a way that their relative volume matches their importance.

Modeling: Creating the illusion of three-dimensional subjects and objects on the two-dimensional television screen through lighting.

Moire: A herringbone-like pattern of video noise, frequently caused by radio frequency interference.

Monitor: (1) To check the audio or visual quality of a recording by listening to it or looking at it. (2) A device used to display an audio or video signal. (3) A television set not capable of receiving a broadcast signal.

Monopod: A single telescoping support tube attached to the base of a camera. Often inserted into a belt pouch and used on portable cameras with rear mounted eyepiece viewfinders.

Narration: Description of a visual scene provided by a narrator, frequently as a voice-over (VO).

Natural Sound (Nat Sound): Sound naturally present on a location that is organically connected to the visual action taking place.

Neutral Density Filter: A filter that reduces the amount of light hitting the camera pickup tube without affecting its color temperature.

Newvicon Tube: An improved vidicon tube developed by Panasonic Company.

Noise: (1) Unintended sound. (2) Unwanted electrical interference. Video noise, or snow, makes the picture look grainy; audio noise is audible as static or hiss.

Noncomposite Signal: A video signal that includes only the video (picture) information, but not horizontal and vertical sync.

Nonlinear Editing: Type of video editing made possible by disc-based editing systems that allow random access to the audio and video information stored on the disc. Differs from sequential linear editing characterized by videotape-based editing systems.

Noseroom: The distance within the television frame between the edge of the subject's nose, seen in profile, and the edge of the frame.

Notch Filter: A special audio filter that eliminates a particular range of frequencies within the signal.

NTSC: National Television System Committee. Organization that set early technical standards for U.S. television line and frame scanning rates, as well as the system for television color.

Objective Camera: The camera acts as an unseen observer of the action and presents a neutral perspective view from outside the scene.

Off-Line: Preliminary stage in video editing process in which a rough cut (or edit) of a program is made, frequently using window dubs of field footage with SMPTE time code.

Ohms (Ω): A measure of electrical resistance.

Omnidirectional: A microphone pickup pattern that is sensitive to sound coming in from all directions.

180 Degree Rule: See *Principal Action Axis*.

On-Line: (1) In video editing, refers to editing the final version of the program or program segment, usually on a high-quality editing system. (2) When using a video switcher, the source that is going out as part of the program that is being broadcast or recorded is on-line.

Open Reel: A metal or plastic device that holds videotape or audiotape. Open-reel tapes must be threaded through the playback and record heads and then fastened to the take-up reel for normal operation. Both 2″ and 1″ videotape recorders use open-reel tape.

Operating Light Level: The amount of light, measured in footcandles, that a camera needs to produce a picture. The optimum light level is the recommended amount; the minimum light level is the smallest amount of light the camera must have, but usually results in an inferior picture.

Optical-Video Transducer: In a television camera, the image sensor (pickup tube or CCD) that changes incoming light into an electrical video signal.

Over the Shoulder Shot: Camera shot, usually of two people. Person in foreground has back to the camera; second person is slightly in the background and faces the camera.

Overlapping: Shooting technique in which dialogue or action at the end of one shot is repeated at the beginning of the next shot. Makes editing easier.

Overlapping Edit: The process in which the end of one shot is erased and recorded over by the beginning of the next shot during the process of editing.

Paint: Adjustment of camera color reproduction to achieve a particular mood or effect.

Page Pull: Digital video effect in which one picture appears to pull another onto the screen.

Page Push: Digital video effect in which one picture appears to push another off the screen.

Page Turn: Digital video effect in which the picture appears to turn like the page of a book, revealing a new picture (or page).

Pan: Horizontal movement of the camera head only. Short for *panorama*.

Parallel Cutting: Cutting between two actions that are happening at the same time in different locations, or between events happening at different points in time. A type of dynamic editing.

Patching: Connecting audio and video inputs and outputs with a cable.

Peak Limiter: An electronic device that pre-vents the audio signal from exceeding 100 percent (0db) on the volume unit meter scale. Also called an *audio limiter*.

Peak White: The highest part of the video waveform, equivalent to the brightest part of the scene being shot. Should not exceed 100 percent on the waveform.

Pedestal: Black level. Control over the reproduction of the deepest shades of black reproduced by the camera. Usually set at 7.5 percent on the waveform monitor.

Persistence of Vision: Perceptual phenomenon that creates the illusion of motion in a movie.

Phone Plug: A large, unbalanced single-pin plug used as a headphone or microphone connector.

Photoconductive Layer: Part of the camera pickup tube that conducts light from the face of the tube to the target.

Physical Editing: Editing film or videotape by actually cutting it and reconnecting the pieces in a different order.

Pickup Pattern: The pattern of directions in which a microphone is sensitive to incoming sound.

Pickup Tube: Vacuum tube inside a television camera that changes light into an electrical video signal.

Ping-Pong: Rerecording time code and audio on different channels on a videotape by making a dub of the original material.

Pistol Grip: A small handle attached to a camera or shotgun microphone.

Pitch: The high or low quality of a particular sound; results from differences in the frequency of sound waves.

Plumbicon: Very high-quality camera pickup tube, often used in three-tube color cameras. A modification of the basic vidicon tube with a lead oxide photoconductive layer. Registered trademark of N.V. Philips.

Point of View (POV): See *Subjective Camera*.

Portable VCR: Lightweight, battery-powered videocassette recorder designed for remote field production.

Portapak: Early term used to describe a small portable camera and VCR recording system.

Postproduction: State of production after field production is complete. Principal component is usually editing.

Poststriping: Adding time code to a videotape that was originally recorded without it.

Potentiometer: Used to increase or decrease the gain amplification) of an electronic signal. Also called a *pot*.

Preinterview: An interview with the potential subject of a program or program segment that takes place before the actual production date. Used to gain familiarity with the subject and to put novice subjects at ease before they appear on camera.

Preproduction: Production planning before the production begins.

Preroll: See *Backspacing*.

Press-On Letters: Commercially available alphanumeric figures composed of precut material to which an adhesive has already been applied.

Pressure Zone Microphone (PZM): Registered trade name of Crown International, Inc., for its boundary microphone with a hemispheric pickup pattern.

Principal Action Axis: Technique of staging for continuity in which the camera stays within an imaginary 180 degree semicircle created by the line formed by the principal action in a scene and thus stays on one side of the action. Also called the *principal vector line* or the *180 degree rule*.

Principal Vector Line: See *Principal Action Axis*.

Prism Block: A glass prism that breaks incoming light into its red, green, and blue components. Found in the highest quality three-tube video cameras.

Processing Amplifier (Proc Amp): A device to correct color quality as well as sync and color burst in the video signal.

Producer: The member of the production team who is responsible for the overall organization of a production.

Production: (1) The shooting stage of the television production process. See also *Preproduction* and *Postproduction*. (2) The television program itself.

Production Assistant (PA): The member of the field production team who serves as a general assistant. Often has responsibility for setting up audio, helping with lighting, carrying equipment, and logging tapes.

Pull Card: A graphic in which one part is removed (pulled) to reveal new information.

Pulse Code Modulation (PCM): High-quality digital audio recording process utilized in some portable VCRs.

Quadruplex: System of videotape recording in which four video heads rotating at high speed scan a 2" videotape. Large format; for many years the broadcast standard.

Question Re-Ask: Technique frequently used in single-camera production; questions asked by an interviewer are recorded onto videotape after interview has been completed.

Radio Frequency (RF): The range of electromagnetic frequencies used to transmit broadcast or cablecast signals. Different frequencies correspond with different channels of reception.

RCA/Phono Connector: A small unbalanced audio connector often used for line level audio inputs and outputs. Also used as a video connector in home video equipment.

Reaction Shot: A cut, usually to a close-up of a person, which shows a reaction to what was just seen or said.

Receiver: A television capable of picking up an RF-modulated video signal.

Record-Run: Operating mode of a time code generator in which time code is produced only when the VCR is in the record mode.

Record Safety: A safety device built into a videocassette to prevent accidental erasure of the tape. A red button on $^3/_4$" cassettes; a small plastic tab on $^1/_2$" cassettes.

Record VCR: In an editing system, the editing VCR. Also refers to any VCR capable of making a recording from a camera or line input, from another VCR, or from off the air.

Reference White: Brightest possible point a television system will reproduce. Should not exceed 100 percent on the waveform.

Reflected Light: The light reaching the camera from the scene.

Reflectors: Any opaque substance, usually bright metal or treated fabric, designed to redirect light back onto a scene. An important part of standard lighting instruments.

Registration: The process of aligning the pickup tubes in three-tube cameras to guarantee accurate image and color reproduction.

Remote Production: Any video production that takes place outside of a television studio. It may be as simple as a single-camera production or as complicated as large-scale coverage of a sports event.

Remote Survey: A survey to gather technical and aesthetic information about a remote location in which a program will be shot.

Resolution: A measure of the amount of detail in a picture.

Retrace: The time during blanking that it takes the beam to move from the end of one line to the beginning of the next (horizontal retrace), or from the bottom of one field to the top of the next (vertical retrace).

Reverse Angle: The technique of videotaping people at complementary angles so that their eyelines converge when the individual shots are edited together.

RF Interference: Audio or video noise caused by proximity to an RF transmitter.

RF Modulator: A device that converts standard electrical audio and video signals into a radio frequency signal that can be displayed on a conventional television receiver.

RGB Signal: Unencoded red, green, and blue video signals.

Ribbon Microphone: High-quality voice microphone designed originally for use in radio. Also called a *velocity microphone.*

Ripple: Computer update of an edit list. When a change in an edit affects the entry and exit points of all subsequent edits, corrections of the edit list ripple through the list.

Room Tone: Ambient noise present on location. Sometimes recorded and dubbed back onto an audio track during editing to preserve sound continuity.

Rough Cut: A preliminary edited version of a program.

Safe Track: The audio track on a videotape that is located in the interior of the tape, away from the outside edge which is subject to damage in use and storage.

Saticon: High-quality camera pickup tube with selenium, arsenic, and tellurium photoconductive layers. Known for excellent resolution and color reproduction. Saticon is a registered trademark of Hitachi-Denshi, Inc.

Saturation: The intensity or vividness of a color. For example, pink is a lightly saturated red, whereas deep red is highly saturated.

Scrim: A type of light diffuser used to reduce the amount of light and make it softer.

Search Dial: See *Joystick.*

Segue: A transition from one sound to another in which one sound source fades or cuts out completely and then the next source fades or cuts in. There is no overlap of the two sounds.

Selective Focus: The technique of keeping some parts of the picture in focus while others are out of focus. Emphasizes depth and draws the viewer's attention to particular elements in a shot.

Servo Lock Warning Light: Warning light on a VCR that indicates when the machine has reached the proper play or recording speed and the picture has stabilized.

Servomechanism (Servo): A variable speed motor used to control various mechanical systems in video equipment.

Shock Mount: A rubber cradle used to attach a shotgun microphone to a boom and insulate it from noise.

Shooter: In video field production, the camera operator. Also called the *videographer.*

Shooting Ratio: Ratio of amount of tape shot to amount actually used in the final production. If 20 minutes of tape is shot to produce a one-minute production, the shooting ratio is 20:1.

Shotgun Microphone: Microphone with an extremely directional pickup pattern, often used to pick up sound at a distance.

Shoulder Mount: A contoured brace attached to the bottom of a portable camera; allows the camera to be carried on the camera operator's shoulder.

Silk: A giant cloth diffuser used to control light intensity and color temperature in outdoor productions.

Skew: Adjustment of the tape tension in a VCR to eliminate picture bending or flagging.

Slant Track: Helical scan recording.

Slate: Audio or video information used to identify the material that will immediately follow on a videotape.

SLP/EP: Standard long play/extended play (six-hour) mode on VHS machines.

Small Format: Portable video equipment characterized by its small size. Tape width is 8mm, $1/2"$, or $3/4"$; camera image sensors are $1/2"$, $2/3"$, or $1"$.

SMPTE Time Code: Society of Motion Picture and Television Engineers Time Code. A binary electronic signal that is recorded onto videotape. Identifies each frame in terms of hours, minutes, seconds, and frames; aids in computer editing. Two main types of time code are longitudinal time code (LTC) and vertical interval time code (VITC).

Soft Light: A floodlight with an aluminized cloth reflector stretched over a frame; produces a bright shadow-free light.

Software: (1) A computer program that contains a set of commands that allow a computer to perform various tasks, such as word processing, video graphics generation, etc. (2) A video program or program segment; as opposed to video equipment which is called "hardware."

Sound: (1) A pattern in the vibration or movement of molecules of air. (2) Any aural component of a program that is intentionally present.

Sound Bite: (1) Voice segments of the subject of an interview (most common meaning). (2) A sound-on-tape (video and audio) segment of a person speaking on camera. (3) Any sound-on-tape or voice-over use of an individual's voice within an edited program.

Sound Effects (SFX): Prerecorded or live sounds that are added to a production, often to reinforce the visuals or to convey a sense of place.

Sound Perspective: Matching loud sound with close objects and quiet sound with far away objects so that sound and picture seem to be the same distance away.

Sound Presence: Characteristic of the quality of a close sound that distinguishes it from a far away sound; can be created by placing the microphone very close to the sound source.

Sound on Sound: Special audio dub feature on some consumer VCRs. Allows an existing audio track to be rerecorded along with a new audio input.

Sound on Tape (SOT): Picture and synchronous sound recorded onto videotape.

Source VCR: In an editing system, the playback VCR.

SP: Standard play (two-hour) mode on VHS and S-VHS machines.

Split Edit: An edit in which sound and picture are edited individually rather than simultaneously. Two separate edits are made on the same piece of tape—one on audio, the other on picture and one follows the other in time. Also called *L edits* or *L cuts*.

Split Screen: Special effect in which two images are simultaneously displayed on the television screen. Usually activated by stopping a horizontal wipe at the halfway point.

Spotlight: Lighting instrument that produces a narrow beam of hard, focused light. May have a variable or fixed beam.

Standby Switch: Switch found on many cameras that reduces the camera's power consumption. Allows the camera electronics and image sensor to warm up, but does not cause the image sensor to produce an image.

Stand-Up: Sound-on-tape segment where the reporter is seen on camera and talks directly into the camera. Commonly used in electronic news gathering.

Steadicam: Camera mounting system that allows a camera operator to carry a camera and achieve extremely smooth camera movement. Registered trademark of Cinema Products, Inc.

Sticks: A wooden tripod.

Still Video Recorder: Video recording device that uses a magnetic floppy disk to record still video images.

Story Outline Script: Script format used for magazine-style production. Often includes a description of the story a list of locations to be used, essential visual material to be recorded at the various locations, and the names of individuals who will appear in interview segments.

Storyboard: A script that contains illustrations of the principal visual elements of a production.

Stripe Filter: Color separation device found on the face of the image sensor in single-tube/CCD cameras; breaks incoming light into its red, blue, green, and luminance components.

Subjective Camera: The camera acts as a participant in the scene. The perspective presented is that of a participant rather than an observer. Also called *point of view (POV)*.

Subtractive Color: Color theory concerned with mixing pigments, paints, and dyes. Subtractive primary colors are magenta, cyan, and yellow.

Supercardioid: A very directional microphone pickup pattern that is sensitive to sound in a very narrow angle in front of the microphone. Characteristics of shotgun microphones.

Superimposition: Special effect in which two video sources are combined through the use of a video switcher. Both sources appear on the screen simultaneously, and are somewhat transparent since neither is at full strength. Formerly used to superimpose titles; most title graphics are now keyed over the background video.

S-VHS: Super VHS. $\frac{1}{2}$" video recording format with greatly improved luminance and chrominance recording capabilities in comparison with conventional VHS format.

S-Video Connector: Video input/output

connection on monitors and VCRs used in conjunction with 8mm/Hi8 and S-VHS systems in which luminance (Y) and chrominance (C) signals are processed separately. Such systems yield better color purity and image detail than conventional signal processing and display.

Sync Generator: A device that generates horizontal and vertical sync pulses. Typically used to drive the scanning beam when several cameras are used simultaneously in conjunction with a video switcher; it synchronizes them with all the other equipment used in the production.

Sync Pulse: The synchronizing signal that controls the scanning of individual lines of information (horizontal sync) and individual fields of video information (vertical sync).

Talent Release: A standard agreement signed by an individual who appears in a video production. Gives the program producer or production agency permission to use the subject's image and/or voice.

Tape Log: A list and description of every shot on a particular videotape.

Tape Speed: The speed at which the tape is pulled through the VCR.

Tape Transport Controls: Buttons that control the movement of a videotape within a VCR. Typical controls include PLAY, STOP, FAST FORWARD, SEARCH, REWIND, RECORD, and PAUSE.

Target: Electrically charged part of the camera pickup tube that is scanned by the electron beam.

Target Object: The end point of an eyeline. The object or person that someone is looking at.

Technical Director: Crew member who operates the video switcher in multiple-camera television production.

Technical Editor: Usually a production subordinate who executes the editing decisions that have been made by someone else. More concerned with the operation of the editing system from a technical standpoint than with making creative editing decisions.

Telecine: Special television camera and film projector used to transfer film to video. Also known as a *film chain*.

Telephoto Lens: A lens with a long focal length and a narrow angle of view. Magnifies a scene by making distant objects appear to be large and close.

Three-Point Lighting: Traditional lighting technique that utilizes a key light to establish the form, a back light to separate the object from its background, and a fill light (or lights) to reduce the intensity of the shadows created by the key.

Tilt: Vertical (up and down) movement of the camera head similar to the movement of the head when a person looks up or down.

Time Base Corrector (TBC): Electronic device used to correct timing errors in the video signal on a videotape as it is played back.

Time Code: Electronic information recorded onto videotape that identifies each video frame in terms of hours, minutes, seconds, and frame number. The two principal types of time code are SMPTE time code and 8mm time code.

Time Code Character Generator-Inserter: Converts time code readout into video information that can then be inserted into the picture on a monitor or rerecorded with the video information on another videotape.

Time Code Generator: Electronic component that produces time code.

Time Code Reader: Displays time code as a visual digital readout in hours, minutes, seconds, and frames.

Time of Day Time Code: Time code generator that is referenced to a 24-hour clock and runs continuously day and night. Typically found in large production houses where one time code generator feeds time code simultaneously to all the VCRs in the facility.

Timed Cut: Editing technique in which shot length is determined by time rather than by content. A cut or series of cuts, each of a certain duration.

Tone Generator: An audio oscillator that generates an electronic tone used to set the levels on audio equipment.

Track Pitch: The width of the track of video information on a videotape. Track pitch is affected by the width of the video head and the speed at which the tape moves through the machine.

Tracking: Adjustment that controls the way in which the video heads line up with the tracks of video information on a tape. The video heads must be precisely aligned with the video tracks to produce a clear and stable playback picture.

Tracking Control: A device that adjusts the position of the video heads in relation to the tracks of video information on the tape. Used to optimize the level of the playback signal.

Tracking Meter: Meter that displays the strength of the video signal in playback. Maximum meter display indicates that the heads are tracking correctly over the tracks of video information.

Tracks: (1) The areas of video, audio, and control track information on a tape. (2) Music, voice, or sound effects that are recorded onto the audio channel of a videocassette so that they can later be edited into the edit master tape.

Transverse Scan: Tracks of video information laid down in vertical lines on the tape. Characteristic of 2″ quadruplex recording.

Trim: To add or subtract frames from an edit point after it has been entered into the control unit.

Tripod: A three-legged device used to support a camera. Tripods contain legs (which may telescope), a head (where the camera is attached), and may include wheels (a dolly) to allow easy tripod movement. Also called *sticks*.

Truck (Left or Right): Horizontal movement of the camera and its support in front of a scene.

Tungsten-Halogen Lamp: Lighting instrument in which a quartz bulb is filled with halogen. The filament is tungsten. These bulbs burn at a constant color temperature of 3,200 degrees kelvin and are the industry standard for professional lighting equipment.

UHF Connector: A threaded, barrel-type connector used for video inputs and outputs.

Umbrella: Special fabric umbrella used to soften and diffuse the quality of light produced by open-faced spotlights and floodlights.

Unbalanced Line: Inexpensive audio cable or connector widely used on portable audio and video equipment; susceptible to electrical and RF interference.

Unity: Principle of graphic material design in which all materials act together in support of the major theme or purpose of the program.

VCR: See *Videocassette Recorder.*

Vectorscope: Special oscilloscope used to monitor the color television signal.

Velocity Microphone: See *Ribbon Microphone.*

VHF Twin Lead Adapter: A small device used to connect the VCR output to the antenna inputs on the back of a television. Also contains a 300-ohm to 75-ohm matching transformer to match VCR output and antenna input impedance levels.

VHS: Video home system. The most popular $1/2$″ consumer videocassette format.

Video: The picture portion of the television signal.

Video Black: A black video signal that contains horizontal and vertical sync pulses along with color burst. Also called *crystal black*.

Video Field Production: Video production that takes place in a location outside of a television/video production studio. Usually refers to single-camera productions shot to be edited in post-production.

Video In: Line-level video input; where the video signal feeds into a piece of equipment.

Video Insert: See *Insert Edit*.

Video Out: Line-level video output; where the video signal comes out of a piece of equipment.

Video Player: A playback-only VCR that does not contain recording circuitry.

Video Player-Recorder: A VCR that has the capability to play back and record a videotape.

Video Signal: An unmodulated electrical signal containing the synchronizing and picture information that form the television picture.

Video Switcher: Production device that allows several video sources to be mixed and manipulated. Used to perform dissolves, wipes, and other special effects.

Videocassette: A videotape that has been packaged in a cassette housing.

Videocassette Recorder (VCR): Videotape recorder that records the video and audio signal onto a videocassette.

Videographer: In video field production, the camera operator. Also called the *shooter*.

Videotape: Oxide-coated plastic (polyester or mylar) used to record the video and audio television signal.

Vidicon: Once widely used camera pickup tube. Vidicons are relatively inexpensive and produce a color picture somewhat inferior to that produced by Plumbicon or Saticon tubes.

Viewfinder: A small television monitor attached to the camera. Used by the camera operator to frame the scene being shot. Also called *electronic viewfinder*.

Voice-Over (VO): Narration that is delivered from off camera. The voice of the narrator is heard over background visuals, but the narrator is not seen.

Volume Unit (VU) Meter: A meter indicating audio levels in a standard calibration of signal strength.

VTR: Videotape recorder. See also *Videocassette Recorder*.

Watt: A unit of electrical power. Watts = amps × volts.

Waveform: How the video signal looks when it is displayed on a waveform monitor, a special oscilloscope designed to display the video signal.

White Balance: Adjustment of the relative intensity of the chrominance channels in a color camera to allow the camera to produce an accurate white picture in the light available on location. Compensates for differences in the color temperature of light.

Wide-Angle Lens: A lens with a short focal length and a wide angle of view.

Wind Screen: Foam cover placed over a microphone to eliminate wind noise. Also called a *wind filter*.

Window Dub: A copy of a videotape that includes the time code display in a black box, or window, keyed into the picture information.

Wipe: A transition in which one screen image is replaced by another. The second image cuts a preselected hard- or soft-edged pattern (such as a circle, square, diagonal, or diamond) into the frame as the transition takes place. Accomplished with the use of a video switcher.

Wired Microphone: Any microphone connected to an input via a cable.

Wireless Microphone: A microphone that sends its signal to a receiver via RF transmission rather than through a cable. Also called a *radio microphone*.

Writing Speed: The speed at which the video heads hit the videotape, determined by the rotation speed of the heads, the speed at which the tape is pulled through the VCR, and the size of the head drum. In general, the higher the writing speed, the better the recording quality.

Wrong Field Edit: An edit that does not correctly join together the fields of information from two different frames of video, resulting in a curved black line that appears for an instant at the top of the frame.

XLR Connector: A three-pin connector used on professional-quality equipment for audio inputs and outputs. Also called a *Cannon connector*.

Z-Axis: The dimension toward and away from the camera; the imaginary line from the camera passing through the object.

Zebra Stripe: Type of camera viewfinder video level indicator.

Zoom: Apparent motion created by Zooming the lens in or out. Brings the scene closer to, or moves it father away from, the viewer.

Zoom Lens: A variable focal length lens.

Zoom Ratio: The ratio of the wide angle and narrow angle focal lengths on a zoom lens. A zoom lens with a wide angle focal length of 12 mm and a narrow angle focal length of 120 mm has a zoom ratio of 10:1. Also called *zoom range*.

Zoom Ring: A device that controls the focal length adjustment on a zoom lens. May be automatic or manual.

Bibliography

Books

Adams, Michael H. *Single-Camera Video: The Creative Challenge*. Dubuque, IA: Wm. C. Brown, 1992.

Alkin, Glyn. *Sound Techniques for Video and TV*. 2nd ed. London: Focal Press, 1989.

Alten, Stanley R. *Audio in Media*. 3rd ed. Belmont, CA: Wadsworth, 1990.

Armer, Alan A. *Directing Television and Film*. 2nd ed. Belmont, CA: Wadsworth, 1990.

Berger, Arthur Asa. *Scripts: Writing for Radio and Television*. Newbury Park, CA: Sage, 1990.

Blank, Ben, and Garcia, Mario R. *Professional Video Graphic Design*. Englewood Cliffs, NJ: Prentice Hall, 1986.

Blumenthal, Howard J. *Television Producing & Directing*. New York: Barnes & Noble, 1987.

Breyer, Richard; Moller, Peter; and Schoonmaker, Michael. *Making Television Programs: A Professional Approach*. 2nd ed. Prospect Heights, IL: Waveland Press, 1991.

Brown, Blain. *Motion Picture and Video Lighting*. Boston: Focal Press, 1992.

Browne, Steven E. *Videotape Editing: A Post-Production Primer*. Boston: Focal Press, 1989.

Burrows, Thomas D.; Wood, Donald J.; and Gross, Lynne. *Television Production: Disciplines and Techniques*. 5th ed. Dubuque, IA: Wm. C. Brown, 1992.

DiZazzo, Ray. *Corporate Scriptwriting*. Boston, Focal Press, 1992.

Eargle, John. *Handbook of Recording Engineering*. 2nd ed. New York: Van Nostrand Reinhold, 1991.

Gaskill, Arthur L., and Englander, David A. *How to Shoot a Movie and Video Story*, 4th ed. Dobbs Ferry, NY: Morgan and Morgan, 1985.

Hartwig, Robert L. *Basic TV Technology*. Boston: Focal Press, 1990.

Harwood, Don. *Video as a Second Language: How to Make a Video Documentary*. Queens, NY: VTR Publishing, 1979.

Hausman, Carl. *Institutional Video*. Belmont, CA: Wadsworth, 1991.

Hewitt, John N. *Air Words: Writing for Broadcast News*. Mountain View, CA: Mayfield, 1988.

———. *Sequences: Strategies for Shooting News in the Real World*. Mountain View, CA: Mayfield, 1988.

Hilliard, Robert L. *Writing for Television and Radio*. 5th ed. Belmont, CA: Wadsworth, 1991.

Holsinger, Erik. *MacWEEK Guide to Desktop Video*. Emeryville, CA: Ziff-Davis Press, 1993.

Huber, David M. *Audio Production Techniques for Video*. Boston: Focal Press, 1992.

Hyde, Stuart. *Television and Radio Announcing*. 6th ed. Boston: Houghton Mifflin, 1991.

Jacobs, Bob. *How to Be an Independent Video Producer*. White Plains, NY: Knowledge Industries, 1986.

Kenney, Ritch, and Groome, Kevin. *Television Camera Operation*. Burbank, CA: Tellem Publications, 1987.

Kybett, Harry, and Delton T. Horn. *The Complete Handbook of Videocassette Recorders*. 3rd ed. Blue Ridge Summit, PA: Tab, 1986.

LeBaron, John. *Making Television: A Video Production Guide for Teachers*. New York: Teachers College Press, 1981.

Lewis, Colby, and Green, Tom. *The TV Director/Interpreter*. Rev. ed. New York: Hastings House, 1990.

Mathias, Harry, and Patterson, Richard. *Electronic Cinematography*. Belmont, CA: Wadsworth, 1985.

Mayeux, Peter E. *Writing for the Broadcast Media*. Boston: Allyn and Bacon, 1985.

Medoff, Norman, and Tanquary, Tom. *Portable Video: ENG and EFP*. 2nd ed. White Plains, NY: Knowledge Industries, 1992.

Merrill, Joan. *Camcorder Video: Shooting and Editing Techniques*. Englewood Cliffs, NJ: Prentice Hall, 1992.

Millerson, Gerald. *The Technique of Lighting for Television and Film*. 3rd ed. Boston: Focal Press, 1991.

———. *The Technique of Television Production*. 12th ed. New York: Hastings House, 1990.

———. *Video Production Handbook*. London: Focal Press, 1987.

Nisbett, Alec. *The Use of Microphones*. 3rd ed. London: Focal Press, 1989.

Orlik, Peter B. *Broadcast-Cable Copywriting*. 4th ed. Boston: Allyn and Bacon, 1989.

Quick, John, and Wolff, Herbert. *Small Studio Videotape Recording*. 3rd ed. Reading, MA: Addison-Wesley, 1980.

Richards, Ron. *A Director's Method for Film and Television*. Boston: Focal Press, 1992.

Ritsko, Alan J. *Lighting for Location Motion Pictures*. New York: Van Nostrand Reinhold, 1979.

Roth, Cliff. *The Real Facts About Desktop Video Editing*. Aliso Viejo, CA: Future Video Products, 1992.

Sambul, Nathan J. (Ed.). *The Handbook of Private Television*. New York: McGraw-Hill, 1982.

Shetter, Michael. *Videotape Editing*. Elk Grove Village, IL: Swiderski Electronics, 1982.

Shook, Frederick. *Television Field Production and Reporting*. 2nd ed. New York: Longman, 1989.

Smith, David L. *Video Communication*. Belmont, CA: Wadsworth, 1991.

Utz, Peter. *Today's Video: Equipment, Setup, and Production*. 2nd ed. Englewood Cliffs, NJ: Prentice Hall, 1992.

———. *Video User's Handbook*. 3rd ed. Englewood Cliffs, NJ: Prentice Hall, 1989.

Walters, Roger L. *Broadcast Writing: Principles and Practices*. New York: Random House, 1988.

Whittaker, Ron. *Video Field Production*. Mountain View, CA: Mayfield, 1989.

Wiese, Michael. *Film and Video Budgets*. Rev. ed. Westport, CT: Michael Wiese Film Productions, 1988.

———. *The Independent Film & Videomaker's Guide*. Rev. ed. Westport, CT: Michael Wiese Film Productions, 1986.

Wilson, Stephen. *Using Computers to Create Art*. Englewood Cliffs, NJ: Prentice Hall, 1986.

Wurtzel, Alan, and Acker, Stephen. *Television Production*. 3rd ed. New York: McGraw-Hill, 1989.

Yoakam, Richard D., and Cremer, Charles F. *ENG: Television News and the New Technology*. 2nd ed. New York: Random House, 1989.

Zaza, Tony. *Audio Design: Sound Recording Techniques for Film and Video.* Englewood Cliffs, NJ: Prentice Hall, 1991.

Zettl, Herbert. *Television Production Handbook.* 5th ed. Belmont, CA: Wadsworth, 1992.

———. *Sight Sound Motion: Applied Media Aesthetics.* 2nd ed. Belmont, CA: Wadsworth, 1990.

Periodicals

Industrial Photography. Melville, NY: PTN Publishing Company.

Presentation Development & Delivery for the Visual Communicator. Melville, NY: PTN Publishing Company.

Videography. New York: PSN Publications.

Videomaker. Chico, CA: Videomaker Inc.

Video Systems. Overland Park, KS: Intertec Publishing Corporation.

Index